THE GULF TANKER WAR

To Nabaweya and Mohammad
Khalil with best wishes

Nadir

4. 8. 2000

The Gulf Tanker War

Iran and Iraq's Maritime Swordplay

Nadia El-Sayed El-Shazly

First published in Great Britain 1998 by
MACMILLAN PRESS LTD
Houndmills, Basingstoke, Hampshire RG21 6XS and London
Companies and representatives throughout the world

A catalogue record for this book is available from the British Library.

ISBN 0–333–71642–6

First published in the United States of America 1998 by
ST. MARTIN'S PRESS, INC.,
Scholarly and Reference Division,
175 Fifth Avenue, New York, N.Y. 10010

ISBN 0–312–21116–3

Library of Congress Cataloging-in-Publication Data
El-Shazly, Nadia El-Sayed, 1936–
The Gulf tanker war : Iran and Iraq's maritime swordplay / Nadia
El-Sayed El-Shazly.
p.   cm.
Includes bibliographical references (p.   ) and index.
ISBN 0–312–21116–3
1. Iran–Iraq War, 1980–1988—Naval operations.   2. Sea-power–
–Iran.   3. Persian Gulf Region—Defenses.   4. Persian Gulf Region–
–Strategic aspects.   I. Title.
DS318.85.E4 1997
955.05'42—DC21
97–35534
CIP

This book is printed on paper suitable for recycling and made from fully managed and
sustained forest sources.

10   9   8   7   6   5   4   3   2   1
07   06   05   04   03   02   01   00   99   98

Printed in Great Britain by
The Ipswich Book Company Ltd
Ipswich, Suffolk

'Historians of diplomacy will find in the recent Iraqi decision to continue diplomacy by other means the failure of the 1975 Algiers agreement, an accord which was to have rectified what the Iranians saw as the intolerable one-sidedness of the treaty of 1937, which the Iranians had agitated for to adjust what they claimed was the patent unfairness of the 1914 border demarcations, which were called for in the protocols of 1911 and 1913, which were to implement an 1847 treaty, which was negotiated to amplify certain articles of an 1823 treaty, which confirmed a 1746 treaty, which confirmed the 1639 treaty of Zhigad, which left basically intact the 1555 treaty of Constantinople, an Ottoman–Safavid treaty which roughly defined what is the international if somewhat violated border between Iraq and Iran.'

(Dr Bruce Hardcastle, address at the 1980 Middle East Studies Association Conference, in Ghareeb, 1983, p. 60)

'Nonbelligerent powers may wring their hands at this latest spectacle of slaughter, but in most cases their grief lacks conviction. The unpleasant fact is that this war suits almost everyone except those actually being killed, wounded or bereaved. It is probably true that both belligerents can be more confident of staying in power while the war lasts than after it finishes. It is certainly true that Kurds claiming autonomy on both sides of the border, aided by each other's governments, are able to hold their own much better than they could hope to if peace came. True, too, Turkey is doing excellent business with both sides; that Syria and Israel can confront each other with relative serenity so long as Iraq is occupied to the East; that the small Gulf states feel more threatened by the victory of either side than by the war's continuation; that OPEC would find it even more difficult to hold the present oil price if Iran and Iraq resumed full production; and that the United States can enjoy better relations with moderate Arab states so long as the latter are more worried about Iran than about Israel.'

(*Times* in *International Herald Tribune*, 'Gulf War: Unconvincing Grief', 19 March 1985)

'There are 22 million Kurds, by far the largest stateless nation in the world. They were among the greatest losers from the early 20th-century European taste for drawing lines, through sand and mountains, where no borders had existed before. As imperial Britain and France contended for political influence, and oil, they created a Middle East map which dismembered the Kurdish-populated territory into four main chunks: Iraqi, Iranian, Syrian and Turkish. Britain, in particular, insisted on millions of Kurds being joined to Iraq against their will, because Britain controlled Iraq and the Kurdish area contained the Mosul oil wells. Intermittently, ever since, as it has suited us, the West has encouraged the Kurds to rebel, or exhorted them to remain quiet.'

('The West must be ready to confront Saddam', editorial in *Independent*, 3 September 1996)

Contents

List of Tables

List of Maps

List of Charts

Preface and Acknowledgements

The subject of this text could benefit anyone with an interest in the Middle East at large, and the Gulf area in particular, where conditions and events in one country echo across the region and even beyond. It is written in the English language, the vehicle that would attract as large a readership as possible amongst Western intellectuals, but in this case from the vantage point of someone who was associated for most of her life with diplomatic, military and political circles in Egypt and elsewhere, and strove to have an understanding of the rationale and dynamics of policy-making in our part of the world. In writing it I had in mind to answer some of what was published in the West, and while now and then the themes were meant to be thought-provoking, I tried my best to be dispassionate, though it was said that it is almost impossible to pretend to be neutral.

The groundwork for this book was launched in Egypt. Among the first helmsmen who assisted me with constructive suggestions were my next-door neighbour, H. E. Muhammad Hafez Ismail, the elder statesman and *éminence grise* of diplomacy, who headed National Security, Central Intelligence and Foreign Affairs at critical times in contemporary Middle Eastern history; Professor 'Ali-Eddin Hilal Dessouky, Dean of the Faculty of Political and Economic Sciences, Cairo University; Admiral Adel Ayad, Head of Maritime Studies and Deputy Director, Nasser Higher Military Academy; Admiral Yousry Qandeel; General Tal'at Musallam, Director of Military Studies, Centre for Strategic Studies, *Al-Ahram* daily; and Professor Raymond Baker at the American University in Cairo. Chief among those who navigated with me the mined waters of the topic was Professor Earl (Tim) Sullivan, Chairman of the Department of Political Science, American University in Cairo, who spent endless weeks on the project. During these preliminary phases, their advice was a valuable contribution, and I am fully indebted to each of them.

Research was also started in Egypt, where I was allowed access to a number of semi-public libraries, and where the assistance granted to me was beyond the customary service provided to others. I am thankful to each and every one of their staff – in particular to Mona 'Essawy, Omneya Sirry, and Ivonne Luxor at the American Cultural Center in Alexandria. But first and foremost my gratitude goes to Admiral 'Ali Gad, Navy Commander-in-Chief, who honoured me with the only membership offered to a female civilian at the navy's Central Library. My thanks also to Admiral Galal Yasseen, Deputy Director of Egypt's Military Intelligence, who facilitated my entry into the library of the Nasser Higher Military Academy, and also enabled me to attend a symposium on the Iran–Iraq War at its Defence College – the only woman permitted to do so since its creation; to my favourite cousin, Ambassador Ahmad Aboul-Gheit, *Chef de Cabinet* of the Minister of Foreign Affairs, who supplied me with published documents and bulletins, as well as details on the evolution of Security Council Resolution 598, which entailed a year of diplomatic efforts behind the scenes at the United Nations, during his service with the Egyptian Mission there, at the time of the Iran–Iraq War; to General Ahmad 'Abdel-Halim, Deputy Director of the Centre for Strategic Studies, Egyptian Ministry of Defence, for helpful data; to General Samir Barakat, for references from his private collection; and to Ambassador 'Abdel-Rehim Shalabi, Deputy Director of the Institute for Diplomatic Studies, Ministry of Foreign Affairs, who allowed me to research at the library.

Making a most appreciated exception, the London Head Office of Lloyd's Register for Shipping provided me with documents which were not available to the general public. The statistical information, which contained a complete record of ships damaged in the Gulf during the Iran–Iraq War, was of immense value and became the empirical foundation of the book. In recognition, my thanks to Mr R. Gregory, Principal Surveyor, North African Area; to Mr O. H. A. Hamdy, administrator of Lloyd's Alexandria Office; and to Mr David J. Turner, Regional Manager.

Throughout the project, my brother, Ismail El-Shazly, was wholeheartedly dedicated to my support in every possible way. Among other contributions, I owe him the creation of the set of charts – the cornerstone of this work and pivotal to the analysis. My appreciation also to Dr Muhammad 'Awad and Dr Noha 'Adli for their technical assistance in the layout and production of maps, charts and tables.

I subsequently moved to London where, from the start, I had the privilege of continuous encouragement and moral support from Sir Anthony Parsons, the distinguished British diplomat and renowned authority on Gulf affairs. During the most crucial phases of the project, I had the benefit of constructive recommendations from Dr Anoushiravan Ehteshami, Director of Graduate Studies, Centre for Middle Eastern and Islamic Studies, University of Durham. My sincere gratitude to both. For his contribution to focus and finesse of the final work, my thanks to Professor Charles Tripp, Chairman of the Centre of Near and Middle Eastern Studies, School of Oriental and African Studies, University of London.

Research was facilitated in Britain by the fact that its unfettered media allow Middle Easterners to have access to news of their area more rapidly than if they lived in their own country; beside the national press, numerous Arabic-language publications appear. London also enjoys a large diplomatic presence, sizeable Iraqi and Iranian communities, and constantly hosts Middle Eastern and other foreign dignitaries, business people, scholars and journalists. Furthermore, as an old colonial power, Britain houses several specialized libraries, and has many experts among academia and in the Foreign Office, with profound insight and valuable information on the Middle East. Warm thanks are due to those who generously gave of their time, in the course of long interviews, and entrusted me with their thoughts or participated with valuable suggestions.

During the course of my research, interviews and discussion-meetings gave me an opportunity to meet members of the Iraqi and Iranian expatriate community, including Iraqi opposition politicians. This enabled me to observe the *nuances* of details between the various Iraqi opposition parties and groupings, which gave me added insight into the points of friction or agreement between them, rooted in either ethnic and/or religious loyalties, or brought about by different political ideologies and/or agendas. They also provided me with vital information on Iraq's domestic conditions over the past two to three decades – whether political, military, social or economic – in addition to relations with neighbouring countries. Some of this information was not published hitherto, except maybe in some of their party newspapers. A personal debt of gratitude is owed to those Iraqis and Iranians who decided to talk despite fear for their safety, and helped to place earlier findings and recent occurrences into their context with more precision. By unveiling confidential information, they had less to gain and more to lose than me. And by allowing the viewing of their unique audio-visual, photographic and documentary material, they demonstrated a great measure of courage, risking retribution abroad or persecution of relatives left behind. However, I alone bear responsibility for the opinions expressed and the conclusions reached in the text.

Footnoting was based on the Harvard Method for Social Sciences, and names were transliterated according to the way they are pronounced in Arabic, and not how such names usually appear in English-language texts, having in mind to preserve their meaning, except for names of cities and countries, where I used English names, such as Cairo, not *Al-Qahira*, Jordan, not *Al-Urdun*. For example, the words Tariq (proper name, as in Tariq 'Aziz, and also meaning 'knocker') and *tareeq* (path or road), should not be written in the same manner, as this would distort their meaning; and Rasheed, Hameed, Rashid and Hamid are four different names.

Finally, I dedicate this book to the memory of my father, Professor El-Sayed El-Shazly, who imperiled his life when he consented to become the prosecution's main witness in the 1948 Arms Scandal Trial, and instilled in me a strongly rooted sense of justice, inspiring me to pursue truth and challenge prejudice everywhere; and to my mother, who kept his flag flying and navigated his ship after his premature passing. I dedicate it equally to the memory of my husband, Admiral Fouad Abou-Zikry, twice Commander-in-Chief, whose second-cherished family, the navy, became mine as well. My gratitude also to my beloved brothers and children, and many dear friends, without whose enthusiastic and unwavering support this work would not have been possible.

NADIA EL-SAYED EL-SHAZLY

List of Acronyms

AAA	anti-aircraft artillery (also triple A)
AAM	air-to-air missile
AAW	anti-aircraft warfare
AIFV	armoured infantry fighting vehicle
AIPAC	American Israel Public Affairs Committee
APC	armoured personnel carrier
ARE	Arab Republic of Egypt
ASM	air-to-surface missile
ASW	anti-submarine warfare
AWACS	Airborne Warning And Control System
BCCI	Bank of Commerce and Credit International
bd	barrels per day
BKO	Babak Khoramdin Organization (Iranian)
BNL	Banca Nazionale del Lavoro
CAP	combat air patrol
CARDRI	Committee Against Repression and for Democratic Rights in Iraq
CBM	confidence-building measures
CENTCOM	Central Command (USA)
CENTO	Central Treaty Organization
CIA	Central Intelligence Agency (USA)
CIC	Combat Information Centre (USN)
C-in-C	Commander-in-Chief
CIS	Commonwealth of Independent States
CIWS	close-in-weapon system
CJTFME	Commander, Joint Task Force Middle East (USN)
CW	chemical weapons
DAMP	docking and assisted maintenance period
DWT	dead weight tonnage
EC	European Community
ECC	European Economic Community
ECM	electronic counter measures
FAC	fast attack craft
FFG	guided missile frigate
FGA	fighter ground attack

FLIR	forward-looking infrared radar (night-vision gear)
FO	Foreign Office (UK)
FPSO	Floating, Production, Storage, Offloading system (tanker turned oil-rig)
G7	Group of seven most industrialized countries
G77	Group of less developed countries
GATT	General Agreement on Tariffs and Trade
GCC	Gulf Cooperation Council
GDP	Gross Domestic Product
GNP	Gross National Product
Harm	high speed anti-radiation missile
HASC	House Armed Services Committee (USA)
HFAC	House Foreign Affairs Committee (USA)
HMS	Her Majesty's ship (RN)
HoC	House of Commons (UK)
ICJ	International Court of Justice
ICO	Islamic Conference Organization
ICP	Iraqi Communist Party
IFF	identification friend or foe
IIAF	Imperial Iranian Air Force
IIN	Imperial Iranian Navy
IISS	International Institute for Strategic Studies
IKDP	Iraqi Kurdistan Democratic Party
IMO	International Maritime Organization (formerly IMCO)
INA	Iraqi News Agency
INC	Iraqi National Congress
IPC	Iraqi Petroleum Company
IR	infrared (missiles or radars)
IRC	Islamic Revolutionary Council (Iran)
IRGC	Islamic Revolution Guards Corps (Pasdaran)
IRGCN	Islamic Revolution Guards Corps Navy
IRI	Islamic Republic of Iran
IRIN	Islamic Republic of Iran Navy
IRNA	Islamic Republic News Agency
IRP	Islamic Republican Party (Iran)
JCS	Joint Chiefs of Staff (USA)
JTFME	Joint Task Force Middle East (USN)
KDP	Kurdistan Democratic Party (Iraq)
KDPI	Kurdistan Democratic Party-Iran

KOTC	Kuwaiti Oil Tanker Company
LCT	tank-landing craft
LDC	less developed country
LGB	laser-guided bomb
LSL	landing ship logistics (stores)
LSM	landing ship men
mbd	million barrels per day
MBT	main battle tank
MCM	mine counter measure
MCMV	mine counter measure vessel
MEED	*Middle East Economic Digest*
MERIP	*Middle East Research and Information Project*
METF	Middle East Task Force (USN) (also MIDEASTFOR)
MKO	*Mujahedeen-e-Khalq* (Iran)
MoD	Ministry of Defence
MP	Member of Parliament
MRL	multiple rocket launcher
MSO	minesweeper operation
NAM	Non-Aligned Movement
NATO	North Atlantic Treaty Organization
NBC	nuclear, biological and chemical
NIC	newly industrialized country
NLA	National Liberation Army (Iranian in Iraq)
NM	nautical mile
NPT	(Nuclear) Non-proliferation Treaty
NSPG	National Security Planning Group (USA)
OAPEC	Organization of Arab Petroleum Exporting Countries
OPEC	Organization of Petroleum Exporting Countries
OpOrder	Operations Order (USN)
P5	UNSC 5 permanent members
PB	patrol boat, also
PC	patrol craft
perm3	US–UK–France (inner group in UNSC)
PFP	Partnership for Peace
PKK	Kurdistan Workers' Party (Turkey)
PLO	Palestine Liberation Organization
POW	prisoner of war
PRC	People's Republic of China

PUK	Patriotic Union of Kurdistan
RAF	Royal Air Force (Britain)
RC	Regional Command (*Ba'th* Party, Iraq)
RCC	Revolutionary Command Council (*Ba'th* Party, Iraq)
R&D	research and development
RDJTF	Rapid Deployment Joint Task Force (also RDF, USA and GCC)
RGC	Republican Guard Corps (Iraq)
RICER	Radar and Combat Information Centre Equipment Room (USN)
RN	Royal Navy (Britain)
ROE	Rules of Engagement
Ro/Ro	Roll on/Roll off
RPG	rocket-propelled grenade
SAIRI	Supreme Assembly of Islamic Revolution in Iraq (Iraqi)
SAM	surface-to-air missile
Sat-Int	satellite intelligence (USA)
SCR	(UN) Security Council Resolution
SDC	Supreme Defence Council (Iran)
SEAL	sea, air and land commandos (USN)
SIPRI	Stockholm International Peace Research Institute
SLOC	Sea Lines of Communication
SMB	submersible buoy
SOSUS	acoustic surveillance system
SSM	surface-to-surface missile
SUCAP	surface combat air patrol
TacAir	tactical air (contingency or plan)
TAO	Tactical Action Officer (USN)
TBM	tactical ballistic missile
TIC	tactical information coordinator (USN)
TOW	tube-launched optically-tracked wire-guided
UAE	United Arab Emirates
UAR	United Arab Republic
UNCLOS	United Nations Convention on the Law of the Sea
UNSC	United Nations Security Council
USAF	United States Air Force
USCG	United States Coast Guards

USG	United States Government
USMC	United States Marine Corps
USN	United States Navy
USS	United States Ship
VLCC	very large cargo carrier
VTOL	vertical takeoff and landing (fixed-wing, other than helicopter)
WMD	weapons of mass destruction

Introduction: The War Iraq Started and Could Not End

By 1984, and after four years of its inconclusive war with Iran, the Iraqi leadership realized that its army could not achieve a decisive victory. The strategic and political objectives which Saddam Hussein had hoped to obtain by mounting a *Blitzkrieg* type of operation against the Islamic Republic of Iran (IRI) in September 1980, were clearly out of reach.

In the Iran–Iraq War, Iraq could not match Iran's large reservoir of manpower, nor its strategic depth, or its economic strength. Iraq enjoyed superiority in airpower only. Therefore, its most viable option was to capitalize on this to end the war. Hence came into being what came to be known as the Tanker War, whereby Iraq hoped to achieve the following intermediate objectives:

1. weaken Iran's economy by reducing its oil-export capacity;
2. internationalize the war;
3. and, to a much lesser degree, reduce pressure on its ground forces.

During the Tanker War, Iraqi aircraft attacked strategic targets, such as tankers carrying Iranian oil, oil refineries and oil-export terminals. The military strategist Clausewitz summarized the logic of exhaustion that drove the Iraqi strategy as a continuous effort to wear out the 'physical powers' of the enemy until its government is deposed, or to bring about an erosion of its will to fight and 'be forced into signing a peace treaty' (Clausewitz, 1968, pp. 123, 128, 368).

It was assumed that exerting continuous pressure would either force the Iranians to end the fighting or pave the way towards the removal of the government in Tehran and its

1

all-powerful spiritual leader, Ayatollah Khomeini. Thus, negotiations would open with a new regime, with Baghdad unques-
tionably in a better position to achieve its aims.

Iran's economy, like Iraq's, is almost totally reliant on overseas earnings made on the sale of crude oil. Oil revenues, especially after the quadrupling of prices in the early 1970s, are
the most important source of foreign currency earnings. By attacking targets connected to its oil industry and export, the
Iraqi command hoped to create economic difficulties in the
IRI, leading to the inability of the government to import hardware for the war and food for a population that had become
increasingly restive. It was believed that these hardships would
erode the combatants' will to fight, and either compel the
Iranian rulers to call for a ceasefire and agree to negotiate, or
destabilize the regime.

In Clausewitz's judgement, warfare is 'an instrument of
policy' by the mere fact that the decision to start a war is
usually taken by the political organ of government, namely, the
cabinet. He regarded war as 'diplomacy somewhat intensified',
in so far that it continued negotiations in 'a more vigorous
way', using as its tool 'the sword in place of the pen' and as its
means battles in lieu of diplomatic memoranda (1968, pp. 13,
24, 26, 101, 140, 382, 406). In starting the Tanker War, Iraqi
actions conformed to these classic formulations of strategic
theory that link war and politics.

When diplomatic negotiations break down, and a peace settlement seems unattainable, war is used as a last resort. 'War as
an extension for diplomacy by other means' sometimes
becomes the only alternative left to compel the opponent to
reach a settlement. In this case, the original motive of the war
and its ultimate objective are the signing of an agreement.
Therefore, the clear knowledge of the relationship between
policy and war leads to the realization that political and military interests hardly differ. Offensive wars are fought for the
attainment of political or economic objectives, and their strategy does not merely determine the timing and the location of
the battle, but also the resources and means used to attain pre-
determined and specific aims. Thus the inquiry into wars and
battles and the assessment of their strategies become part of
the general study of politics and international relations.

Regional wars during the twentieth century generally had one feature in common: they were usually relatively short-lived encounters. The eight-year Iran–Iraq War was an exception, being the longest military conflict between two less developed countries (LDCs) since the end of the Second World War. Yet, despite the fact that human casualties and material costs were staggering, the combatants failed to achieve their full objectives. And although the Gulf region was perceived by both superpowers as a highly geostrategic area, the conflict neither raised the level of tension between them, nor seriously affected the global balance. Likewise, it did not have an adverse effect on the international economy.

From the very first week of military confrontation, the IRI Navy (IRIN) succeeded in controlling the western and northwestern theatre of naval operations in the Gulf. For the duration of the Iran–Iraq War (22 September 1980–4 August 1988) Iraq was hardly able to use its seapower, except sporadically and in brief encounters. Sea denial capabilities were exercized by Iran, and, as a result, while Iraq was deprived of the export of its oil through the Gulf, Iran maintained the flow of its own trade. Thus, Iraq was faced with a grave geostrategic problem: the commodity its economy was dependent upon had to be exported through neighbouring countries, on whose willingness it had to rely.

Six days after the start of the war, in his 'Address to the Nation', Iraq's president offered peace. He made it conditional, however, on 'Iran's recognition of Iraq's territorial rights; the cessation of Iranian interference in Iraq's internal affairs; a mutual pledge to adhere to good neighbourly relations; and the return of three islands in the Gulf (the two Tunbs and Abu Musa), seized by Iran in 1971, to their rightful Arab owners' (King, 1987, p. 5). Rebuffed by the Iranian refusal to stop military operations, and with the war stagnant on the front for over three years, the Iraqi leadership resorted to a deliberate escalatory strategy to attack civilian targets in the Gulf, by exploiting their superiority in airpower.

The Tanker War strategy was from the outset conceived as a means to end the war. By inflicting a devastating blow on Iran's economy, Saddam Hussein assumed that from an Iraqi position of relative strength, he could persuade the Iranian leadership to negotiate a peace settlement, and bring about a solution to the pending disputes.

Any assessment of the Tanker War strategy will depend on the analysis of two key questions:

1. The soundness of the Iraqi strategy – did it make maximum use of the resources available while exploiting Iran's weaknesses?
2. The effectiveness of the Iraqi strategy – did Iraq success- fully use military means to achieve its overriding political ends?

This study argues that Iranian actions made an Iraqi escala- tory strategy, which largely relied on its airpower to strike Iranian oil-related targets, the best available option for the Iraqi regime. The Iranian position for agreeing to a negotiated settlement centred on the removal of the head of government and the *Ba'thi* regime, the withdrawal of Iraqi troops from Iranian territory and a compensation of $50 to $150 billion, the admittance of Iraqi *Shi'ah* of Persian ancestry who were deported from Iraq, and the trial of Iraq's leader 'as a war criminal' (Helms, 1983, p. 84; and according to *SIPRI* 1987, p. 301, Ayatollah Khomeini later demanded the increase of war reparations to $300 billion; see also Daly, 1985, pp. 152–3; and Osman, 1988, pp. 28–9).

At that time, there were strong reasons for scepticism in Baghdad that Tehran might seriously consider making a deal to solve the long-standing dispute. And there were no signs that Iraq's government would seriously contemplate the pre- requisites set by Khomeini in return for a peace treaty. From Baghdad's perspective, given these harsh terms, and in view of the IRI's refusal to agree to a ceasefire and of its escalation in demands, Saddam Hussein's only feasible option – at this stage of political and military stagnation – was banking on the adop- tion of a new strategy in order to break out of the impasse.

Discussion of the effectiveness of the Iraqi Tanker War strat- egy is fraught with controversy. Its analysis faces the researcher with a challenging task: a ceasefire was declared in the summer of 1988 with the IRI's acceptance of the United Nations Security Council Resolution (UNSCR) 598. Was the cessation of hostilities a result of the four-and-a-half-year

Tanker War? Did Iraq achieve its three intermediate objectives? Although the Iran–Iraq War was first and foremost a ground war, a reasonable argument can be made that Saddam Hussein's use of the Tanker War strategy contributed to the ceasefire outcome and assisted in bringing the Iranian regime to negotiations. This preliminary hypothesis may, of course, be revised. It is presumed that, as new evidence is published in the future, other factors may help to elucidate Tehran's acceptance of the ceasefire.

While research for the book drew on classical strategic theory, associated with Sun Tsu, Clausewitz, Mahan, Beaufre, Liddell Hart and others, the fundamental orientation was empirical. To determine the soundness of the Iraqi strategy and evaluate the degree of its success, several factors had to be taken into account.

Different sets of indicators were used to refute or confirm the proposed hypothesis. A set of charts was compiled, illustrating the attacks on ships sailing in the Gulf during the 56 months under study. Vertical intersections on the graphs, coinciding with each month, present significant diplomatic, political and military events related to the Tanker War, within the domestic, regional, and international settings. These were analyzed in order to find correlations and insights into the Tanker War strategy, to determine the degree to which it succeeded and/or to expose its weaknesses (see Charts A6.1–A6.10).

The topic was approached using the following ideas. Liddell Hart pointed out that grand or higher strategy co-ordinates and directs 'all the resources of a nation' or an alliance 'towards the attainment of the political object of the war' (Liddell Hart, 1967, pp. 335–6). Expressed in simpler form, a country's strategy is determined by its vital interests, dictated by its security considerations, and designed to promote its national objectives. A successful strategy is one that has clear aims, and is based on a correct assessment of one's own, as well as the adversary's strengths and deficiencies. Assets should be fully deployed, always with a clear understanding of the constraints imposed by one's liabilities. The country's mobilized resources should be concentrated and brought to bear against the enemy's weaknesses, with the aim of inflicting maximum damage. Thus, the formulation and execution of a strategy depends upon political, economic, military, social and diplomatic factors, some of which remain constant while others continually vary.

Liddell Hart defined strategy as 'the art of distributing and applying military means to fulfil the ends of policy' (Liddell Hart, 1967, p. 335). In other words, a nation's military strategy should be sustainable militarily, economically, politically, socially and diplomatically. This is especially relevant in a protracted war, when operations are carried out at a low level of intensity, but over an extended period of time. It is also a strategy that takes into consideration intangibles, such as the will to fight, training, leadership flair, the maintenance of high morale, and the backing of the population.

A credible and practical military strategy should have well-determined aims but remain flexible. Although focused, it must allow for variations, and explore separate alternatives, in order to employ these when conditions alter. It should permit the rearrangement of priorities for the attainment of its objectives and the re-structuring of plans accordingly. On the tactical or operational level, it is vital that a strategy concedes a measure of freedom of action to field commanders; rigid limitations should not be placed on them, and they must be allowed to use their own initiative in response to new situations.

This study was empirical, based primarily on Lloyd's Register of Shipping records (hereafter cited as Lloyd's). The London Head Office made an exception by providing a complete inventory of ships attacked and disabled in the Gulf during the Iran–Iraq War. This record, which is not generally available to the public, lists merchant vessels hit from September 1980 and up to 4 August 1988 – the date on which a ship was hit for the last time in the Tanker War.

Primary sources also consisted of interviews with Egyptian, Iraqi, Iranian and Western military analysts, politicians, diplomats and scholars, familiar with the topic; official documents; verbatim records of UN meetings; and maps. In addition, papers and lectures on the subject, contributed by diplomats and analysts at conferences, were used as source material. Data were also obtained from international relations and security conference reports, in addition to unpublished theses presented by Egyptian officers to the Nasser Academy for Higher Military Studies, some of which were cited.

Moreover, methods of data collection included historical research of relevant secondary material, such as publications that dealt with the topic directly or indirectly. Apart from private collections, these were obtained from the following establishments:

- Academy of Maritime Transport, Alexandria, ARE.
- American Cultural Centers, Cairo and Alexandria, ARE.
- American University in Cairo, ARE.
- British Council, Cairo, ARE.
- Egyptian Naval Forces, Central Library, Alexandria, ARE.
- Nasser Higher Military Academy, Central Library, Cairo, ARE.
- International Institute for Strategic Studies, London, UK.
- Ministry of Defence, Centre for Strategic Studies, Cairo, ARE.
- Ministry of Defence Library, Whitehall, London, UK.
- Ministry of Foreign Affairs, Institute for Diplomatic Studies, Cairo, ARE.
- Royal Institute for International Affairs, Chatham House, London, UK.
- University of Exeter, Central Library, Exeter, UK.
- University of Exeter, Centre for Arab Gulf Studies, Documentation Unit, Exeter, UK.

While research for the book was empirical, the framework was strategic theory, using parameters drawn from the 'classics', such as Sun Tsu's *The Art of War*, Clausewitz's *On War* and Paret's (1986) compendium of strategic theory, considered a textbook on the subject. The main reason for relying on the 'classics' is that although there have been modern works on the subject, most of these have been influenced by military-strategic thought in ancient texts, as Liddell Hart and Till confirmed, and as is demonstrated in Paret's manual. Also, by using the 'classics' in a contemporary political-military setting, it was possible to gauge their relevance to modern military strategy and doctrine.

In addition, the majority of recent books on strategy were written in the context of a Cold War bipolar nuclear world, where North Atlantic Treaty Organization (NATO) and Warsaw Pact forces confronted each other, supported by a developed superstructure for the research, development and manufacture of the platforms and weapon systems for their arsenals. Their scenarios could hardly apply to a regional war, fought between two LDCs, using conventional weapons. Also, LDCs rely on imports for the bulk of their armoury, and are therefore constrained in the design and implementation of their strategies by the degree to which they have access to hardware, training and technical support, as most have immature military/industrial bases.

Sun Tsu's *Ping-Fa* (*The Art of War*) was probably first published between 400 and 500 BC. In his foreword to Sun Tsu's translated version, Liddell Hart commented that this small book contained as many of the fundamentals of strategy and tactics as he had covered in all his twenty, or more, books. *The Art of War* was thought to have been read by Napoleon, and its concepts strongly influenced Chinese, Japanese and Russian military doctrine. Reading through the text, one cannot help but admire Sun Tsu's grasp of basic strategic theory and his insight in the employment of tactics. Although written so long ago, the precepts of the Chinese philosopher are applicable to modern conventional warfare, such as the 'limited wars' and the 'expanding torrent' theories that were clarified by Liddell Hart. The former was applied by Iraq in its initial attack on the IRI in 1980, but the latter it did not use. Liddell Hart also developed Sun Tsu's themes of 'indirect approach' and of 'mobility and flexibility' in action (see Section 2.3).

Sun Tsu's comprehensive work drew attention to the influence of particular factors on the successful conduct of war. Some of those cited were sound planning, organization, discipline, logistics, deception, surprise, and the choice and study of the geographical area where the battle was to be won. His description of secret intelligence personnel is remarkable, as he lists five types of agents: in place, double, expendable, penetration, and deception agent – the equivalent of the present-day officer in charge of disinformation.

In addition to being a perceptive strategist with an eye for detail, Sun Tsu was a moderate. He preferred the enemy to be

subdued without fighting, and if a war was inevitable, he advocated economy of time, cost, effort, lives and casualties to the
enemy – which seems to have been Iraq's strategy in the beginning, but which was discarded later, when it resorted to the extensive use of chemical weapons (CW). Whilst Sun Tsu
cautioned against attacks on cities, Iraqi troops assaulted
Iranian towns, at the onset of war, and both Iraq and Iran
launched the 'war of cities', hitting each other's urban areas
with missiles, later on.

Unlike Sun Tsu, Clausewitz found 'moderation in war an ab-
surdity', and the abhorrence of war contemptible. His three-
volume work was published in 1832 by his widow, one year
after his death. Clausewitz's *On War* revealed the input of a
soldier-philosopher whose concern was divided between the
attainment of political goals by diplomacy or by other means,
namely war. He also examined the causes of war, and explored
the psychological, social and political effects of warfare on
human beings.

Apart from being one of the most profound and detailed
works on military strategy and tactics, *On War* is a valuable reference for students of international relations. Clausewitz's
thesis that 'politics and war form an indivisible whole', and
that the military and the political were two equally important
components of warfare, permeates the fabric of the book, and
his ideas have not lost their relevance in current international
relations.

The fundamentals of maritime strategy were primarily
drawn from Mahan's *The Influence of Sea Power Upon History*
(1957) and Gorshkov's *The Sea Power of the State* (1979), which
was believed to be 'certainly one of the most extensive analyses
of the subject to appear since 1945' (Till, 1987, p. 54). Mahan
explored the history of European seapowers, to demonstrate
how maritime interests and history influenced each other. He
pointed out the principles to be observed before hostile fleets
were brought into contact, and the conditions that affected
seapower, such as the geographical features of a country, the
character of its people and the nature of its government.

He extrapolated general principles from the description of
particular naval battles, and whereas, 'in the light of the experience of both wars, the thinking of Mahan and company was
refined by more modern writers . . . the doctrine they put

forward seemed to many to have been entirely vindicated'
(Till, 1987, p. 9). His maxims, published a century ago, are
applicable today, such as the importance of sea denial capabilities and the defence of seaports, the relationship between
seapower and a sound economy, and the connection between
the size of a seapower and a country's interests. He also explained the strategic value of controlling straits, and the
methodology of naval battles and combined operations (see
Section 2.3), which at that time meant army/navy. His inquiry
into blockade, siege, convoying, securing of sea routes, control
of seas, access to foreign bases, and measures to be taken in
defence and in offense reveal a full understanding of the main
conditions and factors that impact on present-day warfare,
whether military, economic or moral.

Similarly to Sun Tsu, Mahan stressed the qualitative over the
quantitative element in military forces and was also a propo-
nent of short wars. Like Clausewitz, he believed in the concentration of military power and guarded against the dangers of
stretching one's forces too thinly. But Admiral Mahan had a
definite objective when he wrote his book, namely, to persuade his countrymen to play a greater role in the world naval
arena. He estimated that this course of action might eventually
lead to conflicts with the European maritime powers, hence
his selectiveness in the choice of examples drawn from history.

Admiral Sergei Gorshkov, who served as Commander-in-
Chief (C-in-C) from 1956 to 1985, is widely regarded as the
creator of the modern Soviet Navy. Acknowledged to be his
country's most brilliant naval strategist, he transformed the
navy from a coastal defensive force into a global seapower.
Partly using the same method as Mahan, namely, drawing conclusions from the lessons of the past, he refuted some of the
American strategist's theories, but agreed with him on a
number of other issues, such as the military-economic link,
the influence of the nature of government on seapower, and
the correlation between a country's interests and the size of its
seapower.

His views were analogous to those of Clausewitz, in that he
regarded war as a science and an art, and shared his belief that
military force, in his view the fleet, 'fulfils an important role as
an instrument of policy of the state in peacetime and is a
potent means of achieving the political ends of armed struggle

in wartime' (Gorshkov, 1979, pp. 152–3). Seapower is the obvious tool for attaining foreign policy objectives in peacetime, as it can advance and retreat on the large expanses of the open seas, without creating the complications that territorial occupation by ground troops would generate. And if it does not fulfil its mission, it can quietly withdraw without the loss of face.

Published in the last quarter of the twentieth century, Gorshkov's treatise appreciated the value of scientific progress, which he believed to be 'a military-technical revolution' extraordinary in its 'scope and depth' in comparison to previous improvements. He saw its impact on sea warfare beyond the present century, and its effect in spheres such as command-and-control, with the setting up of sophisticated communication networks.

Gorshkov's maritime strategy is logical and imaginative, albeit positional. This was a result of the dearth of warm water outlets and the scarcity of Soviet foreign naval bases. With no vital interests at stake beyond the borders and the string of countries adjacent to it – considered as a cordon sanitaire – the Soviet Union developed as a land power, unlike Britain, the United States and Japan, which evolved primarily as sea powers, having vital economic, political and diplomatic interests in distant areas. Consequently, naval strategy was designed for the protection of the Soviet Union's approaches, and merely as an extension of the total military strategy. The fleet was developed accordingly. It played a subordinate role, in defence of the army's flanks, whilst the United States Navy (USN) and the Royal Navy (RN) developed offensive naval forces, on a global scale, to protect commercial interests, vital to their existence and to that of their allies. Apart from these reservations, his work is comprehensive, clear, to the point and detailed.

Geoffrey Till's *Modern Sea Power: An Introduction* defined concepts such as sea control, maritime interdiction, inshore operations and naval diplomacy. They were dealt with in a less philosophical manner but with more clarity, and in an up-to-date setting. The description and uses of – and defence against – weapons such as mines, torpedoes, rockets and ballistic missiles were of particular interest. Till based his observations on examples from naval history, as had his two illustrious predecessors. But his were contemporary, for the most part, and thus more suited to a modern-day study of the interaction between politics and warfare.

The role of seapower as an isolated phenomenon in the Iran–Iraq War was not given emphasis in the literature on the conflict, and it rarely constituted the body of a text. The author will not overestimate the importance of seapower in the overall history of the war; rather in this study, naval actions will be assessed. The substance of this book, therefore, aims to fill an important gap in existing publications on the Iran–Iraq War, by demonstrating the appropriate weight of the naval dimension and the impact of the Tanker War on the events of the eight-year conflict.

The formulation and execution of a strategy is dependent upon political, economic, military, geographical, social and diplomatic factors, as well as the intangibles. As they are strongly interconnected, it would be impossible to analyze each component separately, in order to assess the strategy as a whole. Therefore, the book was not divided into chapters analysing each factor in isolation; instead – apart from the introduction and the conclusion – it contains seven chapters, the first half of which set the stage and its background for the Tanker War, while the second deals with the main topic.

The first chapter examines in detail the information in Lloyd's Register for Shipping, and presents interim conclusions. The analysis of the data made possible the compilation of a number of statistical tables. More significantly, the information was used to draw up chronological charts with the purpose of examining links between the Tanker War and other occurrences. The causal relationship between the conduct of the Tanker War and various other military, political, economic and diplomatic factors provided the final assessment of the Iraqi Tanker War strategy in subsequent chapters.

The following chapter focuses on the main protagonist, Saddam Hussein's Iraq, facing the newly established Islamic regime. Its domestic policies are presented against the background of evolving political trends, within the country and beyond its borders. It also details domestic, regional and global conditions that influenced Saddam Hussein to thrust his armies into Iran in 1980.

The first two sections of Chapter 3 are devoted to an analysis of the alternative options to war and a summary of the start of full-scale military operations. The chapter then furnishes a geopolitical account of the events that led to the period under scrutiny, within the regional and global environment. It also discusses Iraq's initial military strategy, and includes a critique of its preparations for and its conduct of the war during the first few weeks. It ends with an overview of the Iran–Iraq War at large, up to the implementation of the Tanker War strategy in 1984.

The fourth chapter lays the ground for the remainder of the text by presenting geographical and geostrategic descriptions of the theatre of operations, namely, the Arab/Persian Gulf, referred to in the text as the Gulf. It also illustrates how the combination of Iraq's geopolitical and geostrategic vulnerabilities was used against its national security interests. Additionally, it offers a historical analysis of political and military foreign power involvement in the Gulf area, reinforced later on, at the height of the Tanker War; after the re-flagging of Kuwaiti tankers in 1987, this led to an escalation in the size and operations of alien fleets in the Gulf and to the internationalization of the war (see Maps 6.1 and 6.2). The chapter concludes by highlighting the Gulf's geopolitical and geostrategic regional and global significance.

A picture of naval activities in the Gulf would be incomplete were the capabilities and the potential of indigenous navies overlooked. Thus Chapter 5 presents a detailed analysis of the chronological data on the naval arms race between the Gulf countries, up to the start of the Iran–Iraq War. It interprets the reasons behind it, and defines the difficulties facing them in establishing new navies (see Map 5). It also presents the order of battle of the Iranian and Iraqi navies at the start of operations in 1980, and up to the end of hostilities in 1988 (see Tables 5.1 and 5.2). In addition, it profiles naval engagements between both navies, prior to the start of the Tanker War. The last three sections explain the concept behind the Tanker War strategy, detail the French–Iraqi deal for the acquisition of *Exocet*-fitted *Super-Etendard* fighter aircraft, and the rationale behind their use as an instrument in conducting naval warfare.

Chapter 6 offers a factual chronology of the phase under scrutiny, within the Iran–Iraq War at large. It relates the military evolution of the Tanker War against the background of an evolving domestic, regional and global political, economic and strategic setting. More importantly, it highlights the causal relationship between the Tanker War, on the one hand, and on the other, the various military, political, economic, geographical, social, psychological and diplomatic factors that were influenced by, or impacted upon what took place over the waters of the Gulf. It also presents incidents of special interest in the evolution of the Tanker War.

The final chapter starts with furnishing the rationale behind Iran's counter-strategy in the Tanker War, then examines the turn of events which brought about the internationalization of that war. It includes the USS *Stark* incident, political discussions among decision-makers in various capitals over the re-flagging of Kuwaiti tankers, the expansion of foreign fleets in the Gulf region and the intensification of their naval operations. In the final stages, the increased confrontation between the USN and the IRIN resulted in the acceptance by Tehran of UNSCR 598, two weeks after the downing of an Iranian civilian aircraft by the USS *Vincennes*.

Although the preceding chapters included an evaluation of the themes under discussion, the conclusion presents an overall view of the military-strategic dimension of the Tanker War, and evaluates Iraq's Tanker War strategy in the face of conflicting evidence. With references to strategic theories, two subjects were addressed in this context: the effectiveness of Iraq's strategy in reaching its ultimate political aim, through the achievement of its three intermediate political and military objectives; and, to a lesser degree, the performance of the Iraqi pilots, and the extent to which they made efficient use of the weapons and delivery systems at their disposal. The text concludes with final analyses and brings events up to date. It is an epilogue – not only to the Tanker War – but also to the second Gulf War, in that it reviews issues of a general nature, and reports on developments regarding the Kurdish issue and warns of its regional impact.

From the outset, it should be understood that Iraq and the Iraqi people, and President Hussein and his henchmen are distinct entities which are separated in the analysis. Accordingly, the words Iraq or the Iraqis should not be understood in the text as synonymous with or an equivalent for the Iraqi government, Baghdad or the regime, nor should the discussion of the interests of Iraq imply that these were necessarily compatible with those of the country's leadership.

In LDCs in general, including Middle Eastern countries, there are handicaps in the study of governments and politics. Amongst these one could enumerate the scarcity of published material, inadequate statistics, and gaps in archives. Added to these are cultural and political dissimilarities, and in some cases, the researcher's ignorance of the local language. There is also a marked distrust of strangers, which limits the opportunities for interviews with decision-makers, members of political opposition groups and laymen alike. Western reasoning and comparability, as tools of traditional political analysis, are mostly inadequate in the Middle Eastern setting. And while power is understood to be concentrated in the rulers' hands – whether monarchs or presidents – elite groups are permitted to retain a degree of influence; the difficulty lies in the lack of a clear delimitation of power, so as to ascertain the extent of an individual's input into the political system.

The most demanding part of the research was gaining access to some of the interviewees, as it proved extremely difficult to have a rapport based on trust with dissident Iraqis and Iranians. Members of both communities were subjected to intimidation or political assassinations, and, understandably, were suspicious of strangers seeking to meet them. But with patience and perseverance, it was possible to hold discussions with a number of Iraqi and Iranian émigrés. However, one had to contend with the difficulty of filtering the information, because of their strong anti-regime sentiments. Other sources included active or former Middle Eastern and Western officials and diplomats, some of whom spoke candidly, while others were constrained because of their official functions and their countries' declared policies. The corroboration of all testimonials was essential, and in most instances, facts revealed by any one source were verified.

More importantly, an analysis of recent wars meets with grave difficulties in acquiring information. In the case of the Tanker War, the dearth of intelligence reaching the West from both countries was the key problem in assessing Baghdad's and Tehran's political directions, and consequently, the design and implementation of their military strategies. This view was supported by *SIPRI 1987*, stating that the 'Iraq/Iran War has not generated the huge professional literature on "military lessons" that other recent conflicts . . . have. In large part that reflects the lack of confirmed information' (p. 307).

Due to the autocratic nature of both governments and to their heavily controlled mass media, the information disclosed was selective and hence suspect. Claims and counterclaims, namely, the casualty figures and the extent of damage concerning the same incident, had to be compared. As a rule, Iraqi figures of Iranian losses were wildly exaggerated, while both countries played down their own casualties. For reasons explained in Chapter 6, the Iranians draped their actions in strict silence. Therefore, any conclusions reached must remain tentative.

Before the analysis of Iraq's strategy was undertaken, a preliminary inquiry should have pieced together the visible and obscure background elements of the central stage. Obviously, the swordplay between Iran and Iraq over the Gulf waters cannot be dissociated from the backdrop of bilateral and international overt and covert relations, and the war could not have continued for eight years if a large number of countries had not armed the two sides, despite the embargo. The primary purpose of the study would have been to concentrate on the connection between concealed but major policy shifts, resulting in secret arms sales to either Iran or Iraq, which was the most controversial element in this investigation.

Military strategy cannot be understood or explained by the mere examination of military conduct. An interdisciplinary study and the necessity for a broader approach need to be emphasized in order to comprehend and rationalize a particular strategy. Warfare, economics, politics, international relations, diplomacy and geography are strongly linked. Their interrelation makes it impossible to separate and analyze the military component in isolation from others. This fact faces the researcher with the gigantic task of trying to unravel an intricate fabric, consider each thread in relation to others and examine the dynamics between them – while published information on most of these factors that are part and parcel of that equation appeared scarce.

In the case of the Tanker War, some of the facts were impossible to confirm, and the scarcity of concrete evidence made the task of assessment more demanding. For instance, arms transfers to both warring countries were difficult to verify because of the arms embargo and the flourishing clandestine arms trade that followed. Also, oil sales were hard to quantify, because of the large volume of crude lifted on tramp steamers and sold illicitly on the spot market.

In the event that the research failed to uncover certain aspects, it is hoped that the shortcomings will be absolved for precisely that reason, namely, the inability to gain access to official records, the consequent dearth of documentation within reach, and the fragmentation of news stories published in the press. However, because this dissertation is multi-textured, in so far that it extends to various fields, it should be of interest to a broad number of other researchers, and provide them with food for thought. The exploratory work undertaken has offered some answers, but perhaps more importantly, it has shed light on numerous questions. These will eventually stimulate others, guide them to further research, and to a deeper insight into the issues raised. Hopefully, they will appreciate the degree of impact that the themes which were brought together had on each other – some of which were seemingly disparate, but in reality connected – and they may be able, in future, to reveal the policy implications that these linkages may have had.

1 The Tanker War: An Empirical Survey

The first half of the book lays the ground for the main topic, up to the adoption of the Tanker War strategy in 1984. It introduces the newly established regimes in Baghdad and Tehran, and discusses the reasons behind Saddam Hussein's decision to wage war on Iraq's neighbour to the east. It also furnishes a geopolitical account of the period preceding the Iran–Iraq War, a geographical and geostrategic description of the Gulf, a precis of earlier foreign power involvement in the area, and an overview of the first four years of the conflict. The second half interprets the reasons behind the naval arms race between the Gulf countries, explains Iraq's rationale for the adoption of the Tanker War strategy, reports on its start and progression, describes Iran's counterattacks, and details the process of negotiations on the re-flagging of Kuwaiti tankers and its political and military evolution. This chain of events resulted in the enlargement of foreign fleets in the Gulf, ultimately leading to skirmishes between Iranian and USN units, with spiralling clashes, starting from August 1987, and Tehran's acceptance of UNSCR 598.

The purpose of this study was to detect links between the Tanker War and political, economic, military, geographical, social and diplomatic factors. Its basis, therefore, was to determine the causal relationship between the maritime campaign, conducted by Iraqi aircraft over the waters of the Gulf, and events elsewhere. In order to investigate that connection, within the general progression of the Iran–Iraq War, and ascertain that it either impacted on these events, or was influenced by them, figures of Iraqi and Iranian strikes on tankers were essential. Based on the combination of estimates of their hits, computed in this chapter, and facts in the next ones, some of the questions asked were the following:

- Which of the above factors led to the containment of the Tanker War, and/or resulted in the escalation in the number of attacks at a particular time?
- Were the lulls or the excessive levels of intensity meant to exert leverage domestically, regionally or globally?
- Was the degree of the severity of hits at a certain time in reaction to external diplomatic pressure, or in response to domestic political and/or economic constraints, or meant to put into action a certain process?
- How did the Tanker War, the ground war and the missile war on the cities interact?
- How did arms transfers – or the lack thereof – influence military operations?
- Was there a correlation between the foreign naval presence in the Gulf and the Tanker War?

Table 1.1   Ships Hit by Nationality and Type, 1984

Flag	Tanker	Cargo	Other
Bahamas	1	–	–
Britain	1	–	–
China	–	1	–
Cyprus	2	3	–
Greece	4	3	–
India	2	2	–
Iran	3	6	–
South Korea	–	1	1
Kuwait	4	–	–
Liberia	8	3	–
Norway	1	–	–
Pakistan	1	–	–
Panama	5	9	1
Saudi Arabia	3	–	1
Singapore	–	2	–
Spain	1	–	–
Sri Lanka	1	–	–
Turkey	1	1	–
Total	38	31	3

Table 1.2   Ships Hit by Nationality and Type, 1985

Flag	Tanker	Cargo	Other
Belgium	1	–	–
Cyprus	4	–	–
West Germany	–	2	–
Greece	4	–	1
Iran	1	–	4
Italy	1	–	–
Japan	1	–	–
North Korea	1	–	–
South Korea	–	1	–
Kuwait	1	2	–
Liberia	8	–	–
Malta	3	–	–
Panama	2	4	–
Saudi Arabia	1	–	–
Singapore	–	–	2
Sri Lanka	2	–	–
Turkey	3	–	–
Total	33	9	7

The foundation of the empirical research for this book was Lloyd's Register of Shipping record, two lists of which were published in 1988, in addition to a third updated 1991 edition, which listed a small number of Iranian vessels that did not appear in the earlier index. A rapid examination of the first register, which logged ships in alphabetical order, revealed that the total of ships damaged from 1980 to 1988 did not correspond to the number of times ships were hit on the second list, which recorded ships chronologically, and where 73 names of vessels appeared more than once. Of these, 54 were hit twice, 12 three times, and five four times. Two were struck five times, and both were Iranian tankers: the *Dena*'s attacks occurred over ten months only, between 29 September 1986 and 1 July 1987; and the *Kharg 4* sustained her hits during 18 months, between 10 February 1987 and 1 July 1988. A further in-depth probe, described below and in later chapters, confirmed that these were periods when the Tanker War was particularly intense.

Table 1.3   Ships Hit by Nationality and Type, 1986

Flag	Tanker	Cargo	Other
Britain	1	–	–
Cyprus	17	1	–
France	4	–	–
West Germany	–	–	1
Greece	6	–	–
Iran	10	1	1
Kuwait	2	1	–
Liberia	22	1	–
Malta	8	–	–
Netherlands	–	–	1
Norway	2	–	–
Philippines	2	–	–
Panama	9	–	1
Qatar	1	–	–
Saudi Arabia	3	–	–
Singapore	–	–	1
Turkey	2	–	–
UAE	–	1	–
Unknown	1	–	–
Total	90	5	5

Only the portion spanning the period from January 1984 to August 1988 was used, as it fell within the scope of the Tanker War study. The findings in the Lloyd's chronicle from September 1980 to January 1984 figure in some of the tables and in supplementary estimates below. Two tables and a chronology of ships hit between 1980 and 1984, published by Danziger in *Proceedings/Naval Review 1985*, are added in the appendix (Tables A1, A2 and Appendix A4), in addition to another table compiled by Brown-Humes (1988; see Table A3).

A swift inspection of the types of vessels listed confirmed that no warships of any flag were entered, as Lloyd's only register merchant ships insured against damage, including that caused by hostile acts. Additional inquiry revealed that in some cases, the Iranian authorities did not report damage sustained by their merchant vessels, but data to corroborate

Table 1.4   Ships Hit by Nationality and Type, 1987

Flag	Tanker	Cargo	Other
Australia	–	–	1
Bahamas	3	–	–
Bermuda	1	–	–
China	–	1	–
Cyprus	19	2	–
Denmark	2	–	–
France	–	1	–
West Germany	–	1	–
Gibraltar	1	–	–
Greece	12	2	–
Hong Kong	1	–	–
India	2	–	–
Iran	28	4	3
Italy	–	1	–
Japan	4	–	–
South Korea	1	1	–
Kuwait	2	2	–
Liberia	26	–	–
Maldive	–	1	–
Malta	3	–	–
Norway	3	–	–
Pakistan	1	–	–
Panama	14	1	2
Philippines	–	1	–
Qatar	–	1	–
Romania	–	1	–
Saudi Arabia	4	–	–
Sharjah	–	–	1
Singapore	2	–	2
Spain	2	–	–
Turkey	–	1	–
USA	2	–	–
USSR	1	1	–
Total	134	22	9

this evidence were impossible to obtain. The following study was mainly based on Lloyd's figures, as this register is the most authoritative.

Table 1.5   Ships Hit by Nationality and Type, 1988

Flag	Tanker	Cargo	Other
Bermuda	2	–	–
Cyprus	8	2	–
Denmark	3	–	–
Greece	3	–	–
Hong Kong	1	–	–
India	1	–	–
Iran	12	4	1
Liberia	13	–	–
Malta	1	2	–
Norway	7	–	–
Panama	5	1	1
Romania	1	–	–
Saudi Arabia	1	–	–
Sharjah	1	–	–
Singapore	4	–	1
Spain	1	1	–
Total	64	10	3

To simplify tables:
Tankers include liquid gas tankers and ore/bulk/oil carriers;
Cargo include Ro/Ro, bulk and general dry cargo;
Others include supply, support, research and fishing vessels and tugs
(Compiled from Lloyd's, 1988 and 1991).

Further research revealed that a record of British-owned ships, some of which flew flags of convenience, damaged by Iranian action between 1 August 1986 and 25 January 1987, was published in May 1987 by the Defence Committee, entitled *House of Commons Third Special Report,* hereafter cited as *HoC Report.* Except for two vessels, the *Berge Saga* and the *Isomeria,* the list corresponded to Lloyd's. The two ships were taken account of in the charts and tables, except those specifying the types, as the HoC inventory did not indicate whether the vessels were tankers, cargo or other.

Initially, tables were prepared by breaking down the number of ships hit between January 1984 and August 1988 into lists of ships hit by nationality and type (Tables 1.1–1.5).

A second set of tables compares the total number of tankers hit to the total number of ships hit by flag per year, including all types, such as cargoes, tankers, roll-on roll-off (Ro/Ro), tugs, fishing vessels, and supply, support and research ships (Tables 1.6–1.10).

A third list of the total number of ships hit was compiled and computed to create a chart covering the 56 months under study, regardless of who made the attack. To determine the nationality of the attackers, Lloyd's index was scrutinized to establish how many assaults the Iraqis were responsible for, and whether the Iranians were retaliating. Each entry included the name, age, flag, tonnage and type of vessel, as for example, tanker, bulk carrier or general dry cargo, in addition to the date and location of the attack. If the date was unknown, the letter 'R' indicated that no date of casualty was available.

Table 1.6　　Ships and Tankers Hit (by Flag), 1984

Flag	Ships	Flag	Tankers
Panama	15	Liberia	8
Liberia	11	Panama	5
Iran	9	Greece	4
Greece	7	Kuwait	4
Cyprus	5	Iran	3
India	4	Saudi Arabia	3
Saudi Arabia	4	Cyprus	2
Kuwait	4	India	2
Turkey	2	Bahamas	1
South Korea	2	Britain	1
Singapore	2	Norway	1
Bahamas	1	Pakistan	1
Britain	1	Spain	1
China	1	Sri Lanka	1
Norway	1	Turkey	1
Pakistan	1		
Spain	1		
Sri Lanka	1		
Total	72	*Total*	38

The location was mentioned 'at sea, off . . .', 'in port', 'at long . . . and lat . . .' (longitude and latitude) or 'RES.WTRS' (restricted waters), as in the instance when vessels were detained in the Shatt, at the start of armed conflict in 1980, or hit in narrow approaches, such as the Khor Musa channel.

The extent and nature of damage were recorded as LT (war loss/damage during hostilities) followed by letters denoting the casualty category:

- **FX**: fire/explosion, when these were the first feature reported;
- **CN**: collision, striking or being struck by another ship, regardless of whether under way, anchored or moored, but did not include striking underwater wrecks, or hitting against the seabed;
- **CT**: contact, striking or being struck by a drilling rig or platform, regardless of whether the ship was in fixed position or in tow, but did not refer to another ship or the seabed;
- **WS**: wrecked/stranded after knocking the sea bottom or colliding with an underwater wreck;
- **HM**: hull/machinery damage resulting in either repairable damage or total loss;
- **XX**: miscellaneous included ships that were totally lost or damaged, which for want of sufficient information could not be classified; and
- **MG**: missing, when the ship's fate was unknown and only after a reasonable period of time had lapsed and no information had been received.

These entries were followed by the severity of categories, such as:

- **SER**: serious;
- **RPD**: non serious and repairable or repaired;
- **TL** : total loss; and
- **CTL**: constructive total loss (also **COTL**).

Next came a summary of the sequence of events when information was available. Thus, some entries included:

- the number of human casualties killed or missing;
- and/or the weapons used in the assault, as, for example, mine, missile, bomb or rocket;

- and/or the nature of the delivery system, such as aircraft, frigate, helicopter-gunship or gunboat;
- and/or the nationality of the attacker;
- and/or environmental pollution caused by collision with a loaded tanker, resulting in an oil spill;
- and/or the port the ship was towed to for repairs;
- and/or whether she was sold and broken up.

This information was thought to lead to the disclosure of the identity of the attacker. But closer scrutiny revealed that Asian and even some Arab harbours in the Gulf extended their facilities to all ships, regardless of their capital's official policy. Consequently, this indicator had to be discarded.

The flag of the ship hit was also believed to expose the nationality of the attacker. Hence, a list was compiled of the number of Iranian vessels struck. The first difficulty arose with

Table 1.7　　Ships and Tankers Hit (by Flag), 1985

Flag	Ships	Flag	Tankers
Liberia	8	Liberia	8
Panama	6	Cyprus	4
Greece	5	Greece	4
Iran	5	Malta	3
Cyprus	4	Turkey	3
Kuwait	3	Panama	2
Malta	3	Sri Lanka	2
Turkey	3	Belgium	1
West Germany	2	Iran	1
Singapore	2	Italy	1
Sri Lanka	2	Japan	1
Belgium	1	North Korea	1
Italy	1	Kuwait	1
Japan	1	Saudi Arabia	1
North Korea	1		
South Korea	1		
Saudi Arabia	1		
Total	49	*Total*	33

Table 1.8   Ships and Tankers Hit (by Flag), 1986

Flag	Ships	Flag	Tankers
Liberia	23	Liberia	22
Cyprus	18	Cyprus	17
Iran	13	Iran	10
Panama	10	Panama	9
Malta	8	Malta	8
Greece	6	Greece	6
France	4	France	4
Kuwait	3	Saudi Arabia	3
Saudi Arabia	3	Kuwait	2
Norway	2	Norway	2
Philippines	2	Philippines	2
Turkey	2	Turkey	2
Britain	1	Britain	1
West Germany	1	Qatar	1
Netherlands	1	Unknown	1
Qatar	1		
Singapore	1		
UAE	1		
Total	100	Total	90

the discovery that no Iraqi-flagged ships appeared on the Lloyd's Register. Readings in other sources had shown that, with the absence of Iraqi ships trading in the Gulf, the Iranians started striking at ships flying the flags of Iraq's Gulf Arab allies.

Closer investigation indicated that there were twelve cases of 'mistaken identity', when Iraq or Iran attacked 'friendly' vessels; therefore, this inquiry was also abandoned.

Two such examples included the *Safina Al Arab* (LT, FX, FX, SER), hit 120 miles south of Kharg on 25 April, and the *Al Ahood* (LT, FX, HM, FX, FD, CTL), struck on 7 May (for the political implications, see Section 6.1.4). Both were towed, sold and broken up. Although the missile did not explode, the *Safina Al Arab*'s starboard side was torn open with the hull plates bent inward around a 24-square-yard gaping section. The cut in the *Al Ahood* was described by a British reporter for

Table 1.9   Ships and Tankers Hit (by Flag), 1987

Flag	Ships	Flag	Tankers
Iran	35	Iran	28
Liberia	26	Liberia	26
Cyprus	21	Cyprus	19
Panama	17	Panama	14
Greece	14	Greece	12
Japan	4	Japan	4
Kuwait	4	Saudi Arabia	4
Singapore	4	Bahamas	3
Bahamas	3	Malta	3
Malta	3	Norway	3
Norway	3	Denmark	2
Denmark	2	India	2
India	2	Kuwait	2
South Korea	2	Singapore	2
Spain	2	Spain	2
USA	2	USA	2
USSR	2	Bermuda	1
Australia	1	Gibraltar	1
Bermuda	1	Hong Kong	1
China	1	South Korea	1
France	1	Pakistan	1
West Germany	1	USSR	1
Gibraltar	1		
Hong Kong	1		
Italy	1		
Maldive	1		
Pakistan	1		
Philippines	1		
Qatar	1		
Romania	1		
Sharjah	1		
Turkey	1		
Unknown	2		
Total	151	*Total*	134

Note: Two 'unknown' ships appears in *HoC Report*, 1987.

the *Times* as 'the size of a London bus . . . The superstructure has been twisted back and outwards over the stern and the crews' quarters have simply melted down as if they were made of plastic rather than iron' (in Danziger, 1985, p. 165). Both were gutted by blazing fires which raged twice, due to the accumulation of gas and the high temperature of the steel. On the *Safina Al Arab*, 8000 tons of oil were destroyed, and 34 000 on *Al Ahood*. It took two and five days, respectively, to extinguish the fires (Lloyd's; and *Navy International*, July 1984, p. 434 and table p. 433).

Names of harbours were cited when ships were hit while berthed at Iranian piers or anchored at Arab wharfs. But when vessels were attacked while sailing in the Gulf, the latitude and longitude were indicated. Generally speaking, whenever the target was an Iranian, a Kuwaiti or a Saudi ship, the attacker's nationality was thought to be obvious – but, as explained above, this proved to be inconclusive evidence.

For the investigation to be of value, statistics had to be as thorough as possible, and it was essential to discover who hit whom. The list of the total number of hits was broken down into three categories – 'Iraq', 'Iran' and 'Unknown'. The last was too long for the results to be of any significance. Consequently, it was thought that determining the location of the ship hit would reveal the nationality of the aggressor.

The problem of determining whether the assault was carried out by Iraqis or Iranians was complicated in the cases when a vessel was disabled whilst sailing in international waters, with no mention made in the report as to the identity of the assailant. This difficulty was compounded by the fact that tankers from many countries and those flying flags of convenience lifted crude oil from Iranian as well as Arab terminals. For instance, the *Texaco Caribbean* (LT, SER), which struck a mine eight miles off Fujairah on 10 August 1987, 'was an American-owned ship flying the Panamanian flag and chartered to a Norwegian company to transport Iranian oil. At least one ship attacked in May [1987], the *Golar Robin*, had loaded part of its oil in Saudi Arabia and was on its way to load the rest in Iran when it was hit' (*Newsweek*, 24 August 1987, pp. 8–9; and Lloyd's).

At the time of the preliminary exploration for this study, Admiral Adel Ayad, who was Head of Maritime Studies and

Table 1.10   Ships and Tankers Hit (by Flag), 1988

Flag	Ships	Flag	Tankers
Iran	17	Liberia	13
Liberia	13	Iran	12
Cyprus	10	Cyprus	8
Norway	7	Norway	7
Panama	7	Panama	5
Singapore	5	Singapore	4
Denmark	3	Denmark	3
Greece	3	Greece	3
Malta	3	Bermuda	2
Bermuda	2	Hong Kong	1
Spain	2	India	1
Hong Kong	1	Malta	1
India	1	Romania	1
Romania	1	Saudi Arabia	1
Saudi Arabia	1	Sharjah	1
Sharjah	1	Spain	1
Total	77	*Total*	64

Source: Compiled from Lloyd's, 1988 and 1991.

Deputy Director at the Nasser Higher Military Academy, reasonably deduced the following:

> During the Iran–Iraq War, tanker operators chose to have complete freedom to determine their own routes through the international waters of the Gulf; they avoided travelling through areas which could expose their ships to danger and selected zones that they regarded as safe. Therefore, ships sailing to or from an Iranian port hugged the country's seaboard, and those calling at Arab harbours manoeuvred their way along the peninsula's shores for security (Ayad, Interview, 14 June 1990).

As mentioned in Chapter 4, the Gulf's shipping channels are not wide. With the increase in the volume and commercial value of maritime transport, countries bordering on international straits sought to regulate ship traffic (see Map 1.1). In the case of Hormuz, the *modus operandi* was established by the United Nations body which oversees world shipping, though none of its recommendations is mandatory. The International Maritime Organization (IMO, formerly IMCO), whose headquarters are located on the South Bank in London, determined five zones separating the Iranian and Omani seaboards:

- one navigation channel, seven to eight nautical miles (NM) wide, is used for tankers in ballast to enter the Gulf to the right of the separating area;
- loaded tankers sail into the Indian Ocean in another channel, of the same width, to the left of the separating area;
- one belt of two to three NM in width, separates them;
- and two sectors, five to six NM broad, are adjacent to the Iranian and Omani shores, and used by these countries for coastal navigation (Nasser, 1988, p. 8).

Explaining this in simpler terms, vessels entering the Gulf, under normal conditions, sailed in the eastern channel, closer to Iran, while those exiting skirted Oman through the western lane. In principle, the strategic implication of this mode of operation was that the Omani coast seemed to outweigh the Iranian in importance, since loaded tankers were within reach of Omani long-range coastal artillery. But in fact, throughout the Iran–Iraq War, Oman restricted the movement of Iranian ships, and how close to its shoreline they could sail. It opposed Iranian intrusion into its territorial waters, and allowed ships of all other nationalities to transit the strait on its side of the channel (Wachenfeld, 1988, p. 192).

The deviation from normal practices by ships transiting Hormuz was confirmed by a former Iranian merchant marine officer. He affirmed that while serving on the *Iran Rezvan*, hit on 25 October 1981, the ships normally transited through the channels estimated as safer, regardless of other considerations and despite the *modus operandi*. He also recounted an incident, when his ship changed the usual course, taken by Iranian craft, and sailed in the direction of the Arab coast, but was called to order by an Arab PB and summoned to alter her route (Pourzanjani, Interview, 17 May 1991). Also, in May

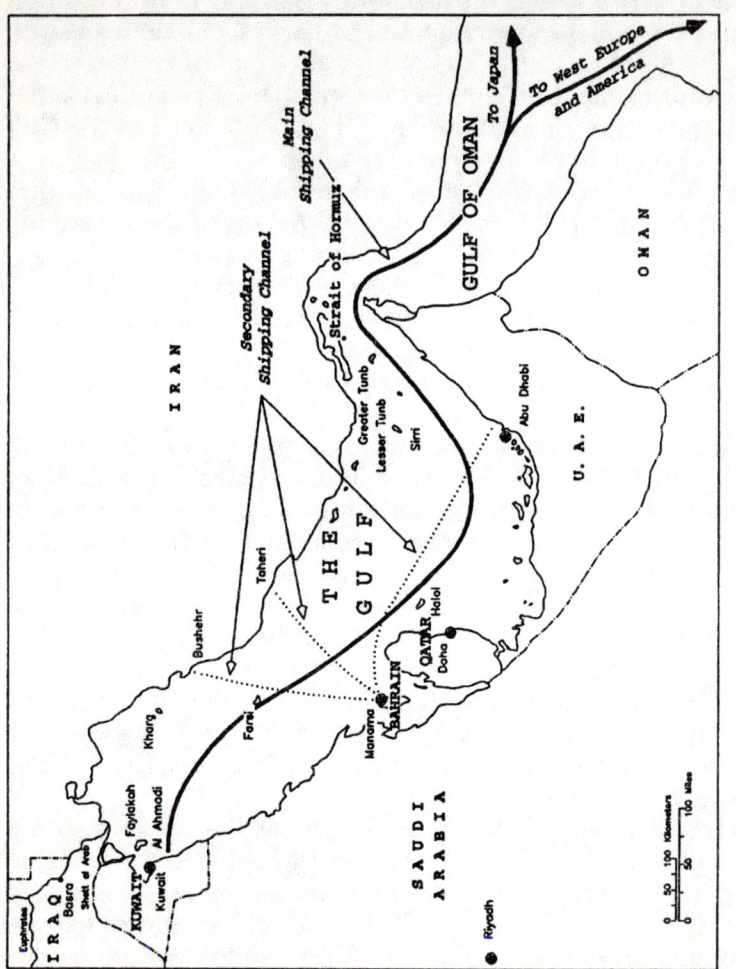

Map 1.1   Shipping Channels in the Gulf

1984, the GCC states advised tankers sailing to and from their ports to navigate within the 12-mile-wide belt of their territorial waters (*Wall Street Journal*, 23 May 1984).

Therefore, having in mind the new setting and the adjustments made to the *modus operandi* established by the IMO, pinpointing the geographical location of tankers hit by unknowns was to be used as an indicator to establish which of the belligerent forces had attacked. But cases of mistaken identity appeared here too. On 27 March 1984, an Iraqi *Exocet* hit the Greek tanker *Filikon L* (LT, SER), steaming 40 miles south-west of Kharg (see Section 7.1.3). The missile lodged in her hull, six feet above water level. None of her 26 sailors were hurt, and she continued her voyage, sailing through the Strait until she reached a location in the northern Arabian Sea. There, at the request of the owner, four seamen from the USN explosive ordnance disposal team, on board the destroyer USS *O'Brien*, safely disarmed the unexploded missile. Ironically, the tanker had lifted 80 000 tons of Kuwaiti oil bound for Sicily, but because of her location at the time of the attack, close to the Iraqi-declared exclusion zone, the pilot probably assumed she was carrying Iranian crude. She was attacked again on 16 November 1987, while sailing off Ras Al-Khaimah, again loaded with crude oil of Arab provenance – but this time by Iranian gunboats (Brown-Humes, 1988, p. 32; Daly, 1985, pp. 157–8; Danziger, 1985, p. 165; Lloyd's; *Navy International*, July 1984, p. 432 and table p. 433; and *Jane's Intelligence Review*, May 1992, p. 218).

Other cases of mistaken identity included the Iranians' hit on the British tanker *British Renown*, on course on 14 June 1984 to off-load Iranian oil from the *Tiburon*, which had been struck by an Iraqi missile 13 days earlier. On 27 February 1985, they also mistakenly struck the Greek tanker *Captain John G P Livanos* (LT, RPD), in ballast and chartered by Iran for the shuttle service to Kharg (Brown-Humes, 1988, p. 32; Danziger, 1985, p. 165; and Hooton, 1992, pp. 218–19).

The preceding rather formidable task led to the identification of attackers in most cases. A minority, however, remained 'unknown'. The targets were hit while sailing in international waters, outside the territorial waters of the two countries at war, or of Iraq's Gulf allies. They totalled seven

out of 463 assaults during the period under observation, or
3.2 per cent. The targets hit by an 'unknown' were as follows:

- one in August out of a total of 72 in 1984: the Panamanian
  tanker *Cleo I* (LT, FX, SER) in ballast and struck by a
  missile 70 miles north-east of Qatar;
- one tanker in March and one in May out of a total of 49
  in 1985, both attacked by aircraft, the second, 78 miles
  from Doha: the Sri Lankan *Royal Colombo* (LT, RPD),
  loaded with 123 000 tonnes of crude, hit by a missile, and
  the Japanese *Japan Aster* (LT, RPD);
- one in December out of a total of 100 in 1986: the
  Maltese tanker *Free Enterprise* (LT, SER), struck by a
  missile at an unknown location;
- one in May and one in October out of a total of 165 in
  1987: the Panamanian tanker *Stilikon* (LT, FX, RPD)
  caught fire after being attacked, and the master of the
  Australian fishing vessel *Shenton Bluff* (LT, SER) was killed
  when the boat was struck by a missile 100 miles north
  north-east of Bahrain;
- and the Maltese bulk carrier *Alga* (LT, RPD), loaded with
  urea, was struck by a missile 15 miles east of Farsi Island
  on the first day of 1988, out of a total of 77 casualties up
  to 4 August 1988.
  A number of damaged ships had to be dealt with on a
  case-by-case basis in regard to their inclusion in charts
  and various tables. These were as follows:
- one of the Iranian casualties, the Korean-made minelayer
  Iran Ajr (LT, FX, FX, FD, SER) was neither included in
  Table 1.11 nor in the charts, having been hit by the USN
  (see Section 7.4.6), but was listed in Tables 1.4, 1.9 and
  1.13;
- the Iranian bulk carrier *Iran Javad* was recorded in
  Lloyd's 1991 list as reported lost during hostilities
  in 1984, with no other references, and was therefore
  not listed in Table 1.11 nor in the charts, but figures in
  Tables 1.1, 1.6 and 1.13;
- the Iranian bulk carrier *Anis*, also reported in the 1991
  Lloyd's list, but with details of the date and place of
  attack, was included in all tables and in the charts;

- the Iranian passenger/Ro/Ro/cargo/ferry *Iran Hormuz* and the PB *Talash,* both of which figured in the 1991 list as being hit in 1986, but reported about two years later, without any mention of date, time, area or circumstances of attack, were not included in the charts, but listed in Tables 1.3, 1.8 and 1.13;
- the tanker *Dynasty* (LT, RPD), hit on 25 November 1986, and again on 27 May 1988, was taken into account in the charts and tables that do not refer to the flag, as her nationality was unknown. There have been several vessels of the same name, according to a letter from the Regional Manager of Lloyd's, in response to an inquiry (Turner, 11 December 1991);
- the five tankers *Happy Kari* (LT, FX, SER both times), hit on 18 December 1987 and again on 11 February 1988, *Berge Big* (LT, SER), hit on 23 December 1987, *Igloo Espo* (LT, FX, SER), hit on 15 January 1988, *Petrobulk Ruler* (LT, FX, HM, SER), hit on 3 February 1988, and *Berge Lord* (LT, RPD), hit on 18 March 1988 and again on 4 August of the same year, listed under the Norwegian Independent Shipping Registry, were included as Norwegian in tables listing the flag of ships hit;
- the Iranian supply ship *Bargir* (LT, SER), referred to in the 1988 Lloyd's list as having caught fire after being struck by missiles off Kharg Island, and her sailors suffering eight deaths on 20 March 1985, did not appear on the 1991 list; she was retained in all charts and tables, the reason being that the Iranians often carried out repairs on their stricken vessels without having recourse to Lloyd's insurers. In fact, several of the Iranian casualties listed in Lloyd's carried the entry 'details of damage not reported';
- *Al Khalij* (LT, SER) was removed from the 1991 Lloyd's list, although the 1988 record showed that she was attacked by Iranian gunboats firing rocket-propelled grenades (RPGs) in the Strait of Hormuz on 27 May 1988, hence, she was included in the charts and tables that do not refer to the flag nor the type of ship, as these were not entered;
- four bulk carriers which sustained serious damage through collision, while in convoy from Booshehr to

Bandar Khomeini on 1 July 1984, were entered as casualties caused by Iraq, although none received a direct hit, as in the melee precipitated by their attempt to avoid the attacking Iraqi aircraft, *Al Kabeer* (LT, SER) collided with *Sitia Venture* (LT, WS, SER) and *Al Tahir* (LT, SER), and the latter collided again with *Five Oaks* (CN, SER);

- and in the *HoC Report*, two vessels listed as hit by the Iranians did not appear in Lloyd's. These were the *Berge Saga*, hit on 12 January 1987 and the *Isomeria*, hit 13 days later. The latter also appeared in an article by Cordesman and a paper by Ayad. They were entered into Table 1.9, as 'unknown', and Table 1.11, but were not listed in Table 1.4, as neither their flag nor their type was indicated.

At this stage, the most important step was made possible. Table 1.11 was subdivided into ten half-yearly charts, each categorizing Iraqi, Iranian and unknown attacks per month, except for the last one, which covered two only. Some of the figures differed from a table of attacks on ships, published by O'Rourke in *Proceedings/Naval Review 1989*. The numbers of

Table 1.11   Iraqi and Iranian Hits Per Month 1984–8

	Iraqi attacks					Iranian attacks					Unknown attacks				
	84	85	86	87	88	84	85	86	87	88	84	85	86	87	88
J	1	4	4	8	6	–	2	2	7	8	–	–	–	–	1
F	4	3	6	5	5	–	4	2	3	6	–	–	–	–	–
M	7	8	4	3	6	1	3	8	3	13	–	1	–	–	–
A	3	1	7	4	–	1	–	2	2	5	–	–	–	–	–
M	6	1	5	3	9	4	2	3	8	5	–	1	–	1	–
J	4	–	3	2	3	1	1	4	5	3	–	–	–	–	–
J	10	2	3	3	4	2	–	–	4	4	–	–	–	–	–
A	4	1	8	4	–	1	2	8	4	1	1	–	–	–	–
S	5	1	5	12	–	1	1	3	12	–	–	–	–	–	–
O	7	1	4	11	–	2	2	4	10	–	–	–	–	1	–
N	–	3	9	10	–	–	1	2	10	–	–	–	–	–	–
D	4	1	4	14	–	6	2	–	17	–	–	–	1	–	–

Iraqi assaults for the months of February, March and April, and the Iranians' for March, May and June corresponded in both tables. But O'Rourke listed Iraqi hits as eight in January, seven in May, one in June and 11 for July and August combined, while Iranian strikes were recorded as seven in January, February and April respectively, and ten for July and August combined.

So far, the charts only indicated the intensity of battle, but did not disclose the types of weapon or weapon-systems used, or the nature of the target hit, nor the degree of damage caused. An inquiry was made to find patterns by depicting whether identical or dissimilar weapons were fired, and whether the same or different weapon-systems were used. This could disclose the platforms Iraq and Iran relied upon for successful operations, or the weapons they favoured. Assessment of these data could also reveal the effectiveness of arms and delivery-systems used, the precision in targeting and the adequacy of defense systems. Whenever possible, the details were drawn from Lloyd's, in addition to the calculations effected to discover the nationality of the attacker. Hooton recorded the following: fixed-wing aircraft, 19 in 1984, 16 in 1985 and 1986, 42 in 1987, and 38 in 1988; rotary-wing aircraft, three in 1985, 21 in 1986 and one in 1987; warships, four in 1986, 23 in 1987 and six in 1988; and ten mines, two *Silkworms*, two *Pasdaran* and two unknown in 1987 (1992, Figure 2, p. 220).

The material helped to assess the performance of Iraqi pilots and the degree to which they made efficient use of the aircraft and arms at their disposal. It also revealed the responses of the shipping companies, the ships' captains and the ships' insurers to the Iraqi and Iranian attacks; and last but not least, the Iranians' retaliatory actions against Iraqi and, at a later stage, American attacks.

Other sources compensated for the gaps, such as *Flottes de Combat, SIPRI, Military Balance* and *Jane's Fighting Ships* yearbooks; the yearly *Middle East Journal, Proceedings/Naval Review* and *Keesing's*; articles in specialized journals, such as *Naval Forces, Navy International, Jane's Defence Weekly, Defense Nationale* and *Proceedings*; newspaper and magazine reports, books, theses, in addition to interviews with Western and Egyptian military analysts, whose identity cannot be disclosed because of their official capacity.

Table 1.12   Weapons Used in Attacks Against Ships 1984–8

		1984	1985	1986	1987	1988
Missiles	IRAQ	39	25	50	55	12
	IRAN	15	16	27	18	2
Explosives	IRAQ	–	–	–	–	–
	IRAN	–	1	–	–	–
Rockets	IRAQ	–	–	1	–	–
	IRAN	–	–	–	2	5
Machine-guns	IRAQ	–	–	–	–	4
	IRAN	–	–	2	8	–
Cannons	IRAQ	–	–	–	–	–
	IRAN	–	–	2	–	–
Mines	IRAQ	–	–	–	–	–
	IRAN	–	–	–	10	–
RPGs	IRAQ	–	–	–	–	–
	IRAN	–	–	–	6	5
Bombs	IRAQ	–	–	–	–	1
	IRAN	–	–	–	1	–

Source: Compiled from Lloyd's, 1988 and 1991.

At the outset, Table 1.11, which covers the whole of the Tanker War phase, did not reveal any patterns that might be analyzed off-hand, and no reasons for the high and low frequencies of hits could be found. Its analysis led to four observations:

(i)   The chart seemed similar to a spaced-out cardiogram or a seismogram with alternating peaks and lows. Its examination showed sudden bursts of hostility followed by relative lulls.

(ii)   The periods of high and low frequency occurred in all four seasons, and did not relate to weather conditions, contrary to the situation on the main battlefront, where seasons and temperatures determined the time for ground force combat, in so far that fighting rarely took place during the rainy season in winter, or at mid-day during the scorching summer heat. For example, the highest peaks were on the following dates: the apex of the Tanker War was in December 1987, with figures climbing to 31 hits; September 1987 witnessed 25 hits; October 1987, 22; and March 1988, 19. The low intensity periods were as follows: one hit only during each of the months of January 1984, April 1985, June 1985 and August 1988, and the diagram showed a flat for November 1984, when no losses were recorded.

(iii)   The number of casualties per year were far from similar during the duration of the Tanker War, when 1987 was the fiercest period, with 166 hits, followed by the first half of 1988, with 78, then 1986 with 101, 1984, with 72, and the year 1985 with 48 only.

(iv)   There was a marked upward trend in the number of hits. Until mid-1986, their total never exceeded 15 per month. The second half of the Tanker War saw figures soaring, culminating in 31 hits in December 1987, averaging one tanker hit every day. In 1987, 60 per cent of the total of vessels were hit during the last third of that year. Most of the high peaks fell between mid-1987 and mid-1988.

According to estimates reached, the first year of the Tanker War started with one Iraqi hit in January, followed by four in February. The Iranian response came in March with one hit, followed by another in April. Figures for 1984 show a climax in July with ten Iraqi hits compared to two by Iran, and another peak in March with seven Iraqi hits and one by Iran. Iran's retaliatory acts gained some momentum in May and December, as it carried out four and six attacks, respectively, compared with six and four by Iraq. November witnessed a lull in the fight. The year ended with 55 Iraqi assaults on shipping, compared to 16 only in 1983, whilst Iran carried out 19 attacks the same year and none in 1983. Of the ships hit, one sank while 27 were broken up and sold (see Section 7.1, and Charts A6.1 and A6.2).

The figures in Lloyd's 1988 publication, which slightly differed from the 1991 revised list, were confirmed by *SIPRI 1987*, (p. 302) and Hiro (1989, p. 284). But small discrepancies appeared between these and O'Rourke, who listed Iranian attacks in 1984 as 18, and none in 1983, while the Iraqis' were

Table 1.13   Ships Hit by Flag by Belligerent, 1984–8

Iraqi attacks		Iranian attacks	
Bahamas	1	Bahamas	3
Bermuda	2	Belgium	1
Britain	1	Britain	1
Cyprus	44	China	1
France	1	Cyprus	14
West Germany	1	Denmark	5
Gibraltar	1	France	4
Greece	13	West Germany	4
India	1	Greece	22
Iran	80	Hong Kong	2
Italy	1	India	6
North Korea	1	Italy	1
South Korea	2	Japan	4
Kuwait	1	South Korea	3
Liberia	41	Kuwait	13
Malta	14	Liberia	40
Netherlands	1	Maldive	1
Norway	1	Malta	1
Pakistan	1	Norway	6
Panama	28	Pakistan	1
Saudi Arabia	4	Panama	25
Singapore	7	Philippines	3
Spain	2	Qatar	2
Sri Lanka	1	Romania	2
Turkey	6	Saudi Arabia	14
		Singapore	8
		Spain	3
		Sri Lanka	1
		Turkey	2
		USA	2
		USSR	1

Source: Compiled from Lloyd's 1988 and 1991, with two additions from the *HoC Report*, 1987.

53 in 1984, and 16 the previous year (1989, p. 43). Karsh was at variance with all, citing 37 by Iraq and 17 by Iran (1987, p. 29).

In 1985, Iraq assaulted eight targets in March compared to three by Iran, four in January and three in February, with Iran scoring two and four respectively. During the rest of the year, activity on both sides was restrained, with one or two vessels hit every month by either side, except in November, when Iraq hit three targets. Lloyd's listed 48 ships hit, and research uncovered that of these, 26 were caused by Iraq, 20 by Iran and in two cases, the assailant remained unidentified (see Section 7.2, and Charts A6.3 and A6.4). According to O'Rourke (1989, p. 43) and Hiro (1989, p. 284), Iraq hit 33 ships and Iran 14, totalling 47 ships, a figure with which O'Ballance concurred (1988, p. 194). Of the ships hit, two went down while 12 were broken up and sold.

The 1986 charts showed a sharp increase of hostile actions by both countries, with figures rising to nine hits by Iraq in November, and two by Iran. The highest toll that year, in terms of the total number of hits, was in August, when each struck eight targets. In March, Iran's curve peaked again, with eight hits, while Iraq scored four. Spring and autumn were characterized by fierce campaigns, while the start, the middle and the end of the year witnessed moderate levels of activity. The total of targets hit came to 101; Iraq struck 62 vessels, Iran 38, while one was struck by an anonymous aggressor. Here again, Hiro was at variance with these figures. He reported that 66 ships were hit by Iraq, twice the number for 1985, and 41 by Iran, three times those for 1985, totalling 107 (1989, p. 286); O'Ballance put the total of ships attacked at 98 (1988, p. 194); and O'Rourke counted a larger number of ships, bringing the total to 111, 66 of which were attacked by Iraq and 45 by Iran (1989, p. 43). Of the ships hit, three sank while 19 were broken up and sold and one half was cannibalized (Lloyd's, see pp. 43–4).

The last quarter of 1987 was the most turbulent so far, and the year's figures were more than double the previous one, with Iranian and Iraqi totals almost neck to neck. The highest numbers were in December, when Iran hit 17 targets and Iraq 14; followed by September, with Iraq and Iran scoring 12 hits each; in October, Iraq hit 11 and Iran 10, while both hit 10 targets each, in November. The other months were characterized by low levels of intensity, never crossing the threshold of five, except for a maximum of eight hits by Iraq in January and the same number by Iran in May, and seven strikes by Iran in January. The year ended with 85 hits by Iran, outnumbering Iraq's 79 for the first time, and two were unaccounted for. Once again, Hiro's approximation did not correspond with these results (1989, p. 287). He estimated that Iraq carried out 76 strikes and Iran 87, totalling 163, while Lloyd's specified 163, in addition to two vessels listed in the *HoC Report*. Dainville compiled a list of Iranian hits which read 17 in 1984, 11 in 1985, 37 in 1986 and 90 in 1987 (1988, p. 63). Again, as in the entries for the previous year, O'Rourke's figures showed larger numbers of ships assaulted, totalling 181, of which Iran 'out-gunned' Iraq for the first time by carrying out 92 strikes, to Iraq's 89 (1989, p. 43). Four of the stricken ships sank, one was stranded, and seven were declared total losses and either used for oil storage or decoys to deflect attacks on other tankers – which demonstrated creativeness on the part of the Iranians, albeit belatedly in the course of the war (Lloyd's).

The 1988 charts demonstrated a continuing trend in high intensity, climaxing in March with 13 strikes by Iran and six by Iraq. The last high peak was in May, with nine hits by Iraq and five by Iran. From May on, a downward tack indicated that the conflict seemed to die down, then ceased after 4 August 1988, when the Tanker War ground to a halt. Iran's hits, for the second consecutive year, outnumbered Iraq's by 44 against 33 and one unknown, the total adding up to 78 hits in seven months, the period that ranged second in severity in the relentless war over the Gulf waters. For the third successive year, O'Rourke's figures outnumbered all the other sources, listing 52 attacks by Iran and 38 by Iraq, bringing the total to 90 (1989, p. 43; see also Hooton, 1992, p. 219, Figure 1, which recorded a total of 208 attacks from 1984 to 1988). The last casualty was the Norwegian tanker *Berge Lord* (LT, RPD), loaded with crude oil, and attacked by Iranian gunboats 25 miles off Dubai. Of the total of vessels attacked, one sank, another was scuttled and one was laid up to serve for oil storage (Lloyd's).

The Tanker War raged on for 56 months, but despite its fierceness, especially in the last stages, only 11 ships sank, while 68.5 were declared total losses. The previous inquiry led to the following figures and observations:

- In the first three years of the Tanker War, Iraqi hits exceeded Iran's. Out of a total of 75 strikes in 1984, Iraq carried out 55, Iran, 19, and one was unaccounted for. The following year's total dropped to 48, while the gap between numbers of Iraqi and Iranian attacks closed, with 26 and 20, respectively, and two by 'unknowns'. The third year witnessed figures spiralling to a total of 101, of which Iraq's share was 62, Iran's 38 and one by an 'unknown' assailant. In the last two years, Iran 'out-gunned' Iraq with 85 against 79 attacks in 1987, with two 'unknown', out of a staggering total of 166. This demonstrates that Iran improved its capability to inflict damage on the targets it chose to attack. Lloyd's listed 163, and two more were mentioned in the HoC Report, while the International Association of Independent Tanker Owners maintained that the number of ships disabled in the Gulf in that year alone were 274, with a loss of 64 lives (O'Ballance, 1988, p. 216). The last phase of the campaign against shipping showed a 4:3 ratio to Iran's advantage, with 44 hits against Iraq's 33 and one 'unknown', thus totalling 78 over seven months only.

The violence of the conflict or its moderation were associated with factors enumerated in the opening paragraph of this chapter, and will be explained in subsequent chapters. The figures reached in this investigation will reveal the links between the Tanker War and incidents surrounding it that were relevant to its conduct.

- Of the total of 463 damaged freighters entered in Lloyd's register between 1984 and 1988, only 11 among them ran aground: one in 1984 and 1988, respectively, two in 1985, three in 1986, and four in 1987, showing a steady, albeit slow increase; in addition, one stranded in 1987 and one was scuttled in 1988. The delayed reaction of the world community in interfering to put an end to the Tanker War could be ascribed to the low percentage of 2.4 per cent of vessels sunk.
- During the 56 months under research, of the 68.5 vessels that were declared total losses, some were broken up and sold, while Iran used a few for oil storage, others as decoys to deflect incoming missiles, and one half in 1986 to repair a damaged ship. The half came about because the accommodation, the emergency generator, the

control, pump and engine rooms in the aft section of the Iranian tanker *Minab* (LT, FX, CTL), hit on 27 April, were destroyed by fire; and the salvaged fore section was attached to the aft section of the tanker *Mokran*. During the course of the war, cannibalization was a practice that Iran performed occasionally. Thus the percentage of ships declared total losses was 14.4 per cent of the total of ships damaged.

- Some Arab harbours in the Gulf extended their facilities to all ships, and tankers owned by Iraq's allies lifted Iranian oil, despite their capital's declared policy. It demonstrated that business interests often outweighed political considerations, a fact confirmed at a later phase in the investigation, when a list was compiled of the nationality of ships trading with, and attacked by, both Iraq and Iran (Table 1.13).

- The damage sustained by Iran's merchant fleet was far higher in comparison to the Gulf Arabs'. Its casualties came to 80, or 17.3 per cent of the total, while Iraq's allies' came to 36, showing a 7.8 percentage of the sum of ships disabled. These were listed by Lloyd's as 14 Kuwaiti, 13 Saudi, four Bahraini, two each from Sharjah (sic) and Qatar and one from the UAE (sic).

- Tanker traffic was not affected by Iraqi and Iranian attacks for a number of causes. Overproduction in oil-exporting states, induced by a worldwide demand, combined with an overcapacity of the tanker fleet, encouraged shipping companies desperate for business, to dispatch their vessels to the war zone. Other reasons fall beyond the scope of this book, but will be briefly cited. Owners of ageing tanker fleets, registered with poorly regulated countries, motivated them to send their old tankers to the Gulf. These were mostly flying flags of convenience, manned by cheap and poorly trained crews, and had structural defects (see Table A5).

2 The Main Protagonist: Saddam Hussein's Iraq Facing Khomeini's Iran

2.1 IRAQ'S GEOPOLITICAL PROFILE

From the sixteenth century onwards, Mesopotamia was part of the Ottoman Empire, until Britain inherited its Middle Eastern dependencies. At the death of the 'Sick Man of Europe' – a term invented by Russia's Nicholas I in alluding to the Ottoman Empire – the British troops expelled the Turks and captured the territories. Despite occupation in 1916, present-day Iraq was not colonized in the legal sense of the word. Created in 1921, the same year Reza Shah took part in a rebellion in Persia, Iraq was administered by Great Britain, under a League of Nations mandate, then granted independence on 3 October 1932.

With their eyes on the prospects for oil, and the security of the new Imperial air route to India, Singapore and Australia, the British needed stability in the Gulf. Ruling the territories themselves was too costly. Winston Churchill, who headed the Colonial Office, devised a plan whereby a new state would appear on the world's political map, with a member of the Hashemite dynasty established as monarch. Faysal bin Hussein bin 'Ali's ancestry went back to the Prophet Muhammad's daughter, Fatima, who married her father's cousin 'Ali, the fourth caliph, during early Islam. He was a Prince of Mecca, the holiest site in Islam, and had a short spell as King of Syria, from March to August 1920, until the French deposed him. He was crowned King of Iraq in recognition by the British of his role in fighting against the Ottomans in the Arab revolt, during the First World War. The Hashemites ruled the Hijaz, in the western Arabian peninsula, until December 1925, when the country was over-run and wrested from them by 'Abdul-'Aziz bin Sa'ud, the founder of the Saudi Arabian kingdom.

Iraq was cobbled together out of three former Ottoman *velayet* (provinces or administrative regions), inhabited by people with great ethnic and religious diversity: Mosul in the north, with a majority of *Sunni* Kurds in the town of Kirkuk, and *Sunni* Arabs constituting a plurality in the town of Mosul; the mainly *Shi'i* Arabs in Basra, in the south; and Baghdad in the centre, with a mixed Arab *Sunni* and *Shi'i* population. Iraq's main ethnic groups are the Arabs and the Kurds, beside a colourful patchwork of minorities, which include the Turcomans and the Christian Assyrians and Chaldeans. The motif is compounded by sectarian divisions within its main religion, Islam, into *Sunnis* and *Shi'ah*, some of whom are of Iranian origin. Iraq has also other minorities, such as Sabaeans and Yazidis, who adhere to a medieval cult, which is neither Christian nor Muslim, and has around 150 000 disciples, two-thirds of whom are in Iraq and nearly all of them Kurds. Jews had small communities scattered here and there, though most lived in Baghdad. A further complication is tribal allegiance, in addition to the other loyalties.

Iraq's population resembles an ethnic quilt of diverse elements, with little in common in cultural heritage or political history. Harbouring peoples with a variety of distinctive cultures, civilizations, languages and religions enriches a country; however, it does not guarantee stability. Finding a collective identity is crucial, because all too often ethnic and religious differences are used as a mantle to conceal struggles for political dominance, or over economic resources.

The newly created state remained Western-oriented and was the prime mover behind the founding of the short-lived Middle East Treaty Organization, better known as the Baghdad Pact. Formed in 1955 with Turkey, it was joined later by Britain, Iran and Pakistan. On 14 July 1958, the 21-year-old King Faysal II, crowned merely three years earlier, was killed and mutilated. The ruling Hashemite dynasty, which only lasted through four generations in Iraq, was overthrown. Brigadier 'Abdul-Karim Qasim became the republic's new prime minister, serving under the collective leadership of a three-member *Majlis al-Siyadah* (Supreme Council), which included a *Sunni*, a Kurd, and a *Shi'i*.

Although Britain recognized the new government 18 days later, Iraq withdrew formally from the Baghdad Pact in

March 1959, and set in motion a policy of alignment with Moscow, Beijing and other socialist countries. In 1961, following Kuwait's independence, Qasim moved to annex the sheikhdom. He based his claim on the argument that under Ottoman rule, Kuwait was part of *velayet* Basra, but his attempt was thwarted by the swift dispatch of British land and sea forces, who were later replaced by Arab League (Egyptian) troops.

Qasim's became a one-man rule as a result of the withdrawal from government of a number of parties, in addition to adulation by the people and flattery by the mass media. However, at the beginning of his premiership, he instituted political and social democratic practices through the creation of women's and youth organizations, labour syndicates and peasant co-operatives. He also introduced land reform, and proposed a constitution which acknowledged the equal partnership of Kurds and Arabs in the nation. Most importantly, he renegotiated the terms of the concession deal with the Iraqi Petroleum Company (IPC), founded in 1914 – one of the major reasons behind the selection of Baghdad as the venue for the creation of the Organization of Petroleum Exporting Countries (OPEC) on 14 September 1960. It grouped the five founders – Iran, Iraq, Kuwait, Saudi Arabia and Venezuela, with Qatar as an observer – after a draft agreement, named the Ma'adi Pact, was signed by their representatives at the Cairo Yacht Club, in the Ma'adi suburb (Butti, 1992 and 1970, pp. 38, 61; Skeet, 1988, pp. 16–22; Sluglett-Farouk and Sluglett, 1990, p. 218; and Yergin, 1991, pp. 522–3).

On 8 February 1963, a second coup, led by *Ba'thi* and Nasserite Arab unionist officers, established another military government, handing the premiership to General Ahmad Hassan al-Bakr, and the presidency to Colonel 'Abd al-Salam 'Arif, a member of the Free Officers, who broadcast the first communiqué of the 1958 revolution. Under Arab and international pressure, Iraq recognized Kuwaiti independence and sovereignty on 4 October 1963. Both countries signed a treaty whereby Iraq accepted Britain's 1923 boundary, although no physical demarcation had been carried out on the ground. The agreement was subsequently registered and published by the UN in document 7063, UN Treaty Series, 1964. According to a leading Iraqi contemporary political historian, the Iraqi government consented to sign the agreement in return for the payment of $30 million by Kuwait (Butti, Interview, 26 December 1994).

The *Ba'th* Party has been in power since July 1968, when another coup removed the second of the 'Arifs; General 'Abdul-Rahman, who had succeeded his brother when the latter died in an air crash on 13 April 1966. It was staged under the leadership of al-Bakr, who retained the presidency and the premiership, and founded and chaired the seven-man Revolutionary Command Council (RCC). The year after, he designated as its vice-chairman the man who was to succeed him in a palace coup ten years later, Saddam Hussein.

In July 1979 Saddam Hussein established his *de jure* authority in Baghdad, by removing his mentor. As al-Bakr's relative and vice president, he had been Iraq's strongman since the mid-1970s, and had challenged his benefactor's power on more than one occasion. He eliminated potential rivals from the party's leadership and replaced them with his relatives and in-laws from the northern Dejla (Tigris) town of Takrit. This trend was reinforced over the years, until the most sensitive posts in the inner core of the power structure were exclusively staffed by relatives on whose loyalty he could count.

After assuming power, President Hussein's political influence became as absolute as that of the Shah of Iran, especially from the late 1960s and up to the latter's dethronement. Their decisions were never questioned, whether they banned political parties, manipulated elections and turned parliament into a rubber-stamp legislature; or selected high officials, party members, senior officers, top executives and diplomats whose loyalty to them was the major criteria. Both established their reputation on Machiavelli's diktat, that a prince should better be feared than loved, and had an undisputed mandate over the sacking and even the physical liquidation of their appointees. Both of them also sought legitimacy through the past. The Shah had traced his line of descent 2500 years back to King Cyrus, and a few years later, Saddam Hussein was compared in songs and poems to King Nebuchadnezzar, who about 2500 years earlier captured Jerusalem and ruled an empire that comprised the territories that today represent Iraq, Syria, Palestine, Jordan, Lebanon and portions of Iran. The Iraqi president had parts of Nebuchadnezzar's ancient city of Babylon reproduced on the same site, with his own mark stamped on millions of specially prepared bricks. As the war against Iran unfolded, it was called *Qadisiyat Saddam*, in reference to the Muslim Arabs' victory over the Sassanid army at Qadisiyah, in the Faurat (Euphrates) Valley, in 637 AD. The Iraqi president was portrayed as the new Salahuddin, a Takriti like himself, but of Kurdish origin, who at the Battle of Hittin defeated the Crusaders in 1187 AD, and was depicted as the modern-day King Hammurabi (1792-1150 BC), as well. Finally, in a letter to the Egyptian President Husni Mubarak, he even went so far as to claim the Quraishi Hashemite House, the Prophet Muhammad's family, as his ancestry, and whenever he addressed King Hussein of Jordan called him 'cousin' (Abd al-Jabbar, 1992, p. 4; Bulloch and Morris, 1991, pp. 43–5; O'Ballance, 1988, p. 15; Rondot, 1990, pp. 48–9; and *Independent*, 21 September 1992).

In the 1980s, Saddam Hussein personally controlled one of the world's largest military forces, and had no qualms about turning this powerful machine against his own people. For his safety, he trusted solely *Jihaz al-Himayah al-Khas* (Special Protection Apparatus), also called *al-Haras al-Jumhuri al-Khas*, a 20 000-strong core of the Presidential Guard, each of whom had been carefully hand-picked. Composed of 13 battalions, each 1300–1500 strong, he entrusted its command to his son Qusay. To consolidate his power, the president also relied on several highly developed security organs that checked and spied on each other, under the overall charge of his elder son 'Uday. They included *Jihaz al-Mukhabarat al-'Ammah* (General Intelligence Apparatus), *al-Istikhbarat al-'Askariyah* (Military Intelligence), *Mudiriyat al-Amn al-'Ammah* (General Security Directorate) and *Maktab al-Amn al-Qawmi* (Bureau of National Security) (Al-Khafaji, 1992, pp. 16–17).

These tightly knit networks extended to all activities within Iraq, and pervaded the opposition movements abroad. In a mirror-image of Imperial Iran's SAVAK, their agents infiltrated educational and governmental institutions, factories, the armed forces, news media and student groupings at home and abroad, and clamped down on any opposition. Jailing, systematic torturing and killing were common place. Although the connection between their infiltration by agents and the fragmentation of the Iraqi opposition movement cannot be established, there was a growing sense that its penetration led to its weakening. The only material evidence to corroborate the politicians' suspicions were memoranda captured from Intelligence offices in Iraqi Kurdistan, in the early 1990s, as well as a record of names of Iraqis abroad, alleged to be *mu'tamaneen* (informers, recruited as agents through persuasion or threat). Published in an Iraqi opposition newspaper in London, the list was said to have been smuggled out by a former Intelligence officer, who defected to the West (see also Korn, 1992, pp. 6, 28–9, 39–46, 65).

The autocratic nature of Iraq's ruler was disclosed in all Iraqi opposition organs, in the English-language press, as well as in interviews with former cabinet ministers, officers, and *Ba'th* members, who became disillusioned with Saddam Hussein's practices and escaped to the West. They concurred that the main element of his power was terror, and although he embarked on costly adventures, with hundreds of thousands of people's lives at stake, he was merciless with members of his entourage who criticized his actions. By so doing, they signed their death warrant. Consequently, under the policy of *targheeb wa tarheeb* ('reward and terror', the immoderate equivalent of carrot and stick), his appointees were forced to conform to his directives (see also Korn, 1992, pp. 1, 5–7).

Put in simple language, Saddam Hussein totally controlled the home turf through repressive measures that included summary arrests, mass executions and the destruction of entire villages. He implicated most members of his inner circle in these activities, so as to forestall a palace coup, and as the *mu'tamaneen* multiplied, no one felt safe. In order to strangle free expression decisively, the security organizations pursued and rooted out members of the resistance. Political executions became routine within Iraq and in foreign countries that harboured former associates or political opponents. To name but a few, Tawfiq Rushdy and former Prime Minister 'Abd al-Razzaq al-Nayif were killed in the early 1980s, in South Yemen and Britain, respectively; the cleric, Sheikh Sayid Mahdi al-Hakeem, was assassinated in Sudan in January 1988; the former head of Intelligence, Majid 'Abd al-Karim, was murdered in Stockholm in 1988: and, according to Saddam Hussein's son-in-law, Saddam Kamel Hassan, after his defection to Jordan on 8 August 1995, the murder of Sheikh Taleb al-Suhail al-Tamimi in Beirut, in April 1994 was also ordered by Baghdad's security apparatus (see also the additional list of victims in Korn, 1992, pp. 41–6).

Iraq's president stamped his authority on every aspect of life. Professional associations, youth leagues, women's societies, and sports clubs were headed by his supporters. Any demonstration of dissent within these organizations was suppressed by the government's curb on the freedom of speech, assembly and expression. Only persons with a strong belief in the *Ba'th*'s political philosophy and personally loyal to Saddam Hussein were allowed to be employed in the media. Political dissenters, especially the intellectuals, stood no chance of contesting government policies in a democratic exchange of views through legal channels. Those who chose loyalty to their consciences over allegiance to the government were branded as traitors and considered saboteurs, and some even paid with their lives for what they had written. Most were persecuted because of their beliefs, or brutalized because of their defence of others. None of the editorial writers and news reporters were immune from being seized off the streets, at their offices or homes, without warrants for their arrest. While they were detained without trial, their publications' equipment was routinely confiscated. Arbitrary and frequent abductions and systematic torture succeeded in bringing to heel some of those who condemned these measures but had no courage left to fight. Those who could not turn a blind eye 'voted with their feet', and chose to denounce the government from their countries of exile (see also Korn, 1992, pp. 61–3, 65, 80–1). Hence, an impotent opposition was bred by the political straitjacket that enwrapped the country. Currently, with the high degree of media censorship and thought-control, the publication of opposition newspapers, clandestinely circulated and eagerly passed on to other readers, provides the people with their only window to news from the outside world.

Saddam Hussein views his people with indifference and suspicion, and the outside world with hostility. He is remarkably insensitive to domestic public opinion, and does not plunge into crowds. These traits and habits distance him from mainstream social, economic and political concerns. Apart from television coverage or photo opportunities to mark a special event or relay a political message, the president is a virtual recluse, and never lives in the same residence for long. It was even confirmed, in a personal communication, that he often slept in other people's homes, especially after the second Gulf War. His moves were orchestrated in a manner to confuse any potential assassination plotters. Three cavalcades, of twelve identical armoured black Mercedes saloon cars each, roll out of his residence and take different routes, while helicopters hover overhead.

Iraq's president did not derive his authority from a grass-roots political movement, and at first, *Ba'th* Party membership did not include a sufficiently large number among peasants or the working class; it was elitist and had a power structure that was rigidly hierarchical. While the officers' corps became gradually Ba'thized from the late 1960s, the government pursued an active policy of *tab'eeth* during the Iran–Iraq War, when huge numbers of workers, peasants, students and teachers were compelled to join the party and drafted into the army (Dawisha, 1986, pp. 22, 26; and Korn, 1992, pp. 24–6).

In his appointments to key positions, the president drew heavily on Takritis, and strengthened his alliances with them by inter-marriages. Firm dedication and absolute loyalty to his person overrode all other considerations. Examining ministerial, ambassadorial and other sensitive posts, one can hardly fail to notice family and friendship connections. Although Takritis total only about five per cent of the inhabitants of the province of Salahuddin, they are the socio-economic and political elite, and form the inner core of the Iraqi power structure. Were an Iraqi *Who's Who* available, the reading of its entries would have been fascinating, though a little confusing and quite overwhelming.

On a lower rung in the political structure, the middle class is his other power base, especially the officer corps, civil servants and businessmen, mainly drawn from Takrit and encouraged to join the *Ba'th* Party. In addition, Saddam Hussein allied with powerful clans and influential families – a custom prevalent in the Arabian peninsula's tribal societies. By joining him, they derived power and authority for themselves as individuals, and were able to obtain privileges for the groups they belonged to. One such clan were the Jabburs, who numbered between one and 1.5 million. Apart from their size, their attraction lay in the fact that they were partly *Sunni* in the north, and *Shi'i* in the south, and inhabited a large area, which extended from around Mosul and Takrit, down to the west of Baghdad, except for the city of Samarra'. The clan included Muhammad Hussam al-Jabburi, the former Air Force Chief, and Defence Minister Marshal Sa'di Tu'mah 'Abbas al-Jabburi, who was blamed for Iraq's defeat and relieved after *Operation Desert Storm* (Karadaghi, 1993).

To lull the population into believing that he did not favour the *Sunni* Arabs in selecting officials, and to deflect criticism that he relied solely on relatives and friends, Hussein appointed a small number from other ethnic and religious communities. Whereas they were perceived as being on the higher rungs of the hierarchy, they were neither allowed a free hand in the running of the administrations that were entrusted to them, nor were their postings of a sensitive nature, such as intelligence and security. For instance, Kurds were represented by Taha Muhy-al-Din Ma'ruf, member of the RCC; Dr Umid Midhat Mubarak, the Minister of Health and member of the Professional Bureau in the *Ba'th*; and Mukarram al-Talabani, former Minister of Irrigation and member of the Central Committee of the Iraqi Communist Party (ICP), who now lives under virtual house arrest since the collapse of the *Ba'thi*–Communist alliance in 1979. Vice-President Taha Yasseen Ramadan al-Jazrawi, half Kurdish and half Arab *Sunni*, was a member of the RCC since its establishment in 1968, and commanded the Popular Army. A Christian, Deputy Prime Minister Tariq 'Aziz, member of the *Ba'th* RCC and the Regional Command (RC), was formerly Foreign Minister. Sa'dun Hammadi, a former Minister of Economic Affairs, then Prime Minister, is a *Shi'i*; he became Presidential Advisor after being dismissed in September 1991, and replaced by another *Shi'i*, Muhammad Hamza al-Zubaidy, until the president took over the premiership in July 1994.

The total lack of democracy in Iraq left the arena open for a single person to drag his country to war, without the need to debate such a momentous decision with others. It is usually possible to foretell the actions of countries, but in a dictatorship such as Iraq, this is virtually impossible because it is ruled by the whim of one man. Saddam Hussein, as portrayed beforehand, was a law unto himself and ruled by presidential decree. He did not have to sell his policies to an electorate.

His government and military commands were impotent. The National Assembly was an emasculated parliament. And the domestic state-controlled audio-visual and printed press distilled the news to manipulate public opinion.

Iraq shares borders with Iran, Turkey, Syria, Jordan, Kuwait and Saudi Arabia. Its area is 434 934 square kilometres, subdivided administratively into 18 provinces. The population was estimated at around 15 million, at the start of the Iran–Iraq War, and increased to above 18 million in the early 1990s, though the figures of the official census were unavailable. The judicial system includes civil, religious and criminal courts, beside 16 special courts for political and security offences, which hold 'kangaroo' trials. But there is effectively a total absence of the rule of law where disapproval with the leadership or its policies is concerned. The RCC, headed by Saddam Hussein, is the highest executive and legislative body, and appoints the president and the council of ministers. But for all practical purposes, Hussein has the political clout, and there is no separation of government and party. The National Assembly, established in 1980, is composed of 250 members, but parliament's rights were circumscribed by the encroachment of the President, and does not serve as a democratic body that requires accountability by bureaucrats or cabinet ministers. It is in no position to influence the government, and functions merely as a consultative assembly to confer on matters referred to it. Supported by the obedient mass media, it stresses the pluralistic nature of the polity and assists the regime to placate disaffected sectors of society by projecting a superficial democratic discourse (Dawisha, 1986, pp. 26–7; Korn 1992, p. ii; and Sluglett-Farouk and Sluglett, 1990, p. 279).

In countries where economies are primarily based on the export of one commodity, the public sector is usually buttressed at the expense of the private. This leads to the government's greater involvement in manufacturing industries and foreign trade, and to the strengthening of the ruler's power over society, the economy and politics. He enhances his role through reliance on informal networks of clans and families or members of a particular class.

In Iraq, the system of government is highly centralized and suffers from structural shortcomings, such as heavy intervention in economic policies, a large and inefficient bureaucracy, and rampant corruption. The economy was largely based on the production and export of crude oil, and its revenues accounted for more than 95 per cent of foreign currency earnings. With the quadrupling of oil prices in the early 1970s, the state was able to pursue an ambitious development strategy by means of public expenditure. It led economic growth by modernising existing industries, and also by investing heavily in agriculture, the development of urban real estate, the infrastructure and the services industries, starting with communication, electricity and motorway networks. The technological industrial evolution and the substantial infrastructural development were of paramount importance when Iraq turned later to privatization, and the newly launched enterprises profited from the favourable conditions created by the state (Sluglett-Farouk and Sluglett, 1990, pp. 217, 230, 250–1, 253, 265–6, 277, 279).

While developing the civilian sector, the government increased its arms purchases, and, despite the embargo on Iran and Iraq during the 1980s, 46 countries provided them with hardware, of which 38 supplied both sides. According to a study conducted by MEDNEWS, 207 companies in 20 countries supplied Baghdad with non-conventional military components, tools and materiel to enhance its military manufacturing capabilities. Indigenous production of spare-parts, ammunition and light weapons culminated in the modification of the ex-Soviet *Scud-B* missiles, renamed *al-Hussain* and *al-'Abbas*, with ranges of 375 and 560 km. This was made possible with Swiss, German, Brazilian, Egyptian and Argentinian assistance. German, American, Italian and French firms contributed the technology and the components for nuclear, biological and a broad range of chemical (NBC) programmes and for the manufacturing of long-range missile and artillery shells. Britain provided spare parts for British tanks, seized from the Iranians, and some weapons and NBC protective equipment; International Military Services, a company owned by the Ministry of Defence (MoD), helped build a weapons complex to prepare *Exocet* missiles (O'Ballance, 1988, p. 149); and parts for surface-to-surface missiles (SSMs) were exported via Jordan and Egypt – the warheads, discovered by UN inspectors after the second Gulf War, were filled with

nerve gas (*Independent* 12 and 22 June 1993) and it emerged
later that the Iraqis used chemical weapons against Allied
troops in the Second Gulf War (Dispatches, 15 May 1997).
Whilst Iraq remained the USSR's biggest client among LDCs,
other countries involved in arms sales to Baghdad, in its drive
to diversify supplies, included Austria, Czechoslovakia, East
Germany, France, Hungary, Italy, Jordan, Kuwait, Libya,
Poland, Saudi Arabia, South Africa, Spain, and Sudan. From
the mid-1980s, and in spite of a drop in oil prices, the industry
shifted emphasis to prestige projects. Oil revenues were lav-
ished on ludicrous manufacturing ventures, which became
almost entirely geared to military production. Shortly before
the end of the Iran–Iraq War, in July 1988, petro-chemical and
military manufacture were placed under the newly created
Ministry of Industry and Military Industrialization, headed by
Hussein Kamel al-Majeed, Saddam Hussein's son-in-law and
distant cousin (Sampson, 1991; Sallinger and Laurent, 1991,
tables pp. 295–304; Schmidt, 1991, pp. vii, 1–2 and tables
pp. 10, 14, 15, 17, 19; Slugglett-Farouk and Slugglett, 1990,
p. 274; Karsh, 1987, p. 45; and excerpts from Russian Ministry
of Foreign Economic Relations Report in *Hayat*, 14 August
1993).

With the on-going Iran–Iraq War, Iraq's financial burden
continued to grow, and its external debt bill rose, estimated to
have reached between $84 to $94 billion by 1988. The government was unable to pursue a development strategy based
solely on the public sector, and consequently, had to raise
money through privatization. After heavy state involvement in
all aspects of the economy, it was forced to undertake a programme of controlled economic liberalization. This appeared
as a move towards democratization in the West, notwithstanding that the public sector was to remain predominant, with the
private sector as a complement. The state, in fact, was highly
selective and helped to create a new class of entrepreneurs.
The persons most involved in commercial transactions were
either the ruler's immediate family, in-laws and assistants, or
their children.

Similarly to other LDCs, specifically those where public
accountability lacks, nepotism and corruption became
characteristics shared by many of Iraq's senior officials. They
were granted commissions on transactions, particularly those

involving weapons, and pay-offs for manufacturing licences and other permits, all of which enabled them to carve a niche for themselves and become part of the affluent business community. Their privileged status allowed them to either monopolize imports, exports, trade and to some extent manufacturing, or demand shares in concerns owned by others. This led to unequal partnerships, where the initial financiers became junior shareholders, with the consequent weakening of their socio-economic position. Their payments were included in the costs of the finished products, and the consumers bore the brunt of having to purchase imported or locally manufactured goods at highly exaggerated prices. Inflation soared, caused by the combined effect of market manipulation and commissions. While the profits of the elite multiplied, the society was further polarized into rich and poor, and the embryonic class of businessmen was comfortably ensconced among the super-rich bourgeoisie in the top socio-economic layer. A similar process took place in pre- and post-revolutionary Iran, in Egypt after the mid-1970s, and in Syria after the mid-1980s, leading to conditions comparable to those that plagued the Iraqis.

To preserve its hold on a large section of the economy, the state admitted persons who were either part of the established socio-political system, who profited from their connections, and to whom democratic changes and the dispersion of prerogatives were detrimental; or those with sufficient resources to contribute to the development of the nation's productive capability, but with insufficient influence and bargaining power to demand political liberalization.

Evidently, democratization was not on Saddam Hussein's agenda. While the authorities painstakingly promoted Iraq's image as a genuinely modernized country, regardless of the fact that political liberalization had hardly ever kept pace with economic change, the Western press perpetuated the myth of Iraq as a democratic state. And although it was tarnished by political murders that were never solved, disappearances that were never investigated, and grievous human rights violations that were ignored, the foreign media publicized the illusory veneer of modernity, cunningly crafted by Iraq's president. At the same time, exiled Iraqi intellectuals, who unleashed their long-standing hostility against the regime in their writings, were slighted when they tried to shatter the misleading image, and exposed the oppression visited upon their people.

As the second Gulf War demonstrated, one of the lessons of the Iran–Iraq War is that if the international community, as a whole, does not check a dictator at an early stage, the price of doing so later can be costly. They armed a ghoul they could no longer overpower, while their studied silence about the terror and carnage – especially in Iraqi Kurdistan – continued for more than a decade. The world thus stands accused of arming Saddam Hussein and of complacently watching him from the ringside waging war against both Iran and his own people.

It is crucial to emphasize this point because throughout the Iran–Iraq War, and up to the invasion of Kuwait, when Saddam Hussein was the West's 'darling', media reports accused members of the Iraqi opposition of exaggerating the extent of corruption and repression within the country. Some even threw a blanket of silence over his attack on Halabja and Shalamja, using chemical weapons (CW), whilst others confirmed the military report, issued by Washington at the time, denouncing Iran over the mass gassing of the two Kurdish towns. They pictured the Iraqi government as a model in the Middle East when it embarked on economic liberalization and privatization, developed its infrastructure, promoted women in public office and promised wider political participation. Beside these modernizing aspects, the secular model of new Iraqi nationalism, namely, Ba'thism as reinterpreted by Saddam Hussein during the Iran–Iraq War, appealed to Western politicians and journalists, who hoped it would offset Khomeini's exemplar of Islamic government.

Normally liberal analysts were either selective in the subjects they wrote about or indifferent to them. They neither demanded of their governments to press Baghdad to cease violating human rights, nor exposed the Iraqi president who only paid lip service to his pledge to create new political parties and lift the ban on old ones. In the aftermath of the second Gulf War, the same newspaper columnists and analysts, who time and again emphasized Iraq's steps towards democratization, lurched with ease to a spasm of indignation. They entered a contest to demonize Saddam Hussein and dent the Iraqi peoples' image, and in both cases, competed in highlighting the trivial and the irrelevant. When they switched later, they did not separate the two distinct issues of Iraq and its people from the president and his entourage. While Iraq-bashing became fashionable, they did not cast as much as a cursory glance at the Iraqis' predicament. They failed to recognize that Saddam Hussein provoked the world with his decision to invade Kuwait and his determination to annex it, while his war-weary people were propelled into another war, after a short peace lull, and had no means of protesting.

2.2 IRAQ'S POLITICAL PARTIES AND THE OPPOSITION-IN-EXILE*

The assessment of foreign policy shifts is unrealistic in the absence of an understanding of internal circumstances, whether political, economic or social – an argument that is more relevant in the case of decisions regarding war. The most prevalent assumptions for the adoption of the Tanker War strategy by Iraq were discussed earlier, namely, that four years after the start of full-scale military operations, any preconceived hopes to vanquish Iran, that Saddam Hussein may have harboured earlier, were brutally dashed. Furthermore, domestic conditions also played a role in the Iraqi leader's determination to launch the new strategy.

It is believed that growing disapproval among a segment of the Iraqi population was one of the factors that led to the adoption of the Tanker War strategy, albeit a negligible one, since public opinion has not been one of Saddam Hussein's main considerations. Some segments of society and a number of political opposition parties resented the growing number of Iraqi casualties and the occupation of Iraqi territory by Iranian troops. In order to understand internal conditions that determined the resort to an alternative strategy, a review of Iraq's political parties is worthwhile.

After the sun set on the Ottoman Empire, *Hizb al-Nahdah* (Renaissance Party) and *Hizb al-Akha' al-Watani* (National Party) represented Arab aspirations in Iraq. This movement reached its apogee at the end of the Second World War, with the establishment of *Harakat al-Shabab al-Qawmi al-'Arabi*

Note: see A11 for update.

(Pan-Arab Youth Movement) and *Hizb al-Istiqlal* (Independence Party). In 1952, Michel 'Aflaq's *al-Ba'th al-'Arabi al-Ishtiraki* (Socialist Arab Revival Party) championed Arab unity and socialism, and attracted the younger generation of members in the old parties. The leftist trend emerged in the early 1920s, supported by Marxist intellectuals. In the beginning, they influenced public opinion mainly through rubrics, which were truculent writings against British imperialism. Their movement took shape in the mid-1930s, with the establishment of *Jama'at al-Ahali* (People's Group) and the ICP in 1934, but the government occasionally pursued and imprisoned their leadership, and in 1949 executed a few of its heads. After World War Two, three parties were established: *al-Hizb al-Watani al-Dimuqrati* (National Democratic Party), *Hizb al-Ahrar* (Liberal Party) and *'Usbat Mukafahat al-Sahyuniya* (League Against Zionism) (Butti, 1992, 1985, pp. 38, 85–94, and 1969, pp. 38–40, 65, 91; also Rondot, 1990, pp. 47–8).

In 1957, four parties reached an understanding on future policies. *Al-Hizb al-Watani al-Dimuqrati, Hizb al-Istiqlal, al-Ba'th* and the ICP allied under the name of *Jabhat al-Ittihad al-Watani* (National Union Front), followed by the signing of an agreement between the ICP and the Kurdistan Democratic Party (KDP) to support it. The Front's members maintained that it was responsible for the revolution that toppled King Faysal II in 1958, while the thesis generally accepted by Western historians, based on reports by the British ambassador in Baghdad, viewed the removal of the Iraqi monarchy as resulting from a military coup; but it should be remembered that diplomats' accounts are usually compliant with the status quo power. A minute-by-minute examination of events established that a small force of about 3000 troops started a rebellion. Contacted by the Free Officers, prior to their move, opposition leaders mobilized the masses. Around 100 000 people immediately surrounded the palace, blocked the streets and precluded any attempt by monarchists to rescue the royal family (Batatu, 1992, pp. 106–17; and Sluglett-Farouk and Sluglett, 1990, pp. 48–9).

The Front was short-lived and collapsed. Despite its support for the revolution, the ICP was excluded from the new cabinet. The remaining parties were pitted against each other over the union with the newly-established United Arab Republic (UAR), joining Egypt and Syria. The pan-Arab *Ba'th* and *Istiqlal* championed the proposal, whilst *al-Hizb al-Dimuqrati*, the ICP and the Free Officers favoured a federation. While pan-Arabism was only encouraged by the mainly *Sunni* urban population, the *Shi'ah* and the Kurds rejected the ideology on sectarian and ethnic grounds, seeing no advantage in uniting with other countries, whose peoples were predominantly *Sunni* Arabs.

In 1970, Iraqi Kurdistan's autonomy was declared with the signing of the 'March Proclamation' by the KDP's leader, mullah Mustafa Barzani and the *Ba'th*. Three years later, *al-Jabhah al-Wataniyah wal-Qawmiyah al-Taqaddumiyah* (National Progressive Front) was formed with the incorporation of the ICP. The KDP withdrew the following year, and the ICP five years later, a short time before Saddam Hussein took power. From then on, the *Ba'th* dominated the entire socio-political structure, and the KDP and the ICP in the north, and *al-Da'wah* in the south initiated armed struggle (Butti, 1992).

Although the majority of Iraq's population are Muslim, Islamic parties emerged relatively late on the political scene, and did not play as prominent a role as secular ones, until the last decade, when they became more active in the opposition to the present regime. The movement crystallized by 1982, when the main parties grouped, giving birth to the Supreme Assembly of Islamic Revolution in Iraq (SAIRI) (see A11).

To strengthen the fragile fabric of his population during the Iran–Iraq War, President Hussein gradually shifted emphasis from *Ba'thi* pan-Arabism to Iraqi nationalism and continuously stressed the secular nature of his government. Borrowing from *Ba'thi* dogma, his philosophy basically underlined non-intervention in religion on the part of the government, and opposed the use of religion for political purposes to encroach upon the state (Ghareeb, 1983, pp. 62–3). Whilst the government's professed policy was to create a new national identity, it in fact guaranteed its survival by exacerbating sectarian and ethnic cleavages (Al-Khafaji, 1992, p. 15).

Sectarian discord, sparked by *Sunni* predominance in the socio-economic and political structures, and later exacerbated by the Iran–Iraq War, led to the creation of a large number of new *Shi'i* parties. However, Iraqi Islamic parties are dissimilar to the Iranian: firstly, because different political trends are represented in their factions, such as the pan-Arab *Ba'th* and *Qawmiyun*, in addition to liberal and, paradoxically, even leftist groups; and secondly, because the majority of their members believe in the separation of religion and government – unlike the Iranians, who adopted *velayet-e-faqih* (rule of politics by religion) (Butti, Interview, 26 December 1994).

The Iran–Iraq War devastated the opposition in more ways than one. It shattered the organizational structures of the parties, decimated its members, and obliterated communication between those in exile and those who remained behind. The *Shi'ah* sought refuge in Iran, where they regrouped, and whence they founded and administered underground networks in southern Iraq. And the leftists established bases in the northern mountains, where they identified with the Kurdish cause, and carried out sporadic guerrilla attacks. These ground to a halt when their camps were routed by *Operation al-Anfal* in 1988 (Abd al-Jabbar, 1992, p. 12).

The war also atomized the opposition into three main tendencies. Some Kurds and most *Shi'i* parties promoted the slogan 'my enemy's enemy is my friend'; they stepped up their anti-government activities and frequently collaborated with Tehran in secret, by serving as guides for Iranian troops in Iraqi Kurdistan, in the north, and in the predominantly *Shi'i* south. The pro-Syrian Iraqi *Ba'th* and a faction from the ICP, with some *Shi'ah*, backed Iraq's war effort but showed no support for the government. And most leftists and communists advocated the recourse to negotiations, and blamed Baghdad and Tehran for having gone to war; after 1982, they condemned Saddam Hussein, declaring him personally accountable for the start of hostilities, and were amongst the first to denounce the US' and Gulf states' responsibility for goading the Iraqi leader into attacking Iran. In allying with Iran, the Kurds ignored that Tehran abruptly withdrew its succour on more than one occasion, and the *Shi'ah* disregarded Khomeini's own stress on Iranian nationalism in his drive against the Shah, and again in the war against Iraq (Abd al-Jabbar, 1992, p. 4).

By monopolizing the slogans of patriotism and nationalism, the President was able to undercut the opposition's struggle against the government. Their stance attracted more repression, and resulted in their loss of legitimacy among Iraqis, having sided with the enemy they were fighting. Thus, during the 1980s, the Iraqi leader's opponents were incapable of devising and implementing a dual-pronged policy that opposed both him and his war. By the end of the decade, a number of dissidents were seeking a face-saving formula to return to their fatherland and be reintegrated into the government-approved political structure (Abd al-Jabbar, 1992, pp. 3–4; and Ghareeb, 1983, pp. 69–70).

After the failure of successive Kurdish rebellions from 1921, in response to the establishment of the new Iraqi state, and up to Mustafa Barzani's revolt in the mid-1940s, the Kurdish movement was strengthened with the establishment of the KDP in 1946, the Kurds' main representative until the mid-1970s. Under the motto 'Democracy for Iraq and true autonomy for Kurdistan', they established their first front in Iraq. *Al-Jabhah al-Kurdistaniyah al-'Iraqiyah* (Iraqi Front of Kurdistan), founded in 1988 by eight of the main Kurdish groups, the ICP and the Assyrian Democratic Movement, it sought to enlarge the portion freed from central control in Iraqi Kurdistan (Butti, 1992 and Interview, 26 December 1994).

In order to reach a well-defined aim – despite slight ideological differences between the parties – unique historical conditions dictate the need to initiate political coalitions. These should be based on clear socio-economic strategies, and must represent diverse political trends that respond to the aspirations of all social and economic groups. Iraqi opponents of the regime formed a front under the name of *al-Jabhah al-Wataniyah wal-Qawmiyah al-Dimuqratiyah* (National Democratic Front) in Tripoli, Libya in 1981. It collapsed after a few months, and a new front was established, which comprised the main national and democratic powers and the Kurdish movement. It lasted a few years and broke down as a result of feuds in Iraqi Kurdistan – essentially between members of the ICP and various Kurdish factions – which claimed the lives of several scores of their followers. In December 1990, a loose coalition of opposition parties and groupings signed an understanding with the broad aim of overthrowing the regime. They formed the Committee for

Joint Action, but it foundered for a want of democracy. With a collective leadership of five, each of whom was empowered to veto, two seats were given to Islamic parties, whilst both Kurdish parties shared one seat, the *Qawmiyun* and the pro-Syrian *Ba'th* another, and the ICP and the socialists had the fifth. The political groups multiplied subsequently, and from 17, they now number over 60, most of which represent pan-Arabs, Islamists or Kurds, but their effectiveness is impaired by constant political sniping.

Political repression had forced government opponents to seek asylum abroad. By relying on regional and outside powers for financial, political and diplomatic support, they were perceived as sympathetic to the interests sponsoring them, which jeopardized their credibility. Saddam Hussein used this against them, targeting the *Shi'i* parties in particular, and branded them as unpatriotic during the 1991 uprising. He claimed that they opposed other Iraqis on orders from foreign capitals, especially Tehran, Riyadh and Damascus. Furthermore, by banking on American, European, Iranian or Syrian tanks to remove the government, they failed to organize and lead the only effective means of resistance, namely, internal revolt.

Most new opposition parties share a characteristic common to a number of LDCs. They are loose gatherings, formed around a particular person, some of whom small dictators, disguised as democrats. Their members are held together less by their programmes, which are imbued with generalities, than by the personality of the founder. With the strong personal element of following, political discourse takes the form of wrestling between leaders, and is often overshadowed by ethnic, sectarian and tribal rivalries.

While political dissent in other Arab countries is basically bipolar, the picture is much more complicated with regard to Iraq. Parties have mushroomed to a degree that one is often unable to distinguish the differences between them. Numbering more than five dozen by the late 1990s, it is difficult to remember their names. It is no overstatement to say that almost all ethnic and sectarian communities created parties covering the whole spectrum of political doctrines, ranging from the far left to the far right. Their potential was diffused at a time when dissident Iraqis were eager for the unification of the movement, not its fragmentation.

Table 2.1   Iraqi Opposition Organizations and Parties

1.1   Organizations and Associations

–   **Iraqi National Congress** (INC) is ruled by a Presidential Council, based on ethnic and religious affiliation, and Salah al-Shaikhli, a former RCC member, was official spokesman, but resigned and edits *Al-Wifaq al-Watani*'s *Baghdad*. Al-Barzani represents the Kurds, Dr Muhammad Bahr al-'Ulum, the *Shi'ah*, and al-Naqeeb, the *Sunnah*. Chaired by Dr Ahmad al-Chalabi, the Executive Committee represented all parties, and had 25 members, widened to 27 shortly later. Some joined in their personal capacity: al-Naqeeb, Bahr al-'Ulum, al-Chalabi, 'Amer 'Abdallah, the former ICP minister, Taleb Shibeeb, 'Abdul-Hussein Sha'ban (withdrew) and Hani al-Fekeiki, Vice-Chairman (a *Shi'i* who opposeed Saddam Hussein in the RC since 1968, and sectarian and ethnic intolerance, withdrew in January 1996, then succumbed to cancer a year later; denied burial in Iraq, the man who dreamt of unity with Syria, was entombed in Damascus, in accordance with his wish, on the 24th anniversary of the Ramadan war). A Constitutional Advisory Council, headed by General 'Arif 'Abdul-Razzaq, allowed those not nominated in other committees some representation. The INC published the weekly *al-Mautamar*, edited by Muhammad 'Abdul-Jabbar, which folded in mid-June 1997 for lack of funds. Its members were:

1.   *Al-Hizb al-Dimuqrati al-'Iraqi* (Iraqi Democratic Party).
2.   *Al-Wifaq al-Watani* (National Accord).
3.   Association of Iraqi Democrats (froze membership, then withdrew in 1996).
4.   Assyrian Democratic Movement.
5.   *Harakat al-Mujahedeen* (Fighters' Movement).
6.   *Hizb al-Da'wah al-Islamiyah* (Islamic Call or Invitation Party) (withdrew in 1994).
7.   *Hizb Kadeheen Kurdistan* (*Zahmet Kishan* in Kurdish, Toilers of Kurdistan Party).
8.   Iraqi Communist Party (suspended activities, then withdrew in 1995).
9.   Iraqi National Turcoman Party.
10. Islamic Movement in Kurdistan.
11. *Jund al-Imam* (the Army of the Imam).
12. Kurdish Democratic Party (KDP).
13. *Majlis al-'Asha'ir al-'Iraqiyah* (Council of Iraqi Tribes).
14. *Munazzamat al-'Amal al-Islami* (Islamic Action Organization).
15. National Reform Movement.
16. Patriotic Union of Kurdistan (PUK).
17. Supreme Assembly for Islamic Revolution in Iraq.

–   **Arab Nationalist Movement.** Based in Syria, it comprises *Hizb al-Ba'th-Qiadat Qutr al-'Iraq* (Iraqi Regional Command), *al-Hizb al-Ishtiraki-'Iraq* (Iraqi Socialist Party) *al-Tajamu' al-Wahdawi al-Nasseri* (Unionist Nasserist Gathering), *al-Harakah al-Ishtirakiyah al-'Arabiyah* (Arab Socialist Movement), *al-Hizb al-Qawmi al-Wahdawi* (National Unionist Party) and *al-Qawmiyun al-Mustaqillun* (Independent Nationalists). Its monthly organ, published in Syria, is a tabloid called *Al-Watan*.

–   **Iraqi Coordinating Committee for Dialogue and Follow-Up (ICCDFU).** A committee of members of an Opposition Conference, held in London in April 1993, mainly for members of the opposition who did not participate in the INC, because they were critical of its sectarian, racial and federational inclination. Its membership includes prominent opposition figures such as Sa'd Saleh Jaber (FIC),

Sheikh Mahdi al-Khalisi (Islamic Movement of Iraq), 'Arif 'Abdul-Razzaq (INC Assembly), and the prominent journalist Sami Faraj 'Ali and others.

–　　**Majlis al-'Asha'ir al-'Iraqiyah** (Council of Iraqi Tribes). Led by Sami 'Ezar al-Ma'jun and Hussein al-Sha'lan, and based in Syria and Europe, it has connections with both *Sunni* and *Shi'ah* tribes, which took part in the 1991 uprising.

–　　**Supreme Assembly of the Islamic Revolution in Iraq** also called **Supreme Council of the Islamic Revolution in Iraq (SCIRI)**. Headed by Ayatollah Muhammad Baqer al-Hakeem, based in Iran, is an umbrella organization which claims to represent the *Sh'iah*, who make up between 55 and 60 per cent of Iraqis. Its 10 000-strong military arm, the *Badr* Brigades, currently under the control of the Iranians, is nominally led by the Ayatollah's younger brother, 'Abdul-'Aziz, and largely made up of Iraqi *Sh'iah* PoWs, captured by the Iranian troops during the first Gulf War. Its organs are the by-monthly newspaper *Nida' Al-Rafidhayn*, published in Damascus and *Al-Shahadah* and *'Lewa' Assadr*, published in Iran.

1.2　Political Parties

Democrats and Independents
–　　**Association of Iraqi Democrats**, led by Muhammad al-Dhaher, the group's delegates participate in INC conferences and the Executive Committee, although it is not a political party. It is a cluster of an independent-thinking community, whose objective is the removal of the regime, and who share national, democratic and liberal values. Its London-based periodical magazine, *Al-Demuqrati*, was edited by the poet Buland al-Haydari, until his death in August 1996.

–　　**Free Iraqi Council (FIC)**, chaired by Sa'd Saleh Jaber, the son of the former prime minister of Iraq, who signed the Portsmouth Treaty with Britain in January 1948, leading to an uprising and its cancellation, thus forcing him to escape. Its policies correspond to those of the former New *Ummah* Party, and its membership comprises middle-class intellectuals, for the most part. Established in early 1991 in London, it contemplates a democratic and pluralistic government, capable of rebuilding the economy, but is not a member of the INC. *Al-'Iraq al-Hur*, a newspaper, was published monthly, but now appears periodically.

–　　**Harakat al-Islah al-'Iraqiyah (Iraqi Reconciliation Movement)**, led by al-Naqeeb, it groups independent nationalists.

–　　**Al-Tajamu' al-Dimuqrati al-'Iraqi (Iraqi Democratic Assembly)**, led by Saleh Dugla, its membership consists of ex-communists and a majority of intellectuals, who aim to establish a democratic parliamentary regime in Iraq. The monthly newspaper *Al-Ghad al-Dimuqrati* is its organ.

–　　**Iraqi Communist Party**, founded in 1934, it was headed by 'Aziz Muhammad, until the 5th National Congress in 1993, then replaced by Hameed Majeed Moussa. It has former roots in Iraq, and its members were part of the Iraqi administration until the late 1970s. It issues the bi-monthly newspaper *Tareeq Al-Sha'b*, and in London, publishes the monthly magazine *Risalat Al-'Iraq*, of which a periodical in the English language also appears.

–　　**Iraqi Democratic Movement (IDM)**, based in Dubai and the UAE, it has contacts within Iraq and elsewhere in the Middle East. Professionals form the bulk of its membership, but it has no specific hierarchy, and is administered by a Central Committee of six.

– **Iraqi Free Officers** are connected with al-Naqeeb's Iraqi Reconciliation Movement, and have support among officers within Iraq. Hussein al-Jabburi, one of its prominent members, was one of several officers poisoned by the regime in the spring of 1992. The group, which attempted to assassinate the president at least once, includes Tawfiq al-Yasseri, Ahmad al-Samarra'i, 'Aziz al-Yasseri and Safa' al-Battat, who was poisoned with thallium, in 1995, and treated in London.

– *Al-Harakah al-Malakiyah al-Dasturiyah al-Iraqiah* (**Monarchists**) based in London, and headed by Sharif 'Ali Bin al-Hussein, a descendant of the last Hashemite rulers of the Hijaz, and the son of princess Badi'ah and a cousin of King Faysal II of Iraq, who was killed in the 1958 revolution, at which time Sharif 'Ali's family sought refuge in the Saudi Embassy. Born in Baghdad in 1956, he holds a degree in agricultural economics and has some experience in banking. The Royalists, who have some support among the exiled Iraqi community, are seen as a possible compromise to resolve the difficulties which tend to fragment the opposition movement (El-Shazly, 1993, pp. 8–9; and see A11). In 1996, their fortnightly magazine *Al-Dasturiyah*, replaced a monthly newspaper, also published in London, named *Al-Malakiyah Al-Dasturiyah*.

Islamic Parties and Groups

– *Ahl al-Bait* is a *Shi'i* social, religious and cultural foundation, based in London, and its guardian is Bahr al-'Ulum.

– *Hizbal-Da'wah al-Islamiyah*, founded by Ayatollah Baqer al-Sadr, who was executed, with his sister Bint al-Hoda by Saddam Hussein in 1980, is led by Sheikh Muhammad Mahdi al-Asefi, Dr Ja'far al-Adeeb (Abu Bilal), Sheikh Nasiri and Sa'id al-Haiyi. It is active in southern Iraq, and claims to have made a number of assassination attempts on the Iraqi president. But like other groupings, it suffers from internal splits. Alongside SAIRI, it has influence in Najaf and Karbela'. Its organs are the weekly newspaper *Al-Rafidhayn*, published in London and Syria, *Al-Mawgef*, published in Syria, *Sawt al-'Iraq*, published in London, and *Al-Jihad*, published in Iran.

– **Al-Khoi Foundation** is a religious charitable organization, established by Ayatollah al-Khoi, the *Sh'iah Marja'* of Najaf, in the 1970s, and is currently run by his sons. The eldest of these was put under house arrest with his father until his death in a car accident, in suspect circumstances, in the summer of 1992. The Foundation cooperates with the opposition to Saddam Hussein.

– **Democratic Islamic National Association**, led by Sa'd Yousef, this small party is based in Tehran, and appears to be distancing itself from SAIRI.

– *Harakat al-Mujahedeen* (**Fighters' Movement**), based in Syria and led by Bayan Jaber, it was created by *al-Da'wah* members to increase their membership in the INC, and publishes *Lewa' Al-Sadr*.

– **Islamic Accord** (formerly *Muhajjereen*) moved its base from Tehran to Damascus, after disagreements with the Iranian authorities. The group currently plans to expand its activities in Britain.

– **Islamic Bloc**, led by Muhammad al-Alusi, is a small *Sunni* fundamentalist movement, connected with a foiled plot by the Muslim Brotherhood against the regime in the 1970s, and suffers from divisions, which led to resignations.

– *Al-Harakah al-Islamiyah fil 'Iraq (Al-Khalesseen)* (**Islamic Movement of Iraq**), led by Sheikh Mahdi al-Khalisi, a member of ICCDFU, was founded in 1978, but plays a minor role.

–   ***Al-Hizb al-Islami*** (**Islamic Party**), led by Dr Usaina al-Takriti, is a *Sunni* party, with a branch in Kurdistan.

–   ***Harakat Jund al-Imam***, led by Sheikh al-Khafaji and Sami al-Badri.

–   ***Munazzamat al-'Amal al-Islami***, led by Ayatollah Muhammad Taqi-Eddin al-Mudaressi, Ayatollah Muhammad Shirazi and Sheikh Muhsin al-Hussaini, it has a large membership within SAIRI, but its leadership feel that the Assembly retains far too much control. *Al-'Amal Al-Islami*, its weekly newspaper, and *Ashaheed* are published in Tehran.

Pan-Arab Parties

–   ***Al-Harakah al-Ishtirakiyah al-'Arabiyah*** (**Arab Socialist Movement**), led by 'Abdul-Elah al-Nasrawi.

–   ***Al-Hizb al-Ishtiraki-'Iraq*** (**Iraqi Socialist Party**), led by Dr Mubder al-Waiyes, it is based in Damascus, and was originally part of the Committee for Joint Action. Its members are mostly Arab nationalists.

–   ***Al-Hizb al-Qawmi al-Wahdawi*** (**National Unionist Party**), led by Ahmad al-Habbubi.

–   ***Al-Qawmiyun al-Mustaqillun*** (**Independent Nationalists**), previously led by the moderate al-Naqeeb.

–   ***Al-Tajamu' al-Wahdawi al-Nasseri*** (**Unionist Nasserist Gathering**), led by Dr 'Abdul-Hameed Sherif.

–   ***Al-Wifaq al-Watani*** (**National Accord**), led by Dr Ayad 'Allawi, it includes numerous former members of *al-Ba'th* Party, and while their main base is in London, the group's membership spreads to Europe, Turkey, Syria and Saudi Arabia. They are reputed to have maintained contacts with *Ba'thi* officials and officers within Iraq, and hope to dislodge Saddam Hussein from within, by using these connections. The party publishes the weekly newspaper *Baghdad* in London and Damascus.

–   ***Hizb al-Ba'th*** (***Qiadat Qutr al-'Iraq***) (**Iraqi Regional Command**), led by Dr Fadhel al-Ansari, it publishes a monthly magazine entitled *Sawt Al-Jamaheer*.

–   **Iraqi Democratic Accord Assembly** is a London-based group, which is not a member of the INC. It is led by Salah 'Omar al-'Ali, a Takriti and former member of the RCC, who disagreed with Saddam Hussein in the early 1970s. He aims for the dislodging of the president, without the elimination of the existing power structure controlled by the *Ba'th* and the Takriti elite. It publishes *Al-Wifaq* weekly newspaper in London.

1.3   *Parties and Groups Based in Iraqi Kurdistan*

Al-Jabhah al-Kurdistaniyah al-'Iraqiyah (**Iraqi Front of Kurdistan**) grouped the following parties, until the elections in May 1992:

–   **Assyrian Democratic Party**, publishes the monthly newspaper, *Al-Ashuri*.

–   ***Hizb Kadeheen Kurdistan*** (in Kurdish, *Zahmet Kishan*, **Toilers of Kurdistan Party**), led by *mullah* Qader 'Aziz, it publishes the monthly newspaper *Al-Rayah*.

–   **Kurdistan Communist Party-Iraq**, formerly a regional branch of the ICP, it was founded during the 5th National Congress of the ICP in 1993. Karim Ahmed is its current secretary-general. The party is influential throughout the area, and maintains friendly relations with the other Kurdish parties. Its weekly newspaper is entitled *Rigai Kurdistan* (The Path of Kurdistan).

–   **Kurdish Democratic Party (KDP)**, led by Mas'ud al-Barzani, it has a large organization inside northern Iraq, based mainly on tribal support in the Badinan area bordering Turkey. It is more traditional than the PUK, which split from it. Although widely respected as a courageous tribal fighter, its leader has difficulties with some of his relatives within the Barzani and neighbouring tribes. In the elections in Iraqi Kurdistan in May 1992, the KDP gained 51 per cent of the vote. In July 1993 the Unity Party of Kurdistan (UPK), an amalgamation of three smaller Kurdish parties, merged with the KDP. The *Khabat* weekly newspaper is its organ.

–   **Patriotic Union of Kurdistan (PUK)** draws much of its support from the areas around Sulaymaniyah and north-eastern Iraq, bordering on Iran, and has many supporters among the Kurdish intelligentsia. It is well organized, and towards the end of the Iran–Iraq war had almost as many fighters on the ground as the KDP. The PUK came second to the KDP in the 1992 elections, with 49 per cent of the vote. It publicizes itself strongly and its leader, Jalal Talabani, travels widely on behalf of the Front. It publishes the weekly newspaper *Al-Ittihad*.

–   **Unity Party of Kurdistan (UPK)** comprises three of the smaller Kurdish parties: the Kurdistan Popular Democratic Party (KPDP), the Kurdistan Socialist Party of Iraq (KSPI) and the Popular Alliance of Socialist Kurdistan (PASOK), who united to form the UPK, under the leadership of Muhammad Mahmud (Sami) Abdul-Rahman, leader of the KPDP, after the Kurdish elections of May 1992, and merged with the KDP in the summer of 1993.

Other Groupings

–   *Al-Harakah al-Islamiyah fi Kurdistan al-'Iraq* (**Islamic Movement in Kurdistan**), led by Sheikh 'Ali 'Abdul-'Aziz, but its spiritual leader is Sheikh 'Othman 'Abdul-'Aziz. It is a *Sunni* group, based in Halabja, near the Iranian border.

–   **Kurdish Conservative Party**, formed by a younger generation of Kurds, it includes a number of tribal leaders. In the past, they called for the independence of the old *velayet* of Mosul from Iraq.

–   **National Turcoman Party**, founded after the 1991 uprising.

–   *Al-Ittihad al-Islami fi Kurdistan al-'Iraq* (**Islamic Union in Iraqi Kurdistan**), which has strong links with Egypt's Muslim Brotherhood and Turkey's Islamic *Refah* (Welfare) Party, considers itself an extension of the 1950s Iraqi Muslim Brotherhood in its flexibility and repudiation of violence, and believes in the reshaping of policies, whether social or cultural, to conform to Islam.

–   *Hizbollah al-Thawri al-Kurdi* also called *Harakat al-Nahdah al-Islamiyah* (**Revolutionary Kurdish Party of God**) has minor activities, supported by Iran, and is led by Adham al-Barzani, the nephew of Sheikh Mohammad Khaled al-Barzani, the most prominent tribal religious personality.

Source: Compiled from various sources.

Note: See A11.

In 1992, a number of these parties combined under the leadership of the INC umbrella organization. They held two conferences, a restricted one in Vienna in June, then an expanded meeting, attended by 281 delegates, in 'liberated' Iraqi Kurdistan. It was inaugurated on 26 October, after overcoming Kurdish apprehension. The Kurds feared a backlash by surrounding countries, on whose goodwill they increasingly relied for their lifeblood, and also for another practical reason: delegations had to enter Iraqi Kurdistan through one of the three neighbouring countries.

Before the Salahuddin conference, a list of the five dozen parties was compiled, and percentages given to each. The proportion was equated with a quota apportioned to each group to send representatives, though some leaders were invited for their personal status. The Islamic groups had 35 per cent, the Kurds 25, the *Qawmiyun* 18, the Turcomans six, the socialists and liberals four each, the Assyrians and the Communists three each, and two per cent were given to tribal envoys. Some parties refused to send delegates, such as the Syrian-supported *Qawmiyun*, who demanded 30 per cent, while others obtained more seats, by claiming a larger membership among their ranks.

In spite of ideological disagreements, the delegates achieved an understanding on general policies, such as the acceptance of a federation, the duration of the interim government, human rights and democratic elections (though some *Shi'ah* had reservations on the last point). After public discussions and consultation behind closed doors among party leaders exclusively, consensus was reached to designate an executive committee, responsible for daily management. A *Shi'ah*-inspired proposal to have a six-member council was ruled out, and a Presidential Council of three participants was selected. Mirroring the set-up after the 1958 revolution, it was based on ethnic and religious affiliation, and not on political loyalties. Al-Barzani represented the Kurds, being acknowledged as the leader of the largest party. The *Shi'ah* elected Bahr al-'Ulum, a non-controversial cleric from a respected family, who emigrated to the West, and lacked strong ties with Islamic parties. He won by default, due to the absence of al-Hakeem, who resided in Tehran. The third member was General Hassan al-Naqeeb, a *Sunni* from an upper middle class land-owning family, who lived in Syria, and was enlisted as a well-known military figure, having served as Deputy Chief of Army Staff. Earlier, he had been Military Attaché in Washington between 1958 and 1960, when he joined the *Ba'th* Party, then its Military Bureau, three years later. He was one of three officers who sentenced Qasim to death at the Iraqi Broadcasting Station, along with 'Abdul-Ghani al-Rawi and al-Bakr, who later became President, and who, at the time, refused to sign the sentence. Al-Naqeeb served as commander of Iraqi Forces in Jordan during the 'Black September' incidents in 1970, and as ambassador to Spain, until he defected from Sweden to Iraqi Kurdistan, in 1978, where he later organized military resistance against Baghdad.

Damascus and Tehran rejected the decisions reached at both conferences, accusing them of being Western-oriented and aimed at Iraq's break-up. At a meeting held in Damascus in December, the Syrian-supported factions questioned the integrity of the INC leadership, and maintained that the delegations sent to Vienna and Arbil were not representative of opposition trends within Iraq. They failed, however, to set up an alternative grouping. In addition, some of the leaders who attended the October meeting subsequently denounced it and repudiated the final arrangement – which brought into question the suitability of the system employed.

This in no way means that democratic dissent is harmful. But the weakness of the Iraqi opposition movement is partially attributable to their inability to devise a formula for a council acceptable to the majority of Iraqis at home and abroad. By disregarding political affiliation and maintaining ethnic and religious representation, they risk an outcome similar to the one in Lebanese politics. Known as the 'confessional system', proportional representation by religious faith is applied to government appointments. All officials are selected on confessional grounds, regardless of efficiency. More often than not, in order to reach consensus on nominees, people of lesser merit are selected, and as a rule, they serve their community's interests, and not Lebanon as a nation.

The INC is more pluralistic than other alliances formed so far, and includes parties with roots and weight in Iraq. Whilst the Tehran-supported *al-Da'wah*, pro-Syrian pan-Arabs, some Saudi-backed independents and a number of leftists were not at Vienna, simply because they refused to participate, they were represented in the Executive Committee at Salahuddin, except for the Syrian-based *Qawmiyun*. The INC is committed to the establishment of a democratic government, after removing the present regime, and continues to be the most comprehensive umbrella grouping. Furthermore, despite criticism and internal disputes, as well as regional and international constraints, it survives as an opposition coalition, and almost constantly attempts to remedy to its shortcomings. It has the added advantage of making the opposition's views known to the world, whereas internal protest is muzzled.

However, growing disagreements, involving the secrecy surrounding the source and disbursement of INC funding, the scarcity of meetings and the lack of consultation between the chairman and the members of the Executive Committee led to the withdrawal of *al-Da'wah*, the ICP, the Association of Iraqi Democrats and others. Some independents, such as Hani al-Fekeiki and 'Abdul-Hussein Sha'ban, either froze their membership or withdrew in protest at the one-man decision-making within the leadership. Although these developments weakened the INC, it continued to function within the larger opposition movement, and al-Chalabi, supported by some Western capitals, was frequently invited to attend negotiations, such as those involving mediation between the feuding Kurdish parties.

But exiled political activists neither resolved their battle for power, nor delivered to their people their long-held hope for a democratic government in their multi-ethnic and multi-sectarian nation. Amid political posturing, they are at variance on the nature of the future government. Apart from the Kurds, who strongly back a secular federation, the other parties are uncertain whether to maintain the parliamentary republic, create a presidential republic, restore the monarchy, or establish an Islamic theocracy based on the Iranian model. The opposition's record of bellicosity over differing agendas yields little to encourage belief that cooperation between them is possible. It somewhat explains why President Hussein has survived so far, having escaped – within one decade only – two of the bloodiest wars in contemporary times and uprisings in 14 of Iraq's 18 provinces.

2.3   SADDAM'S ASSESSMENT OF KHOMEINI'S IRAN

Because Iraq initiated full-scale military operations in 1980 and the Tanker War in 1984, Iran's counterattacks have been dealt with in the text as a response. Because this study focuses on Iraq's military strategy and political objectives, and does not claim to equally assess Iran's, the preceding two sections examined Iraq's geopolitical profile and political economy in some detail, showing how its power structure sparked competing political forces, within and beyond the borders of the country, some of which with military means, albeit limited – all of which were relevant to the subject. As Iran was not the core of the study, this section reviews the Iraqi president's perception of the enemy he was about to contest, and offers a condensed review of Iran's historical, geographical, political and military conditions.

Iran shares borders with Iraq, Turkey, Afghanistan, Pakistan and the former Soviet Union. Its area and population make it one of the major states in the Middle East, and certainly the largest among the Middle Eastern oil-exporting countries. Its area is over one million square kilometres, more than half of which is desert. Iran's population stood at 45.2 million and exceeded the combined figures of all other Gulf states, while Iraq's was 15.4 million (*Military Balance 1986–87*, pp. 96–7). Like Iraq's, Iran's ethnic composition is heterogeneous. The intricate ethnic pattern includes a majority of *Shi'i* Persians (60 per cent), in addition to *Sunni* Arabs in Khuzistan in the south (five per cent), *Sunni* Kurds in the west (ten per cent), *Sunni* Turcomans in the north (ten per cent), and Baluchis in the south-east (ten per cent), apart from other minorities such as Zoroastrians, Jews, Armenian Christians and *Baha'is*. In addition to having linguistic, ethnic and sectarian diversity, the mountain ranges and the desert have distanced the inhabitants of the different provinces from each other. Except for the region of Tehran, the concentration of the population in the outlying provinces has facilitated cross-border contacts between Iran's minorities and those in neighbouring countries (*Ahram 1987*, p. 148; *Statesman's 1986–87*, p. 691; and *World Defense Almanac 1986–87*, p. 251).

Shahinshah Muhammed Reza Pahlevi succeeded his father Reza Shah, an officer in the Cossack Brigade, who took part in a bloodless rebellion in 1921. Colonel Reza, first appointed prime minister by the *majlis* (parliament) in 1923, overthrew the weak Qajar monarch and founded the Pahlevi dynasty, two years later. His coup was encouraged by the Russians, his deposition was brought about by an Anglo-Russian invasion, and his son's return to power after the Mussadeq take-over was aided by the American Central Intelligence Agency (CIA). As a consequence, Muhammed Reza's legitimacy became questionable, in so far that his dynasty was recently founded and that he owed his throne to the assistance offered by foreign powers, on more than one occasion.

To resolve his double-barrelled problem – the heterogeneity of his population and the legitimacy of his throne – the Shah initiated a campaign to revive the Persian character of his country, especially during the final years of his reign. The resuscitation of Iran's ancient glory led to a fashionable national renaissance movement, epitomized, worldwide, by the Persepolis extravaganza. He foisted the Imperial Persian calendar on his people, and added to his title the name Aryamehr (Light of the Aryans). The Shah's third consort, Empress Farah, patronized a drive to de-emphasize Islam and adhere to the Persian culture by using the arts as a means of expression, especially in schools, through the teaching of history and poetry, and in theatres. Later, this proved to be counterproductive with his Muslim population, who resented the destruction of their cultural heritage and traditions (Parsons, Interview, 1 March 1988).

Up to 1975, the Shah used tactics that achieved a double gain, namely, the solution of the Kurdish question and the internal subversion of Iraq. In an attempt to destabilize the Iraqi government, he funded the Iraqi separatist Kurds, on condition that they fight their Iranian brethren (Alam, 1991, pp. 357–8, 391, 394, 398–9). This policy was also pursued by the Turkish authorities, who link aid to the KDP with the repression of Turkey's Kurdistan Workers' Party (PKK), and by the present regime (see statement published on 19 June 1979 by Dr Sadegh Tabatabai, Official Spokesman for the Iranian government in Ghareeb, 1983, p. 64).

In his quest for internal and regional control, the Shah launched a policy of *rapprochement* with the Soviet Union, in the 1960s. The shift enabled him to readjust his defence posture towards the Gulf, and not to the north. Mostly buying from the West, he established a formidable base of strength, in some respects stronger than a few NATO members, armed with the latest technology that money could buy. During the 1973–8 Five-Year Plan, almost one-third of Iran's total budget allocations, or nine per cent of the gross national product (GNP) went on arms purchases. In 1976, Iran's defence apportionment was the same as China's and eight times that of Iraq, whose armed forces were about half the size of Iran's (Halliday, 1979, pp. 71–2; and O'Ballance, 1988, p. 10). A report predicted that the Imperial Iranian Air Force (IIAF) would become

> one of the most modern in the world, including the F-14A with Phoenix missile system, F-4E, F-4D, RF-4, F-5E, P-3F, and C-130H aircraft . . . [and that] the Iranian Government is considering a buy of 250 to 300 of either the F-16 or F-18 fighter aircraft, from 2 to 6 AWACs, additional 747 aircraft, between 4 and 10 E-2C 'Hawkeye' electronically equipped aircraft and 12 HH-53 long range search and rescue helicopters (US Congress, Senate, Committee on Foreign Relations, *US Military Sales to Iran*, 94th Cong, 2nd sess, July 1976, in Zonis, 1991, pp. 7–8).

Nevertheless, in 1980, there was a flood of evidence, based on the views of highly qualified foreign observers, presenting Iran's picture as one of military weakness, economic chaos, and increasing public disaffection, and that the time of the start of full-scale operations by Iraq was well-selected, as it had 'a flourishing economy, political stability, increased international acceptability reflected in its role in the non-aligned movement, and foreign-exchange reserves of some US$ 35 billion' (Chubin, 1986, p. 311; see also Karsh, 1987, p. 13).

Iraq also had access to weapons, spare parts, ammunition, technical assistance and training facilities, primarily in the USSR, but also in France, Italy, Britain and elsewhere. In Iraq, foreign experts – mostly Soviet – advised on training plans; and the French and Indians trained the air force and maintained its hardware while French and Italian personnel supervised the training of air defense and naval crews. At the start of the war, it had a significant stockpile of weapons, and had increased its army from ten to twelve divisions. Saddam Hussein's evaluation of Iraq's strengths and his adversary's weaknesses, coupled with the crescendo of destabilization, seemed to have been instrumental in his decision to go to war.

However, Sir Anthony Parsons, who headed Britain's mission at the UN in the 1980s, and was Ambassador to Tehran in the late 1970s, held the view that the war started more because of the American hostage crisis than for any other reasons. He added that Iraq's ruler was advised to wage war by Iranian émigrés, on the grounds that Iran was in total chaos and internationally isolated (Parsons, Interview, 1 March 1988). This gave credence to private disclosures of Arab politicians, to the effect that the US government (USG) – directly or through Middle Eastern allies – encouraged Hussein, after the unsuccessful American attempt to release the hostages in April 1980 (see also Jawdat, 1983, p. 97). It is to be noted that a large number of former politicians, probably yearning for their past ascendancy, as well as thousands of officers from the Iranian *ancien régime*, were sheltering in Iraq. It is likely that they called on Iraq's president to use his powerful war machine to embark on a military intervention and dislodge the newly created republican government.

It was also hoped that an Iraqi victory would check the spread of Muslim extremism to other countries and hence undercut the political effects of its ideology. News surrounding the eruption of a scandal involving the US administration, now known as Iraqgate, revealed that before Iraq's attack on Iran in 1980, National Security Advisor Zbigniew Brzezinski was of the opinion that 'Iran should be punished from all sides'. Gary Sick, who served at the time as his deputy for Iranian affairs, disclosed that Brzezinski 'made public statements to the effect that he would not mind an Iraqi move against Iran' (*Independent*, 27 May 1992).

After their revolution, the ruling elite in Tehran repeatedly encouraged the espousal of true Islam as a socio-political force, and their statements called for the destruction of hereditary regimes and the adoption of Tehran's Islamic political philosophy. They summoned Muslims to shed imported Western materialist values, and to search for the fundamentals of their religion in their own past history, and establish governments based on the Iranian model. They denounced 'the stooges of the Great Satan', and incited Muslims to overthrow those whom they labelled as 'tyrannical rulers who were not true believers, and who bartered their people's independence and sovereignty for rapid modernization' (Hooglund, 1987, p. 17; see also Khalaf, 1987, pp. 19–20). The concept of an Islamic *ummah* was floated, with Tehran as the capital of the true believers' community, rejecting the nation-state and calling for the erosion of state boundaries (Chardin, 1987, p. 61; and Chubin, 1986, p. 309).

Whereas his predecessor policed the Gulf region and kept a strong deterring military force, Imam Khomeini, who became nominal head of state in 1979, waged a sharp ideological war, by sanctioning *jihad* (struggle in God's Path). The concept is largely interpreted as holy war by Muslim laymen and Westerners alike, but covers a wide range of endeavours, with spiritual self-improvement as the starting point, followed by the reform of others through prayer and by conveying Islam's message; only when these fail, are Muslims invited to use their swords, and only as an act of last resort. His campaign of rhetoric, far from mild, aimed to enlist Muslims around the world to remove their governments, by pronouncing them as illicit.

The Ayatollah's perception of threats and his use of means underlay his decision to de-emphasize the role of the armed forces. He perceived threats as mostly cultural, and feared the corruption of the Islamic faith by non-believers. Khomeini mistrusted the professional military, vilified them as pro-Western and suspected them of loyalty to the Shah. Perceived as a threat to the consolidation of the newly established theocracy, 12 000 officers – most of whom among the top echelons of the armed forces – were either executed, jailed or purged, while some fled into exile. Between February and March 1979 alone, about three dozen generals were executed and over 500 senior officers dismissed, which decapitated the armed forces. In June and July 1980, young commanders were appointed to various armed services, and a revolutionary militia was created, as a counterbalancing force (Hunter in Naff [ed.], 1983, p. 171; Karsh, 1987, pp. 13–14; and Taha, 1984, p. 42). Designated as 'The Guardians of the Revolution', the now-famous *Pasdaran* volunteers lacked training and discipline in the beginning.

Their capabilities were further weakened by a shortage in hardware and spare parts, in addition to bitter rivalries and feuds between their command and that of the regular defence forces (O'Ballance, 1988, pp. 40, 51, 59; Ahram 1985, p. 121; Chapin, 1988, p. 67; Chubin, 1986, pp. 309–10; Hanks and Cottrell, 1981, p. 103; Daly, 1985, p. 152; Danziger, 1985, p. 165; 'Abdel-Halim, 1986, pp. 18–19, and 1985, p. 30; and Muhsin in CARDRI [ed.], 1986, pp. 229–30).

Iran's military capabilities were also significantly reduced. Conscripts deserted, and ground troops numbered between 100 000 to 150 000 from 285 000, airmen 65 000 to 70 000 from 100 000, and the navy's strength fell from 28 000 to 22 000 (O'Ballance, 1988, p. 20; and Karsh, 1987, pp. 14–15). Contracts for weapons, negotiated by the Shah, were cancelled, and it was reported that the *mullahs* even tried to sell back to the US some of the F-14 aircraft (Chubin, 1986, p. 309). Also, part of the armament had become obsolete. Because of Washington's arms embargo, many of Iran's American-made fighters were grounded, and some ships were non-operational because of a shortage in spare parts. The sophisticated weapon-systems were badly affected and most were in disarray and disrepair, especially in the navy and the air force, as the American experts deleted computerized data showing the location of spare parts in the depots (Karsh, 1987, pp. 15, 46). It took the Iranians about two years to restore the computer catalogue and trace the weapons, ammunition and spare parts in the various storage sites (O'Ballance, 1988, pp. 52–3, 103). The training programmes were discontinued when the American personnel left Iran. The services had a shortage in maintenance teams for the more sophisticated platforms and weapon-systems, especially in the navy and air force, and expert opinion confirmed that some of the platforms were inoperable, as the Iranians lacked the experience and did not have the resources to maintain them. According to a self-exiled Iranian naval officer, the troops were undisciplined, and the majority of the armed forces were demoralized, except for the sailors, who were in better form, in comparison to other servicemen (see also Hunter in Naff [ed.], 1985, p. 171; 'Abdel-Halim, 1985, p. 49; and O'Ballance, 1988, pp. 20–1, 23, 52–3).

Consequently, at the start of the war in 1980, only part of the impressive Imperial Defence Forces remained, while Iraq was considered the fourth military power in the world, and the second oil-producing state, after Saudi Arabia. But Iran managed later to acquire US-made arms, abandoned in Vietnam, when the American troops left hastily. In addition, it was able to arrange clandestine sales with a number of other countries, including the United States, in contravention of the arms embargo declared by its own government on 4 November 1979.

Iran, like Iraq, is a hydrocarbon-rich state, and its economy is largely dependent on oil revenues. Its oil industry, however, was damaged by a combination of several factors, which precluded its efficient organization and productivity. The purging, detention and emigration of the higher echelons of management affected sound planning, workers had become politicized and disorderly during the revolution, and imports of oil by the US and gas by the USSR were reduced. The situation was compounded by Khomeini's desire to organize economic development according to *shari'ah* (Islamic law, in accordance with the holy *Qur'an*, and also as defined in the Prophet Mohammad's *ahadeeth* [authenticated pronouncements] and his *Sunnah* [practices]). Iran thus attempted what no other country had been able to manage, which was to maintain absolute control over an economy, tuned to comply with basic Islamic precepts, while keeping it integrated in the world market system.

The picture of domestic Iranian politics was not brighter. The leadership was divided, and central authority seemed weakened. Vying against each other, power struggles abounded in governing circles between the conservatives and the more 'liberal' members among the clergy, and between them and secular officials, represented basically by intellectuals and technocrats. On more than one occasion, Iran's spiritual leader had to interfere to end squabbles, usually siding with the *mullahs*.

Resistance to the government mounted from parties and groups that were alienated by its policies against them, and terrorism became widespread in Tehran and some of the main cities. The most organized was the communist *Tudeh* (Masses) Party, founded in 1941. It was banned after the Shah's countercoup against Mussadeq, and a number of its most militant members were placed under arrest. Except for a short period

of revival in the early 1960s, its members had to go underground or operate in exile, after political activities were outlawed in 1963. These conditions were similar to Iraq's in the
late 1970s.

The *Fedayeen-e-Khalq* (People's Guerillas) was an offspring of
the *Tudeh*, and had always embraced Marxist dogma since its
inception. The *Mujahedeen-e-Khalq* Organization (MKO)
(People's Fighters) were Islamic at first, then became secular
and published attacks on Islam. Subsequently, although still
Marxist–Leninist, they couched some of their appeals in religious forms, especially when targeting the *'ulama* (clerics) and
the *bazaaris* (tradesmen, who were a significant economic
segment of society, with influence across Iran, and particularly
Tehran, especially before, but also after the revolution). But
an alliance with Khomeini or others became impossible, since
he was considered as conservative as the Shah, and had prohibited his disciples from cooperating with any Marxists.
Founded in the mid-1960s, both groups started their guerilla
activities in 1971, carrying out isolated clandestine operations,
political assassinations, and bombing campaigns, targeting
banks, police stations, and other public buildings. In the early
1980s, the MKO sought asylum in Iraq, and their military
bases continue to be equipped, financed and supported by
Baghdad.

Groupings who had taken part in the revolution but were
not given a role in the administration, were aggrieved. Former
bureaucrats were resentful, having been sacked or demoted.
The minorities, who saw an opportunity to ask for rights,
became restless. And the vast majority of the urban poor were
disaffected by the scarcity and high prices of consumer goods
and the drop in the standard of public services.

Whilst Saddam Hussein's strategy to bring about cohesion
in Iraq was based on a national secular government,
Khomeini's was on the opposite side of the spectrum, namely,
the Islamic indoctrination of the masses, and government by
the application of *shari'ah*. Nationalism and its appendages,
such as state sovereignty and boundaries, were derided by
Khomeini. His vociferous campaign against other Muslim
regimes seemed to consider secular Iraq as his prime target. It
became clear from his bellicose statements that his objective
was to remove the regimes in the Gulf Arab states and to

create surrogate governments there. He promised to lead the march to Baghdad to free the Iraqi people, and ordered a *jihad* to oust its 'evil and atheist' leadership. *Shi'ah* groups were mobilized to carry out sabotage and assassination missions in Iraq, the most notorious of which was the attempt on the life of Deputy Prime Minister Tariq 'Aziz on 1 April 1980, for which *al-Da'wah* claimed responsibility.

Subversive rhetoric was only one of the weapons that Khomeini relied on. He also orchestrated an aggressive campaign to destabilize the secular regime of Saddam Hussein, and incited Iraq's armed forces and people to rise against the government. On 7 April 1980, the Iranians bombed al-Nassiriyah University, killing a number of students, and the following day, hand-grenades exploded among those following the funerary cortege. That same day, Khomeini called upon all Iraqi *Shi'ah* to topple their President, and summoned *Shi'i* servicemen to defect from their units. Then on 16 April 1980, Tehran Radio broadcast the news that the Revolutionary Islamic Army for the Liberation of Baghdad was established.

Cross-border attacks escalated '(240 by some accounts), largely initiated by Iran', (Daly, 1985, p. 152) and '249 violations of Iraqi airspace by Iranian aircraft' were reported (Osman, 1988, p. 23). On 4 September 1980, the towns of Khaneqeen, Mendeli, Zarbatia and Naftkhaneh came under Iranian artillery fire, causing human and material losses. For the following fortnight, Iran intensified the bombing, using heavy artillery and airraids on densely populated residential areas and on Iraqi and foreign merchant ships sailing along the Shatt al-'Arab. On 19 September, the Iranians set ablaze the oilfield of Naftkhaneh, and the following day, general mobilization was proclaimed by President Bani Sadr.

War seemed unavoidable.

3 The Enduring Contest of Wills

3.1 WERE THERE OPTIONS OTHER THAN WAR?

On 17 September 1980, Saddam Hussein abrogated the Algiers Agreement, brokered by President Anwar al-Sadat of Egypt, King Hussein of Jordan and President Houari Boumedienne of Algeria, which he had signed, as vice-president, with Shah Muhammed Reza on 7 March 1975. Baghdad claimed that Tehran breached the treaty by its support for Iraqi Kurds, subversive activities, border attacks and violation of Iraqi airspace, and the refusal to return the 400 square kilometres in the northern areas of Zain al-Qaws and Saif Sa'id, agreed when the borders were redrafted in the 1975 accord. Predating the Iraqi decision, Sadegh Tabatabai, the official IRI spokesman, announced, on 19 June 1979, that Tehran no longer endorsed the agreement, and almost one year later, on 16 June 1980, it unilaterally abrogated it (Ghareeb, 1983, pp. 61, 64; Gheitany, 1987, pp. 9–12; 'Abdel-Halim, 1986, p. 15; Hunter in Naff [ed.], 1985, p. 172; Jawdat, 1983, p. 91; Karsh, 1987, pp. 12–13; and Osman, 1988, p. 24).

As the confrontation with Iran hovered on the brink of a military clash, Saddam Hussein had four other options, apart from the military response. Firstly, to ignore the Iranian actions. Secondly, to settle the dispute through bilateral negotiations. Thirdly, to present the case to the Hague International Court of Justice (ICJ), or to international UN-sponsored arbitration, as Iraq had suggested in 1961, when Iran abrogated the 1937 Treaty. Lastly, to seek mediation, in accordance with the UN Charter, Article 33 (1) of which stipulates that parties should seek to resolve their disputes through negotiations, mediation, arbitration, judicial settlement, or resort to regional agencies.

The first choice would have eroded the domestic and regional *Ba'thi* base, and weakened its authority, especially in the

82

Arab world, where bitter animosity endured between Saddam Hussein and Hafiz al-Asad, the only two *Ba'thi* leaders, whilst the rewards of a swift victory would bolster the regime's legitimacy at home and abroad.

A summit meeting, before things came to a head, could have strengthened support for a peace course. The necessary steps to settle disagreements would have then been taken. Needless to mention that there was room to negotiate if Iraq's and Iran's leaders had the will to ease tension across their countries' common borders. Establishing direct contact between the two states, before both sides cemented their positions, would have provided a better chance of weighing what may have been diplomatically possible to achieve, without the recourse to an armed conflict. Baghdad had shown its goodwill at the very inception of the new regime in Tehran. It had previously extended invitations to Bani Sadr and Bazargan, Iran's president and prime minister, to visit Iraq and conduct talks on the bases of cooperation between both neighbours. Iraq was also among the first countries to recognize the clerical regime in Tehran, and congratulated Khomeini when the IRI was proclaimed. Also, at the Havana Summit of the Non-Aligned Movement (NAM), the Iraqi president and the Iranian foreign minister had discussed bilateral issues, such as Tehran's political and media assaults on Baghdad, and the revision of the Algiers agreement. Hussein also requested Yazdi to return the three islands, seized in 1971, to their rightful owners, the United Arab Emirates (UAE), and that Iran's Arabs, Kurds and Baluchis be awarded their national rights. Besides, the Iraqi government notified Tehran 193 times to start an exchange of views, related to bilateral relations, and warned it of the serious consequences of political and military hostility. Iran ignored Iraq's diplomatic approach and refused the dialogue.

On 24 December 1979, Baghdad had officially requested the intervention of the UN to revise the Algiers agreement and to assess the legitimacy of Iran's occupation of the three islands ('Abdel-Halim, 1986, p. 17). Arbitration could have possibly resulted in the solution of the territorial dispute, after a more or less lengthy period of time. But nothing guaranteed the outcome, nor the duration of the process, as the Egyptian–Israeli Taba dispute demonstrated. During that period, Iraq ran the risk of being subjected to pressures by the international community to acquiesce to an agreement unfavourable to its interests. More seriously, it would continue to be exposed to Iranian subversion, further incursions across the frontier and attacks on border towns, in addition to infiltration of saboteurs, followed by acts that could cause internal chaos, or slowly undermine the ethno-sectarian structure of Iraqi society (for examples of Iranian subversion, see Jawdat, 1983, pp. 90–1, 93). The unfavourable aspect of arbitration is that parties can neither select their own judges, nor interfere in the procedures, which are usually based on legal precedents, and whilst only one side wins, the ruling is binding, and can lead to renewed diplomatic or military crises.

Mediation, as distinct from arbitration – where both parties can draft their own rules, taking into consideration their strategic interests, and where the terms of the final settlement can be confidential – is a face-saving alternative, where failure is concealed. The presence of other parties, for instance the heads of Gulf Arab states, would have improved the chances of discussions from deteriorating into a charade, mounted to avoid reaching an understanding. Mediators may have created motivation for both parties to proceed with peaceful means. They could have contemplated actions that would be of potential benefit to Iran and Iraq, by demonstrating that their proposals were constructive, whilst the resort to military action could be counterproductive for both countries. They could have also addressed the issue of preventive measures, in order to avoid the problem from flaring up again. If Saddam Hussein had kept his sword sheathed while mediators sought a diplomatic solution, and given the spiritual leader a chance to ponder the effects of war, the bloodshed and devastation may have been averted.

The question of the legality of wars, waged under the assumption that they were defensive strikes, is discussed in numerous works. If one were to refer to Clausewitz's beliefs, Iraq's use of war to coerce Iran into negotiating a lasting settlement was valid, and the escalation of the months-old skirmishes into full-scale war seemed legitimate, given the conditions Iraq was subjected to by Iran (Clausewitz, 1968, pp. 101, 241). Others argued that countries whose security is endangered by unlawful acts are allowed to challenge their assailants and request compensation. While general scholarly opinion is divided on the use of war as a defensive measure, all favour diplomatic protests as the ideal manner to deal with acts of aggression. In the post-UN era, the authors of these publications have based their arguments on the UN Charter, Article 2 (3) of which stipulated that '[a]ll Members shall settle their disputes by peaceful means in such a manner that international peace and security . . . are not endangered'. However, the efficiency of this method of response was questioned by some analysts, and in the case under discussion, it is worth noting that Iraq had sent close to two hundred such protests – all of which had been ignored by Iran.

Article 2 (4) of the UN Charter specified that '[a]ll Members shall refrain in their international relations from the threat or use of force against the territorial integrity or political independence of any State'. Iran encouraged acts of sabotage and terrorism, carried out by *al-Da'wah* members and other Iraqi *Shi'ah* inside their country, and Khomeini instigated revolt among the people and the armed services of Iraq against their government. Whether this destabilization campaign would be considered as an act where force was used against the political independence of Iraq is an open-ended question.

Some argue that Iraq's attack on Iran was a preemptive move, aimed at protecting the *Ba'thi* regime from Tehran's military-political onslaught. While a war waged in self-defence against clear armed aggression is not open to challenge, the justifiability of anticipatory attacks is. (Similar atttacks in the area, when a state has hit before an assault takes place, occurred in the cases of Israel's invasions of Egypt in 1956 and 1967 and of Lebanon in 1978, 1982 and 1993, and Israel's air strike on the Iraqi nuclear plant in 1981.) This view is based on the 1974 UN General Assembly Definition of Aggression Resolution 3314, Article 3 (b) of which stated that aggression included the '[b]ombardment by the armed forces of a State against the territory of another State or the use of any weapons by a State against the territory of another State' (in Wachenfeld, 1988, note p. 199). Article 51 of the UN Charter proclaimed that '[n]othing . . . shall impair the inherent right of individual or collective self-defense if an armed attack occurs against a Member of the United Nations' (see also Wachenfeld, 1988, note p. 194). Given that Iran shelled heavily populated areas in several Iraqi cities, it could be plausibly argued that Baghdad had a legitimate right to self-defence.

Conditions preceding the start of the war, as seen from Baghdad and other Arab and Western capitals too, seemed to lead inexorably towards an armed conflict. However, with the advantage of hindsight after 16 years, the picture that arises differs somewhat from the one described by observers in the earlier literature on its origins. Apart from the fact that general mobilization was proclaimed in Iran on 20 September 1980, the idea that Iraq's president expected an all-out attack, now seems unsound, for several reasons. The Iranian revolution was all too recent, and the regime had not had enough time to stabilize. The newly appointed officials were engulfed in internal problems, and in the process of liquidating members of the Shah's regime, by supplanting the military with the Revolutionary Guards, and dissolving SAVAK, while tracking down its half-million members and replacing them within the intelligence agency with their own men. At the same time, they were dealing with widespread economic problems in industry, and particularly, in the decaying oil sector. They were preoccupied with the future of the country, too, whose government was facing internal dissension and international isolation. They also had to ensure domestic cohesion in the face of mounting resentment by members of parties and social groups who had helped to propel the republic's leadership to power, the year before, but were disregarded when the post-revolutionary administration was created.

With its armed forces in a state of disintegration, it can now be assumed that Iran had no intention of carrying out a full-blown offensive against Iraq at that time. Despite frequent cross-border attacks and constant violations of Iraqi airspace, there was no massing of troops at the frontier. This may have accounted for the swift advance of the Iraqi army, which swept approximately 55 km. into Khuzistan within the first couple of weeks, and the near-absence of serious Iranian resistance – a fact which Saddam Hussein eagerly proclaimed in a speech shortly afterwards, losing no time to flex his muscles. As the unfolding war demonstrated, it took Iran two years to recover, regroup the remnants of its army and expel the Iraqi troops from most of the area they had in their grip, then another two to inch forward, cross the borderline and occupy Iraqi territories.

3.2   THE IRAQIS PLUNGE INTO DEEP WATERS

On 22 September 1980, several squadrons of Iraqi planes overflew the border eastward, droned over ten Iranian airfields and unloaded their lethal cargo, but failed to destroy the aircraft on the ground. The following day, six Iraqi divisions crossed the frontier into Iran, in a swift attack, designed to pierce the enemy's lines. A few hours afterwards, fighting erupted at three points, along a 400-mile front. Supported by intense air attacks, the Iraqi army occupied an arc on the Shatt al-'Arab estuary, in the southern province of Khuzistan/Arabistan. After some resistance by the Iranian division in Ahvaz, supported by *Pasdaran* units, the Iraqi troops reached the outskirts of Abadan, Iran's giant oil refinery. Although they were unable to capture the city, they surrounded it. Continuous bombing and airraids demolished it within a month. They besieged Susangerd and Dezful, seized Khorramshahr, and a detachment moved to Penjwin to prevent attacks on oil installations in the northern areas around Mosul and Kirkuk. They also occupied Mehran and Qasr-e-Shirin, in the central sector, to deter attacks on Baghdad, barely 80 miles away from the border, and to cut the north–south road network west of the Zagros mountains. The remainder of the army was tied up in the north, as Baghdad feared that the Kurds could intensify their operations at any moment ('Abdel-Halim, 1986, p. 22; Musallam, Interview, 10 May 1988; O'Ballance, 1988, pp. 32–7; Karsh, 1987, pp. 18–20; and *Strategic Survey 1985–86*, p. 122).

On 28 September, the Iraqi leader demanded that Iran relinquish sovereignty over an area around Shatt al-'Arab and the three islands in the Gulf, captured in 1971. By making these demands, one could suggest that Saddam Hussein was poised to play the principal role in Arab politics, beside obtaining other advantages. Control over both banks of the Shatt reinforced Iraqi security, and Khuzistani oil sales would raise Baghdad's revenues, since the province held four-fifths of Iran's oil. A quick victory would legitimize and consolidate the regime regionally and internally, and bolster Hussein's status as the undisputed *Ba'thi* leader. The return of the three islands would project him as the moderating force, which kept the IRI in check and protected the weaker Gulf states. Having vanquished Iran, Iraq would be recognized as the regional power which it aspired to be.

The successful thrust into Khuzistan accomplished the most crucial of Iraq's strategic objectives. The expansion of the ten-mile coast on the Gulf secured a defensible perimeter around the Shatt al-'Arab estuary for its exports and imports. This was particularly important for the southern port of Basra, its main harbour and military naval base, being the main link between the interior of the country and the outside world through the Gulf.

The type of war Saddam Hussein chose to wage was a *Blitzkrieg*. But he turned it, very soon, into a *Sitzkrieg*, by committing a grave strategic error, which proved decisive. In the early stages of the war, the military command in Baghdad instructed the troops to stop, thus 'hobbling the army'. Morale fell among the men as they prepared for defence. When an army attacks, the soldiers' morale is high as long as they advance on the enemy's territory. They should continue the momentum and apply pressure until the physical powers of the enemy are exhausted. The destruction of the opponent's offensive capability to the point when his remaining forces are hardly enough to be on the defensive brings about an erosion of the will to fight, and thus accomplishes the political aims of the war. But a 'ruler can bring misfortune upon his army when . . . ignorant that it should not retire, to order a retirement. This is described as hobbling the army' (Sun Tsu, 1976, p. 81).

With minor territorial gains and without inflicting a major defeat on Iran, Saddam Hussein relinquished the privilege to dictate the course of the war and allowed Iran to mobilize its population and reorganize its army. While Baghdad minimized its gains, Tehran had the opportunity to maximize on its superior assets. By bringing them into play, Iran was able to endure a protracted war for the following seven years.

3.3   TOUR D'HORIZON

Much ink has flowed to explain Iran and Iraq's hostility, some ascribing it to the 'historical enmity' between Aryan Persians and Semitic Arabs, or to *Shi'ah* and *Sunni* sectarian differences, while others underscore the cleavage between political beliefs, whereby Muslim non-national fundamentalism, carrying a populist message, opposed secular Arab *Ba'th*ism, with an elitist affiliation. A fourth group highlighted the caustic resentment that Khomeini had against Saddam Hussein personally, as the religious leader had been evicted from Iraq, where he lived as an exile, in accordance with the understanding reached at the signing of the Algiers accord. *Realpolitik* adherents diagnosed the strenuous relations as resulting from a regional contest, and emphasized the hegemonic role that Iran and Iraq aspired to play in the Gulf area. Within the context of a war strategy study, this angle seemed the most logical. However, it would be unrealistic to exclude the other facets, as the sum of all tends to reinforce the Iran–Iraq antagonism. The emphasis on one cleavage only would ignore the dynamic interplay of all, and underrate the potent multi-dimensional animosity.

The war was waged in a highly explosive zone, surrounded by chronic wars, latent tensions and intermittent conflicts. To the west, the Arab–Israeli wars, the bloody factional skirmishes in Lebanon, and the fierce *Ba'thi* political confrontation, which involved Syria's Hafiz al-Asad and Iraq's Saddam Hussein; to the north, the Soviet occupation of Afghanistan; and to the east, the Indo-Pakistani military clashes. The Gulf area itself suffered from patterns of friction disguised under the facade of a cooperation system among its states. Around it, the region was seething with the restiveness of ethnic and religious minorities, who aspired for national recognition. The Kurdish territories, where a nation was made to spread over five different countries, was a cauldron of resentment and bitterness that foreshadowed yet more strife. These tensions, kept latent by the Communist regime in the Soviet Central Asian republics, and by repressive governments around the Gulf itself, subsequently flared into open conflict and violence. The overall global setting was tense too. USA–USSR relations hit an all-time low, and the Cold War was at its chilliest, with each bloc aiding its regional proxies.

By extension, one could argue that the Iran–Iraq War was made possible by the withdrawal of British power from East of Suez in 1971, and its replacement by the US – a process which was already manifesting itself gradually. Nonetheless, the international political milieu at the turn of the 1970s decade allowed Saddam Hussein to wage war against the IRI. In other words, regional and local events in 1979 and the distraction of both superpowers in 1980, steered him towards an armed showdown; and their cumulative effect bolstered him in his determination to thrust his army into Iran.

In February 1979, the dethronement of the Shah of Iran caused the collapse of the American *twin-pillar* strategy, founded on the support of Iran and Saudi Arabia, as a guarantee for stability in the Gulf area. His downfall made possible the Soviet invasion of Afghanistan on 27 December. The Tehran hostage crisis and the presidential elections absorbed the attention of the American public and its administration. In a bid to continue playing a leading regional role – though not through military means but by exporting the new regime's ideology – Iran aided the Afghani *mujahedeen* (fighters in God's Path) and vehemently opposed the occupation. Tehran had thus alienated both superpowers.

The interaction of these two regional crises had some strategic consequences, and caused a slight change in the balance of power. The Gulf – a de facto Western lake – was now closer to Soviet tactical aircraft, stationed in Kandahar, in southwestern Afghanistan. More importantly, the SS-20 missiles, deployed in the south of Afghanistan, could have become a potential threat to American forces deployed in the naval theatre surrounding the Gulf. Besides straddling Bab al-Mandab, between South Yemen and Ethiopia, the USSR projected its military power close to another strategic chokepoint. In the meantime, Washington lost the major vassal it was previously banking on to police the area on its behalf.

Whilst vice-president, Saddam Hussein had distanced Iraq from the Soviet Union and edged closer to the NAM to gain international legitimacy for the *Ba'th* administration. He also sought a *rapprochement* with the Gulf states, who, in spite of previous Iraqi irredentism, felt less threatened by Baghdad than by Tehran. The signing of the Camp David Peace Agreement with Israel, in March 1979, caused Egypt's estrangement from the Arab world. It is possible that Iraq, the country on the second rung in the hierarchy, with a greatly built-up war machine, could fill the vacuum.

It could also be argued that Saddam Hussein planned the attack on Iran to protect and consolidate his newly established government. After taking control over the political corpse of al-Bakr, the new president alleged that several members of *al-Ba'th* Party's RC fomented a conspiracy against the state. In reality, they opposed his takeover of power. Officials, some of whom from al-Bakr's entourage, as well as others, disapproved of the turn that events had taken. Collectively, they represented a powerful body of opinion that the new president could not ignore, and he had to establish, without any doubt, that he did not tolerate challenges. His stern warning that he would not remain indifferent in the face of internal defiance led ultimately to the execution of 22 people, a number of whom were RC members and ministers, such as Minister of Planning 'Adnan al-Hamdani; Minister of Industry Muhammad 'Ayesh; and Minister of Education Ghanem 'Abdul-Jalil. The most prominent among them was 'Abdul-Khaleq al-Samarra'i, who held no ministerial portfolio, but was the strongest man in the RCC and RC leadership, and an opportunity presented itself to dispose of him. The list included Bedan Fadhel, the chairman of the Iraqi Labour Union, Muhammad Mahjoub, Mortadha 'Abdul-Baqi, Muhammad Fadhel, and others.

Rumours reached Saddam Hussein that the senior echelons of the military had misgivings that, beside being nominated Supreme Commander, he was accorded the highest military rank and honours, although he did not emerge from the military establishment. By starting the war, the president hoped to distract them and forestall dissidence within the armed forces. During the war, he claimed that some of them had committed high treason or shown cowardice, and executed them to obliterate latent rebellion within the ranks, once and for all.

Most Kurds had given up their arms to the central government after the Algiers agreement, whilst some fled to Iran, Turkey and Syria. But in early 1979, before the change in the leadership, the Kurdish revolt resumed in the north of the country, in alliance with members of the ICP and other parties. Saddam Hussein saw a chance to seize on their plight – citing the defence of the country at war to crush the rebellion was as good an opportunity as any. During the war, Kurdish demands for autonomy or self-determination were regarded by the government as illegitimate, and Kurds were branded as insurgents, especially when they started collaborating with Iran.

Al-Da'wah Party was founded by the end of the 1970s, and its members devised ways to destabilize the largely *Sunni* and secular regime in Baghdad, right from the moment the new president seized power. Supported by the *Shi'ah*, especially in the south, Saddam Hussein became convinced they were backed by Iran. Under the circumstances, a preemptive strike against their sponsors was thought best.

In addition to ensuring his personal safety, American and regional allies' worries about the implications for their own national security interests from Tehran's post-revolutionary policies came as a bonanza. Fearing a *domino effect*, world public opinion was concerned with the impact of the new republic's ideology on other Muslim countries. Arab heads of states, Iranians from the *ancien régime*, Western politicians, diplomats and media analysts, and members of the American administration were uncomfortable and sceptical about the embryonic Islamic republic. On all sides the war cry mounted. Iranian émigrés, American, European and Arab Gulf rulers alike, each had plausible grounds to use force against Tehran. The counter-arguments were submerged, and for purely practical political convenience, they united with Iraq's new president to topple Iran's new government.

After overpowering internal dissension, the Iraqi leader may have also envisioned himself as the arbiter of the Middle East by neutralizing Iran. By demanding the return of the three Gulf islands and parts of Khuzistan, he presumably stressed the pan-Arab nature of Iraq's policies among his Arab allies. He may also have contemplated championing their cause by challenging Israel later. The disclosures in 1991, concerning the discovery of the supergun and documents on Iraq's potential nuclear capability, revealed that the Iraqi president may have planned to match Israel's US-tolerated thermo-nuclear bomb programme. According to Seymour Hersh in *The Samson Option*, Israel's nuclear arsenal was far larger than the US intelligence reports had estimated, and included as many as 200 nuclear warheads mounted on missiles, artillery shells, and in land mines, some of which were suspected to be deployed in the occupied Golan Heights. The nuclear and chemical laboratories and long-range missiles located by the UN mission in Iraq in 1991 may have enabled Baghdad, in the long run, to manufacture a number of nuclear warheads. These could have eventually become a credible deterrent against an Israeli first nuclear strike against any of the Arab states.

In November, a group of Muslim extremists captured the Grand Mosque in Mecca, and whereas no proof exists to date that Iran sent any *agents provocateurs* or encouraged its seizure, its statements blamed Saudi misrule for the attack. There were also reports of unrest in Saudi oilfields and rioting in the province of Hasa, which has a significant *Shi'i* community. Though Iranian responsibility for the penetration of local opposition groups in largely Muslim countries has often been overstated by analysts, the inspirational appeal of the post-revolutionary Iranian model cannot be ignored. Evidently, the fragile Gulf governments felt severely threatened by what they perceived as militancy. Iran's menaces to encroach on its neighbours thus gave Hussein the opportunity to pose as the protector of the weaker Gulf states. The inclusion of the three islands in his territorial demands should be viewed from this angle. During the Iran–Iraq War, the Gulf leaders' gratitude took the form of generous financial contributions, vital military and logistical support, and virtually continuous political and diplomatic backing.

What made resort to force thinkable and even attractive was the military balance and the conjunction of international forces at the time. Iran appeared to be in chaos, militarily in shambles, divided at home and isolated internationally, yet it persisted in destabilizing and vilifying its neighbours. The opportunity for fighting and defeating Iran might never reappear and the temptation to use the period of the revolution's maximum vulnerability must have appeared tempting.

3.4 IRAQ'S STRATEGY

A week after the initial attack, the Iraqi troops stopped and dug in, an act which raised speculation. Analysts wondered why Hussein's forces had stopped their successful advance, at relatively little cost, when Iran was internationally isolated, internally divided and its economy and armed forces in chaos. The answer lies in the means the president chose to achieve his aims with, namely, the war strategy, and its effective application.

The plan that Iraq used was initially designed by British military instructors at the Baghdad War College in 1941, with the objective of capturing Dezful, Abadan and Khorramshahr in ten days, and the core principle was to rapidly deploy mobile forces to the Ahvaz–Dezful road in order to sever communications (O'Ballance, 1988, p. 48). This the troops failed to do in September 1980, because the strategy implemented was that of a limited offence, in the sense that only part of the forces available were committed, operations were contained in a restricted theatre, and troops confined their attacks to counterforce and not countervalue objectives.

The fact that Iraq did not achieve its political aims, and that it had to change its strategy subsequently and wage a defensive war on the ground, with selectivity in the use of means (chemical weapons), and a total air and missile war, with selectivity in the use of targets (countervalue in addition to counterforce) proves that either the strategy, or its implementation, were flawed. The forsaking of the momentum, created at the start of the invasion, and the conduct of the war during the subsequent stages revealed that the Iraqi leadership was unable to translate the sum of the country's military resources into effective leverage.

Sun Tsu advised that if the aims are limited, the war should be limited in time, space, effort and losses to the adversary, having in mind that the neighbour is the enemy and remains so after the war ends – a concept echoed by Liddell Hart twenty-five centuries later. Another consideration is that besides sharing 733.25 miles of borders, Iran and Iraq have numerous common interests. Tariq 'Aziz, Iraq's Foreign Minister and member of the RCC, explained that the 'military strategy reflects our political objectives. We want neither to destroy Iran nor occupy it permanently because that country is a neighbour with which we will remain linked by geographical and historical bonds and common interests' (in Helms, 1983, p. 78).

Hundreds of thousands of *Shi'i* pilgrims from Iran and elsewhere stream across the border to western Iraq to visit two of their three holiest shrines. Every year, they flock to the golden-domed mausoleum and burial place of Imam 'Ali in Najaf, the Prophet Muhammad's cousin and son-in-law and the supreme figure in *Shi'i* Islam, and to the shrine of Hussein, the Prophet's grandson, killed in Karbela'. It was feared that if

Iraq had opted for total war, they could have become a subversive force that committed acts of terrorism or sabotage. The Kurds, another large community with a potential for manipulation, and who also live on both sides of the border, will be fully discussed in Section 4.3.1. Moreover, both countries are members in various organizations, such as OPEC, UN, NAM, the Islamic Conference Organization (ICO) and the Group of less developed countries (G77), where their mutual interests often dictate that they cooperate on policies.

More importantly, the choice of a limited war strategy may have indicated that the Iraqi leadership was hoping for a better peace accord. The Iraqi restraint in military actions, during the first phase of the war, may be ascribed therefore, to the government's political objective of having fruitful negotiations with the Iranians to settle the long-standing territorial disputes, once and for all. Additionally, by avoiding attacks on civilian targets, the authorities forestalled opposition to the campaign by large *Shi'i* communities in Iraq and in other countries, such as Pakistan, Lebanon and Bahrain.

But a country's wish to conduct a strategy of limited warfare hinges on the willingness of the enemy to accept these restrictions. With the advantage of hindsight and the eight-year stalemated front, one would be tempted to adhere to Clausewitz's theories and defend total war. But geostrategic realities militated against it and may have been a powerful argument against the use by Iraq of a total war strategy. Iraq's three-to-one demographic and territorial handicap made an extended occupation of the entire Iranian territory unthinkable. Even if, hypothetically, the initial assault were successful, Iraq could not realistically subdue Iran for long.

3.5   A REVIEW OF IRAQ'S GROUNDWORK FOR WAR

The success of the initial Iraqi thrust into Iran, followed shortly by orders to halt and revert to a strategy of defence, was widely debated, as mentioned above. The following part is a critique of Iraq's preparations prior to the war, and their impact on the conduct of operations in the early phases.

In parallel with planning for war, the Iraqi leader should have embarked on a diplomatic campaign to legitimize what he had already decided, and to canvass international support, with special emphasis on the Arab world. Centuries earlier, Sun Tsu had recommended keeping on good terms with one's old allies, attempting to acquire new partners and disrupting enemy coalitions, as a tactic in the prelude to war (1976, pp. 9, 68, 78). This undertaking would have maintained the unity of Iraq's alliances, strengthened them, and made them more effective. In his own, as well as in his country's interests, Saddam Hussein should have consulted with Iraq's allies who would possibly be affected by the war. These talks would have offered him the opportunity to vigorously defend the political imperative of his proposed act, by exposing Iran's destabilization tactics, orchestrated by Khomeini. He should have warned them of the *domino effect* on their own countries from the campaign of abuse, and of the impact that the *Shi'ah's* acts of sabotage could have. His allies could have proffered him advice on ways to avert the war, by offering themselves to mediate on his behalf. Alternatively, if convinced of his rationale, he would have ensured that the sheikhs' cheque-book diplomacy would continue. Before his call to arms, Saddam Hussein should have also tried to win over some of the Arab countries who subsequently sided with Iran during the war. By so doing, he would have forestalled the adoption of an adversarial policy by Algeria and Libya. In the case of Syria, he could have struck a bargain, and offered oil at a concessionary price, as Iran did later.

At the outbreak of operations, Iraq would have then secured political support in the international forum, safeguarded the cohesion within the Arab front, and avoided the Soviet arms bans. Furthermore, it would have enlisted the support of its Arab allies to guarantee their financial commitment in the event of Iraqi oil exports being impeded. In fact, Iraq's vulnerability was proven by subsequent events. Its capacity to export oil through its ports and oil terminals was denied from the first week of operations, and two years later, its pipeline across Syria was shut down, thus reducing its exports by 0.8 million barrels a day (mbd) (King, 1987, pp. 17–18).

Whereas Clausewitz required that the ruler be both 'statesman' and 'general' (1968, pp. 25, 156–7, 198), Sun Tsu recommended specialization. In his judgement, the appointment of a strategist and of officers was one of the privileges of the sovereign. He should 'select them and give them responsibilities commensurate with their abilities', and to avoid 'bringing misfortune' to his army, he was required not to interfere in the conduct of war; for his part, the general had to give precise and clear orders to avoid confusion (1976, pp. 94, 81, 83, 58).

In Iraq, there was only one decision-maker, and he broke each of these rules. Despite being given the highest military rank in the country, that of *Muheeb Rokn* (Field Marshal), Saddam Hussein had never received any military training, and was merely awarded an honorary degree by Iraq's Military Academy, in 1970. At the start of the war, he sat at the pinnacle of the power hierarchy. He was president, prime minister, leader of the *Ba'th* Party and chaired the RCC. Similarly to the Shah of Iran, he had an absolute and undisputed mandate over the appointment, sacking and even physical liquidation of ministers, military commanders and public servants.

The autocratic nature of Iraq's ruler was proven in a graphic manner in 1991, by video films found by the *Peshmerga* (Kurdish guerilla fighters, 'facing death' in Kurdish), when they stormed the Kirkuk headquarters of the newly-appointed Defence Minister 'Ali Hassan al-Majeed, Saddam Hussein's cousin. They partly explained the failure of military operations, and why the commanders were terrified, for many years, to express their opinion about the setbacks the Iraqi troops had. The video displayed a meeting of the Iraqi president with his advisers, on the eve of military operations, in 1980. Hussein was seen abusing and shouting down those who objected to his plans. Later sections of the film showed those who had opposed the invasion of Iran being executed. An Iraqi interviewee argued that video films, such as the one referred to here, were often clandestinely circulated by the regime itself, to thwart opposition at any level, whether in the country at large, or among senior politicians and within the armed forces ranks.

According to two highly reliable Iraqi sources, one of whom held a cabinet ministry, while the other had served in the army, appointments to command positions were based on loyalty, with disregard to competence, and Iraqi commanders were commissioned with an eye on their allegiance to the *Ba'thi* doctrine, and vetted for the degree of their devotion to the person of Saddam Hussein. The army structure was top-heavy, with

7000 of senior rank among the officers corps, and the system of command was highly centralized and rigid. Being subject to a long bureaucratic chain of command for each operation, the field commanders were allowed no scope for imagination and spontaneity, and their authority was constrained. In the early stages of war, excessive political control of the military apparatus resulted in a loss of initiative on the part of officers. Like irresolute pawns, awaiting orders that were unclear and slow to come, they lay siege to strategically unimportant towns and villages, and forfeited the opportunity to occupy strategic and easily defendable cities, such as Dezful, Susangerd and particularly Ahvaz, a key oil facility, being a juncture where several pipelines link.

The adoption of Sun Tsu's concept of 'expanding torrent' (1976, p. 43), advocated by Liddell Hart later (Carver in Paret, 1986, p. 803), would have enabled the Iraqis to bypass towns that offered strong resistance, and press forward to expand their territorial gains with fewer casualties. The competent strategist is not only the one who drafts a blueprint, but the one who is alert enough to either devise a new offensive when his first plan fails, or allows others to do so. A flexible strategy permits field commanders, forced by developments on the ground, to rethink and review part or all of their operating instructions. The policy was reversed later on, during the course of the war, and only after the Iraqi troops were driven out of Iranian territory, having suffered serious loss of life. Officers with expertise were later selected for higher military command posts, regardless of their political affiliation. They were allowed to exercise their own initiative in battle and had almost full command and control over their units. Cynics ascribed this new policy to Saddam Hussein's intention to hold others culpable for any defeats that the army suffered in future.

Intelligence about the enemy's political, economic and military conditions is vital for planning for war. Sun Tsu elaborated on the importance of 'foreknowledge', and his disciple Mao Tse Tung advised: 'Know your enemy and know yourself and you can fight a hundred battles without disaster' (in Sun Tsu, 1976, p. 50, see also pp. xi, 8, 44, 84, 149 and the discussion in Section VI, pp. 12–14). Specific information on potential military and strategic targets is necessary for an efficient surprise attack. The ignorance of the Iraqi pilots as to the exact location and disposition of the Iranian aircraft resulted in the failure of their mission to destroy the IRI Air Force on the eve of the invasion. The deployment of reconnaissance aircraft, prior to the campaign, would have robbed the Iranian army of air cover, and aided the Iraqis in the effective conduct of ground battles.

Analysts agree that a strategic plan should determine the time of attack, the geographical location envisaged for the battle, and the qualitative and quantitative force formation used in combat. The selection and correct balance of platforms and weapon systems, and the careful distribution of tasks among the forces empowers them to attain their initial objective. But Iraq seemed to have started the war without a clear military or diplomatic plan, which plainly means that articulate war aims commensurate with the available military resources in Iraq's arsenal were non-existent.

General Tal'at Musallam, who at the time served as Director of Military Studies at the Centre for Strategic Studies, at the daily *Ahram*, and frequently travelled to Iraq during its war against Iran, suggested that the hesitation shown by the troops in taking towns, then evacuating them, or besieging cities, then withdrawing, denoted the absence of a plan designing clear objectives and identifying specific targets. Apart from the decision to cross the border and occupy a very limited strip of territory, the Iraqis did not appear to have had an overall operational plan for combined operations. The three forces – ground, naval and air – did not seem to follow a comprehensive plan based on cooperation and support. Furthermore, Iraq's changes in its initial *limited war* strategy, indicated that no contingency plans existed in the case of failure to bring about negotiations (Musallam, Interview, 10 May 1988).

The Iraqi Military High Command appears to have disregarded geographic conditions in planning for war, despite the prominence given to these in works on strategy, including Kautilya's and Sun Tsu's. The timing of the Iraqi invasion, one month before the start of the rainy season, and the choice of platforms show poor judgement; topographical conditions in all three sectors of operations make it almost impossible for armoured columns to advance. Terrain in southern Khuzistan is marshland, formed by the confluence of the Dejla and Faurat rivers north of Basra. The marshy area forms a triangle between Basra to the south, al-'Amarah to the north, and a point between al-Nassiriyah and Jalibah to the west. The central and northern sectors of the border area are dominated by a jagged range of mountains, with peaks reaching an altitude of over 10 000 feet, and the Zagros ridges run steeply into the surrounding valleys. During the rainy season, roughly from November to February, the Kharkheh and Karun rivers swell and flood large areas. Iraq based its offence on the use of tanks and armoured vehicles, which became bogged down in the marshes, and were also inadequate in hilly and mountainous terrain in the northern battlefields. Some of the armoured columns in the south sector sank, while others were halted and had to be supplied by helicopters – a situation similar to that which arose over a decade later, when the heavily armoured Allied troops were unable to pursue the retreating Iraqi Republican Guards in the marshy southern area. Under the circumstances, apart from being more mobile, the use of Iraqi mechanized infantry would have been more effective, especially later, in the assault on Iranian towns. The tanks and armoured vehicles should have been supplanted by hand-held anti-tank weapons, which would have been useful in firing missiles at surface targets, causing extreme damage at a great range. Sending in commandos, to give the infantry an edge, would also have helped in the battles which ensued in built-up areas. Combat with machine guns and rocket-propelled grenades (RPGs) could have broken the Iranian troops' resistance, especially in the Iraqis' offensives on towns (for a detailed topographical description of the Iran–Iraq border area and how its features constrained ground operations, see 'Abdel-Halim, 1985, pp. 31–2, 34–8, 43, 50–1, 54–5).

In the late 1970s, Iraq started rapidly to diversify its armaments, to lessen its dependence on the USSR, and to modernize its growing army, air force and navy (Schmidt, 1991, p. 1). Diversification is a political decision aimed at enhancing sovereignty. Being dependent on one particular source for arms can partly erode a country's freedom of action, or, in the extreme, bring about its total subjugation.

The policy, however, has its negative aspects, in so far that it faces the services with the problem of standardization. It is difficult for the crews of battle tanks, aircraft or ships to man platforms or use ammunition from diverse destinations, especially if these were provided by both the Western and Eastern blocs. Consequently, the capabilities of a defence force can be weakened by between 40 per cent, and up to 60 per cent, by acquiring materiel from different countries. In addition, huge organizational problems arise with logistics in trying to calculate when and which spare parts are needed, and recording the stocks from different countries for various platforms or weapon-systems (Day, Interview, 5 January 1992).

The effective use of airpower is a decisive element in conventional wars. The Iraqi Air Force hit targets as far away as the Sirri and Larak oil-export facilities only later on in the war; at its start, Iraq lacked this capability. Furthermore, operations were not coordinated between the services, nor even between units of the same service (Karsh, 1987, p. 38). Therefore, prior to the war, Iraq should have procured aircraft with greater combat radius, efficient guided-missile systems and aircraft refuelling capabilities. Equipped with a flexible strategy and a communication system for combined operations, field commanders could have evaluated the opportunities at hand and coordinated modifications in tactics. But by awaiting the 'green light' from Baghdad, changes were likely to be slow and piecemeal and, hence, of limited effectiveness.

In contrast, Iran's successful use of its airpower, especially after the release of some pilots from prison, was critical in slowing down the initial Iraqi advance and in hitting targets inside Iraq ('Abdel-Halim, 1985, p. 55). Also, combined air/navy operations on oil terminals at Fao and Mina al-Bakr, in November, lowered Iraqi oil exports by one-third, and slimmed down shipping traffic in these areas. In addition, the Iranian air strike on Kuwaiti border stations, a few weeks after the start of war, deterred military support by Arab Gulf states for the duration of the conflict.

During the initial battles, Iraq attacked a limited number of counterforce targets, that is, military objectives, such as airfields, troop concentrations, military vehicles, armour, artillery, and military depots and headquarters. Iraq responded in kind only after Iran had bombed strategic targets. A settlement, through negotiations with Tehran, was Iraq's principal war aim. An intensive attack on countervalue targets at the time Iran was still in chaos, such as oil and industrial installations and stores, power generation plants, strategic railway stations, bridges and supply routes, transportation and communication centres, could have changed the course of the war. It would have created disarray in towns and among the troops, and deprived the Iranians from electrical power, without which factories and other vital installations would have been useless. Had strategic bombing been used, the Iranian population might have demanded of its government to consent to negotiations, or would have possibly risen against it, for '[i]f our opponent is to be made to comply with our will, we must place him in a situation which is more oppressive to him than the sacrifice which we demand' (Clausewitz, 1968, p. 104).

Sun Tsu recommended that 'in battle use the normal force to engage; use the extraordinary to win' (1976, p. 91). However, although the Iraqis had 11 divisions (some writers cite twelve), of which seven infantry and mechanized and four armoured, in addition to three special forces brigades, 1740 tanks, 3260 armoured personnel carriers (APC) and 1176 artillery pieces, they only used six divisions and two brigades in their offensive ('Abdel-Halim, 1985, pp. 39–40). They thus failed to commit a sufficiently large force towards the war effort. Along the same lines, Clausewitz explained that 'the superiority in numbers is the most important factor in the result of a combat, only it must be sufficiently great . . . [This factor] will be sufficient to ensure the victory, however disadvantageous other circumstances may be' (1968, pp. 265–6). As mentioned earlier, some of the ground forces were stationed in the north to deter attacks by the Kurds and secure the border with Syria, while the remainder were held as a strategic reserve. During the decade from 1968 until 1978, Iraq's military forces had risen from 80 000 to 200 000. Ground forces were expanded with the creation of eight new divisions, bringing them to 20, only at a later stage of the war, in 1983 (Karsh, 1987, p. 25). They were doubled to 40 divisions, with 700 000 men under arms, by the end of 1986 (Axelgard, 1987, p. 58; Schmidt, 1991, p. 7; and Gamlen, 1989, pp. 64–5). Overwhelming the Iranians with a massive – not rationed – comprehensively-combined force may have compelled their leadership to negotiate.

A small, well-trained and disciplined army, which executes a flexible strategy, can defeat a larger army. Clausewitz, Fuller and Liddell Hart strongly advocated the importance of training, and pointed to its impact on the speed of thought and the rapidity of action. Training was also emphasized by Soviet military doctrine, which Iraq adhered to, according to Western strategists. But the performance of Iraqi pilots belied appropriate preparation. They lacked mobility in manoeuvring and also flew at high altitudes, which did not permit accurate targeting. Massive bombardment, which makes up for precision shelling, was utilized against enemy targets, such as the island of Kharg, only later on in the Tanker War. Furthermore, drill exercises, in conditions as close as possible to the ones encountered in a war situation, enable servicemen to be familiar with, and make maximum use of their sophisticated weaponry. The technical incompetence among the Iraqi ground forces resulted in the abandonment of a large number of almost intact armoured vehicles that needed minor battlefield repairs (Abbas in CARDRI [ed.], 1986, p. 221).

By conducting a surprise attack on Iran, President Hussein may have believed that he could replay the 1941 invasion of Iran by British troops, when Iran's army, magnificently equipped by Germany, broke down straightaway. Or he may have seen a chance to re-stage the 1973 October War, in which Egypt sharply limited its offensive with the aim of bringing about a negotiated settlement. The Iraqi leader planned a swift strike, to be shortly followed by the toppling of the government in Tehran and the start of negotiations, but the conduct of war left him with unfulfilled expectations.

Some analysts ascribed Iraq's inability to achieve its military objectives to the rigidity of Soviet military doctrine, although a consistent theme in Soviet military thought is the importance given to overall superiority in all forms of military capabilities, such as organization, training and weapons acquisition. Hussein disregarded these essential guidelines. One could even go so far as to remark that his troops were betrayed by poor strategic planning, faulty timing, inadequate intelligence, insufficient resources and incomplete training.

A fundamental canon for the success of a military operation is to conceal the attacking force's intentions from the enemy. Iraq was successful in so far that its troops struck at a time when the Iranian forces were chaotic, and according to an Iranian military source, who asked for anonymity, it took his countrymen almost a month to re-group and counterattack. However, the momentum gained at the beginning of operations was wasted later, as explained. It is true that a dilemma exists between the need to achieve surprise and adequate preparations, but the time factor would have been beneficial to Iraq (on the importance of surprise see Clausewitz, 1968, pp. 269–70).

By giving themselves the chance to prepare, the Iraqis would have waged the war on terms far more advantageous to them. Had the political leadership provided its armed forces with the essential requirements for the campaign, they would have been in a better position to translate their military power into the political domain. Or maybe, the Iranian revolution might have run its course, as the Chinese Cultural Revolution did. With time, internal rivalries, political resistance, poor economic performance and decay within the armed forces might have eroded the regime's power and prestige.

3.6   IN PAIN WITH NO GAIN: 1981 TO 1984

From 1981, and for the following seven years, the Iraqi army waged a defensive war around the border area. Since offence is the best means of defence, the Iraqis' posture meant that they could hardly hope to win a victory, and they even risked losing cities and territories they had captured. When these setbacks began to occur, Baghdad launched the new Tanker War strategy.

Immediately after the start of the war, Iran experienced some difficulties. With a drop in oil production, food shortages were observed, and rationing was introduced. Despite the rapid expansion in the numbers of troops, (mobilization instantly raised the regular forces to 200 000 men, growing by at least 1000 a day in Tehran alone, the *Pasdaran* enlisting about 150 000 volunteers), the reverses on the battlefront uncovered an unwillingness on the part of the conventional and non-conventional forces to cooperate and coordinate their actions (Daly, 1985, p. 155; and O'Ballance, 1988, pp. 50–1). The impasse motivated President Bani Sadr to set up a unified command, and he was able to persuade Khomeini to establish the Supreme Defence Council (SDC). Formed on 13 October

1980, the military command was placed under the central control of the Supreme Commander; nonetheless, his leadership was constantly challenged by the three clerics on the seven-man Council, who on most occasions sided with the distinctly autonomous stance taken by the Islamic Revolution Guards Corps (IRGC) (O'Ballance, 1988, p. 51; and Karsh, 1987, pp. 22, 42).

The arms embargo against Iran and Iraq was effective in reducing their fighting capabilities, though Tehran was able to obtain some replacements early on in the war. From the first week of operations, Syria provided Iran with ex-Soviet *Sagger* anti-tank missiles and portable surface-to-air missiles – otherwise known as SAM-7s. While the American hostage crisis still remained unresolved, Washington sanctioned Turkish arms transfers to Iran, on 30 September 1980. From the following year, Tehran also started receiving by air freight ex-Soviet consignments from Libya through Turkey and Greece, Israeli tank spare parts on Argentinean civilian aircraft through Cyprus and Turkey, and Taiwanese and North Korean shipments. On the other hand, Iraq received its first East European arms shipment, one year later, through the port of 'Aqaba, on 7 October 1981 (O'Ballance, 1988, pp. 52–3, 73, 104; also King, 1987, p. 49).

The stalemated battlefront witnessed a series of minor and confused engagements, launched by both sides in 1981. During the last quarter of the year, Iraqi troops were forced to lift the siege of Abadan and pushed back across the Karun river ('Abdel-Halim, 1986, p. 23). Taking advantage of Iraq's involvement in the war, Israel's warplanes destroyed the Osirak thermal reactor in Tuwaitha, near Baghdad on 28 June, claiming that it had succeeded in making weapon-grade plutonium (see details of operation in O'Ballance, 1988, pp. 76–7; also King, 1987, p. 55).

The Gulf States (Saudi Arabia, Kuwait, Bahrain, Oman, Qatar and the UAE), so far content that their two powerful neighbours were absorbed in weakening each other, became concerned about their security and the dangers of the war spilling over. In February, they formed the Gulf Cooperation Council (GCC) to design a strategy for concerted action in internal and external security matters, although the final communiqué stressed the non-military nature of the agreement.

Whilst they attempted to brush aside their mutual distrust, their differences surfaced in their conflicting suggestions and counterproposals. The Saudis stressed cooperation on internal security and a collective defence agreement, with a view to coordinating military procurement policies, but the smaller states were reluctant to endorse these recommendations. Oman contemplated a plan for the creation of a joint naval force to defend the Strait of Hormuz. Kuwait, intent on de-emphasizing defence arrangements, stressed cooperation in economic, cultural and oil policies. In reaction to the new developments, statements from both capitals confirmed that Baghdad and Tehran were rankled at their exclusion from a security regime in the Gulf – an area where each one of them perceived itself as the predominant power (Khalaf, 1987, pp. 20–1, 32; and King, 1987, pp. 34–5).

Iran's domestic scene witnessed a great degree of turbulence. After President Bani Sadr was impeached and Premier Rajai elected to the office, a wave of bombings and assassinations by members of the *mujahedeen* shook the country, claiming the lives of Ayatollah Beheshti and the new Premier, Javed Bahonar. Also, a large number of top military and political leaders were killed: the defence minister met his fate in the battle zone, 74 of the Islamic Republican Party (IRP) leadership died in an explosion in Tehran, and a group of senior army commanders perished in an air crash.

The year 1982 proved to be a watershed. In major offensives, using *human wave* tactics, the Iranian troops regained Dezful, in *Operation Undeniable Victory* in March, and in May, liberated Khorramshahr at a grievous price, drove the Iraqis back to the international border and captured a small area in Musian.

In April, seeking to bring about an end to hostilities, Saddam Hussein promised to evacuate Iraqi troops from Iran. In a meeting which he did not attend in June, the RCC declared a unilateral ceasefire. The following day, using the Israeli invasion of Lebanon as a justification, the President announced the voluntary withdrawal of troops from Iranian territory, with the exception of the area claimed by Iraq. These appeals, as well as those of the UN (in its SCR 514), the GCC, the League of Arab states and the ICO were rejected by Tehran. A mediation attempt by Algeria's Minister of Foreign Affairs was preempted with the shooting-down of his plane.

In a new development on 12 August, Iraq announced a *Maritime Exclusion Zone* around the Kharg oil terminal, two months after Saddam Hussein had warned international shipping to sail clear of the northern Gulf. This appeared to be in retaliation against Iran, as its ally Syria had closed down the pipeline from Kirkuk to the Mediterranean port of Baniyas, on 10 April. It resulted in a substantial drop in Iraqi oil exports, reaching a low of about 600 000 barrels a day (bd), and denied it of $5 billion in revenues. Iraqi aircraft subsequently bombed Kharg and the ships within the zone, and for the duration of the war, the oil terminal became Iraq's preferred strategic target. On occasion, countries at war declare certain areas as hazardous for merchant shipping or aircraft, and prohibit their entry within a specified stretch of water or air space. The most recent examples were the Falklands/Malvinas war in 1982, when the British forces declared a 200-miles *Total Exclusion Zone*, and in early 1984, just about the time the Tanker War started, the US Middle East Task Force (METF), which operated in the Gulf region, also set a five-mile exclusion zone around its ships to prevent attacks by hostile aircraft or naval vessels (see Section 6.1.2). In accordance with the practice, any air or naval craft within the zone is considered as having hostile intent and runs the risk of attack – in a manner of speech, it becomes 'fair game'.

Kurdish insurgency intensified in Iraq and the *Peshmerga* sabotaged the pipeline to Turkey; and the restive *Shi'i* population, mainly concentrated in the south, went on riots against the government. To reassert his control, Saddam Hussein reshuffled the RCC and the cabinet, during a meeting of the *Ba'th* Party Congress. The meeting built to a dramatic conclusion, and the power struggle was finished off by the slaying of the Minister of Health. In a vicious twist, Saddam Hussein brutally gunned down Ryadh Ibrahim Hussein, who was among his inner circle of friends, and who for that reason had the courage to face him. Observers believed that by sacking a few officials, he played to public opinion and indirectly attributed to others the army's reversals and the uprisings. But while some of the military became politically tarnished, and despite defections from within their ranks, they did not, as a reaction against the cabinet replacements, attempt a coup against their leader (Butti, Interview, 26 December 1994). Meantime, in

Tehran, a new ministry for the IRGC/*Pasdaran* was formed, headed by Muhsin Rafiqdust, and SAIRI was established with the specific aim of overthrowing the *Ba'thi* regime in Baghdad.

Major events took place that year in relation to the Arab–Israeli conflict. At the strategic level, Israeli troops overran Lebanon, in what Prime Minister Menachim Begin described as a final 'cleansing of the terrorist nests' and the rooting out of 'international terrorism'. Commenting on the outcome, the *Jerusalem Post*'s editor, and then Defence Correspondent, Hirsch Goodman, wrote that Israel set out to destroy Palestinian terror, and created *Shi'i* terror instead (in *International Herald Tribune* 16–17 March 1985).

On 6 June 1982, the Israeli government used an attempt on its ambassador's life, in London, three days earlier, to launch an invasion against Palestinians in Lebanon, who were not associated at all with the shooting. The attack on Shlomo Argov outside the Dorchester Hotel, which Baghdad seemed to have sanctioned, was carried out by a member of Abu Nidal's Palestinian faction – a group outlawed by Arafat's Palestine Liberation Organization (PLO) (*Independent*, 25 November 1991). The cost in lives of *Operation Peace for Galilee* was more than 17 000 people killed. Mostly civilians bore the brunt of Israeli bombardments and airraids, in addition to over 500 Israeli soldiers. Subsequently, the Lebanese Phalange militia, watched by their Israeli mentors, slaughtered hundreds of Palestinian men, women and children in the Sabra and Chatila camps.

On the political stage, Iraq modified its hard-line posture by accepting Israel's existence in the region, and by indicating that in principle, Baghdad would not oppose a negotiated peace settlement (Axelgard, 1987, p. 128; Devlin in Naff [ed.], 1985, pp. 149–50; and Ghareeb in Axelgard [ed.], 1986, p. 71). This was a far cry from the time when the Iraqi President considered Egypt's signing of an armistice with Israel as a betrayal, championed *Jabhat al-Sumud wal-Tassaddi* (Rejectionist Front), and advocated the expulsion of Egypt from the League of Arab States and from all other Arab and Islamic organizations.

American support for Baghdad started secretly in early 1982, two years before it was publicized, when it was supplied with highly classified intelligence, and removed by Secretary of State Alexander Haig 'from the list of countries supporting terrorism, so enabling it to receive credits and other aid'. In addition to receiving US-made arms directly or through its Arab allies, the CIA allowed American arms dealers to sell Iraq Soviet-made weapons obtained from East European countries (Cockburn, 1992; see also, Hersh, 1992; and Axelgard, 1987, p. 128).

Along the Iran–Iraq border, military stalemate characterized ground operations in 1983. Although Iran mounted several offensives, its troops made modest gains. Iraq's periodic shelling, aerial bombing and firing of SSMs on Iranian cities caused civilian casualties, but were strategically ineffective.

Domestic Iranian politics were dynamic. The government dissolved the pro-Moscow *Tudeh* Party on 4 May, liquidated its leaders and arrested about 1000 of its members. This was followed by the expulsion of 18 Soviet diplomats – all of which risked antagonizing the USSR again. On 20 June, the Navy's commander was also executed. On the economic level, fuel rationing was terminated, on 4 January. It had been introduced when much of the Abadan refinery was reduced to rubble and twisted pipes by massive bombing at the start of the war. An increase in Iran's oil refining capability enabled it to export around 2mbd from Kharg alone, in addition to smaller quantities from other oil-export facilities. By March, and despite a 15 per cent drop in crude oil prices, from $34 to $29 a barrel, its balance of payments surplus, which had reached about $6 billion, enabled it to pay off its foreign debts. Across the border, an oil-for-arms barter agreement, struck between Baghdad and Paris, on 23 May, accounted for Iraq's demand for an increase in its OPEC quota from 1.2mbd to 1.8mbd, in November ('Abdel-Halim, 1985, p. 8; and O'Ballance, 1988, p. 129).

The year witnessed numerous major developments in regional affairs, some of strategic significance. In spite of Turkey's professed neutrality, the Turkey–Iraq Border Security Agreement, signed in April, enabled Turkish troops to cross into northern Iraq to track down Kurdish guerrillas, and prompted the PUK's leader, Jalal Talabani, to agree to a ceasefire with Saddam Hussein in December. Turkey reached a similar understanding with Iran, and its troops were allowed on Iranian soil. A pattern was set in train, whereby Kurdish skirmishes were followed by Turkish military clashes in border areas in Iran and Iraq. It became a permanent fixture and endures until now. US complicity in giving their 'green light' to the Turks has not been established yet, and Middle East observers will have to await the publication of archives or memoirs to link the policy with the one set in motion by Henry Kissinger in 1972 (see Section 4.3.1).

Also in April, the first of the Islamic *Jihad* bombings took place in Beirut. The first *kamikaze* bombing, targeting the USA Embassy in April 1983, resulted in the death of 46 Lebanese nationals and 17 US officials, including several CIA station chiefs in the Middle East. (One of the survivors was Ryan Crocker, a political officer, who became the USA ambassador to Beirut, a few years later.) It was followed on 23 October by two explosions, carefully timed to go off about 30 seconds apart. These were on the US barracks and French military headquarters, and claimed the lives of 241 US marines and 58 French paratroopers, in addition to the two suicide bombers, who rammed their explosives-laden lorries into their targets. It was circulated at the time, that US Secretary of State George Shultz subsequently lost interest in the Middle East, as a result of these bombings. 'It was', he wrote in his memoirs, the 'worst single disaster of the Reagan administration'.

The strategic developments that unfolded were to prove consequential for the whole world. US marines participated in a multi-national force, dispatched to oversee the ceasefire between warring factions. The coalition troops took sides in the civil war, and became a target of hostility. In the words of Sheikh Abbas Moussawi, *Hizb-Ullah*'s leader: 'When America and the West became involved in the Lebanese war, they came here to support the Christian Maronites and the Israeli invasion and so they became part of the internal struggle in Lebanon' (interview in Fisk, 7 October 1991).

As the sequence of events demonstrated, the cycle of terrorism, initiated by Israel, with the tacit succour of the US, engendered more anarchy and violence. Most Middle East observers recognize that, to a certain extent, the Lebanese *Hizb-Ullah* (Party of God) and its offshoot Islamic *Jihad*, as well as the Palestinian *Hamas*, were the outgrowths of Israel's occupation of southern Lebanon and its attacks against members of the PLO in Lebanon and the West Bank. It is also a well-known secret that *Hamas*, who with the others now forms the backbone of resistance to Israeli occupation, was encouraged and supported by Israel after the start of the *intifadah* (uprising) (BBC 1, 5 March 1996). Today, their influence has risen to such an extent that they have become the most feared of the militant groups in the Middle East.

But they are no longer the only ones. Others have mushroomed across the Arab world, and on more than one occasion, the *Hizb-Ullah* and the Afghan connections were evident. The war against the Red Army in Kabul was fought by young multi-national *mujahedeen*, recruited by CIA agents, who spent $3 billion on the operation, based in the Pakistani town of Peshawar (Doyle, 1995). Saudi coffers armed them and US personnel trained the men who later turned against them. In addition, state violence, in the form of collective punishment, forced removals, mass demolishing of houses, detention without trial, and torture of prisoners by Israel, gave birth to a myriad of radical groups across the Middle East and beyond.

A week before these developments, the GCC armed forces had their first joint manoeuvres, code-named *Peninsula Shield I* (not to be confused with the 1990 *Desert Shield* US-led operation). The following month, President Ronald Reagan announced a strategic cooperation agreement – the most important pro-Israeli initiative this far.

Repeated threats by Iran to block the Strait of Hormuz if Iraq's attacks on merchant ships continued, motivated the UNSC, on 31 October, to call for free navigation and trade in the international waters of the Gulf and a cessation of hostilities. The resolution also condemned Iraq for attacking civilian targets. Malta, Nicaragua and Pakistan abstained, while the other 12 members supported the resolution.

On the same day, Iraqi *Puma* helicopters attacked a 12-ship convoy with *Exocet* missiles, damaging the Greek cargo ship *Avra*, loaded with bagged fertilizers. Undeterred by the UN SCR, helicopters struck again on 21 November. The Greek bulk carrier *Antigoni*, loaded with 21 000 tonnes of scrap steel, was hit by a missile low in a hold, in Khor Musa, the narrow channel leading from Bandar Mahshahr and Bandar Khomeini (formerly Bandar Shahpour) into the northern Gulf. The crew of 19 took to a lifeboat and were able to move away five to ten minutes before a huge explosion broke the vessel in two. While the Iraqis claimed that they had sunk seven ships during that attack, and a Greek report stated that several ships in the convoy were damaged, Lloyd's listed the Greek cargo-ship only (see also *Navy International,* January 1984, pp. 44–5).

Worsening conditions in the Middle East prompted the USN's Sixth Fleet to augment its Eastern Mediterranean contingent, bringing it to more than 30 vessels, 250 aircraft and 3200 Marines. The force included the *Eisenhower,* carrying at least 90 aircraft, and the battleship *New Jersey,* armed with *Tomahawk* cruise missiles. They were joined later by the *Independence,* with 80 more aircraft, and five other vessels, in addition to those already deployed close to the Lebanese coast. F-14 *Tomcats,* on air reconnaissance patrols, were frequently fired upon by Syrian anti-aircraft artillery (AAA), resulting in the shooting down of two USN aircraft, in December. The METF was reinforced on 13 October by the dispatch of a task force to the Indian Ocean, including the *J F Kennedy,* carrying 80 aircraft and supported by a contingent of about six ships. *Operation Persian Gulf,* launched by the USN on 15 October, deployed 60 vessels, half of which were provided by Britain, France and Australia (O'Ballance, 1988, p. 56). At the time, the METF comprised five USN warships on patrol duties in the Gulf, in addition to ten more in the Arabian Sea, including the carrier *Ranger.* Their principal duty was to safeguard the international sea lines of communication (SLOCs) leading to the Gulf, in order to ensure that Hormuz remained unobstructed and thus protect their access to the Gulf's oil wells (*Navy International,* January 1984, p. 45; also Karsh, 1987, p. 29).

At a secret meeting between US Secretary of State George Shultz and Iraqi Foreign Minister Tariq 'Aziz, Baghdad was advised to end its support for Abu Nidal's group if it wished to improve relations with the West. It was named among states sponsoring terrorism for sheltering the Palestinian faction which carried out the attempt on Shlomo Argov in London, as well as other actions. Before long, the members of the cell were expelled, and Iraq was struck off the list (Dorril, 1994, p. 349). Also, President Reagan's special Middle East envoy visited Baghdad, and Washington issued a communiqué explaining that the purpose of the visit was the exchange of ambassadors 'if Iraq so wished'. At face value, the move was seen as a 'tilt' towards Iraq in its war against Iran. However, the strategic implications were far more significant. While some observers ascribed the *rapprochement* with Saddam Hussein as a means to bear pressure on his arch-enemy Asad, in order to force Syrian troops to withdraw from Lebanon, others accurately suggested that, on the contrary, the US preferred the Syrian military presence to continue, so as to contain the Muslim militiamen. More importantly, USN warships came increasingly under Iranian air surveillance patrols. Twenty F-4 *Phantoms* had been stationed at Bandar Abbas airfield, near the Strait of Hormuz, and it was feared that the Iranians were planning *kamikaze*-style air attacks on USN vessels in the Gulf. American overtures to Iraq were interpreted as a sign that the administration was willing to support Baghdad, in exchange for guarantees that Iraqi air attacks against international shipping would cease. It was also hoped that Iran would no longer be motivated to escalate and close the Strait (in fact, the French and Iraqi governments had already secured Washington's approval to use Iraqi-piloted French aircraft in attacking Iranian economic targets, which made the USG's foreign policy moves comparable to a pendulum, see Section 5.6) (*Navy International*, February 1984, p. 121; also O'Ballance, 1988, p. 156).

The last quarter of the year witnessed the unfolding of two events in the Gulf area that were to dramatically affect the second half of the Iran–Iraq War. Five French *Super-Etendard* fighter aircraft, armed with anti-ship *Exocet* missiles, were delivered to the Iraqi Air Force. And four days later, Baghdad extended the *Naval Exclusion Zone* (*Navy International*, January 1984, p. 44).

The stage was set for the start of the Tanker War. Its theatre of operations was to be the waters of the Gulf.

4 Power-Play in the Gulf

4.1 THE CHOKED AORTA

The Tanker War was the most crucial phase of the Iran–Iraq War. In its evolution over four years, it involved native and alien naval and air fleets alike. In order to fully explain the strategy and its scope, some extensive description is necessary here. It is also essential to recognize Iraq's geostrategic and geopolitical vulnerabilities to understand the conditions that drove Iraq's leadership to introduce the new tactic.

Sun Tsu was one of the earliest strategists to underscore the relevance of geography in the formulation of a military plan. He recommended the meticulous study of the theatre of operations on both the tactical and strategic levels. In the case of the Tanker War, it entails a survey of the Gulf proper. The 'Gulf region' comprises a larger naval theatre than the one referred to here, and includes adjacent waters, such as the Gulfs of Oman and Aden, the Indian Ocean and the Arabian and Red seas.

When examining a world map and the large expanses of oceans and seas covering almost three-quarters of the surface of our planet, at first glance one nearly overlooks the Gulf. This quasi-closed sea measures merely 92 500 square miles, with a maximum width of 210 miles and a length of 615. The waters are shallow, between 81 and 328 feet, and the average depth is about 100 feet. The wide seasonal variations in temperatures and the restricted flow between the Indian Ocean and the Gulf affect the water's salinity. Coral reefs line the littoral, and a myriad of small islands are scattered almost everywhere. No rivers flow into the Gulf basin, except for the Shatt al-'Arab, Iraq's main approach to the sea, of which 55 miles are now shared with Iran. Just as Gibraltar towers over the waters at the western entrance to the Mediterranean, the only gate into the Gulf from the Indian Ocean and the Arabian Sea is dominated by another rock, Ras Musandam, a jagged and forbidding 3000-feet-high iron-grey volcanic rock.

114

The Gulf waters sweep the shores of Iraq in the north, Kuwait in the north-west, Saudi Arabia, the tiny island of Bahrain and the peninsular state of Qatar in the west, and the UAE (Abu Dhabi, Dubai, 'Ajman, Ras al-Khaimah, Sharjah, Fujairah, and Umm al-Qaiwain) in the south. Iran is the only country situated on the entire north-eastern coastline of the Gulf. Its seaboard stretches 1976 miles, including islands, from the Shatt estuary to the Gulf of Oman through the Strait of Hormuz and on to the Arabian Sea. In the north, the Iraqi southern seaboard is barely 10 miles, and less than 50 miles, if measured around Fao, Majnoon (crazy) and Umm Qasr – most of it unsuitable for shipping. The innermost tip of the Gulf is characterized by mudflats, covered with water at high tide only, and as shallow as ten feet in some areas. This feature made it almost impossible to construct deep-water harbours on its northern coast, and accounts for the offshore erection of the two main oil-exporting terminals of Iraq and Iran at Fao and Kharg.

The Gulf's characteristics make shipping hazardous, save in the internationally recognized lanes, which in some areas are narrow. Conditions lend themselves to several scenarios with various military implications. The many chokepoints enable countries that ring the Gulf to endanger the passage of merchantmen, by laying small minefields in any of the narrow sections of the route; by establishing artillery pieces or anti-ship missile launchers on the islands under their control; by deploying warships to blockade the Strait of Hormuz; or by positioning long-range artillery or anti-ship rocket launchers on the Omani or Iranian coasts at the entrance to the Gulf.

Environmental conditions in the Gulf are unique, characterized by extreme temperatures and excessive humidity, especially during its long summers. Apart from the sultry heat, a haze of dust hangs in the air almost continuously. The summer monsoon season starts at the beginning of April, with visibility dropping to less than a mile. On the clearest of days, horizontal visibility is approximately three to five miles, which makes it difficult for airplanes and ships to identify other craft. Because of the haze, reducing the ceiling of visibility to only about 200 feet, visual identification using a television camera, for instance, is impossible. During the last stages of the Tanker War, and the rise in the number and level of activity of air and naval units operating in the southern Gulf, visibility was crucial for positive identification of the various air and naval fleets. Omani, UAE and Iranian warships sailed in the area, alongside the foreign armada, while squadrons of native and alien aircraft circled above them.

Sand and fine dust particles, carried by the damp and excessively hot wind, damage sensitive computers and precision machinery on board ships, aircraft, and battle tanks, especially when these sophisticated instruments are kept on alert for long periods of time. State-of-the-art equipment, tested for European battlefields, was found to be inadequate for the area in the allies' operations in 1991. During the 1970s and 1980s, weather conditions affected the presence of Soviet warships in the Gulf, and a review of their schedule over a few years revealed that their numbers were far lower in summer (see Section 4.5).

At the eastern end of the Gulf, about 500 miles away from the Shatt, the waves wash the base of the Omani Ras Musandam peninsula, a rugged and barren mountain, which abuts against the Strait of Hormuz. Oman was also provided with a coastline that stretches along the Gulf of Oman and winds close to the Gulf of Aden. These coincidental geographical features create the impression that Oman dominates this chokepoint along with Iran. In fact, it ceded control to its powerful neighbour to the north, in return for sending Iranian troops to fight the anti-royal forces of the Popular Front for the Liberation of Oman, in the early 1970s.

Sprinkled in its mouth are a number of islands, and all the ships that sail through Hormuz have to manoeuvre around them. De facto, they now all belong to Iran. Qishm, Larak and Hormuz face the Bandar Abbas naval and air base; and further west into the Gulf, lie the two Tunbs and Abu Musa, previously owned by Ras al-Khaimah and Sharjah, respectively. Premier then Minister of Court Asadollah Alam, the childhood friend and *confidant* of the Shah of Iran, revealed the emperor's unbending insistence to seize the three strategic islands. The subject was broached incessantly with both the American and British ambassadors, personally or through Alam. While the Shah demanded the two Tunb islands, by establishing his case on their location in relation to the Gulf's median line, he nevertheless claimed Abu Musa, which lay far closer to the

Arabian coast, on the grounds that he was 'sufficiently power-ful to disregard the line' (the Shah in Alam, 1991, pp. 31, 34).

Subsequently, in exchange for the Shah relinquishing his long-standing claim on Bahrain, the British Ambassador to Tehran was instructed to divulge to him the exact time of the British pull-out. At 2200 hours on 30 November 1971, on the same night that the contingent was about to withdraw from the islands, the ambassador asked for an audience with the Shah to inform him of the imminent operation (Ramsbotham, Interview, 12 January 1992). Straightaway, the Imperial Iranian troops were ordered to occupy the Greater and Lesser Tunbs and Abu Musa islands, and landed a few hours before the British cleared them, according to a retired Iranian naval officer.

Conspiracy theory and left-wing observers saw this action as yet another example of collusion between a former colonial power and its proxy, in an area where it still retained interests. British apologists interpreted it as a deliberate act, on the part of the Shah, to embarrass their state. But *realpolitik* analysts interpreted the Shah's move as facing the world with a *fait accompli*. Only when classified government documents are released will light be shed on the real motives, and whether a secret deal was agreed on, what the terms were and what the price was. At face value, the way the incident unfolded led to the conclusion that indeed a barter agreement was struck, and that the century-old pursuit of the 'hotly contested and increasingly unrealistic claim over Bahrain' was finally settled (Alikhani in Alam, 1991, p. 31).

This view was supported by Sir Dennis Walters' account, who wrote that he was approached, in early 1971, by Sir William Luce, who was Sir Alec Douglas-Home's representative for Gulf affairs. Sir Dennis was instructed to meet the Shah to consult with him on two matters that had to be discussed 'with Iran first' before the final withdrawal, and an 'understanding with the Shah . . . [on] Bahrain and the islands of Abu Musa and the Tunbs' had to be reached. Sir Dennis stated that at the end of the talks, 'Iran did gain possession of the disputed islands, as a result of a tacit understanding between the Shah and the British government that this should be done discreetly, and a cash payment made to one of the sheikhs most closely involved' (Walters, 1989, pp. 182–4).

While Sir Dennis did not divulge the details of the deal, Alam explained that Abu Musa was to be divided with Sharjah. As a 'conciliatory gesture', Crescent Petroleum was to retain the right to drill oil in Iran's share of the island and territorial waters. And in return for his good will, its ruler, Sheikh Khalid bin Muhammad al-Qasimi, received an annual allowance from Tehran; accused of collaboration, he was killed by rebels led by his cousin, in January 1972.

In 1971, the British Ambassador to Tehran was Sir Peter Ramsbotham, who was later posted to Washington. Asked to comment on the incident, he replied that he could not remember Sir Dennis's visit to Tehran. But he could clearly recall that Sir William Luce, the distinguished former Governor of Aden, conducted the negotiations which took several months. The talks included several points: the withdrawal of British troops from East of Suez, the formation of the UAE, and the questions of Bahrain and the three islands. The talks were long drawn out and entailed more than one visit to Tehran, and necessitated calling on the Shah, at least once a week. The Americans caused complications over the question of offshore oil around the islands, and various formulae were discussed. During Sir William's visits, he stayed at the residence of the British envoy, who accompanied him on each of the meetings with the Iranian emperor and officials. An agreement was reached, and on the night the British were about to withdraw, the Shah sent off his troops in the British-made hovercrafts to the islands. In the melee, two policemen were killed. Iraq lodged a protest at the UN, asking them to summon the Shah there. As the Iranian monarch felt offended, presuming that the British were behind the protest, it was agreed that an invitation to stay at Windsor and attend the Ascot races would appease him, cheer him up and make him forget his hurt (verbatim Ramsbotham, Interview, 12 January 1992).

Sir Peter's account corresponded with Alam's diaries, in which he continuously referred to the Shah's persistent claim over the islands (1991, pp. 15, 31, 34, note 38, 44–5, 70–1, 83, 85, 94, 101, 103, 113, 147, 153–6, 159–61, 163–5, 174, 182, 185, 189, 238, 244, 413). Unfortunately, due to Alam's preoccupation with arrangements for the Persepolis celebrations from 21 March 1971 to 21 March 1972, there was a gap in the diaries, at a critical historical juncture. It includes the night when the Imperial Iranian Navy (IIN), supported by marines, occupied the islands. About two decades later, in late August 1992, Iran effectively annexed Abu Musa. It jointly controlled the island with the UAE, under a deal agreed with Britain, the country in charge of the foreign relations of the seven sheikhdoms. In the first interference with civilian traffic, a passenger ferry was detained in port for three days, then turned back by the Iranian police detachment. The problem of the three islands is still a heated issue in the Gulf area, and one of the reasons that pit Iran against its southern Gulf neighbours and most of the Arab World.

In any event, despite the outcry in some Arab capitals, and Baghdad's decision to break off diplomatic ties with Tehran on 3 December, the 1971 incident did not arouse world clamour, and the UNSC was neither summoned to take action nor even called into session. By pretending to be unaware of the episode, the world obviously accepted Iran's occupation as a *fait accompli*. Nine years later, these three strategic islands were to be part of Saddam Hussein's territorial war aims.

4.2 HORMUZ: THE CHOKEPOINT

Geographically, Iran dominates the Gulf, which sweeps its seaboard all the way from the Shatt to the Strait of Hormuz, whereas the western shore is shared by all the other Arab Gulf states. The strait's width extends from 20 to 25 miles, and its main shipping channel is five to eight miles wide, and about 300 feet deep. Iran also dominates the strategic gateway to the Gulf, by the fact that Qishm, Larak and Hormuz islands abut the narrowest navigable passage. As the shipping channel winds into the Gulf, a second crescent-shaped cluster of islands (Sirri, Forur, Abu Musa and the two Tunbs) adjoins it. Roughly every 11 minutes, one of the tankers which lift 8mbd of oil crude to Europe, Japan, America and about 60 LDCs have to navigate in close proximity to Iran and Iranian-controlled islands.

The Shah considered the Strait his most prized strategic asset. But he repeatedly referred to its vulnerability in order to justify Iranian military self-sufficiency. He thus ensured the continuous flow of hardware from Britain and America, and secured for his country a qualitative and quantitative edge in arms over all the other Gulf states. By the mid-1970s, he became the largest single purchaser of American arms in the world, and controlled the world's fifth largest military force (Abrahamian, 1980, p. 21; and Halliday, 1979, p. 64). This enabled him to fill the military 'vacuum' caused by the British withdrawal from the Gulf. His role in ensuring the stability of the area was favourably viewed by the major Western powers, who recognized the immense strategic importance of Hormuz, being the most vital international route, leading to the world's main oil reserves, which meant that almost two-thirds of global oil supplies was shipped through it.

The expansion of a network of pipelines across Saudi Arabia and Turkey reduced the bulk of sea-lifted crude, which represents only 17 per cent of the West's imports (Cordesman, 1988, p. 27). However, whether small or medium tankers transit the Strait into the Arabian Sea, then turn into Bab al-Mandab, up the Red Sea and through the Suez Canal into the Mediterranean, or supertankers (VLCCs) sail around the Cape of Good Hope or go east into the Pacific, they must all transit the narrow channel between Oman and Iran. None of the other straits, such as Gibraltar, Bab al-Mandab or Malacca, bear the same degree of strategic significance as the confined waters of Hormuz, the conduit of oil to the world.

During the Iran–Iraq War, the international community of oil-consumers feared the blocking of the Strait by one of the combatants. Iraq would have been unaffected by its closure, since its oil was exported overland. Although one of its intermediate Tanker War aims was to internationalize the war by drawing in concerned parties from outside the region, it was unlikely that it would resort to the closure of the Strait. Such an action would have alienated the countries whose good offices or military intervention it needed to compel Iran to end the war. Furthermore, Baghdad feared to alienate its Gulf allies, whose financial, political and diplomatic support were vital for its war effort. But the Iraqi leadership hoped that Iran would block shipping through Hormuz, and that such an action would precipitate foreign naval intervention. At that time, Westerners feared Muslim militancy, and suspected Tehran's ties with the Lebanese *Hizb-Ullah*, while the Americans were traumatized by the hostages' crisis and their aborted attempt at rescuing them. Consequently, international public opinion suspected Iran of being the only party which would resort to such an act. Especially so, if its oil-export capabilities were crippled by Iraqi attacks, in which case Iran would seek to hurt the economies of Iraq's supporters in the Gulf, or deny the industrialized countries their lifeblood.

In the autumn of 1983, Khomeini and Rafsanjani threatened several times to close the Strait if France delivered to Iraq the aircraft it had requested (see Section 5.6). In a statement broadcast on Radio Tehran, a short time after the Iraqi-French deal to lease the five fighters was confirmed, Parliament Speaker Rafsanjani detailed various Iranian options for retaliation: either to fire on tankers from artillery on Qishm and Larak islands, or bomb them from aircraft overflying the Strait of Hormuz, or alternatively obstruct it by sinking a VLCC. Occasionally, these threats raised speculation in oil markets.

Whether it was realistically feasible, whether Tehran was deterred by pronouncements and counter-threats by Washington, or whether Iran's leadership showed a considerable degree of self-restraint will be explored next. At this stage, a description of the physical features of the Strait, and an explanation of the various methods available to Iran to block Hormuz are essential, in order to form a concrete idea of the seriousness of the threats and counter-threats made. It would also help to ascertain whether the West's fears and the Iraqi hopes were founded on realistic assumptions. Before launching the review, however, it is worth noting that a US Congressional study, completed in 1979, concluded that obstructing the Strait would be virtually impossible and also improbable, as Iran's economy and its people's well-being relied heavily on safeguarding trade through the Gulf (O'Ballance, 1988, pp. 127–8; and *Navy International*, 1984, January, p. 44 and May, p. 310).

A USN captain explained that there were four ways of blocking the Strait of Hormuz. The first plan entailed placing artillery on one or more of the islands, scattered close to the shipping channel. But he believed that a few waves of air strikes would wipe them out. The second option was the use of mines, of which Iran held a large arsenal. But 'the Strait's currents, depth and width probably preclude success', and a minesweeping operation could clear the waters quickly. In addition, Hormuz has a number of narrow passages along both coasts and around the islands, which allowed small-tonnage ships to navigate away from the minefields. Despite these facts, members of NATO were concerned that Iran might resort to mining if the Tanker War resulted in a massive decrease in Iranian oil exports (Daly, 1985, pp. 151, 155–6; see also *Navy International,* May 1984, p. 310).

Sinking vessels in the shipping channel was a technique used during the 1956 and 1967 Arab–Israeli wars, when the Egyptians successfully obstructed traffic through the Suez Canal (for details on the operations see Abou-Zikry, 1986, pp. 221–3, 228–9, 253–5). But because of the differences in width and depth between the two waterways, submerged ships would have been impractical, in so far that they would not have halted navigation through Hormuz (*Navy International,* April 1984, p. 232). The Strait has two main shipping lanes, whereas the Suez Canal had only one channel, except where it flowed into the Bitter and Timsah lakes. Furthermore, an Iranian closure of the Gulf would have defied international conventions, as the Strait adjoins Oman as well. But the Suez Canal runs within Egyptian territory, and under the Suez treaty of 1883, in times of war, Egypt had the right to refuse passage of enemy ships or of neutral ships carrying goods destined to its enemy.

A naval blockade was possible, if Iran had a large enough seapower, capable of protecting its coast while patrolling the strait. The manoeuvre would have had a strategic impact only if it continued over a long period of time. With only three destroyers and four frigates operational, the IRIN would have been hard-pressed to sustain defensive and blockading operations. In contrast, the 'blockade established by the Egyptian Navy at Bab el-Mandeb from 11th October to 13th December was apparently effective . . . A minefield near the Straits of Tiran reinforced a blockade which effectively choked off Israel's Red Sea traffic' (Till, 1987, p. 138), and 'the deployment of Egyptian submarines in the Eastern Mediterranean augmented the effectiveness of the Red Sea blockade' (Day, Interview, 5 January 1992; for the description of the *stop and search* operation at Bab al-Mandab, in a regional conflict between two LDCs, see Abou-Zikry, who devised the plan, 1986, pp. 283–91, 296–300, 306, 322, 351–63, 388–9). Were such an operation envisaged by Iran, the long coastline and the considerable number of harbours, bases and oil terminals would have been more than the weakened IRIN could have handled simultaneously. Even if the fleet had carried out this mission, it would have been for a few days at the most, in which case it would not have had the desired strategic effect.

In this discussion, the American factor cannot be overlooked. It was highly unlikely that the USN, which had a constant presence in the area, would have stood by while the IRIN carried out its threat of closing the Gulf in the face of international shipping. Reconnaissance aircraft, stationed on the carriers deployed in the area, would have warned the US warships in and around the Gulf of any such action. It is therefore doubtless that the USN would have sought to engage the IRIN, and the outcome was all too predictable.

There was also a legal obstacle to such an operation, as the Iranians would have broken international maritime laws concerning free passage for ships in international water lanes bound for neutral non-belligerent countries. At best, this would have been counterproductive for Iran, as it would have been penalized by the countries that had an interest in safeguarding freedom of traffic for trading ships; and at worst, it would have invited foreign naval intervention, which Tehran painstakingly avoided. The conclusion derived is that Iran's threat to close Hormuz was a symbolic gesture, while practically infeasible. The danger that Iran would undertake such a crucial step was a remote possibility – as an act of desperation – but the threats were probably made to deter actions that might completely halt Iranian seaborne trade in the Gulf.

4.3 IRAQ'S GEOPOLITICAL AND GEOSTRATEGIC PREDICAMENT

Iraq, carved out of territories that were part of the disintegrated Ottoman Empire, was afflicted by severe geopolitical and geostrategic problems. The boundaries of the nascent state, like so many frontiers drawn up by colonial fiat, were arbitrarily chosen, cut across ethnic homelands, ran between mutually hostile nations, and thus sowed the seeds for external conflicts and internal strife. Their delineation indicated a considerable lack of insight and consideration, or possibly betrayed undue political scheming.

The Algiers Agreement illustrated more than anything else how the combination of Iraq's geopolitical and geostrategic problems was used against its interests by making the cessation of Kurdish anti-Baghdad activities, instigated, supported and aided by Tehran and Washington, conditional on ceding half of the Shatt's waters. In the introduction to Alam's memoirs, Alikhani acknowledged that '[b]y supporting rebellion among the Kurds and maintaining pressure along the Iraqi border, the Shah managed to force concessions from Baghdad: above all the demarcation of the Iran–Iraq border along the Shatt al-Arab waterway in accordance with Iran's most cherished hopes' (1991, p. 15; see also Ghareeb in Axelgard [ed.], 1986, p. 69).

Reneged five years later, it was exclusively advantageous to Iran, and awarded it its long-standing objective of sharing the entire Shatt with Iraq. At the time of its signing in 1975, it was hugely unpopular with the Iraqi public. It was also a mainstream opinion adopted by the major political parties, not an opposition tactic, supported by one or the other faction. Statements by their leaders confirmed that they were against it, albeit for different reasons. Arab Nationalists felt strongly against the pact, as they considered Arabistan part of *al-ummah al-'Arabiyyah*. The ICP repudiated it, although a number of its members were in the National Front – two of them cabinet ministers. The reason they gave was the territorial sovereignty of their country, but they seized upon the agreement to demonstrate their aversion to the concept of monarchies by attacking the one in Tehran. The Islamic groups, keen to see the Shah removed, found a window of opportunity to blame him, and empathized with Khomeini, who was deported to France at the Shah's request. The Kurds, who had enjoyed Tehran's financial and military succour for a number of years, and had free territorial passage into Iran, lost both privileges because of the conditions enshrined in the agreement.

4.3.1 The Geopolitical Issue

The ailments from which the Kurds suffer now are the result of earlier developments which echo each other from different vantage points. In the course of seven decades, London, Tehran, Tel Aviv, Washington, Ankara and Baghdad, often in collusion, tried to liquidate the 'Kurdish Question', by subjecting the Kurds to extermination. Similarities appear in stratagems devised by Winston Churchill, Shah Muhammed Reza, the Turkish authorities and Saddam Hussein, which led to the wilful killing of hundreds of thousands of Kurds.

The dramatic circumstances from 1989 to 1991 led to the revival of national tendencies and the unravelling of ethnic tapestries. Many parts of the world were on a downward spiral of chaos, as sectarian and ethnic rivalries spread like bushfires. Long before these events, however, Kurdistan was a cauldron of resentment and bitterness that foreshadowed turbulence. But active rebellion was kept under control through a combination of forcible measures, first by Britain, then by Iraq, Turkey and Iran. At different historical stages, open conflict and violence erupted in the region, countered by military repression, mass killings and covert action, especially in northern Iraq and south-eastern Turkey, and to a lesser degree, in western Iran.

Despite the Treaty of Sèvres, signed by envoys of the Allied and Ottoman governments on 10 August 1920, the Kurdish issue, a potential powder keg, was never seriously addressed. Article 64 of the treaty stated that if the Kurdish people aspired for statehood, they should make a request to the League of Nations within one year. Following approval by the Council, Turkey was to relinquish all claims over those territories. But the British feared that the Soviet Union would gain a strategic foothold in the newly established weak state. It was also hinted that the plan was soft-pedalled because the creation of an independent Kurdistan would alienate Arab opinion.

However, logic based on *realpolitik* strongly suggested that the British coveted the oil-rich territory and intended not only to include it in the new kingdom that was about to be founded under their mandate, but to actually create the new state around it. According to a televised programme, based on declassified documents, when the British wrested the territories from the Ottomans, petroleum had been discovered in vast quantities around Kirkuk. They 'wanted to get their hands on it', so they linked the province of Mosul to two other provinces and created the state of Iraq. When the Kurds rebelled, Churchill, the Air Minister, resolved to use aircraft against them, because there were plenty of airplanes; their deployment was more cost-effective than keeping an occupation army on the ground; and an opportunity presented itself to test new arms, such as delayed-action bombs and napalm, and to train pilots for target practice. As political expediency was the concept that dictated the scheme, pilots were not to draw any distinction between attacks on freedom fighters and civilians. Consequently, the Kurdish revolt was quelled in the early 1920s and early 1930s by the Royal Air Force (RAF). Sir Hugh Trenchard, Chief of Air Staff at the time, ordered the operational reports to be 'doctored' to conceal the indiscriminate bombing of villages, the high number of civilian casualties, the extent of atrocities and the tonnage of bombs dropped. The MoD feared that the disclosures would damage the government, as the true details could prompt a public outcry and a call for investigations ('Birds of Death' in *Secret History*, 6 July 1992; also *Independent*, 6 July 1992; and see Omissi, 1990, on the extensive use of the RAF in Iraq).

Churchill assumed that the destruction of Kurdish villages and the creation of large numbers of refugees, suffering hardship and bad weather, would coerce their leaders to negotiate – the identical logic behind Saddam Hussein's aggression almost 70 years later, and the strategy implemented by Israel against the southern Lebanese in July 1993 and April 1996. The people were flushed out by bombing, and those who tried to escape to mountain caves were hunted and cut down by machine-gun fire. After the raids, they returned to be blown-up by the new delayed-action bombs. The operation also marks a peculiar resemblance to the one in the spring of 1991, when the allies relied on airpower to carpet-bomb Iraqi troops, and new weapons were primed, loaded and tested for the first time.

Arthur 'Bomber' Harris, who described the operation, wrote in 1924: 'The Arab and the Kurd now know what real bombing means in casualties and damage. Within 45 minutes a full-sized village can be practically wiped out and a third of the inhabitants killed or injured by four or five machines' (in *Independent*, 6 July 1992). Another pilot commented that 'if the Kurds had not learnt by our example to behave themselves in a civilized way, then we had to spank their bottoms. This was done by bombs and guns' (Gale, televised interview, 6 July

1992). This warning blast from the past reverberates through almost seven decades, when in 1991, an American pilot proudly proclaimed that he was about to 'kick Iraqi asses'.

As a result, the Kurdish population remained fragmented and forced to live in four Middle Eastern countries and in the defunct Soviet Union. Totalling 15 to 17 million in the mid-1980s, the Kurds were close to one-quarter of Iraq's inhabitants, slightly more than one-tenth of Syria's, and about 16 per cent and 18 per cent of Turkey's and Iran's, respectively. Today, excluding those living abroad, one million of them in the former republics of the USSR, and 450 000 in Germany alone, the judgement is that the Kurds now number between 20 and 25 million people, which made them the world's largest nation without a state, and the fourth major race in the Middle East, after the Arabs, the Turks and the Persians. On the whole, they were only helped by their host countries when it was in the latter's best interests to do so, and the Kurds were susceptible to influence and manipulation when it suited their own purposes. They were 'courted and then ignored in the 1970s by an unholy alliance of the CIA and the Shah of Iran, orchestrated by Kissinger', and again in 1984, their rebellion was crushed when external backing was withdrawn (*Independent*, 9 and 27 December 1991; *Independent on Sunday*, 29 September 1991; see also Daly, 1985, p. 152; and *Hayat*, 3 December 1993).

Iraq's socio-political fabric was doomed to be continuously weakened by the restiveness of the Kurds, who were known to be a vocal minority. The arrangement to destabilize and weaken Iraq was agreed during a visit by US President Richard Nixon and Secretary of State Henry Kissinger to Tehran in May 1972, whereby Iran was to serve as a base for the Kurds for future military operations. While the US, Britain and Israel supplied weapons and advisors, Iran mobilized the Kurds, and the Shah was constantly informed of the *Peshmergas'* acts of sabotage against Iraqi pipelines around Mosul and Kirkuk. At the same time, Imperial Iranian ground troops engaged in cross-border attacks, and their British-made *Rapier* missiles shot down Iraqi aircraft. Pre-dating this agreement, Tehran had organized a failed attempt on President al-Bakr's life, and had devised a plan to bring down the Iraqi regime, by bringing together the Kurds and the exiled Iraqi opposition. The Kurds' calls for autonomy and their opposition to the Iraqi state were encouraged and backed for the following three years, but after the signing of the Algiers accord, American and Iranian succour was instantly removed (Alam, 1991, pp. 39, 41, 119, 176, 230, 244–5, 358, 391–2, 399–400, 411, 417–19; and Zonis, 1991, pp. 69–70).

Despite repeated Iraqi denials, a UN investigative committee reported in August 1988, that Iraq made extensive use of CW in the spring and summer operations against Iranian troops, and since then, mounting evidence confirmed that it stockpiled CW and pursued a genocidal campaign against the Kurds. The aim of the operations in 1988 and 1991 was to eradicate the Kurdish movement, by exterminating as many of their fighters as possible, and by disseminating the population, as in 1924. Halabja and Shalamja were gassed in retaliation for assistance proffered to Iran during the first Gulf War, and to curb Kurdish power, especially after they wrested control of 4000 square miles in northern Iraq, in March 1988. A treasure trove of official documents, left behind in Iraqi Kurdistan by the withdrawing Iraqi army, and discovered by members of the KDP, established beyond doubt that Baghdad used CW. This was proven by a memorandum with instructions from the former Iraqi commander in Arbil, addressed to divisions in control of bio-chemical weapons. The INC leadership hope to present a case to the ICJ, with evidence that Baghdad waged a chemical war against its own people, founded on Iraq's violation of its obligations under the Geneva Protocol, recalling that Baghdad subscribed to the Convention in 1972, as mentioned in the 1990 UN SCR 687, labelled 'the Mother of all Resolutions'.

'Ali Hassan Al-Majeed, who previously held the Interior and Defence ministries, had absolute control over Iraqi Kurdistan, and commanded several offensives there. His extensive use of CW against the Kurds, before the implementation of the Iran-Iraq ceasefire, earned him the epithet "Ali *Kemawi*" ('Chemical'). Thousands of families fled to Turkey and Iran, after the devastation wrought by Saddam Hussein's war machine. Up to 4500 villages were wiped off the map when the troops bulldozed them before pulling out. To date, 180 000 people were still missing, as a result of *Al-Anfal* operations in 1988. Several mass graves, discovered by the Kurds in the early 1990s, held corpses of women and children. An Iraqi source revealed that 'Ali Al-Majeed, whom they designate as the 'butcher of Kurdistan and Kuwait' – having been appointed governor of the emirate in 1990 – took the unusual step to associate himself with these operations, during meetings between Iraqi and Kurdish leaders, after the second Gulf War. When Talabani raised the issue of the 180 000 missing, Majeed exclaimed, 'Why are you making such a fuss about these people? After all, they were only 100 000!'.

Al-Majeed led two similar operations, except for the use of chemicals, to smash the uprisings in 1991, killing thousands, of whom a number were massacred after being captured. Three armoured divisions with air cover attacked civilians in Iraqi Kurdistan, and once again, the population fled in fear, seeking safety in the mountains. They were seen on television screens, as they took to the hill tops, on the move along ridges, stuck in the mud of the mountain passes, without food, medicine, water, or shelter – the weakest dying of cold, hunger and dehydration. Television images showed the air-dropped food crates and relief bundles landing on the slopes, with children scrambling and fighting to get a share. According to reports, some were poisoned by the river water contaminated by the Iraqi forces, or shot from helicopters hovering overhead, their bodies torn apart by starving dogs.

But despite the grim stories that shocked public opinion the world over, there was no Western military intervention, bearing in mind that the Kurds did not themselves provoke the disturbances. President Bush was tragically irresponsible in the Spring of 1991, when he encouraged Iraqis to take up armed opposition and rise against Saddam Hussein, then extricated himself and simply dropped them, allegedly because of fears over the dismemberment of Iraq, but most probably because of the political colour of the insurrection in southern Iraq. His act had disastrous consequences and led to regional instability. After letting them down, they bore the brunt of emigration, isolation, exhaustion and famine in a fierce winter. The world stood by as an accomplice to the massacre of the Kurds, and shares the shame of their betrayal.

Iraqi Kurdistan became a besieged region. Over three million people were crowded in the enclave, living in the few towns and villages that were spared. They survived in bullet-scarred houses, some gutted by fire, where rooms were empty shells, except for their scant belongings. Wooden shutters, doors, window frames and furniture were all burnt for cooking and heating, when Baghdad withheld oil consignments to the region – one of the richest in the world in oil reserves. The mountain slopes were shaved clean of trees, used for fuel by the scores of tens of thousands that were still out there, too frightened to return, and who sheltered in tents and caves on mountain tops. Factories ceased to function, electricity, telecommunication and road networks were in ruin, but they were unable to attract investment or tap their oil resources for the repair of their shattered infrastructure.

But in spite of their plight, and despite political differences between the two main leaders, Talabani and Barzani were able to cooperate, and the Kurds established the legal and institutional foundations of an autonomous state. In May 1992, they cast their ballots in an internationally observed election, and restored some of their battered towns and villages. They created local administrative units in the services sectors, such as health, education and economic assistance, but their capabilities were limited by the double embargo, the one against Iraq and the one imposed by Baghdad. A government was set up to administer their homeland, and 30 000 *Peshmerga* were organized into a lightly-armed and semi-disciplined force. They had more form than substance, and while their numbers could be increased to 100 000, they would always be rather impotent with light artillery, hand-grenades and *Kalashnikovs* ranged against Iraqi heavy armour and aircraft. But the shortage in heavy weapons was compensated for by their high spirits. Radio and television stations multiplied, alongside local newspapers, giving them free channels of expression to broadcast current news, and allowing them to keep their culture alive by transmitting their arts. But Iran is increasingly concerned that the television stations foster unrest among its own Kurds.

At its creation, when 15 000 allied troops enforced it, the world's first 'Safe Haven' encouraged one million Kurds to return, although it was not safe and far from being a haven. Part of the no-fly sector remained under the Iraqi government's control, and part of the Kurdish-held territories were outside that zone and beyond Western commitment, and the key cities of Kirkuk and Mosul remained in Saddam Hussein's hands. Proposed by Britain's Prime Minister, John Major, and championed by the US, its establishment has done little to initiate a political solution. It gave the Kurds breathing space and security, albeit limited, but safety for them seemed to be a rare commodity. The mandate for *Operation Provide Comfort* is reviewed every six months by Turkey, and speculation grew as to the Kurds' future every time. They constantly live in fear, and although the overflights from the Turkish airbase of Incirlik have not ceased, they have been brought down from 90 sorties a day to about four. By the end of 1996, there were strong reasons to suspect that the whole operation would grind to a halt. Ground patrols had discontinued, and Turkey's troops and air force had been given *carte blanche* inside the territory.

That is only half the problem. Aid was imperiled when donors closed their purses. Some of the 'blue helmets' were withdrawn from northern Iraq in June 1993, as the organization was far short of funds for the programme. They ensured the security of aid workers and restricted covert operations by Iraqi agents against them, albeit to a limited degree. On many occasions, they were singled out and a number were killed in the course of their duty. The 'blue berets' also guarded the convoys, while *en route* to Iraqi Kurdistan through territories held by Baghdad, thus ensuring that humanitarian aid reached its destination. Nevertheless, many trucks were blown up by timed devices.

In the meantime, Iranian and Turkish ground and air forces crossed the northern and north-eastern Iraqi border regularly to strike at 'rebel' bases, and reinforcements were laying the groundwork for further aggression. Baghdad's troops, massed along the Dejla river on the edge of the Kurdish-held territories, were strengthened by Republican Guards. Awaiting the departure of the allied forces from Turkey to carry out a full-scale assault, they sporadically shelled Kurdish hamlets to disrupt the harvest.

The Kurds' chronicle of persecution forced them to adopt balance-of-power politics to serve their interests, and at various stages in their past, they allied with stronger parties. Their awareness of geopolitical realities served the Iraqi Kurds, when their latitude was increased after the second Gulf War. They cultivated relations with Ankara, Damascus and Tehran, and strengthened their ties with Kurdish parties in these countries. Consultation to bring about political unanimity among the different Kurdish factions, conducted by the Iraqi Kurdish leadership, were moderately successful in eliciting the cooperation of some of the governments in the area. To deflect Turkish or Iranian retaliatory attacks, they were able to influence a number of Kurdish factions not to operate against their home-countries from northern Iraq, and at times, the *Peshmerga* collaborated with Turkish forces in border-policing. Despite being unequal players in the game, their new status enabled them to serve as mediators between Turkish and Iranian Kurdish parties and their governments. One of these instances was a short-lived cease-fire, announced on 17 March 1993 by Abdullah Ocalan, the leader of the PKK, and for which Talabani acted as the catalyst. When it collapsed in June, it alarmed Iraqi Kurds, whose trade lifeline was threatened by the resumption of Turkish–Kurdish hostilities.

In 1994, cooperation between the two main parties in Iraqi Kurdistan collapsed. Bitter confrontation, taking the form of scattered armed skirmishes, at first, were triggered by a trivial dispute between two individuals, belonging to the two Kurdish clans, over a tiny plot of land. The show-down escalated for control of the whole territory, following the status quo, with the Talabani tribe established in the larger towns in southern and eastern Kurdistan, along the Iranian border, and the Barzanis spread across the area in the north and west, adjoining Turkey and Syria. 'Customs duties' on contraband goods entering northern Iraq and on oil exported to Turkey was at the heart of the feud for political and economic influence. Negotiations in different locations, organized by American diplomats and Intelligence officers, with KDP, PUK, INC, Turkish and British participation, produced the 1995 Dublin Agreement and led to a fragile ceasefire. However, in-fighting between the two warlords blighted the region again, and the talks failed. Their miscarriage delighted the Iranian authorities, who, similarly to the Turks, regard themselves as the main player in northern Iraq.

Talabani, since 1995 ensconced in Iraqi Kurdistan's capital, Arbil, seized two valleys held by Barzani, dominating the Hamilton Road, a major contraband route, where the KDP levied 'customs duties'. Profiting from the KDP's 60th anniversary, on 17 August 1996, he attacked with weapons left behind by 1500 Iranian Revolutionary Guards, who crossed the border, in late July, ostensibly in pursuit of Iranian Kurdish 'rebels'. On 20 August, al-Majeed was nominated governor of Kirkuk, with command of a Republican Guard armoured division, deployed from Baghdad and stationed at the edge of the no-fly zone. On 31 August, in response to a request for assistance from Barzani, these troops marched into the Safe Haven. A new round of peace talks, launched the day before at the US Embassy in London, was brought to a sudden halt. Despite the last-minute intervention of Robert Pelletreau, the US State Department's Assistant Secretary for Near Eastern Affairs, conditions deteriorated to the extent of a full-blown civil war between the two main Kurdish tribes, by early September. Their fight was closely monitored by Baghdad, Tehran, Ankara and Damascus – the parties with the greatest vested interest in the outcome. Accused by Baghdad of collaborating with Tehran, Talabani was first dislodged from Arbil, and in September, from the PUK's stronghold, Sulaymaniyah, capital of the third province of Iraqi Kurdistan. By late September, Talabani regained most of his losses, including Sulaymaniyah. In early November, a peace agreement, negotiated by US, British and Turkish officials, was signed in Ankara, allowing the two rivals to hold on to the territories they had controlled since 23 October. The area was to be monitored by a peace-keeping detachment, heavily manned by Turcomans and Assyrians, as advocated by Turkey's Deputy Prime Minister and Minister of Foreign Affairs, Tansu Ciller; and Ankara established unquestionable influence in this geostrategic region by sending its officials to carry out a census in northern Iraq.

4.3.2 The Geostrategic Question

Shatt al-'Arab (Arab River, *Arvand Rud* in Persian), formed by the confluence of the Dejla and Faurat rivers, is about 130 miles long, and runs south to the northern tip of the Gulf. It bordered the Arabistan Emirate, established in 1690, which dominated the northern Gulf with its formidable navy. During the Kabide Period, which lasted 200 years, the emirate controlled the main trade links between the Ottoman and Persian empires, and monopolized trade between the Indian subcontinent and the East African coast. Alerted by the East India Company, British warships attempted at times to curb Arabistan's supremacy by obstructing shipping through the estuary, but were themselves often blockaded. The emirate was conquered by the Persians in 1823 and by the Ottomans in 1837, but the British, in alliance with the Russians, compelled them to withdraw, and handed Muhammarah to the Persians. Nominally independent, Arabistan was stripped of its influence and remained under Persian authority.

Competition for control over the Shatt has a long history, and several treaties between the Persian and Ottoman empires, and later between Iran and Iraq, have not resolved the territorial dispute. The roots of the crisis that entangle Iraq and Iran originated earlier, when their common frontier was not clearly delineated and although an agreement was signed in 1639, giving the Ottomans control over a disputed area, it remained within the grip of the Persians. Border skirmishes in 1818 led to a new agreement in 1823, followed by another in 1837, whereby the Ottomans were forced by Britain and Russia to yield parts of Arabistan, including the cities of Muhammarah (renamed Khorramshahr), and Khidr (renamed Abadan). In return, Persia ceded a slice of land on the border. In the 1911 and 1913 Tehran Agreement and Constantinople Protocol, the Ottomans conceded half of the Shatt waters, off Muhammarah, but otherwise retained sovereignty over both banks of the river. After the establishment of the kingdom of Iraq, a complaint it made to the League of Nations was shelved, but not resolved. The simmering problem was aired again, and three agreements were signed in 1937, with more territorial concessions by Iraq, giving Iran half of the Shatt, along a five-mile stretch up to Abadan. These settlements were unilaterally abrogated by Iran in 1969, and the Shah insisted that the border should run along the *thalweg*, the theoretical median line along the river's deepest channel. As Iranian and Kurdish skirmishes in northern Iraq intensified, Saddam Hussein acquiesced to the emperor's demand, in return for three villages in the Khurmanshah region and non-interference in each other's internal affairs. Iran, however, ignored its part of the agreement with regard to the Sulaymaniyah region, and never returned to Iraq the villages of Zain al-Qaws, Bir 'Ali and Shukra.

The controversy over the Shatt al-'Arab and territories along the Iran–Iraq boundary were discussed in Tareq Ismael's *Iraq & Iran: Roots of Conflict.* The value of the book lay in the fact that it contained a number of translated legal documents on its historical, ideological and political aspects. Also, five maps illustrate how Persia, and later Iran, seized territories, first, close to, then adjacent to the Shatt al-'Arab waterway, demonstrating that part of the Ahvaz region, populated by ethnic Arabs, along with the island of Khidr and the town of al-Muhammarah became part of the Persian Empire, relatively recently, in 1847 (see Ismael, 1982, maps 1–4 pp. 4, 7, 13, 17). The main criticism is that the author did not include the four treaties predating the 1847 Treaty of Erzerum, which also dealt with the problem of the disputed territories, the first of which was signed in Constantinople in 1555. The author also failed to mention the strategic implications of the border changes.

When the British troops first landed in Mesopotamia in 1914, to wrest it from the declining Ottoman Empire, their ships berthed in the river.

> The expedition's political adviser, Sir Percy Cox, warned his superiors that 'the position of our ships . . . from an international point of view, is undoubtedly a weak one'. Cox's warning echoes ironically through more than 60 years of disputes between Iraq and Iran . . . For in this inhospitable part of the world, neither geography nor international law permits any power to feel secure. So long as that has been the case, military conflict was bound to recur – with ever-increasing seriousness as the oil became more precious and the military forces on each side of the Shatt al Arab grew more potent (Wright, 1980/81, p. 275).

The strategic implications of the Iran–Iraq border changes were given predominance by Danziger, who described British and Soviet attempts to build secure ports at Basra and Umm Qasr, and their recognition that Iraq had an 'almost insurmountable problem' which made 'the construction of a naval base almost impossible', as both harbours were 'strategically vulnerable'. Access to Basra entailed sailing 'more than 100 miles . . . skirt[ing] the Iranian border, leaving the approach to the base completely exposed to the . . . Iranians . . . [and]

Kuwait dominates the Iraqi fleet's approaches from two islands located at the entrance to the lagoon, Bubyan and Warba' (1982, pp. 93–5). Wright (1980/81, p. 277) and Ramazani (1988, p. 5) also emphasized the strategic predicament Iraq found itself in as a result of the border changes, brought about when Persian (or Iranian) power rose whilst Ottoman (or Iraqi) power declined. They both shared the belief that Iraq's sense of insecurity because of the vulnerability of its two main ports was well-founded from the strategic viewpoint. While Danziger and the *Financial Times*' Mark Nicholson (19 February 1992) saw this as one of the main reasons for the Iraqi invasion of Iran in 1980, the Iranian-born scholar went so far as to single it out.

King, however, was ambivalent in his discussion of the value of the Shatt, which he regarded as 'a matter of both symbolic and strategic importance . . . a reflection of national power, which helps psychologically, if not militarily', then continued in the same sentence and wrote 'to offset the constraints imposed by Iraq's very limited coastline' (1987, p. 7). This is all the more astonishing, coming from an analyst as able as King, to fail to grasp the national security implications of a 'very limited coastline' for Iraq. A scholar of considerable analytical powers, his paper provided a comprehensive and valuable political overview of the Iran–Iraq War, where domestic conditions, regional politics and international ramifications were artfully interwoven.

Although the dispute over the Shatt predated the creation of Iraq by more than three and a half centuries, its border with the Persian Empire was not reviewed, despite Britain's interest in Iraqi oil, and although its emissaries knew of the impediments to shipping at the ports of Basra and Umm Qasr, because of their vulnerable location, and by the very nature of the seaboard in these areas. While Mahan estimated that 'ships that thus sail to and fro must have secure ports to which to return', Iraq was neither provided with the 'naval strategic position', nor with a 'secure' harbour, both of which were regarded by him as essential for a viable navy (1957, p. 25). One could argue that the disputes between Iraq and its two neighbours, Iran and Kuwait, were partly attributable to this factor, and that therein lay the seeds of the controversies that were to generate two devastating wars.

Sharing access to the Gulf with its two neighbours was complicated further by the fact that none of its oil can be exported to its destination without crossing the land borders into neighbouring states. Thus, Iraq's oil-based economy found itself hostage to Iran, Kuwait, Syria, Lebanon, Turkey and Saudi Arabia, and its prosperity depends heavily – not simply on their friendliness – but also on stability in the area and within these countries. Hostilities with any of its neighbours can affect Iraq's export of oil, as in the instance of its war against Iran. Mere personal animosity, such as that between Syria's Asad and Iraq's Hussein, was in great part the cause of the closure of the pipeline to Baniyas. Internecine strife in Lebanon could stop the flow of crude. Any of these conditions can affect Iraq's oil-export capability to the extent of destroying its economy and bringing the country to its knees. This was in great part why the 1990 UN-mandated sanctions have worked far too well against the Iraqi people.

4.4 COMPETITION FOR PRIVILEGE AND POWER

On the world map, the Gulf appears like a kidney-shaped cul-de-sac of water. In terms of size and geographical characteristics it almost seems insignificant. Yet, over the years, and actually before petroleum gushed out of its soil, major and regional powers vied for supremacy around its shores. The fierce battle to control the Gulf by the main players underlines how the strategic importance of an area is related to and conditional upon their perception of the degree to which events in that area promote, damage or jeopardize their interests or those of their rivals.

The Russian (and later the Soviet) and British empires competed for influence in a region which they viewed as an integral part of the wider geostrategic naval theatre that comprised the Mediterranean and Red seas and the Indian Ocean. The Russians were hard-pressed to gain an outlet to warm waters for their ice-locked fleets and to retain control over a buffer zone around an area close to the glacis encircling them. The British strove to secure their land and naval routes to the Far East generally, and to India particularly. The supervision of their far-flung empire, which provided them with cheap raw materials, entailed the procurement, transportation, maintenance and supply of troops, equipment and facilities. The Gulf remained virtually a British lake from the early nineteenth century, when Britain's resident agent controlled the whole area from his bureau in the Persian port of Booshehr, until Nuri al-Sa'id's government in Baghdad was overthrown in 1958.

In a quest to expand its southern cordon sanitaire, Tsarist Russia gained a foothold in the Caucasian provinces through the treaties of Gulestan in 1813 and Turkmantchai in 1828. Then it occupied Tashkent and conquered Turkestan in 1865, and 20 years later, annexed Merv. Britain, in the meantime, extended its protection over a number of states in the region (Trucial Coast, Qatar, Bahrain and Kuwait), and signed a treaty with Persia in 1919, whereby its advisors were posted throughout the Persian administration at Tehran's expense – a step in preparation for ultimately dominating the empire. This prompted the new Bolshevik regime to dispatch troops to northern Persia the following year. Two years later, a treaty confirmed British supremacy over Iraq, by retaining the right to protect foreign minorities and advise on foreign and financial affairs. In 1930, the Anglo-Iraqi Treaty handed over to Britain the total control of Iraq's military, political and foreign affairs, allowed it to station ground troops and air forces there, and stipulated that its ambassador was to enjoy a permanent position of pre-eminence. Britain's profound preoccupation with its political ascendancy in the Gulf could not be better illustrated than by the following rather peculiar case: After the assassination of the Austrian Archduke Franz Joseph, on 28 June 1914, an event which was to catapult the world into the century's most radical transformation, the subject which was of paramount concern at a House of Commons (HoC) foreign policy debate was the contest over Persia with Russia.

This competition was interrupted for short periods of time, first in 1907, with the signing of the Anglo-Russian Accord, whereby the two powers divided Persia into two spheres of influence, with the Russians retaining the northern part, including Tehran, and the British the southern area. Another pause occurred during the First World War, when Russian, Turkish and British troops occupied parts of Persia, to ensure its neutrality and prevent its government from entering the war on the side of Germany. They cooperated again in an invasion on 25 August 1941, during the Second World War, deposed Reza Shah and installed his son Muhammed Reza on the Peacock Throne. Their association lasted throughout the war to offer logistical support to the Red Army. These were but hiatuses in their continuing battle for control of the area. Soviet troops remained in Azerbaijan and Kurdistan until 9 May 1946, when they were forced to leave the two oil-rich provinces under American pressure.

The discovery of petroleum had introduced a new player into the zone. During the first decade of the twentieth century, the RN had started adopting oil as fuel. By 1910, the US naval command, who were keen to rule the waves, realized that oil became a necessity for warships, as it provided their fleets with greater speed and an expanded steaming radius. Accordingly, ships were constructed in a way that would allow them to be converted from coal to oil, and all the new battleships had oil tanks. American oil companies made their entry in the early 1900s, in a bid to compete for oil-prospecting contracts against British and German companies. The Europeans safeguarded their oil investments around the Gulf and the Caspian Sea with the political and military might of their states, whereas their American competitors did not enjoy any assistance from the US government, until after the Second World War. In time, these conditions were to change gradually at first, then markedly later, when the area's strategic pre-eminence became second only to Europe by the mid-1980s.

By the early 1950s, there were lingering doubts that the US was working out ways of replacing Britain in the area, after the decline of its economic power. It is likely that with the inability of the British to meet their far-flung military commitments, and the diminishing role of its seapower, Washington started designing its new approach to the Middle East – albeit along rather imprecise lines. While it aimed at stripping British influence, it avoided challenging its ally's political power, and was careful not to jeopardize their 'special relationship'. But the gist of the policy became more evident from the beginning of the 1970s, when the British withdrew from East of Suez.

With the start of the Cold War and the polarization of the global system, the Gulf region came to be regarded by both superpowers as a strategically important area, one where their

respective spheres of influence intersected and where their interests conflicted. Geostrategic and geopolitical considerations
were at the root of their competition, as the Soviets viewed the
Gulf zone as part of their southern security belt, whilst the
West considered it the eastern wing for their eastern African
and eastern Mediterranean cordon sanitaire.

Containment became the cornerstone of US global strategy
vis-à-vis the Soviet Union, after George Kennan's 'X Paper'.
Meanwhile, oil had become increasingly vital as the energy
source for industry, transport and war machines, especially for
the non-producing industrial states in the Western alliance.
These two developments made access to oilfields and the
security of SLOCs an overriding strategic concern of all their
governments. They felt threatened by any manifestation of
intent by the USSR to exploit their dependence on Gulf oil,
and contrived to curtail Soviet plans for the establishment of
a presence in that area and in strategic locations along the
naval routes of approach, within the larger geostrategic naval
theatre.

At the same time, the Gulf is close to the soft underbelly of
the Soviet Union – a mere 700 miles away from its southern
border. The ability of the US to preserve the status quo was
viewed by Moscow as inimical to its security interests.
Washington was able to pursue this strategy by strengthening
relations with most of the rulers of the countries overlooking
the Gulf. It succeeded in involving their countries in Western-
sponsored security networks, and also acquired military facilities in the area. Although the Persian government had signed
a treaty of friendship with the Soviet Union in 1921, Tehran
changed sides, moved closer to the US and signed an accord
with Washington in 1947, then a Military Cooperation
Agreement in March 1959. Also, Mussadeq's opposition to the
Anglo-Iranian Oil Company in 1953, was seized upon by the
American prospecting companies to gain an important
foothold in Iran.

The Middle East and Central Treaty Organizations
(CENTO) agreements, signed within four years, were perceived by the USSR as an attempt to encircle it, at the least,
and at worst, in preparation to use member countries as spring-
boards against it. One should bear in mind that the Middle
Eastern signatories were geographically contiguous to or close

to the Soviet Union, and populated by minorities who shared ethnic and religious ties with the majority of people in the southern provinces of Azerbaijan, Turkmenistan, Uzbekistan and Kazakhstan. In addition, the US's government unbending stance not to allow the Soviets to play any part in the resolution of conflicts in the Middle East – an area much closer to them than to America – reinforced their grievances.

The creation of an anti-Western republican regime in Iraq in 1958, followed shortly by withdrawal from the Baghdad Pact in March 1959, and the release of imprisoned Communists renewed Moscow's prospects of playing a role in the region, albeit ancillary up to 1968, when power was seized by the *Ba'th* Arab Socialist Party. To counterbalance Iran's growing ties with the West, Baghdad established Moscow as a primary player in Iraq, with the signing of the 1972 Friendship and Cooperation Treaty. This compensated for reversals in Egypt, where President Sadat evicted Soviet advisers and sought a partnership with the US. From then on, Washington's perception of *Ba'thi* Iraq was equated with that of Nasser's Egypt: At the height of the Cold War, both had allowed the USSR to intrude into the region.

From the early 1970s, Moscow became Baghdad's main arms supplier, and apart from the UN embargo, implemented after Iraq's invasion of Kuwait in 1990, two interludes took place. The first lasted from 1975 to mid-1976, when the USSR was irritated because of the growing animosity between the Iraqi and Syrian *Ba'th* parties, on the one hand, and Iraq's friendly relations with Sadat's Egypt, on the other. Sales resumed when Iraq diversified and placed large orders in France. Arms shipments also ceased in 1980, when Iraq invaded Iran, but recommenced when Iran repulsed the Iraqi troops in 1982 (Schmidt, 1991, pp. 7–9 and tables pp. 13, 17, 18, 19; also O'Ballance, 1988, p. 25).

In the meantime, Moscow's trade relations with Iran flourished. It viewed normal relations with its neighbour as essential to its security, and set in motion a pragmatic policy towards Tehran. In June 1969, the Iranian ambassador to the Kremlin was informed that his country would never be abandoned by Moscow for the sake of Iraq, and in the 1970s, Iran had become its most important Middle Eastern market for non-military wares. Its imports from the USSR were worth $515 million in 1977, which entailed sending an army of 3000 technicians to the monarchy – the largest contingent of Soviet experts in any LDC in the world (Angrand and Rabier, 1989, pp. 98–9; and Alam, 1991, p. 74).

Despite anti-Soviet rhetoric and pronouncements, referring to it as the 'Little Satan', Moscow energized its links with postrevolutionary Iran, and by 1981, trade rose to $1 billion. Again, as during the Shah's reign, relations were complex and ambiguous, with Moscow consistently watching for opportunities to expand its influence, while avoiding forthright confrontation. Exploiting anti-Western feelings in Tehran, Moscow strove to invest into the future, when it would be allowed again as a major player. Although uneasy in dealing with an unpredictable regime, the Kremlin feared its overthrow and replacement by yet another pro-American government. Leonid Brezhnev, who had promoted armed intervention abroad, modified the earlier Soviet doctrine, during the XXVIth Communist Party Congress. He affirmed that in some circumstances, Islam can serve the progressive cause, especially if under a regime which is anti-American and anti-imperialist. Despite the potential destabilizing effect of political Islam on Muslim populations in the southern Soviet provinces, Tehran's potential ability to have a spoiling effect on feudal Gulf states seemed valuable (Angrand and Rabier, 1989, pp. 98–100).

Remarkably, Moscow exhibited a great deal of nonchalance when Tehran aided the *mujahedeen* in Afghanistan, pursued and imprisoned communists, and excluded the *Tudeh* Party from participating in politics. While continuing to provide Iraq with weapons, it arranged for arms, spareparts and ammunition deliveries to Iran during the war. These were transferred through client states such as Poland, Libya, Syria and North Korea. In addition to the obvious economic benefits, the Kremlin pursued its twin-track policy of augmenting its allies in the region and – to the extent possible – limiting American control.

The IRI's policies towards the Soviet Union were not less pragmatic. While it continued political and financial support to the *mujahedeen*, Tehran allowed the installation of an intelligence-gathering station in Baluchistan, to inform the Red Army command of movements across the Afghan-Pakistan border; and in exchange for access to the American F-14 radar system, it was speculated, Iran was granted technical assistance in the form of student scholarships in the Soviet Union, under an agreement signed in 1981. Moscow was able to perform these shrewd balancing acts, as it enjoyed diplomatic relations with both Iraq and Iran (Angrand and Rabier, 1989, pp. 98–100; Campbell, 1984, pp. 79–80).

In the mid-1980s, Moscow improved its relations with other Gulf states, establishing diplomatic links with the UAE and Oman, thus raising the number of Arab Gulf countries which recognized it to four, including Kuwait, which had diplomatic ties since 1963, and Iraq. When Kuwait's request for weapons was rejected by the US Congress, it looked elsewhere, in what could be interpreted as a rebuff to the US government. It turned to the Soviets, who were only too keen to sign arms sales agreements. And again, in 1986, when the sheikhdom seemed to be playing a complex game of bluff with the Americans, its officials approached the Kremlin, which obligingly agreed to re-flag and protect Kuwaiti tankers. The response was positive and swift, while US–Kuwaiti negotiations on the same matter were stalled (see Section 7.2).

Saudi Arabia, despite its fervently anti-Communist policies and the absence of diplomatic relations since 1926, established secret contacts with the USSR. Several Saudi ministers visited Moscow clandestinely, and Aeroflot airliners were allowed to use Saudi airspace (Angrand and Rabier, 1989, pp. 97–102). Much to the chagrin of the US government, unpublicized contacts were made with the other Communist giant as well, and resulted in the sale of Chinese 'DF-3 (CSS-2) intermediate-range ballistic missiles in response to Iranian threats' (Zaloga, 1988, p. 1427). The furore in Washington was prompted by disclosures from Tel Aviv about a secret sale of electronic guidance-systems for the *Silkworms* to the People's Republic. Despite Chinese denials that the Saudi deal included these systems, the Jewish lobby worried that, in a nightmare scenario, some day Israel could possibly be hit by missiles fitted with Israeli-made guidance systems. It is likely that the vehement protestations of the US ambassador to Riyadh, at the time of the crisis, caused his early transfer from the kingdom.

US resolve to play a leading role in the Middle East could be traced to 1954, when the Eisenhower Doctrine was enunciated. It shared one main feature with Nixon's, Carter's, Reagan's and, later, Clinton's also. Their core was intervention in the Middle East to defend US national interests that were perceived to be at stake. Examined collectively, they brought into focus a steady evolving pattern. One by one, they emphasized the high value that the US came to place on the Middle East first, and on the Gulf region, in particular, later. But Washington's status in the Gulf remained fairly uncertain until the Iran–Iraq War, when the USN had an unfettered hand in military operations. The second Gulf War, followed closely by the disintegration of the Soviet Union, ensconced the US as the dominant military, political and economic power in the region. The doctrines enunciated by successive US administrations highlighted the principal preoccupation, which in essence was control of the strategic mineral. The dimension of America's commitment was made evident later by the establishment of the Rapid Deployment Joint Task Force (RDJTF). The swift and decisive military intervention in Kuwait, in 1990–1, confirmed how seriously it viewed its 'responsibilities' in the area, and demonstrated its willingness to strike at any country that challenged *Pax Americana* there (for an interesting examination of the doctrines see Defarges, 1986).

4.5   ALIEN FLAGS OVER THE GULF WATERS

The white ensign fluttered over the entire Gulf at the zenith of the British Empire. From the early nineteenth century onwards, RN warships patrolled the area to protect merchant vessels, flying the red ensign, and to secure the vital trade routes between the British Isles, the Middle East and the Indian sub-continent. A string of friendly harbours were essential, as ships carrying troops and supplies were in need of docks to resupply, or for routine maintenance and minor repairs. Later, with the change from wooden to iron hulls in 1852, and the introduction of steam vessels in the early 1860s, anchorages were needed to refuel at coal stocking points.

While *Pax Britannica* prevailed in the area, St Andrew's cross (patron saint of sailors), rippled in the lazy winds over the Gulf waters merely from 1899 to 1903 (the blue ensign, introduced by Tsar Peter the Great in 1696, three years after he founded the Russian Navy, and abolished by the Bolshevik revolution in 1922, was flown again by Russian units in the post-Communist era, replacing the white banner with the blue band and red star, hammer and sickle). While the presence of Russian warships was short-lived, RN ships were unchallenged by any local or external action, and surrounded by non-hostile states: the Trucial Coast, Bahrain and Kuwait were under its protectorate, while Saudi Arabia, Iran and Iraq were friendly allies; Oman, theoretically independent, could nonetheless be placed among the first group.

The dawn of the twentieth century witnessed Britain as the world's greatest seapower. It had the largest naval and merchant fleets, and its giant ship-building industry dominated the world market. The end of the Second World War heralded the break-up of the British Empire, and the termination of Britain's world status, as its economic descent necessitated the scaling down of defence obligations. In its aftermath, Britain's seapower declined.

The coup de grâce came in the autumn of 1956. After the Suez Canal imbroglio, things were never the same. The crisis inflamed passions and split the country down the middle. It shattered the illusions of grandeur, jeopardized the 'special relationship' with Washington, and affected Britain's standing in the world. Anthony Eden, who served in Churchill's cabinet as Secretary of State for Foreign Affairs, had by now succeeded him as prime minister. His strategic objective in the campaign was the toppling of President Nasser to secure free navigation through the Suez Canal. But the government's proclaimed policy to dispatch a one-hundred-ship task force in the guise of peace-making between Israel and Egypt, while it colluded with France and Israel, divided his cabinet, and the deception prompted resignations at the highest levels of government.

When the Labour Party took office on 16 October 1964, the Treasury estimated that the government had inherited from the Tories a balance of payments deficit of £800 million. Consequently, Prime Minister Harold Wilson resolved to streamline overseas military commitments and recall British forces from the four corners of the world. But he was advised not to relinquish Britain's defence obligations East of Suez, while on a visit to Washington during the same year. US officials persuaded him to continue Britain's role in the Gulf, and linked it with the fundamentals that kept the 'special relationship' alive, namely, financial, political and diplomatic support. Wilson went along with the policy at first, and in 1966, with sterling still under intense pressure, he resolved to abandon Aden the year after, and to focus on maintaining a presence in the Gulf. However, with the devaluation of the pound in November 1967 – a step deferred since winning the elections – he decided to recall British forces from East of Suez. The last major contingent was withdrawn by the end of 1971, and the six small Trucial Coast sheikhdoms (Abu Dhabi, Dubai, Sharjah, 'Ajman, Umm al-Qaiwain and Fujairah) formed the federation of the UAE. Granted independence with Bahrain and Qatar, they joined the UN, along with Oman. Ras al-Khaimah, in objection to Iran's occupation of the two Tunbs, followed one year later (Alam, 1991, p. 185; Ciarocchi, 1987, p. 21; O'Ballance, 1988, p. 9; and *Independent*, 2 January 1995).

As in 1947, when America replaced Britain in the defence of Greece and Turkey after the enunciation of the Truman Doctrine, the USN succeeded the RN in the Gulf to emphasize US determination to safeguard the Western world's interests. Through unpublicized understandings with the Saudi and Bahraini governments, as early as 1947 and 1949 respectively, the US forces had conditional access to a Saudi airfield and a Bahraini port. Except for a short interval, following the 1973 October War, an agreement with Bahrain to rent docks and stores enabled the USN to station the flagship of the METF Commander and two destroyers at the naval facility of Jufair; initially developed by the British, it underwent major expansions after their withdrawal.

In time, US perception of the Gulf region's value shifted from one 'of detachment in the 1960s, to the direct application of its naval forces as a central policy tool in the 1980s' (Ciarocchi, 1987, p. 3). In the wake of the Carter Doctrine, an arrangement was worked out with the Omani authorities, in June 1980, allowing the US Air Force (USAF) and the USN access to airstrips and anchorages, in return for military aid. Muscat/Matrah, with a dockyard and slipway, is Oman's main harbour, and Mina Raysut and Jazirat Ghanam have naval facilities. Masirah Island became an American base, and its jet airstrip, its armaments, munition and fuel depots, and its administrative and training sites were equipped to support

USN vessels, deployed in the Arabian Sea and the Gulf (Taha, 1984, pp. 34–6; and O'Ballance, 1988, p. 157).

While the USN controlled the extensive air-radar and naval base on Masirah, and had 4000 military personnel contracted to Saudi Arabia ('Abdel-Halim, 1985, p. 91), the other Gulf states placed restrictions on the use of their facilities (O'Ballance, 1988, p. 157). Because of the high value that the US government placed on insuring access to oil and on securing the shipping lanes to the Gulf, they had a continuous naval presence in the area. The lack of permanent bases in the Gulf proper, viewed as essential by the Pentagon, led to the establishment of the RDJTF in April 1981. Renamed Central Command (CENTCOM) in 1983, its plans entailed assembling 220 000 and up to 400 000 men from various US services. From the army, 'the 82nd airborne division, the 101st air assault division and the 24th mechanized infantry division . . .; 3 carrier task forces, 1 surface action group . . . eighteen cargo ships (loaded with supplies for 10 000 troops)' from the USN; '2 B-52 bomber squadrons, 12 tactical fighter squadrons, and 9 tactical airlift squadrons' from the USAF; and the Marine Corps (USMC) contributed 'the 7th marine amphibious brigade'. The troops' extensive training programme enables them to intervene rapidly and operate under difficult desert conditions ('Abdel-Halim, 1985, pp. 91–2; see also Freedman, 1985, pp. 64–9; Delcorde, 1986, p. 99; and Daly, 1985, p. 151).

Heavy materiel was pre-positioned on floating barges and container ships, one stationed in the Mediterranean, and 17 at Diego Garcia. The armaments, munitions and supplies were adequate for combat by a Marine Amphibious Brigade for up to one month. Diego Garcia, the only American nuclear base in the Indian Ocean, is a horseshoe-shaped atoll, which forms part of the Chagos archipelago. Despite a 1965 UN resolution requesting Britain not to dismember Mauritius before independence, it purchased the islands in 1966 for £3 million, promising to cede them back when no longer essential for defence purposes. They became part of the British Indian Ocean territory, and Diego Garcia was loaned to the US in 1967 for no payment for 50 years. The base, with its long airstrip and naval dockyard, was useful during the last stages of the Tanker War, and was particularly valuable in February–March 1991, as a refuelling and re-arming site for the B-52s that were bombing Iraqi troops. Despite plans for the contraction of US forces abroad, Diego Garcia is regarded as one of three locations necessary for future defence needs in a 1990 USAF report on security in the coming century (Delcorde, 1986, pp. 99–102; and *Independent*, 11 August 1992).

CENTCOM headquarters assessed the nature of possible threats, such as a Soviet thrust into northern Iran or a popular uprising in Saudi Arabia, then determined the scale of response and the appropriate mix of forces. The Initial Ready Company of the 82nd Airborne Division were equipped and ready to be flown to the area of conflict on a two-hour-alert basis to secure airfields in the area, possibly Dhahran in Saudi Arabia, the largest airfield on the peninsula. These were planned to be followed, 18 hours later, by a force of 4000 men from the Division Ready Brigade. Within ten to 15 days, 16 500 men could be air-lifted and assembled in the Gulf, then reinforced by a division dispatched aboard troop-transport vessels, one month after the alert. In the meantime, the ships stocked with the pre-positioned hardware would have sailed to rendezvous with the forces (Freedman, 1985, pp. 66–7). The Navy and Marine Corps components that were involved comprised 'three carrier battle groups, one surface action group, three amphibious ready groups, and five anti-submarine warfare patrol squadrons' (*US Department of Defense Annual Report to the Congress*, in Ciarocchi, 1987, notes p. 4).

In addition, the METF had a permanent presence in and close to the Gulf, with a minimum of four combatants on patrol, armed with SSMs and SAMs, including *Stingers* (Daly, 1985, p. 157). Also, a carrier battle group, with an impressive array of arms, patrolled the areas close to the Strait of Hormuz, within about 500 miles. Their missions included the evacuation of civilians from Iran in 1979, furnishing support for the rescue operation of the Tehran hostages in April 1980, escorting USN tankers lifting Gulf oil to US forces world-wide since 1984, and monitoring the American merchantmen sailing in the Gulf since early 1987 (Ciarocchi, 1987, pp. 5–6).

Apart from Diego Garcia and limited access to air and naval facilities in some Arab Gulf states, the USN ships and aircraft operated from bases developed by the Soviets at Mogadishu and Berbera. An understanding reached with Somalia in August 1980, allowed access to those airstrips and port facilities. Also, Subic Bay naval base, established in 1901, 50 miles north-west of Manila, had large installations that comprised a repair yard, a training centre and ammunition and supply depots for the Seventh Fleet, which patrolled vital trade routes between the Middle East and East Asia. With the strategic review of future defence needs, and the gradual reduction of US forces overseas, including those stationed in the Philippines, Subic Bay naval base had only about 6000 servicemen left in 1991. In November 1992, US forces vacated their last big base in South-East Asia (Daly, 1985, pp. 151, 157; Delcorde, 1986, p. 99; Ciarocchi, 1987, p. 41; and *Independent*, 22 July and 11 August 1992).

By 1983, elements of the US Seventh Fleet in the Indian Ocean were in the Arabian Sea, within reach of the Strait of Hormuz. The fleet had become sizeable and comprised the carriers *Ranger* and *Midway*, the latter escorted by a 15-ship battle group in 1984 (O'Ballance, 1988, p. 157). The METF established headquarters on board its command ship the USS *La Salle*, manned by a 20-man team from the RDF, with the mission to safeguard American interests in the Gulf and the Indian Ocean area. Because of the absence of permanent land-based stations in the area, the flag-ship was selected because of her command links (*Navy International*, 1984, January, p. 45 and April, p. 232). By 1987, with the intensification of attacks on merchant vessels during the Tanker War, Saudi Arabia extended an 'immense amount of logistical support', according to US officials, Bahrain provided the USN with its 'only base in the region', and Oman's supply depots were used by US forces (*Time*, 26 October 1987, p. 11).

In the meanwhile, Soviet warships were denied access to any of the Gulf ports. The only Soviet ships that sailed in the region were fishing and research vessels, or men-of-war *en route* between European and Pacific bases. From 1968, Soviet units were allowed to visit Iraqi ports periodically to 'show the flag', and following the Friendship Agreement, they had a permanent presence in the waters of the Gulf and the Arabian Sea. In the Indian Ocean, they deployed 'eight surface combatants, two or three attack submarines, two amphibious warfare ships and support ships' (Daly, 1985, p. 157).

From year to year and from month to month, the squadron deployed by the Soviets altered as to components and size, depending on diverse factors, such as regional tensions, naval manoeuvres, ship availability and weather conditions. In 1968, they deployed a squadron of seven ships which increased to 11 in 1969 and 1971, 13 in 1970, 17 in 1972, and 15 in 1973, and on the whole, their flotilla was larger in winter. Between two-thirds and half were auxiliary and other vessels, except in 1973, and they mainly operated from berths in Somalia and South Yemen. After the split with Somalia's President Barre in late 1977, and the eviction of their forces from Mogadishu and Berbera, they developed an anchorage on the Dahlak Archipelago, off the Ethiopian coast (Ciarocchi, 1987, table p. 24 and pp. 22–3, 41–2).

In the 1970s, the Soviet squadron in the region constantly attempted to attain parity with the USN, and its size depended upon that of the Americans. Periods of crises witnessed increases in strength and naval activities by American and Soviet vessels alike. Force levels rose during the Indo-Pakistani, the Arab–Israeli and the Somali–Ethiopian wars in 1971, 1973 and 1977, respectively, and also during the 1978–9 turmoil of the Iranian revolution. But in the summer of 1987, the pattern was interrupted. In early July, Michail Gorbachev invited all foreign countries to withdraw their warships from the Gulf, in a bid to defuse regional tension. Thus, when the USN expanded its battle group and stepped up its activities, the Soviets kept to their initial level of one frigate and six minesweepers and supply ships, at a time when the USN had about 40 warships. Occasionally, a cruiser was deployed, but most of the warships were destroyers and light frigates, such as the *Petya*, except in 1973–4 and late-1977, when the squadron had 'an unusually large number of major combatants'. In Ciarocchi's view, the Indian Ocean squadron's 'limited warfighting capability suggests that it has served primarily a political function', establishing the Soviet Union as an actor with an equal role to that of the US in the region, by demonstrating its intention to safeguard its interests, and by manifesting its support to its allies (1987, pp. 13, 23; see also *Guardian*, 1 November 1987).

However, in the 1980s, other American strategists viewed the relative strength of the USN in comparison to its Soviet counterpart as offset by the deployment of land-based tactical aircraft and the stationing of 50 divisions of the Red Army in

Afghanistan, close to the vulnerable frontier of Iran. They feared that the combined deployment of ground, air and naval forces, close to an area of vital importance to their country's security interests, would cause an erosion of their political influence in the Gulf. In Captain Kevin B. Jordan's view,

[g]iven the Soviet perception of naval power as an extension of land power, the primary purpose of the Soviet Indian Ocean force is to protect the seaward flank in the event of a Soviet invasion of the Gulf states. . . American naval power could not prevent direct intervention by Soviet ground forces. Although the deterrence value of the US force in the Indian Ocean is significant, it is not absolute. In the present situation, the ultimate restrictions on Soviet seizure of the oil fields in the Persian Gulf are self-imposed (1981, p. 30)

During the last two years of the Tanker War, when Soviet warships escorted their merchant vessels in the Gulf, their presence was more visible, though limited in comparison to the Western armada, armed with enormous fire-power. They usually included light vessels of the *Natya* or *Grysha* classes, or larger escort units such as the *Kashin*, *Krivak*, *Udaloy* and *Sovremennyy* types, with a flotilla of support ships (Dainville, 1988, p. 59). After Moscow's prompt response to Kuwait's request to charter three tankers, protected by the Soviet Navy, its presence could not be legitimately questioned by members of the Western alliance, given that their own navies were taking part in the same exercise.

From the Middle Eastern viewpoint, the creation of the RDF, in addition to the deployment of the METF was yet another means of projecting American military power in the area. Even those countries that were labelled as 'moderate', and whose overall policies were pro-Western, doubted whether the main objective of the RDF and the METF was to defend American vital interests against Soviet aggression only, or whether they would also be used against any Gulf country that challenged those interests.

The news that emerged in the autumn of 1991 and the winter of 1992, after the breakdown of the Soviet Empire and the dismantling of the Warsaw Pact, strengthened these misgivings.

The collapse of Communism resulted in the disappearance of the West's traditional enemy. Therefore, containment of the defunct Soviet Union had lost its relevance. Hence, the establishment of foreign bases became a dispensable relic of the past, and the Cold War dogma had clearly outlived its usefulness.

Despite earlier American claims that bases were needed in the Gulf area because of Soviet opportunism, the Bush Administration and Kuwait signed a ten-year memorandum of understanding on defence, on 19 September 1991. The agreement allows the USN and USAF access to Kuwaiti naval and air bases, the stockpiling of American war materiel, and combined exercises. The Pentagon also announced a plan to reconstruct and upgrade the two Kuwaiti airfields of al-Ahmadi and al-Jahra for their use by the USAF, at a cost of $350 to $500 million. 'Washington hopes to reach similar arrangements with Saudi Arabia, Oman, Qatar, the United Arab Emirates and Bahrain' (*Independent*, 20 September 1991), and similar pacts were being negotiated with Britain and France (*San Diego Union*, 26 January 1992). The talks between the UK and Kuwait led to the signing of bilateral technical and military agreements, in February 1992, on the lines of previous understandings with the Trucial Coast states, Qatar and Bahrain. According to a senior source at the Egyptian Embassy in London, an official at the Foreign Office had explained to him that despite Kuwaiti insistence for a provision on defence from both the USA and the UK, this clause was dropped in the bilateral defence cooperation accord. The agreement was non-committal in so far that it only included joint exercises, but did not entail the deployment of forces or the pre-positioning of materiel; and the stationing of the remainder of the forces in the Gulf area and in Turkey were a sequel to the Gulf War and not part of the new understanding, he said.

In early 1992, a study on the future of the US strategic deterrent in the wake of the collapse of Communism was leaked to the press. Prepared by 21 nuclear experts, the published excerpts of the Pentagon report disclosed that it recommended re-targeting nuclear weapons against 'every reasonable adversary' and the formation of a 'nuclear expeditionary force, with bomber and submarine-launched nuclear arms and tactical weapons . . . to prevent the annihilation of US allies and *the seizure of vital raw materials by rival groups*' (*Independent*,

7 January 1992, emphasis added by author). These new developments strongly suggested that American military power may be used, for instance, against a Saudi regime which is no longer willing to remain the moderator of price and supply within OPEC. Traditionally, Riyadh played that role to maintain the output of oil, in order to dampen prices, and influenced members of OPEC to control pricing at a level acceptable to Washington to help restore Western economic growth especially during times of recession in the West.

The news may be alarming to the Gulf states, and may have serious ramifications. It proved that their fears were indeed well-founded, despite Washington's assurances in 1979 not to use nuclear weapons against LDCs which did not possess them, and can only lead to increased attempts on the part of these countries to acquire a nuclear arsenal as a deterrent. The propagation of non-conventional weapons cannot be ruled out and will be hugely destabilizing, bearing in mind the Middle Eastern backdrop and its extreme combustibility – with the US continuing to ensure that the military balance in the area is weighted in Israel's favour, with Israel's quantitative and qualitative edge in conventional arms, arms-manufacturing industry and weapons of mass-destruction (WMD), in addition to its continued refusal to adhere to the nuclear Non-Proliferation Treaty (NPT). The large arsenal of former Soviet short-range nuclear weapons may find their way to 'nuclear threshold' countries in the area, such as Pakistan, Iran, Iraq or Libya, or to oil-rich states willing to pay the price. Moreover, tactical weapons are easily transportable, and it is worth noting that they have not been included in any formal treaties, and their quantity has not been disclosed.

At a time when the end of the Cold War obviates the need for weapons proliferation, a new arms race of a different calibre may start among countries that resent the significance of these developments.

4.6   THE GULF – BOON OR DOOM?

For the foreseeable future, the Gulf area will retain its geostrategic and geopolitical distinction, for it 'is no exaggeration to state that whoever controls these waters will have the ability to regulate the destinies of myriad nations, particularly those of the industrialized countries of the First World' (Hanks and Cottrell, 1981, p. 88). The region has vast oil reserves, and despite research by consumer countries in the fields of energy conservation and alternate sources of fuel, especially renewable ones such as hydraulic, wind and sun energy, oil will remain the preferred source for energy supplies.

The industrialized countries' commercial interests add to the Gulf's importance. Arab countries represent a significant market for foreign-made goods, agricultural produce and machinery, worth $15 billion for America alone, with Egypt and the Gulf states at the forefront. While Saudi Arabia is the US' seventh world trading partner, the Gulf region is a $7 billion market for American goods (Cordesman, 1988, p. 27; and *Hayat*, 11 December 1993). As long as world trade remains one of the fundamental pillars of any nation's prosperity, transport by sea will prevail. Since air transport is not competitive in price – being 17 times the price of sea freight – it will be minimal compared to seaborne cargo, which will remain the foundation of international commercial exchange. Therefore, secure SLOCs are a major concern to Gulf countries and those trading with that lucrative market.

The Gulf states' development programmes offer profitable investment prospects to Western business interests. The expansion of civilian and military infrastructures, as for instance, oil industries and agricultural projects, as well as army camps, airfields, naval bases and depots, are all capital-intensive and will therefore require massive imports. Investment accelerates only in areas of relative stability and security. Given these conditions, protecting international merchant shipping is essential.

Very few areas in the world provide weapons manufacturers the same opportunities as the Gulf area. The Iran–Iraq War accelerated an already active arms race, and the region's position in purchases topped the world's list in the 1980's. During that decade, Iraq topped the Soviet list with $27 billion, followed by Syria; and Saudi Arabia was the US' biggest customer, buying weapons worth $52 billion. The Soviet Union dominated the export market to LDCs, with sales of $108 billion from the mid-1980s to 1992, compared to the US' $45 billion, followed by Britain ($22 billion), France ($20 billion) and China ($12 billion) (see *SIPRI 1993*, pp. 444–5 Tables 10.10 and 10.11).

Viewed through the military/strategic prism, the transport of large numbers of troops with their heavy materiel and supplies is mainly carried out by sea. Although the USAF has an impressive fleet of giant C-5 transport planes that can carry units complete with vehicles for an advance party, heavy equipment has to be sea-hauled. *Operation Desert Storm* was a recent example, and in the words of Admiral of the Fleet Lord Lewin, 'the vital resource, as in both world wars, was merchant shipping. More than twice as many merchant ships as warships provided the logistic support for the Falklands. Of the equipment required by the UK air and land forces in the Gulf, 86 per cent was transported by sea' (letter to the *Independent*, 3 February 1992). The transfer of British and American troops and weapons to Bosnia was another example of a combined air and sea lift. Apart from the logistical problem of carrying out a strategic airlift to a combat area, various political difficulties and complications can arise, if a military campaign involves flying halfway around the globe, as for instance, countries refusing overflights or landing for re-fuelling, for fear of retribution.

The Gulf is also vital for the economies of the countries that border this semi-enclosed sea. They rely almost totally on oil revenues to pay for development schemes and foreign commodities which their populations' well-being depend upon. Given these conditions, the security of the strait of Hormuz is crucial. Most of their economies, however, are inadequate in absorbing the surplus generated by their oil sales, and invest in the northern hemisphere, where countries compete to attract their 'petro-dollars'. They thus lay themselves open to the freezing of assets and consequent financial precariousness, as befell both post-revolutionary Iran and post-1990 Iraq. Being a double-edged sword, investments could be linked to politics and used as a penalty. The most recent example of such a case was that of Professor Mohammad Al-Mas'ari, the Saudi dissident, whose political campaign became an issue that jeopardized British commercial interests in 1996, including *Al-Yamamah* deal.

The Gulf area was an arena for power struggles since the nineteenth century, but from the early twentieth century onwards, there was a redistribution of means and functions. Treaties of friendship and cooperation, and reinforced trade relations, including weapons transfers, substituted military occupation and became the method for control. As the status of Great Britain, the traditional colonial power, was constricted politically, and especially militarily, it was replaced by the US, the champion of Western interests. The USSR continued the role of Tsarist Russia and expanded it by pursuing pragmatic policies towards monarchist and nationalist regimes, as well as radical and Islamic governments.

In geographic terms, the competition for control over Persia/Iran always headed on a North–South course by the Russians/Soviets, and a South-North tack by the British/Americans. These directions were dictated by the understanding they had of their respective national security considerations and of their perception that certain regions lay within their spheres of influence. In spite of the IRI's proclaimed policy of rejecting dependence on either superpower, they continued their efforts to contain or exclude each other while promoting their own influence, but avoided direct confrontation.

Increased Western reliance on Gulf oil, an area close to the USSR, gave an extraordinary importance to the region. Combined with Soviet military power projection in the naval theatre along the SLOCs where oil tankers sailed to their destinations, and in Afghanistan in the 1980s, added to the Western sense of vulnerability.

The rivalry continued even during periods of detente between the US and the USSR, and their role in the Gulf mirrored their overall strategy. Moscow was eager to promote its global policy of an ever-expanding role in LDCs, especially in countries with past histories of colonial subjugation, whilst Washington was intent on containing that role. But the degree of interest in the Middle East varied between the two superpowers. While the US viewed the Gulf as vital to the survival of members of the Western alliance and Japan, the Soviet Union's primordial interests were security-related, with states that touched its borders, such as Turkey, Iran and Afghanistan. Hence, their efforts to intrude into the area illustrated the extent to which they perceived the region's significance, with Washington pressing to establish a permanent military presence in the Gulf, or alternately, military, political and diplomatic supremacy, and Moscow conducting a defensive strategy and an *ad hoc* expansionist policy. Both exploited opportunities to enlist client states, and consistently avoided commitments and risks.

The contest for influence by powers external to the region created alignments which led to inter-state rivalries. Although the proclaimed policy of the Gulf Arab states is presented as being based on cooperation and friendly neighbourly relations, cross-currents are at work beneath the surface. Their rulers share a mutual suspicion of each other, and are separated by jealousies, fears and profound distrust. In the 1990s, the hostility between members of the GCC seemed baffling, as it involved countries who were part of the coalition that confronted Iraq in the second Gulf conflict. The frictions intensified and persist with the encroachment of external powers who sought access to the Gulf and control of this geostrategic area at the exclusion of others, by enmeshing the actors in their security networks. This trend was illustrated in the past by the 1921 Soviet-Persian Treaty, the British-sponsored Baghdad Pact, CENTO, and the 1972 Soviet–Iraqi Treaty. In the 'New World Order', bilateral memoranda of understanding between the Gulf states with the US, the UK, Russia, China and France typified the tendency.

Local instability influenced domestic developments, such as revolutions, which altered the orientation of countries in the alliance structures, and are a reflection of the importance of the area, as in the case of Iraq in 1958 with relation to Britain and the US, and Iran in 1979 with regard to America. US Ambassador Robert Neumann held the view that prior to the military coup, 'Iraq was the Arab country closest to the United States and the backbone of the now-defunct Baghdad Pact . . . Thereafter, relations between the two countries deteriorated quickly, from warm to tense to non-existent' (in Axelgard [ed.], 1986, p. ix). Interestingly, the same description is pertinent to US–IRI relations, although the Iranian revolution was in no way connected to Moscow. In fact, it was the first mass movement in contemporary history not to be influenced by Marxist ideology.

Indigenous ambivalence and vacillation, in other words, the inter-state and intra-state strains in the region became the *raison d'être* of foreign power intrusion and the continued maintenance of alien navies in the Gulf and the surrounding naval theatre. Unable, or unwilling, to solve these tensions regionally, off-stage actors, particularly the US, came to be accepted as key players. This became evident during the 1990 Gulf crisis which established the US as the dominant power in the area.

The struggle for control was made possible by the Gulf nations' weaknesses. They suffer from demographic, political and economic imbalances, and the marginal role they now play in international relations is the consequence of these defects. Demographically, they are mostly heterogeneous and have a high rate of illiteracy. Except for Iran, they are under-populated, harbour large foreign communities, and have adopted a Western model of economic growth, although they continue to be ruled according to traditional systems. Their people use primitive agricultural methods and, in general, lack technical and managerial skills. These deficiencies, in addition to infant productive industries, made them dependent on others for the transfer of technology and the import of skilled foreign personnel, as well as manufactured goods. A casual look at advertisements in Arabic-language newspapers published in London revealed that Gulf states imported men and women from almost all professions, such as judges, teachers, doctors, nurses, engineers, soldiers of all ranks, company managers, skilled and unskilled labour, and even salespersons for boutiques. Their dependence on expatriate experts gave foreign powers the possibility to maintain their influence. Most Gulf states have weak and inflexible political structures and are ruled by autocratic regimes that abhor power-sharing and political participation by the people. Public accountability lacks even in countries where elections are held and parliaments convene. Rulers, sometimes represented by their governments, have a monopoly on oil revenues, a large part of which they squander on extravagant lifestyles. They decide on the policies governing the reinvestment of the large 'petro-dollar' surpluses, which end up in Western countries on both sides of the Atlantic. Western financial capitals benefited from the investment of $670 billion out of the surpluses of oil revenues from Arab Gulf countries, in contrast to the $226 billion devoted to projects within the Arab world, of which only $22 billion were disbursed, showing a 56:1 ratio (*Hayat*, 18 May and 25 August 1993). Finally, a large percentage of their income pays for foreign purchases, including arms, instead of investing in industrial and agricultural projects locally or within the region.

They share the predicament of other LDCs, in that most of them neither have servicemen skilful enough to operate sophisticated weaponry, nor the capability to manufacture the appropriate equipment required for their defence. Their foreign and defence policies remain hostage to others, given that they are not in a position to determine for themselves what their security needs are and have to depend on the willingness of arms-manufacturing countries to provide what they perceive as adequate. Unfortunately, various strategic, political and economic factors impinge on the decisions of governments to sell arms to client states, and these have quantitative and qualitative effects. Weapon sales to Arab countries – even those considered 'moderate', that is, pro-Western – are frequently blocked by the US Congress citing the Arms Export Control Act. The powerful American Jewish lobby and Israel vigorously oppose all sales and thereby consistently succeed in impeding their endorsement. Following are but a few that come to mind among a myriad of cases that illustrate even the 'friendly' Gulf states' predicament. One of the best-known of such examples was the $250 million sale of *Maverick* ASMs to Saudi Arabia, obstructed on 11 May 1987 (Angrand and Rabier, 1989, note p. 101); an earlier request in 1981, to purchase a number of AWACSs was blocked, and in October 1994, the American Israel Public Affairs Committee (AIPAC) prodded the US administration to prevent the sale of satellites to the kingdom (*Hayat*, 12 December 1994), although these were not offensive weapons; while orders placed by Kuwait were decided by US military study committees.

Arguments were always advanced by Israel's allies in Congress that a republican revolution or internal acts of terrorism may, in future, place the arms in the hands of radical anti-Israeli regimes or groups. Moreover, election speeches by candidates for the White House or Congress invariably promise that the qualitative military edge of Israel in the region would not be threatened, and that its supremacy would be maintained. However, in the case of some of the Gulf states with vast 'petro-dollar' surpluses – although some of the items on their 'shopping list' were sometimes refused – it made economic and political sense, albeit cynical, to sell 'glamorous' equipment that had to be manned by specially trained sophisticated troops, which the Gulf states obviously lacked.

Although the Gulf nations played both cards in some instances, they generally seemed wary of the geographical proximity of their powerful neighbour, and mindful of the potential disruptive influence of an atheist communist country, virtually on their doorstep. For example, when both superpowers showed an interest in providing the IRI with weapons, directly or through proxies, as early as the autumn of 1980, Moscow's offer was rejected by Khomeini. As a counterbalance, some Gulf states have shown signs of edging closer to China. Ironically, these were the most vehemently outspoken anti-Communist and fervently Islamic states, namely, Iran and Saudi Arabia, who bought *Silkworm* missiles from the People's Republic. The day may be close when the Gulf region witnesses the dynamic involvement of this player in the arena, especially after Beijing's support for the clause calling for war reparations to Iran in SCR 598; its nuclear collaboration with Tehran, helping to build a reactor; and its tacit sanctioning of Pakistani–Iranian nuclear cooperation.

In regard to the Iran–Iraq War, both superpowers and most major powers claimed to be as neutral in the conflict. Publicly, they embargoed arms to both countries, and repeatedly called for the immediate implementation of a ceasefire and the return to the status quo *ante bellum*. Secretly, both superpowers provided Iraq and Iran with weapons, and a large number of other countries clandestinely shipped arms to either one or both opponents, which raises doubts as to whether they genuinely aspired to an early end to the war. There seems to have been a tacit agreement to weaken both states so as to forestall the emergence of a victor from the war, and thus prevent either country from becoming the leading player in the region. The scheme was summarized by Alan Clark, the former British Minister for Trade and Defence Procurement who 'told a *Sunday Telegraph* journalist in January 1988: "The interests of the West will be served by Iran and Iraq fighting each other – the longer the better."' In the same interview, he said his job was to maximize exports despite the government's proclaimed guidelines, which prohibited the sale of machine tools with military potential to Iraq, in defiance of a ban on such sales (*Independent on Sunday*, 8 November 1992).

Intent on weakening both Iran and Iraq, no effort was seriously made to end the conflict, though both superpowers seemed to concur on preventing the war from expanding and spilling over to other states. Fearing a regional superpower, and also investing in future relations with either victor, they both encouraged the sale of arms to Iran and Iraq, directly or through surrogates, whenever the tides of war changed and became disadvantageous for one or the other, or possibly to undercut a perceived *rapprochement* with the other superpower.

The Iran–Iraq War was another of the many regional wars, fought with armament supplied by the superpowers, whose interests increased only when they perceived a shift in the regional balance of power and then sought to pursue strategic profit or deflect strategic loss. But it was not a zero-sum game for the US and the USSR. Their interests converged in so far that neither wished a victor to arise at the end of the war. In short, their attitude can best be described as a 'blend of wary opportunism, alarm and indifference' (*Strategic Survey 1984–85*, p. 70).

In the post-Cold War era, the Gulf area still retained its geostrategic prominence. According to Madeleine Albright, US Permanent Representative at the UN, 'while the United States is redefining its global role, it is calibrating its relations with the major powers and their relationship to each other. Force is the ultimate arbiter. As America has the most effective airpower, it can make its will felt' (Albright, televised interview, 18 June 1993). It is the only power with the military capability and the permanent naval presence to pose as the defender of the oil-producing Gulf states and the West's interests, by securing their SLOCs. By the same token, and despite protests from the capitals of its allies and others, it is in a position to expand its Gulf market by the implied threat to use its powers of persuasion to control oil supplies and routes. By so doing, trade relations with the Arab Gulf states will complement America's overwhelming political and military might, and have become an integral part of its overall policy towards the region.

5 The Actors, the Plot, the Props

5.1 THE QUEST FOR NATIVE FLEETS

The value of oil for the Gulf countries cannot be overstated; it is the principal, and largely the only commodity that underpins their economies. Soaring oil prices in the 1970s allowed them to envisage forging a self-reliant shield to protect their life–line in their own part of the world. They started an arms build-up, with naval forces as one of its components, despite, or maybe motivated by, the presence of foreign fleets patrolling their waters.

Fear from neighbours who displayed ominous signs of assertiveness, such as Iran, Iraq or Saudi Arabia – whether real or imagined and encouraged by arms dealers – created unease within some of the smaller states, and played a role in sparking their arms procurement programmes. The chronic Iran–Iraq and Iraq–Kuwait border disputes and their disruptive effect were detailed earlier. Iran's claim over Bahrain, although settled by agreements, may still be simmering. The three Gulf islands, also part of the latter settlement, have not been renounced by the UAE; the controversy over them was bluntly escalated by Iran in the autumn of 1992, and continues to this day, despite mediation efforts.

Saudi Arabia is also involved in a number of border disputes. In 1977, it annexed Umm al-Maradim and Qarawa, the two islands between it and Kuwait. The Buraymi Oasis is the subject of a controversy with Abu Dhabi. Qatar, the country with the smallest population in the area, is justified in fearing its neighbour, in particular after the frontier dispute erupted into the open in late September 1992, when a Saudi detachment attacked a border post. In the diplomatic wrangle which followed, Qatar dismissed the 1965 border agreement, which was never officially ratified, and the Saudis declared it an inadmissible unilateral act. Despite Saudi endorsement of the old colonial boundary, Oman has reasons to feel vulnerable, with Saudi ambitions to control an outlet to the Arabian Sea through a corridor across its territory. The longest border dispute in the Arabian peninsula is the one between the desert kingdom and Yemen, dating back to the war in the 1920s. Following the 1934 Treaty of al-Ta'if, Yemen lost three provinces to its neighbour. Despite a British declaration in 1965, the frontier was never officially recognized, and the conflict intensified with the discovery of oil reserves in these territories. Another case is mainland Oman, which is separated from the Musandam peninsula by the UAE. The Hawar Islands issue was also one of the disputes that clouded the horizons of the Gulf since the 1930s; the cluster of reefs and sandbars, located half a mile from Qatar and 12 miles from Bahrain, were claimed by the former but given by Britain to the island sheikhdom. In April 1986, the controversy over the potentially oil-rich islands erupted into open conflict, and the dispute was taken by Qatar to the ICJ in July 1991. The dispute provoked armed skirmishes in September of the same year, and in April 1992, Qatar extended its territorial claims by 12 miles.

The borders were artificially created along purely arbitrary lines, and imposed relatively recently by the colonial power. Most were unacceptable to the Gulf states, and the controversies led to simmering disputes with periodic border clashes. Originally, the boundaries' description was phrased with strategic vagueness, and they were for the most part undelineated. The frontiers run along vast featureless deserts and lack demarcation signs on the ground or unalterable landmarks, such as rivers or mountain ranges. On some of the maps, the lines between points *A* and *B* were referred to as just south of *X* town to south of *X* location. Sometimes, strings of palm trees were marked on the maps as reference, with predictable implications for controversy over possible alterations. The disputes were complicated further by the fact that many of the original maps were not sketched to scale. It is therefore reasonable to assume that the Gulf states' anxieties were compounded by the manner in which borderlines were drawn in the sands, and that British mapmakers thus generated the likelihood for conflict. The problems cited may have given rise to legitimate security concerns and the consequent arms race.

In some LDCs, the possession of technologically advanced arms is regarded as a status symbol. The quest for prestige was often a factor behind the purchase of sophisticated weaponry – especially so if dissension already existed between rulers. In the Gulf, most rulers are driven by political rivalry and personal suspicion. Furthermore, fear of infiltration from across the border, followed by acts of sabotage or subversion, demanded more vigilance and dictated their need for weapons. Internal security considerations, because of political, ethnic or religious tensions, also played a role.

These factors, as well as the eagerness of arms-manufacturing countries to absorb the Gulf states' foreign exchange surpluses, led to an arms race. Strategic interests, designated as legitimate security concerns of allies, also motivated governments in both the Western and Eastern camps. It was suggested that political considerations played a role, and that 'the sale of advanced technology and armaments, and the continued recycling of "petro-dollars" is essential if the basis for American influence and power in the Persian Gulf is to be maintained' (Jordan, 1981, p. 31). Such motives were especially apparent in the policy of the former Soviet Union, where war materiel was often sold to allies or prospective client-states at well below the market price.

The build-up of naval forces is the most capital-intensive among the various services of the armed forces. Some indicators can be used for a comparison of an estimate of cost, but it is sometimes difficult to quantify expenditure on any of the branches within a defence force. Numerous elements enter into the equation, such as the following:

– The value of the platform (ship, aircraft, battle tank) and its life-span, in order to plan for its replacement, as it is a rapidly diminishing asset. The life-span is usually 30 years for RN ships and 20 for RAF aircraft, but LDCs try to operate them longer, because of budgetary constraints.
– The price of weapons (guns, rockets, missiles) and their life-span, as they become inoperable or unreliable after a few years.
– The cost of spare parts, which must be replaced periodically, if the platform or weapon-system is to remain effective; they are lifed at X-hours of performance and have a shelf-life of

up to 5 years, then have to be sent back to the manufacturers to be checked.
- The price of the ammunition for war and practice, in which respect LDCs are usually issued with more practice ammunition because of the low level of literacy and technical training among their manpower.
- The fee for training maintenance crews, which is vital because the platforms and weapon-systems will cease to be reliable if the expertise to change spare parts and carry out routine repairs is unavailable; the time is inversely related to the degree of literacy among recruits.
- The cost of servicing the platforms and weapon-systems, depending on their frequency and level, as the lack of upkeep causes them to degenerate and decay faster.
- The initial expenditure for support facilities and their subsequent running costs, which consist of headquarters, communication centres, subsidiary power generation plants, supply stores and vehicles. They also include shore bases, logistic replenishment tankers and other support vessels for the navy, airfields and fuel depots for the air force, campsites for ground forces, and logistic backing for all three, but especially for the ground troops.

Before a country establishes a defence force, it must identify its enemy, evaluate the nature of the threat, estimate the level of response and envisage the theatre of operations. Since political influence and military capability are closely linked, major or regional powers also consider the political role they wish to play, and weigh the degree of commitment to that posture. A country needs to balance obligations and resources – in other words, to blend its political imperatives with military needs – so as to be able to calculate the mix of forces in quantitative and qualitative terms, within a certain affordable budget. In simpler terms, it must determine how many and which types of ships, aircraft and armour are adequate for its defence needs, and how many and which types of defensive or offensive weapons these platforms are fitted with. In the face of budget constraints, the choice between versatility and scale is imperative to determine the force structure within the country's financial confines.

According to Commander Keith Day, who spent ten years of his navy career as an aviator in the Fleet Air Arm, including serving in the Gulf, each of the services has its advantages and shortcomings, and so do the platforms operated by their men. While an aircraft is more versatile and manoeuvrable in contrast to a battle tank, enemy territory is not really occupied except by ground troops. As ships are larger in size and can be fitted with a considerable number of weapon-systems, their fire power is stronger and equals several aircraft or tanks. Furthermore, ships can have an almost constant presence, such as the nuclear-fuelled submarines, while aircraft have to fly back to their airfields for refuelling. Even if an air force has mid-air refuelling capabilities, the crew can sustain a specific number of flying hours only, after which it must be replaced.

On the question of expenditure, Commander Day explained that all the elements in the equation had to be taken into consideration, but that the build-up of a navy was certainly costlier in terms of initial disbursements. These include the purchase of naval vessels and the establishment of adequate shore facilities. The unit price of a ship is high compared to that of a similarly-armed aircraft or armoured vehicle. Therefore, depending on the weapon-systems, a frigate or a destroyer would roughly equal in price 130 fighter aircraft or about 210 main battle tanks (MBT). The difficulty in establishing a new navy lies in the fact that while an air force or an army can gradually assemble their hardware, with an eye on the budget at their disposal, the creation and development of a navy is more capital-intensive. Newly-founded air forces or armies can phase over several years the transfer of hardware to their squadrons or battalions, buying only a few aircraft or MBTs and artillery pieces at a time, but a ship cannot be transferred in instalments.

Furthermore, if a ship is to have a long life-span, it has to follow a rigorous and regular maintenance schedule and have access to shore facilities, which are costly to construct. Ships require in-life refits every ten years, and major renovations every five; a warship can then, for instance, have the sonar updated or a completely new weapon-system installed. Every one to three years, they have to enter dry docks and undergo a docking and assisted maintenance period (DAMP), which involves scraping the bottom and painting, repairs and replacement of equipment, among other minor servicing. DAMPs are comparable to a car's 12 000-mile service, except that a ship covers about 20 times that mileage. The expenditure on maintenance is difficult to quantify, as it varies widely.

The purchase of munitions and spare parts is another item to be considered. Although the price varies enormously from ship to ship, the normal practice is to buy two-years' stock with a newly-contracted ship. This usually amounts to ten per cent of the vessel's price, on top of the bill. Another ten per cent is allowed for practice ammunition, which is cheaper than war munitions, and is usually disbursed from the ship's annual training allowance, after the vessel becomes operational within its native service. With an on-going war, the consumption of spare parts and ammunition obviously increases.

Ground forces are the most labour-intensive of the three services, and the easiest and least costly to establish, being the most inexpensive of the services in terms of hardware and training. In LDCs, despite the high rate of illiteracy, infantry soldiers assimilate easily the handling of their fairly simple arms. But apart from troops and crews to man the armour, an army needs great numbers of engineers to build bridges or lay and clear mines, as well as highly-experienced personnel, specially trained in organizing logistics. Many armies extended themselves and failed in their campaigns because of the lack of proper logistics. The over-stretching of Iraqi forces between 1980 and 1982 is one of the most recent examples.

The air force is the second most labour-intensive service, as pilots can only fly for very short periods of time, and have to be replaced by others. A small crew in a fighter aircraft handle a highly complex platform, equipped with sophisticated systems, ranging from guns and radars to air-to-air (AAM) and air-to-surface missiles (ASM). Furthermore, aircraft have to be constantly checked and serviced by large ground teams. Regardless of the high cost of creating and maintaining a capable air force, armed forces may have to expand that service, in future. *Operation Desert Storm* undoubtedly demonstrated the successful use of helicopter-gunships and fixed-wing aircraft, which seem to have superseded the MBT's task.

In the navy, the ship is handled by a crew that is not changed as in an aircraft, and only about two-thirds of its vessels are operational at any one time. This means that, in any one mission, four vessels are required if one is to be kept on patrol, while one is being serviced, one is on its way to do so, and the fourth is sailing to relieve the one on patrol. Naval crew need good shore-training facilities, to a greater degree than others, such as diving chambers and a great number of attack teachers. The air force train some of their more specialized crew on simulators, but the navy has intensive training in bigger and costlier simulators.

Training is of the utmost importance, as half of the effectiveness of a weapon depends on the person who handles it. But here too, each service varies in the extent of training that its personnel needs. Whereas the price-tag to instruct a RAF jet-fighter pilot is around £5 million, and a communications instructor above £800 000, an infantryman costs the army around £5000. And while an air force squadron commander requires from 12 to 15 years' training, a private acquires a few months' guidance on uncomplicated equipment, and mainly needs his muscles to carry his weapon, the ammunition and spare parts, as well as his rations (Day, Interview, 5 January 1992).

Unfortunately, in their race to match each other's ever-increasing power, and in their contest for the latest technology, the Gulf states outspent each other. For instance, in 1980, per capita expenditure on arms in the tiny state of Qatar was $2809 – the highest in the world; and in 1984, the Saudis came second with $2525, thus more than double the US figure of $1001 (*Military Balance* in Khalaf, 1987, p. 21). While the prosperity brought by 'black gold' was wasted on arms, it was obviously doubtful that any of the tiny states could seriously hold out for long against an attack from one of the powers that overshadowed them. The less-than-brief struggle of the Kuwaiti Armed Forces, on the first morning of Iraq's invasion in August 1990, and their inability to act at least as a 'trip-wire' force, was a glaring illustration.

The states overlooking the Gulf lack a deterring naval force, capable of protecting this vital area and the SLOCs leading to it. This, they could have achieved by responding to Oman's recommendation, in May 1981, to form a joint GCC navy. Coupling this to the Saudi proposal to coordinate military procurement policies would have facilitated integration and absorption. Various problems have to be addressed until such a navy could be regarded as cohesive, efficient and credible, such as restructuring, training and command and control.

These could be overcome if the political will exists among the GCC rulers to embark on confidence building measures (CBM). Since their security interests are fundamentally the same, the confrontation and settling of disagreements over individual issues should be their priority. This has to be followed by continual consultation, a careful study of the nature of the threat, the concrete planning for contingencies, and a clearly-designed concept of their collective security aims.

Efforts in that direction must emanate from the states bordering the Gulf, and not be imposed by external powers. Security networks brokered in the not-so-distant past by foreign parties have not been credible, and were consequently short-lived. The creation of a strong navy would provide the Gulf states with the capacity to act independently of Western powers, and form the foundation of a reliable deterring regional force, based on cost-saving collaboration. It seems an opportune time in light of recent developments; the economic problems that burden the US and Europe have reduced the US armed presence abroad, with countless military installations being closed, reduced or put on standby.

The combined Gulf navy must firmly aim at pulling in Iran and Iraq, the two states that could be potential aggressors, and should render the encroachment of one of the dominant states on another unthinkable. The working of such a coalition seems hard to imagine in practice, and it may sound incredible to group former enemies such as Iran, Kuwait, Saudi Arabia and Iraq in a security network. The suggestion may trigger an avalanche of protest in the beginning. As unprecedented a proposal as it may sound, incorporating Iran and Iraq with the GCC states is pivotal to the success of the scheme, and would be very much in the interests of the international community, in so far that it would constrain transgressions by the major regional military powers.

The idea may seem implausible, especially to the frail states who already have simmering border disputes with their more powerful neighbours. They may find it impossible to adhere to and be signatories of the same defence pact, and perceive themselves as being at the mercy of the regional superpowers. This will require the alleviation of the weaker states' fears – with some cajoling and arm-twisting, these may be overcome. It would also necessitate that all concerned parties display statesmanship and a determination to reduce turbulence in this geostrategic area.

The two Gulf wars face the area with the problem of addressing the creation of a security structure that would diminish the threat of a third war in the region. Setting up a new military regime will entail extremely difficult negotiations, and may need the orchestrated efforts of the states that border on the Gulf, as well as the countries who have a stake in its stability.

Throughout the region, territorial disputes are flaring up, fuelled by either strategic or economic interests, or chauvinistic trends. Open confrontation has raised the level of apprehension and given birth to the notion that people there are sitting on the edge of a volcano. The countries concerned should first confront reality and respond forcefully to the challenge, then – through the pursuance of CBM – strive towards an acceptable level of political collaboration. Success will generate trust and lead towards military cooperation. Failure will encourage already strong pressures towards hegemony. In the end, the script of the agreement should be drafted in a manner to highlight the convergence of interests and thus bring about cohesion.

Perestroika unleashed a chain of events which not only tore down the Berlin Wall, but split the Soviet Empire, readjusted the world alliance system and defused local crises. The most recent Gulf War reordered another coalition structure. In their aftermath, peace between Israel and its neighbours is no longer a dream, and the West, represented by NATO, has discarded confrontation with Eastern Europe, and opted for cooperation under the Partnership for Peace (PFP) scheme. With these momentous developments in mind, is the creation of a joint Gulf navy that includes both Iraq and Iran beside the GCC states inconceivable?

The winds of war have blown twice over this tiny expanse of water. To subdue any future storms and steer the Gulf ship towards tranquil waters, its states have to take charge of their security collectively and exclusively.

5.2   NAVIES OF THE CAST

Until the early 1960s, the Gulf witnessed Iran's naval predominance among its neighbours, having purchased, in 1949, two used vessels from Britain, a *Loch*-class frigate and an *Algerine*-class minesweeper. Iraq, the only other country with any naval craft, had four small and ageing coastal patrol boats (PB), purchased in 1937, which, evidently, were insignificant in comparison to Iran's nascent navy. The status quo was temporarily disrupted with the transfer of 12 Soviet P-6 class fast torpedo boats to Iraq between 1959 and 1960. In theory, Iran's two larger ships could have been challenged by Iraq's new acquisition, with the speed, manoeuvrability and sheer number of its craft.

These conditions did not continue for long. To shift the naval balance to its advantage again, Iran placed orders for four new American corvettes in 1961, one British Second World War vintage destroyer in 1964 and four new British frigates in 1966. A gentleman's agreement with the Johnson administration in 1964 allowed Iran to use American credits to purchase any arms necessary for its security requirements. Two of the four quick-response naval craft, the PF-103 class, were delivered in 1964, and the two other ones, in 1969. The British *Battle*-class destroyer was armed with 4 *Seacat* SAMs. Her transfer, three years later, marked a new stage in the naval race, with Iran's becoming the first Gulf navy to acquire guided missiles. The destroyer was modernized again between 1975 and 1976 to carry eight American *Standard* medium-range SSMs, and her load of four *Seacat* SAMs was quadrupled. The British frigates, each fitted with nine *Seacat* SAMs and five Italian short-range *Sea Killer-2* SSMs, were delivered between 1971 and 1972, in addition to two ex-USN Second World War destroyers of the *Allen M Sumner (Fram-2)* class. The latter were armed with eight *Standard-1* SSMs, and replaced the very first two ships Iran had started its navy with, which were retired from service (Angrand and Rabier, 1989, p. 105; and Danziger, 1982, pp. 94–6).

Additionally, orders were placed in 1974 for 12 French *Kaman*-class fast attack craft (FAC), fitted with medium-range American *Harpoon* SSMs, of which nine were transferred by 1979; and six US *Spruance*-class destroyers, of which two were cancelled in 1976. Orders placed between 1977 and 1979 included three *Tang*-class submarines, six Type-209 class submarines and 12 F-122 class missile frigates, but these were not delivered. Neither was the armed supply ship *Kharg*, completed in Britain and handed over to an Iranian crew in April

1980, but not permitted to sail, as the government refused to assign the necessary documents. The purchases had been prompted by the Shah's desire to enlarge the navy by five-fold, as he viewed the 'Security Perimeter of Iran' expanding to encompass 'the north-west quadrant of the Indian Ocean', after the withdrawal of the British forces from the Gulf (O'Ballance, 1988, pp. 13, 23).

As a result of these major purchases, Iran's defence budget, which was $78 million in 1954, rose to $241 million a decade later, and for the year 1971 exceeded $1 billion. The years 1953–70 showed an approximately 15-fold increase, from $57 to $844 million. The military budget for 1972 increased by 29 per cent, that for 1973 by 11 per cent, to reach $1.525 billion. In 1974, it climbed to $3.68 billion, showing a 141 per cent increase. In 1977, it escalated to $9.4 billion, and in 1978 it reached a peak of $9.94 billion. In comparison, Iraq's defence budget for 1979 was $2.2 billion (*US Congress Subcommittee on Foreign Assistance Staff Report*, 'US Military Sales to Iran', July 1979, in Angrand and Rabier, 1989, p. 105; also Halliday, 1979, pp. 71–2, 94–5; and O'Ballance, 1988, pp. 14, 28).

While it increased the navy's capabilities with the transfer of units equipped with the latest technology, and modernized older vessels, weapons and communication systems, Iran also embarked on projects to develop various bases along the Gulf's coast, and located navy headquarters in Khorramshahr (see Map 7.1). The Shah's ambition to limit the presence of foreign navies in the Gulf, and eventually become the sole protector of shipping throughout the region, was made evident by the upgrading of a string of bases, and his interest was further demonstrated by his frequent visits to attend naval manoeuvres. There were bases in Khosrowabad, in the northern Gulf, in Bandar Abbas, close to the Strait of Hormuz, and in Bandar Pahlevi, on the Caspian coast. In the early-1960s, construction was started on a coastal road to link Booshehr harbour to the Baluchi port of Chahbahar, close to the Pakistani border, on the Makran coast. The development of Chahbahar, at the far south-east end of the Gulf, and the occupation of the two Tunbs and Abu Musa were crucial for the future projection of Iran's seapower into the Indian Ocean, as anticipated by the Shah. Throughout the 1970s, hundreds of millions of dollars were invested to transform it from a tiny and neglected port into a large and modern naval and air base, designed to become 'Iran's gateway to the Indian Ocean' (Alam, 1991, pp. and notes 103–4, 14, 170, 229, 252, 290–1, 395–6, 419, 434, 477; also O'Ballance, 1988, p. 15; and Hunter in Naff [ed.], 1988, p. 164).

The 1970s witnessed an intensification of the naval race, with Iraq trying to pick up the lag, and other Gulf countries joining, as well, though Iraq's purchases were a trickle in comparison to the hardware that was pouring into Iran. In 1969, Saudi Arabia bought three German modern torpedo boats, and in January 1971, Oman ordered three British gunboats. In January 1972, Saudi Arabia placed an order for six US corvettes fitted with missiles, and four tank landing craft (LCT), under an agreement covering a 10-year period. At that time, Kuwait had about 18 small PBs, armed with machine guns only.

Between 1972 and 1976, the substantial rise in oil revenues enabled Baghdad to pay for more hardware, and it bought six Soviet *Osa-1*-class and eight *Osa-2* FACs armed with the effective and now-famous *Styx* SSMs. In addition, two ex-Soviet Navy T-43 class ocean minesweepers, with mine-laying capability, made the Iraqi Navy the first among the Gulf countries' to acquire this ability, in addition to their potential use to police political and economic exclusion zones. In the meantime, in April 1974, Oman ordered four more British gunboats.

The last three years of the 1970s saw a further escalation in the naval race. In 1977, Kuwait assigned Japan to build a naval base, including a dockyard, completed five years later. Within the ten-year Saudi-US agreement, signed in 1972, Saudi Arabia ordered four 815-ton PCG-1 corvettes, armed with eight *Harpoon* SSMs, and nine 348-ton missile FACs, fitted with four *Harpoons*. The UAE states, who had formally unified their armed forces on 6 May 1976, joined the race by ordering six German TNC-45 class missile boats armed with two *Exocet* SSMs, delivered in 1980. Oman modernized its first three gunboats by having them equipped with two short-range *Exocet* SSMs, and thus entered the missile race. After the loss of one of the boats in a hurricane in December 1978, it ordered a larger one as a replacement.

Table 5.1   Iranian Naval Order of Battle

At the start of the Iran–Iraq War in September 1980, the navy comprised:

1   DESTROYER (ex-British *Battle*-class). Transferred 1967.
     Armament: Missiles: Standard SAM (had limited SS capability)
                      Guns: 4 4.5 inch
                                       2 40 mm Bofors
                                       4 23 mm AA
                      ASW: 1 3-barrel Squid A/S mortar

2   DESTROYERS (ex-USN *Sumner, Fram II*-class). Transferred 1971–2.
     Armament: Missiles: Standard SAM-9 (had limited SS capability)
                      Guns: 4 5-inch
                                       2 23 mm AA
                      Torpedoes: 6 324 mm Mk32
                      ASW: 2 *Hedgehog* Mk10
                                       1 AB 204 Helicopter

4   FRIGATES (Vosper Mk 5 *Saam*-class). Delivered 1971–2.
     Armament: Missiles: *Seakiller* SSM
                                       Seacat SSM
                      Guns: 1 4.5-inch
                                       2 35 mm Oerlikon
                      ASW: 1 3-barrel mortar Mk-10

4   CORVETTES (ex-US PF-103-class). Transferred 1964.
     Armament: Guns: 2 3-inch
                                       2 40 mm Bofors
                                       2 23 mm
                      ASW: depth charges (4 projectors, 2 racks)

9   FAST ATTACK CRAFT (*La Combattante* [*Kaman*] class). Delivered 1977–8.
     Armament: Missiles: *Harpoon* SSM
                      Guns: 1 3-inch Oto Melara
                                       1 40 mm Bofors

4   LARGE PATROL CRAFT (ex-USCG *Cape*-class). In service 1956–9.
     Armament: Guns: 1 40 mm Bofors
                      ASW: 2 depth charge racks

3   LARGE PATROL CRAFT (ex-USN PGM-71-class). In service 1967–70.
     Armament: Guns: 1 40 mm Bofors
                      ASW: depth charges (4 racks)

3   COASTAL MINESWEEPERS (ex-USN 292 and 268-class). Transferred 1959–62.
     Armament: 2 20 mm Oerlikon

2   INSHORE MINESWEEPERS (ex-US *Cape*-class). Transferred 1964.
     Armament: Guns: 1 12.7 mm machine gun

2   LANDING SHIPS (Logistics [LSL] *Hengam*-class). Built by Yarrow to merchant
     ships standards. In service 1974.
     Armament: Guns: 4 40 mm Bofors
                                       2 12.7 mm machine guns
                                       122 mm multiple rocket launcher (MRL)
                                       fitted later

5   LANDING SHIPS (Tank, *Iran Ajr*-class). Japanese-built to commercial design.
In service 1978.
Armament: Guns: 2 12.7 mm machine guns

2   FLEET SUPPLY SHIPS (INS *Bandar Abbas* and *Booshehr*). German. In service 1974.
Armament: Guns: 2 23 mm
                                   8 14.5 mm machine guns

2   WATER TANKERS. Built in Bombay. In service 1978–9.

2   ACCOMMODATION SHIPS (former Italian liners *Raffaelo* and *Michel-Angelo*).

1   REPAIR SHIP (ex-US *Amphion*-class). Transferred on loan in 1971. Purchased
1977. Non-operational.

A number of vessels and/or armament may have become temporarily non-
operational because of the departure of foreign maintenance personnel (no
information available as to the capabilities of Iranian teams to maintain the vessels)
and to the lack of new spare parts and/or ammunition, due to difficulties in military
equipment resupply. Despite the arms embargo, some spare parts found their way to
Iran and others were cannibalized from similar units and systems. Iran also has
indigenous ammunition manufacturing.

Not listed are a large number of auxiliaries and small vessels, including small
patrol craft, tugs, tenders, service craft and hovercraft. The Iranian Coast Guard also
operated coastal and inshore patrol craft, many of which were subsequently taken
over by the IRGCN. By 1980, the manpower in the navy was 20 000 men.

Known additions to the fleet during the course of the war included:

1980

5   CARGO VESSELS, 2 of which specialized explosives carriers.

1981

3   FAST ATTACK CRAFT (*La Combattante* [*Kaman*] class). One was captured by
anti-Khomeini dissidents off Cadiz, in an operation led by Admiral Kamal
Habibullahi, former C-in-C IIN, but subsequently surrendered to the French at
Toulon. Not armed with *Harpoon* SSM.

1984

1   FLEET REPLENISHMENT SHIP (INS *Kharg*). Built at Swan Hunter on lines of
British RFA 'OL' class oiler but carrying stores and ammunition in addition to fuel.
Finally released to Iran after much discussions on the grounds that it was not suitable
for use in the war against Iraq.

1984–85

3   LANDING CRAFT (Tank). Built in Holland. Merchant ship design and
ostensibly ordered for civilian use.

50   FAST ATTACK CRAFT: approximately 40 13 m and 10 11 m Swedish-built
Boghammer. These craft, with maximum speed of about 45 knots, were the principal
weapon of the IRGCN. They were variously armed with multiple rocket launchers, a
12.7 mm machine gun and SA-7 or *Stinger* SAM.

1985

2   LANDING SHIPS (Logistic [LSL] *Hengam*-class). Built by Yarrow to merchant
ship standards and handed over without armament. Later fitted with Bofors MRL.

1986

5 LANDING SHIPS (tank, LST). Built at Inchon, South Korea to merchant ship standards.

1987

1 MIDGET SUBMARINE. Origin unknown, may have been developed in Iran. It was almost certainly not used operationally.

3 FAST ATTACK CRAFT (*Chaho*-class). Delivered from North Korea 1987. Armed with 2 23 mm guns, 2 14.5 mm machine guns and a 40-barrel MRL. Their main engines were in extremely poor condition but may have been replaced.

1988

1 MIDGET SUBMARINE built in North Korea.

1 LANDING SHIP (Logistic, *Foque*-class). Built in Bandar Abbas.

Iran also had a large number of miscellaneous small craft, including Rotork, Boston Whalers and inflatables, principally for use with the IRGCN. Many of the small craft were produced locally.

A conservative estimate of war losses is as follows:

1 FRIGATE INS *Sahand* (Vosper Mk 5 Saam-class). Sunk by USN in 1988.

2 CORVETTES INS *Milaniam* and INS *Khanamuie* (PF-103). Believed sunk by Iraq in 1982.

2 FAST ATTACK CRAFT (*La Combattante* [*Kaman*] class). INS *Peykan* sunk by Iraq in 1980 and INS *Joshan* by USN in 1988.

1 LARGE PATROL CRAFT (*Cape*-class). Believed sunk by Iraq.

3 LANDING SHIPS (Tank, *Iran Ajr* class). Two believed sunk by Iraq in 1980. One (INS *Iran Ajr*) caught red-handed on mine-laying operation by the USN in 1987, captured and scuttled.

1 COASTAL MINESWEEPER (ex-USN 292 and 268-class). Reported sunk by Iraq in 1980-1.

There is some confusion over 3 PGM-71 Large PC, all three being reported as sunk during the war, but later reports indicated that they in fact survived.

(Aggregates based upon the following: interviews with Western navy expert; *Flottes de Combat*, *Jane's Fighting Ships*, *Jane's Defence Weekly*, *Proceedings*, *Proceedings/Naval Review* and *Military Balance*)

Table 5.2   Iraqi Naval Order of Battle

In September 1980, the navy comprised:

1   TRAINING FRIGATE. Built in Yugoslavia. Entered service March 1980.
    Armament: Guns: 1 57 mm Bofors
                                1 40 mm Bofors AA
                                16 20 mm Bofors AA
               ASW: 1 depth charge rack

12   FAST ATTACK CRAFT (4 Soviet *OSA-1* and 8 Soviet *OSA-2*-class). Transferred
     1971–7. Formed the core of the fleet.
     Armament: Missiles: 4 *Styx* SSM
                         Guns: 4 30 mm

12   FAST ATTACK CRAFT (Soviet P-6-class). Transferred 1959–71.
     Armament: Guns: 4 25 mm
                   Torpedoes: 2 21-inch tubes

5   COASTAL PATROL CRAFT (Soviet *Zhuk*-class). Transferred 1974–5.
    Armament: Guns: 4 14.5 mm AA

2   LARGE PATROL CRAFT (Soviet *Poluchat*-class). Transferred 1966.
    Armament: Guns: 2 14.5 mm AA

3   LARGE PATROL CRAFT (Soviet SO-I-class). Transferred 1962.
    Armament: Guns: 4 25 mm
                   ASW: 4 rocket launchers
                               Depth charge racks
                               Mine-laying capability (20 mines)

2   OCEAN MINESWEEPERS (Soviet T-43-class). Transferred 1962.
    Armament: Guns: 4 37 mm AA
                                 8 12.7 mm machine guns
               ASW: 2 depth charge throwers
                               Mine-laying capability (20 mines)

3   INSHORE MINESWEEPERS (Soviet *Yevgenya*-class). Transferred 1975.
    Armament: Guns: 5 20 mm AA

4   INSHORE MINESWEEPERS (Yugoslav *Nestin*-class). Transferred 1978–9.
    Armament: Guns: 5 20 mm AA
                                 Mine-laying capability (24 mines)
                               Influence and mechanical sweeping equipment

3   LSM (Soviet *Polnochny*-class). Transferred 1977–9.
    Armament: Guns: 4 30 mm AA
                 Rockets: 2 122 mm rocket launchers

1   SALVAGE VESSEL (Yugoslav *Spasilac*-class). Transferred 1978.
     Not listed are a number of auxiliary and small craft such as tugs and fire and
diving tenders.
     By 1980, the navy's manpower was 4000 and scheduled to expand to 28 000, with
the absorption of the units on order.
     Known additions to the fleet during the course of the war included:

1981

4   FRIGATES (*Lupo*-class) and 6 CORVETTES (*Asad*-class, guided-missiles) ordered
from Italy, but not delivered.

1983

3　AMPHIBIOUS WARFARE SHIPS, delivered from Denmark, commercial Ro/Ro vessels of 3681 GRT modified to act as LSLs. They handled tanks of up to 55 tons.

1984

1　REPLENISHMENT OILER (Italian *Stromboli*-class). Delivered.

2　FAST ATTACK CRAFT (Soviet *OSA-2*). Delivered.
　　An estimate of the state of the navy after one year of the start of the war follows, and so far as can be ascertained, this situation did not change significantly throughout the war:

OSA FAC:	of the original 12, one was believed trapped in Basra, at least 4 were destroyed by enemy action, the surviving based at Umm Qasr.
P-6 FAC:	of the original 12 probably 6 were destroyed at Basra.
5 *Zhuk* PC:	at Umm Qasr.
2 *Poluchat* PC:	at Basra.
3 SO-1 PC:	at Basra.
2 T-43 OMS:	at Basra.
3 *Yevgenya* IMS:	at Basra.
3 *Polnochny* LSM:	two at Umm Qasr and one probably at Basra.

(Aggregates based upon the following: interviews with Western navy expert; *Flottes de Combat, Jane's Fighting Ships, Jane's Defence Weekly, Proceedings, Proceedings/Naval Review* and *Military Balance*)

Between 1977 and 1979, four Polish-built ex-Soviet Navy *Polnochny*-class LCTs were transferred to Iraq. The vessels were fitted with rocket launchers and guns. Thus Iraq became the first of the Gulf countries to be able to land tanks in a combined operation. It had also ordered, in 1978, a Yugoslav training frigate, armed with four SSMs, which was delivered in 1981, despite the arms embargo imposed after the start of the Iran–Iraq War.

In 1979, one British 2000-ton landing and command ship was transferred to Oman, and an order was placed for two more large missile FACs. Bahrain, who began plans to establish a navy in 1975, entered the race by ordering two German TNC-45 class missile boats, armed with four *Exocet* SSMs, as well as two gunboats. The same year, Iraq's shopping list was impressive and included six French FACs, three Soviet *Foxtrot*-class patrol submarines and ten Soviet gas-turbine-powered *Nanuchka*-class missile corvettes.

In early 1980, Iraq signed a contract with Cantieri Navali Reuniti, worth more than 1.5 billion lire, for the building of four 2000-ton modified *Lupo*-class turbine-powered frigates, armed with eight *Teseo* (Italian *Otomat* Mk-2) over-the-horizon SSMs and eight Italian *Albatros* SAMs. The *Hittin* was launched at Ancona on 27 July 1983, and the *Musa Ibn Nusair* and the *Tariq Ibn Ziyad* at Muggia on 8 July and 16 December 1983,

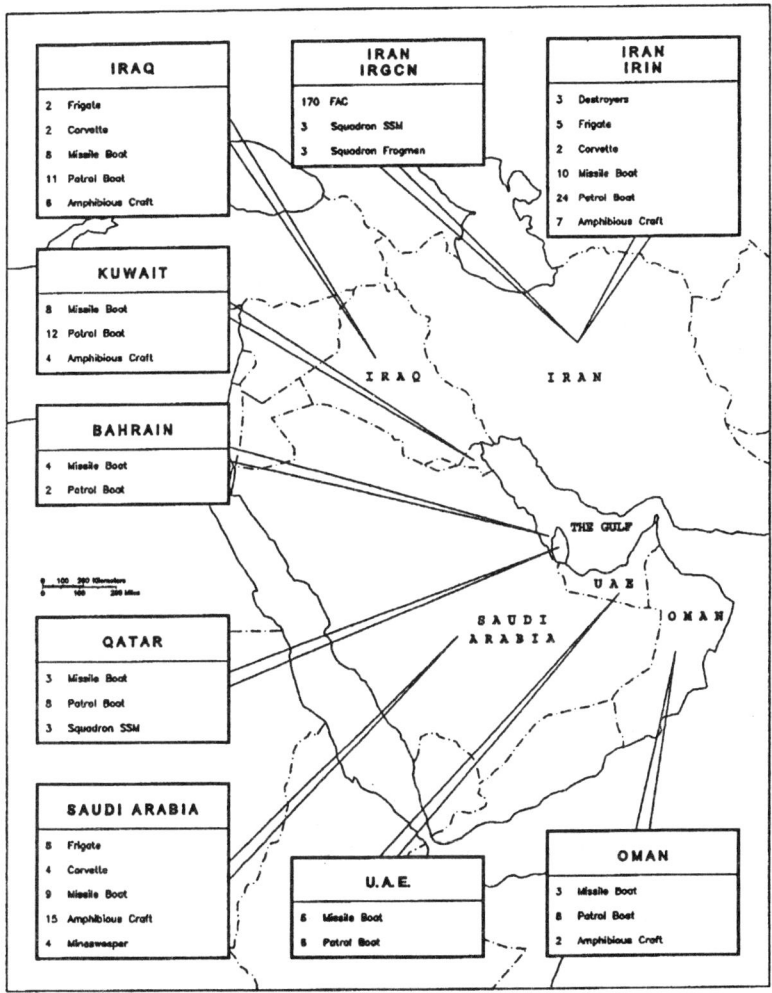

Map 5.1   Gulf Navies

respectively, but none were delivered. The sale also included six 650-ton *Asad*-class guided missile corvettes armed with four *Teseo* SSMs. The deal was held up by the US until 1981, because of its objections and its refusal, therefore, to deliver the American-made gas turbines. The *'Abdallah Ibn Abisah*, the *Khalid Ibn Al-Walid*, the *Sa'ad Ibn Abi Waqqass* and the *Salah Al-Din Al-Ayubi*, fitted out at the Breda yard at Porto Marghera, and the *Dhi Qar*, the *Al-Qadisiya* and the *Al-Yarmuk*, built at Riva Trigosa, were completed between 1985 and 1987, but none were delivered because of problems over payment and crew training. The fleet oiler *Agnadeen*, ready for delivery, was moored at Muggia (Taha, 1984, pp. 34–7). In August 1989, Iran announced that it would never permit the delivery of these ships to be completed.

In 1980, Bahrain ordered two British missile FACs, with Kuwait placing an order for eight German ones. Qatar, the last of the Gulf countries to join the race, ordered three French *La Combattante*-class missile FACs in September. Saudi Arabia signed the largest contract for naval hardware that France was ever awarded, worth FFr 14 billion, for four frigates armed with eight long-range *Otomat* SSMs and *Crotale Navale* SAMs, two logistic replenishment tankers and 24 *Dauphin* helicopters, to be delivered between 1985 and 1988 (Danziger, 1982, pp. 93–8; and Taha, 1984, pp. 34–40).

But suitably-trained manpower, an essential factor, was virtually absent in the Gulf countries' race to establish naval forces, although 'the effectiveness of any navy depends more on the quality of its manpower than on the numbers and types of its vessels. In this respect, all the Gulf states suffer from equally serious weaknesses' (Danziger, 1982, p. 98). When the GCC armed forces had their first joint manoeuvres in 1983, in the UAE desert, Sultan Qabus, the only Gulf leader with formal military training, detected the flaw and commented that having sophisticated arms was beneficial, but not without learning to use them. Especially visible at the higher echelons of the officers' corps, appropriate training was also lacking among the crews who would man the ships, handle the weapons, and service them. This drawback enabled foreigners to be given sensitive posts at all levels of the services' structures. Under such circumstances, one cannot overlook the factors of divided loyalty and security risks. For example, in the early 1970s, British officers were seconded to the UAE and Oman, but were directly responsible to their own government. Their responsibilities included training military personnel in Sharjah and organizing visits of British troops to the UAE. RAF officers manned the staging post at the Omani offshore island of Masirah, and in conjunction with British ground troops, operated and protected Salalah air base. In the mid-1970s, the Iraqi Navy was commanded by an Egyptian-trained Syrian officer who defected to Baghdad; the Bahraini Navy was headed by a retired Pakistani officer; the Omani Navy employed large numbers of British and Pakistani naval personnel, and its C-in-C was a British officer; and the Qatari Navy hired British personnel, and recruited heavily from Pakistan, whose pilots flew their squadron of *Sea King* helicopters, equipped with *Exocet* missiles (Taha, 1984, pp. 34–7; Alam, 1991, pp. 300-1; and personal observation).

Because of high illiteracy rates in LDCs, their service personnel need more time than others to fully absorb the handling of modern military equipment. Unfortunately, most arms agreements do not address this problem in full, and recipient countries find themselves heavily reliant on the presence of foreign staff. In the Gulf Arab states, these 'advisors' in fact ran the services, drew up the operational and contingency plans, manned the defence systems, maintained the hardware and trained the men. Furthermore, up to the second Gulf War, about two-fifths of the 14 million GCC inhabitants were foreign workers, relied upon to discharge the chores which the native population balked at doing. In Kuwait, for instance, the *bedoun* ('without', in Arabic, meaning those without nationality) formed the bulk of troops because they coveted citizenship, which most of whom were denied anyway.

The training of local forces to operate modern platforms and weaponry should become a priority in arms deals. Furthermore, the problem of educating cadets should also be addressed by establishing national naval academies within the Gulf region, as their scarcity in the area forces governments to dispatch them to foreign academies. Conscription should be introduced in countries where the population refrains from volunteering to enlist in armed forces, such as Kuwait, where recruitment drives attract limited numbers. Also, less sophisticated weapons may be better suited for LDCs in general, including the Gulf countries. Being less expensive than 'high-tech' arms, acquiring them would release more funds for economic and social development, and also prevent security risks that a heavy foreign presence may cause.

At the outbreak of the Iran-Iraq War in 1980, Iran's navy had a quantitative and qualitative edge over Iraq's in materiel (see Map 5.1; and compare Tables 5.1 and 5.2). With the purging of the higher echelons of the Iranian officer corps after the revolution, and the departure of American person-nel, the navy lacked senior officers, instructors and trained crews and maintenance teams. Consequently, some of its so-phisticated units and weapon-systems became inoperable. In Iraq, the less sophisticated Soviet hardware in the naval arsenal was easier for crews from an LDC to handle. A study of the Iraqi Navy's procurement programme suggested a ten-dency towards acquiring a large number of small inexpensive craft, which were economical to operate, and therefore indi-cated an appreciation of cost-effectiveness. FACs and patrol craft (PC), with the dual characteristic of speed and ma-noeuvrability, were well suited for a restricted naval theatre of operations, such as the northern Gulf. They formed the core of the nascent fleet, in addition to two ocean minesweepers, armed with guns and/or torpedoes, and/or anti-submarine warfare (ASW), and/or mine-laying capability. With the trans-fer of 12 additional FACs, armed with *Styx* missiles, seven minesweepers and three LCTs, Iraq increased its navy's firepower and potential. In the 1970s, the Iraqi Navy became the second of the Gulf countries', after Iran's, to possess sea-launched missiles, and the only one, until the start of the war, to acquire mine-laying and tank-landing capabilities (Danziger, 1982, pp. 94–8).

Although none of the Italian frigates and corvettes were de-livered, the orders placed by Iraq in the late 1970s and early 1980s revealed an ambitious programme for a potentially fast-growing navy, with the inclusion of three Soviet *Foxtrot*-class patrol submarines, ten Soviet *Nanuchka*-class missile corvettes, six French FACs, four Italian *Lupo*-class frigates, six Italian *Asad*-class corvettes, three amphibious warfare ships, two more Soviet FACs and one oiler. The naval build-up reflected a transformation in Iraq's regional policy and in the perception of its future role in the Gulf, founded on ideological, economic and strategic bases. It indicated a change in its interests and aims, as well as an understanding of the obstacles facing it, and may be attributed to a conjunction of events.

The gradual compression of Egypt's war machine after the Camp David Agreement, at a time when Iraq's expanded, presented Saddam Hussein with the opportunity and the means to play a leading role among Arab rulers. In addition to being the Eastern flank of the Arab world, Iraq also aspired to play a dominant role in the Gulf, by substituting the weakened Iranian Navy with its own in patrolling and policing its waters. By projecting its power, the Iraqi Navy would thus assert the Arab character of the Gulf, and become the protector of the more vulnerable states. The paramount advantage of the anticipated naval build-up was to remove the danger of Iraq's economy being at the mercy of Iran's seapower. Military and naval operations during the first nine weeks of the Iran–Iraq War demonstrated, in a blatant manner, how vulnerable it was. They were to prove that without a strong navy to defend its exposed offshore oil terminals and harbours 'the Iranian Navy could have operated with virtual impunity against Iraqi ports and oil facilities at or near the coast . . . and could have inflicted greater damage on a totally unprotected Iraqi merchant fleet' (Dowdy, 1981, p. 117).

5.3 EARLY FIRES OVER THE GULF WATERS

Throughout the history of mankind, preparations for an imminent war have always been veiled in a shroud of secrecy. Prior to the start of combat, the fear of allowing the enemy to discover the general strategic plan, and thus turn it to his advantage, prompted nations to conceal facts related to the onset of combat. These consist, for instance, of political or military alliances negotiated in secret, the manufacturing or procurement of new types of arms, and the stockpiling of additional quantities of weapons, ammunition, spare parts, raw materials and components for industrial purposes, and foodstuffs. They also include strengths and weaknesses in the forces, and the location of military installations and troops. To the layman, camouflage is the most obvious of these practices.

After the outbreak of military hostilities, accounts of on-going battles are either suppressed and/or selectively reported or broadcast. Information that could be valuable to the enemy is concealed, and details that are detrimental to the country's interests are covered up. News of damaged military or strategic installations, or distinctive public buildings which bear a special value nationwide, as well as figures of human casualties are sometimes withheld for their adverse effect on the population's morale at large, and particularly for their impact on the troops.

Disinformation, suggested by Sun Tsu (1976, p. 146), was also used with the advances in communications in contemporary times. Governments and military commands around the world had recourse to tactics of deception, although Westerners have always been led to assume that this method was the Soviet Union's private preserve. The most recent example of the practice was shown by *Operation Desert Storm*. At some press conferences, reporters were prevented from asking any questions and were merely handed prepared statements. But generally, the military spokesmen seemed to be coached on how to deal with members of the press, and gave evasive and bland answers. After the establishment of the 'media pool', under the all-powerful control of the military command, some of the communiqués were so replete with nebulous or 'doctored' facts, that while the majority of correspondents readily agreed to publish them, some were so enraged that they were privately disparaging of the guidelines. When word got round, and it became obvious that they disregarded them, they were subsequently hindered from flying to zones of action and barred from attending press briefings because of their 'undisciplined behaviour'.

A decade earlier, one of the main features in reports of engagements between the Iranian and Iraqi navies was the flow of conflicting reports and the lack of concrete evidence as to the claims and counterclaims of casualties. Iraqi and Iranian losses of warships, as a result of naval engagements, were both hard to establish. Losses resulting from Iraqi actions were difficult to verify because they were wildly exaggerated by Baghdad and rarely admitted by Tehran. There were several instances of Iranian vessels reported by Iraq as sunk, but which reappeared later in the war. As an illustration, on 9 February

1983, and between 4 and 12 September, then again on 21 November of the same year, Iraq asserted that its navy had sunk or destroyed 16 enemy vessels in all, but Lloyd's reported only two ships damaged.

Also, a number of Iraqi naval units were in Basra when the war began in 1980, and were either destroyed by direct hits or in the crossfire between ground troops, or trapped by the closure of the Shatt al-'Arab waterway – but not damaged in naval engagements. During the period from late 1980 to the end of 1983, a number of ships were hit by both armies, but most were casualties of attacks on other targets. Iraq hit 23 commercial vessels in attacks on Iranian oil terminals and Iran hit five, according to *Proceedings/Naval Review 1985* (p. 162). Lloyd's listed a far larger number of merchant ships detained, damaged or sunk during the same period. As a result of the blockade of Iraqi ports by the Iranian Navy at the outbreak of hostilities, 59 merchant vessels were detained: 31 in the Shatt waterway, 21 in Basra, five in Umm Qasr, and one each in Khor al-Zubair and Abu-Flus. Also, 60 ships were hit, of which nine sank: 18 at Bandar Khomeini, 17 at Khorramshahr, 12 at Umm Qasr, two at Fao, one each in the Shatt, at Kharg and Basra, and one at an unknown location. Of the ships lost, six sank at Bandar Khomeini and three in the Khor Musa channel. Some entries did not mention the weapons used, others cited sea-mines or attacks carried out by ground artillery or aircraft firing rockets or missiles.

The main sources of information available for the war coverage were Tehran's and Baghdad's reports, published or broadcast in their heavily controlled mass media. By their accounts, they destroyed each other's naval forces several times over, and were their reports reliable, in the first few weeks of hostilities, 'Iran [would have] lost more than 76 naval craft of various descriptions, or more than 56% of its inventory, Iraq [would have] lost fewer vessels, 42, but that represents 66% of its naval inventory' (Dowdy, 1981, p. 115). But an Iranian naval officer, who was among a group arrested in 1982, managed to escape to Europe and gave his estimate of the losses. In a press conference on 31 July 1984 in Bonn, he revealed that the IRIN lost one-fifth of its naval units and four-fifths of its helicopters, and that they were short of munitions. He also disclosed that discord within the armed forces, fuelled by ideological divergence, prevailed on two levels: between the regular forces and the *Pasdaran*, on the one hand, and on the other, between individual officers – those appointed by the *ancien régime*, whose loyalty to the Islamic values propagated by the present government was not in evidence, and those commissioned after the revolution (in O'Ballance, 1988, p. 150).

Reporters were not allowed on the scene while action was taking place, but in some instances, international media representatives, war correspondents, defence attachés and diplomats were taken to specific sites, by one or the other of the warring sides. This was usually done to disclaim the other party's allegations of capturing an area, or alternatively, to assert control over newly won territory. In the case of tanker casualties, information was provided by the ships' masters and seamen to Lloyd's or to other national or international merchant marine organizations and insurance companies. However, the Iranian authorities sometimes withheld information regarding their own losses, some of which was publicized later on.

Another characteristic, common to both Iran and Iraq, especially in reporting naval battles, was the dearth of information on the numbers and categories of warships engaging each other, or on weapons used in combat. Types of ships reported to be disabled or sunk were observed operating in other areas, hundreds of miles away – such as Iranian frigates sighted near the Strait of Hormuz after Baghdad reported hitting them at the northern tip of the Gulf during the same week. It is difficult to conclude whether mistaken identification in regard to the class of a ship was by design, or whether because – in the heat of battle – some craft appeared from a distance like others in size, and therefore had the same silhouette. Hence, to evaluate the efficiency of weapons utilized and to appraise the competence of crews proved a perplexing task. Furthermore, Tehran's reports often omitted to name the harbours attacked or to specify the location of battles, thus compounding the difficulty of assessment because of the lack of information on the setting in which the naval engagements took place – in other words, the geographical features of the theatre of operations.

The evaluation of the tactics used by both navies was therefore daunting. The inference drawn from the information available is that surprise attacks seem to have been effective;

but with the absence of confirmed evidence on the number of ships sunk or disabled, it was difficult to ascertain the degree of success. Also, Iraqi combined operations – during which they deployed helicopter gunships with naval vessels in defensive missions – were successful. Why the Iraqis did not mount combined offensive attacks on Iranian naval bases during the first phase of the war, using the element of surprise, and taking advantage of the initial disarray in their enemy's forces in order to neutralize the Iranian edge in seapower, is an open question. Various hypothetical answers were given by strategists, such as Soviet doctrinal rigidity; a rationing of the air force for use later, or the lack of proper training of pilots and the fear, therefore, of high casualties; or simply, the absence of an overall plan for combined offensive operations. The latter reason appears to be the most plausible, and aircraft seem to have been called upon to perform missions on an ad hoc basis only.

A study of newspaper reports by Dowdy established that only three major naval engagements were recorded between the Iranian and the Iraqi navies. During the first hours of the Iran–Iraq War, Iraqi merchant ships sailing on the Shatt were harassed by Iranian gunboats. Units of the Iraqi Navy responded by attacking and destroying five of the vessels. Three more were later shelled and wrecked by Iraqi artillery fire. On the second and third day of the war, minor naval engagements took place, when Iranian units assaulted Iraqi PBs, in the mouth of the Shatt, and hit shore facilities on Fao. In response to an air strike on their base at Khor 'Abdallah, where some of their craft were sheltering, the Iraqis bombed the naval outpost at Khosrowabad, south of Abadan. Baghdad claimed that Iran lost eight more of its gunboats against the loss of one Iraqi PB.

On 24 September 1980, units of the Iranian Navy carried out a major operation and bombarded Iraq's main port, Basra, along with two oil terminals, Khor al-'Amayah and Mina al-Bakr, the offshore facility near Fao. The Iraqis asserted that these battles cost Iran two frigates and seven gunboats, whilst the Iranians claimed that they had destroyed four Iraqi units. The following day, Iranian warships attacked Khor 'Abdallah again. They were engaged by the combined deployment of Iraqi FACs and helicopter-gunships, in an attempt to defend the base. Again, discrepancies appeared between the reports, broadcast by both capitals, as to the number of vessels lost on either side. Iraq proclaimed that the encounter cost Iran three frigates and two gunboats; whilst Iran announced that its navy destroyed eight of Iraq's craft, six of which were missile-launching FACs, and admitted the loss of two gunboats and a minesweeper.

During the last two days of November, the Iraqi and Iranian navies engaged each other in what was considered the main naval battle in the Iran–Iraq War. Iran used warships and commandos in an attempt to capture Mina al-Bakr, but was repulsed by the deployment of Iraqi naval and aircraft – another of the rare instances, during the course of the eight-year war, when combined operations were carried out by the Iraqi forces. Tehran alleged that its forces captured the offshore terminal and sank four enemy missile boats and seven gunboats. Baghdad denied the claim and alleged that its forces successfully repulsed the attack, which resulted in the sinking of four Iranian units, one of them a frigate. In a reprisal attack four days later, Iraqi naval craft attacked and shelled an Iranian naval base at the entrance of the Khor Musa channel, and reported that their units withdrew after setting ablaze four Iranian warships (Dowdy, 1981, pp. 114–17; see also O'Ballance, 1988, pp. 45–6).

The Iran–Iraq War was the latest example of full-scale war between two LDCs engaging each other with albeit limited naval resources. Their hardware was procured from distinctively diverse sources, and their navies adhered to dissimilar military doctrines, but naval battles aroused little interest, although their navies' performance was worth comparing. The Eastern Bloc, headed by the USSR, was Iraq's main supplier until the late 1970s, when a shift appeared, which signalled a desire to start diversifying, by looking towards the West, in addition to retaining the East. It involved France, Denmark and particularly Italy, with the order placed for Cantieri Navali Reuniti. The US and UK were Iran's main suppliers, but smaller orders were also contracted with shipyards in Japan, West Germany, India and Italy, and after the start of the war, with Holland, Sweden and North Korea.

The naval aspect was limited geographically and in time, and naval engagements took place around the northern-most tip of the Gulf and only during the last quarter of 1980. This was due to the disparities between the seapower of both combatants. The geostrategic element, described earlier, enabled Iran to establish a string of ports and naval bases on its extended seaboard, while Iraq's limited coastline, barely a few miles long, made it virtually landlocked. It lacked secure naval bases with defensible peripheries around any of them, and its harbours were conveniently accessible and an easy target for attack and blockade. Therefore, for the duration of the war, Iraq's navy kept a low profile, remaining mainly in the Khor 'Abdallah channel or based at Umm Qasr.

Another factor in the equation was the difference in materiel between the Iraqi and Iranian navies, in both quantitative and qualitative terms. By comparing Tables 5.1 and 5.2, at the onset of the war in 1980, it can be seen that Iraqi naval capabilities in numbers and types of craft were obviously modest in comparison to Iran's. Furthermore, the demographic disparity between both countries allowed Iran to draw on a considerably larger pool for its navy's manpower.

Lastly, with regard to international relations and balance-of-power politics, both superpowers and most major powers consistently perceived Iran as the country to court in the Gulf area. Viewing Iran as the 'prize', it was not only given political and diplomatic backing, but no interference was attempted to curtail the hegemonic role it exercised over the waters of the Gulf. This trend was beneficial to the IIN. According to Admiral Fouad Abou-Zikry, who headed an Egyptian Navy delegation which in January 1976 visited Iranian bases on both the Gulf (Khorramshahr, Bandar Abbas, Bandar Shahpour) and the Caspian Sea (Bandar Pahlevi), the IIN prided itself in having acquired the most up-to-date warships from American shipbuilders, some types of which had not yet been introduced into the USN's own fleets.

The status quo, which was maintained to Iran's advantage, facilitated the procurement of materiel necessary to buttress its armed forces' deterring capabilities with. It enabled its navy to acquire units and weaponry suitable for the preservation of its role as the dominant seapower in the region. In so far that the West was concerned, the trend appeared to start in the mid-1950s, and seemed to be reinforced, following the emergence of an Iraqi regime which espoused policies that were favourable to Moscow and anti-Zionist. The occupation of the three islands in the mouth of the Gulf, the participation of Iranian forces in quelling the Dhofar rebellion in Oman, and aid to Iraqi Kurds to destabilize the Iraqi regime were but a few examples of Iran being encouraged to play the role of the policeman in the area. The tendency continued, especially before, but also after the downfall of the Shah, albeit in an ambivalent manner.

The Iran–Iraq War was multidimensional and included the Tanker War, the missile war on the cities, and minor naval engagements, along with the ground war across the border, which certainly was its main manifestation; it involved more troops and armour, and they definitely played a consequential role in the overall military confrontation. However, from 1984, when Iraq escalated air strikes against Iran's oil export capability, eventually expanding its range of attacks to raid the Sirri and Larak islands by 1986, the focus of attention shifted to the waters of the Gulf.

5.4 IRAQ'S TANKER WAR STRATEGY

The conduct of the Iran–Iraq War, up to late 1983, revealed to the Iraqi government a stark reality: it had been incapable of converting military power into political leverage, and failed to compel Tehran to recognize that it was futile to continue fighting. So far, Iraq's use of 'war as an extension of diplomacy by other means' had been fruitless, and Iran consistently refused to face Iraq across a negotiating table. Not only was Baghdad unable to break the Iranians' resolve, but the war hardened their stance. Tehran rejected several ceasefire proposals, except on its own terms, which entailed installing a government that it could control. This it meant to achieve by either carrying the war into Iraq, or by calling upon Iraqis to remove the regime themselves.

Hopes of a conclusion to the conflict were receding, and the Iraqi leadership seemed to face a bleak future. Considerable anxiety prevailed in Baghdad that with a protracted conflict still in prospect, the spoils of war – in domestic and regional political terms – could be lost. It was conceivable that a political rift among the military elite or popular discontent risked affecting Saddam Hussein's prestige, or threatening the whole *Ba'thi* regime and even endangering his own life. Iraq's President may have also feared a change of attitude among Arab Gulf rulers. Apprehensive of the instability and financial drain caused by the on-going war to their own countries, they could have agreed to compel him to step down, or at least ceased political and diplomatic backing – and more importantly for the continuation of war, withheld financial and logistical support.

Furthermore, the defensive posture adopted by the Iraqi army a few weeks after it initiated full-scale war, could not possibly lead to a military breakthrough, 'limiting itself to reactions to Iranian activity, rather than using its material superiority to dictate the course of the war' (Chubin, 1986, p. 312). The Iraqi leadership had hoped to wear down the Iranian troops by subjecting them to barrages of artillery and tank fire, and causing colossal losses in human lives. However, this had not weakened their resolve to continue fighting, and the attrition did not diminish their leaders' commitment to the continuation of armed conflict. In his earlier calculations, Saddam Hussein did not perceive the revolutionary zeal that animated the Iranians, who were convinced that they were fighting for the defence of Islam. He failed to foresee that the impact of combat was a force that rallied them around their spiritual leader, and that most of them did not doubt him when he declared, on 31 October 1982, that 'war can be as holy as prayer when it is fought for the sake of defending Islam' (Hiro, 1989, p. 92). Up to this point in time, warfare had consolidated the government in Tehran, and this too Saddam Hussein did not anticipate.

The Iraqi high command had underestimated 'Iran's high tolerance for casualties and costs and . . . the symbolic role the war . . . play[ed] in the Islamic republic . . . Iran [wa]s better able politically (with a broader popular base) and economically (with a larger GNP and no foreign debt) to outlast its neighbour' (Chubin, 1986, pp. 312, 316). By 1984, Iraq's GDP was $27 billion, while Iran's was $157.6 billion; and Iraq's debt was estimated at $45 to $50 billion (*Military Balance 1986–87*, pp. 96–7). In contrast, Iran was able to curb its trade deficit of $3.2 billion at the start of the war and turn it into a surplus of $6.3 billion, by 1983, and cut down its foreign debt from

$15 billion, by the end of the 1970s, to $1.1 billion. This it achieved by applying austerity measures and strict import controls, by reducing the defence budget, and improving oil output (Hiro, 1989, p. 111).

Iran's offensives, although costly in terms of human casualties to its own troops, had dislodged Iraq from territorial gains made at the start of military operations in 1980. The Iraqi military commanders had become masters at entrenching their troops in carefully reinforced positions, but, nevertheless, their marked improvement in setting up series of fortified parallel lines of defence did not prevent the Iranian troops from wresting away territories in a salami-slicer method. Iran gradually but steadily gained ground by instalments, as it were, and by 1982, Iraq had been forced to retreat to its original frontiers, except for a few pockets along the border.

The first motive for the adoption of the Tanker War strategy was to make Iran reel under an economic crisis. The most effective way to overcome Iran's refusal to cease warfare, as envisioned by Baghdad, was to maximize pressure on it by weakening its oil-based economy. Unable to procure weapons for the on-going war, nor to import food and consumer goods for the population, the Iranian leadership would then be forced to seek a negotiated settlement for the long-standing territorial dispute. The Iraqi Tanker War strategy, which capitalized on its 'air superiority of 4 or 5:1' sought to bring that superior asset into play and transform it 'into meaningful political leverage' (Chubin, 1986, p. 312). The second tenet of the Tanker War strategy was based on the strong belief that when Iraqi aircraft effectively reduced the quantities of Iranian oil shipped out of the Gulf, Tehran would be more amenable to international persuasion to end the war and negotiate.

> Iraq has thus sought a total, not selective, end to the war. In its quest for this end, Iraq has sought to mobilize international pressure against Iran by indulging in attacks on tankers in the hope that the threat of widening the war might concentrate the minds of the international community, or at least inhibit shippers from buying Iranian oil (Chubin, 1986, p. 316).

Also, the asymmetries in geostrategic depth and manpower were a handicap to Iraq in a protracted war. It had a demographic numerical inferiority of approximately 1:3, as Iran's population stood at 45 200 000 while Iraq's was 15 400 000 (*Military Balance 1986–87*, pp. 96–7). Because of the unwillingness of the leadership 'to engage in the sustained carnage of the early months of the war, a theatre for low-risk prosecution of the war became desirable. One possibility was the Gulf itself' (Daly, 1985, p. 155).

In Danziger's judgement, 'there [wa]s nothing new in Iraq's missile attacks on Gulf shipping. As far back as October 1967, two Russian-made SS-N-20 *Styx* surface-to-surface missiles launched from Egyptian fast attack craft sank the Israeli destroyer Elath' (1985, p. 166; see also Cordesman and Wagner, 1990, pp. 19, 105–6; Nitze *et al.*, 1979, pp. 15, 21; O'Ballance, 1988, p. 204; Till, 1987, pp. 26, 78, 161; and for details see Abou-Zikry, 1986, pp. 259–63, 318). At the time of the incident, on 21 October 1967, Admiral Fouad Abou-Zikry had just been promoted from Head of Naval Operations to C-in-C, Egyptian Naval Forces. The sinking of the 1710-ton *Elath*, the prize of the Israeli Navy, which was to revolutionize contemporary naval strategic thought and impact on the formation and procurement programmes of LDC navies, was his brainchild. The *Elath* episode clearly demonstrated that radar-guided antiship SSMs, launched from small inexpensive FACs, which were less well detected on enemy radars than large units, could cause havoc to large expensive vessels, such as destroyers, frigates, and cruisers. Another advantage is the relative safety of the attacking craft in that she is easily manoeuvrable and could launch her long-range missiles from a distance, and even operate under a protective SAM or AAA security umbrella within her home port.

Iraq already owned four *Osa-1* and eight *Osa-2* FACs fitted with *Styx* SSMs, of which four *Osa-2* were sunk during the Iran–Iraq War (*Jane's 1984/85*, p. 252). These were the same type used in the sinking of the *Elath*. The reluctance of the Iraqi military command to deploy them in operations against Iranian vessels may be attributed to the absence of secure harbours, to which the boats could withdraw after completing their tasks, 'depending on two naval bases whose access is entirely controlled by foreign (and, in one case, hostile) countries' (Danziger, 1982, pp. 97–8). Another theory related to Iraq's marked naval inferiority *vis-à-vis* Iran's seapower, manned by 22 000 sailors in contrast to Iraq's 3300 (O'Ballance, 1988, pp. 20, 29; and see Tables 5.1 and 5.2, where Western naval sources indicated that by 1980, Iranian Navy manpower was 20 000 and that of Iraq 4000).

Since the beginning of operations in 1980, Iran had been able to cripple the port of Basra, blockade Shatt al-'Arab and Umm Qasr, and carry out sea-control and maritime interdiction in the Gulf waters, in the face of the Iraqis. For the remainder of the war, the Iraqi fleet was bottled up in home waters, and could not challenge the Iranian navy. But while the IRIN retained control of the sea, the Iraqi Air Force had the command of the sky above it. The Iranian Air Force had declined to the degree that it was no longer a potent force that could challenge the Iraqis. Its inability to defend its air space and its oil facilities – let alone strike at Iraq's overland oil-export pipelines – demonstrated the extent of its malaise. Hence Iraq realized that its airpower was the only effective force it could rely on to conduct a maritime campaign against Iran's off-shore oil facilities and oil shipments. Using *Super-Etendard*, *MiG*-23BN, *Mirage* F-1 fighters and *Super-Frelon* helicopter-gunships, Iraq relied on its airpower to cripple Iran's lifeline.

5.5 BAGHDAD'S RATIONALE

In 1980, the Iraqi armed forces entered Iran by the logic of both military and political opportunism, though it would also be tempting to argue that Saddam Hussein stumbled into the war through a combination of conspiratorial obsessiveness, megalomania and a sense of being under threat. On the other hand, the Tanker War's main purpose was political, in so far that it was expected to put pressure on Iran, in order to force it to sign and observe an agreement favourable to Iraq's national security interests.

In preparation for the imminent Tanker War, Baghdad undertook a number of diplomatic initiatives to deflect world criticism and improve its economic position. Washington's attitude, so far, was that of deliberate neglect, as the on-going war had neither directly nor seriously threatened its interests. Iraqi officials tried to secure the Reagan Administration's tacit support in August 1983, by admitting that their economy had suffered. In order to bring the war to an end, they explained, the Iranians had to be made to feel that its continuation was becoming too costly for them, too. The Tanker War strategy would become part of an overall process – including sanctions and mediation efforts – of breaking the Iranians' will to continue fighting, and convince them to agree to a ceasefire, followed by negotiations. Subsequently, the US State Department sent its Deputy Assistant Secretary Placke and Ambassador Rumsfeld to Baghdad, in the aftermath of *Hizb-Ullah* bombings in Beirut and explosions in Kuwait. The central themes of the meetings were the demonstration of US support for Iraq, the inadmissibility of an Iranian victory, and arrangements for contingency plans, in the event of an Iranian attack on other Arab Gulf states (Saunders in Naff [ed.], 1985, pp. 72–3).

Iraq's diplomatic forays were successful in other capitals as well. Fearful of the eventual spread of *Shi'i* revolutionary movements in moderate Arab countries as a result of a weakened Iraq, its European creditors agreed to reschedule its debts. Its Gulf Arab supporters increased the flow of funds that sustained Baghdad, and Saudi Arabia and Kuwait underwrote the Iraqi war effort to the tune of $100 million a day, according to an Iraqi contemporary historian (Butti, Interview, 26 December 1994). Moreover, Iraqi negotiators were successful in augmenting their quota within OPEC, and thereby increased the bulk of oil exports. In parallel with the diplomatic initiatives, Iraq undertook economic measures to stretch its budget, by cutting down imports by 40 per cent and shelving part of the development plan (Saunders in Naff [ed.], 1985, pp. 72–3).

Technically speaking, attacks on merchant ships started on 7 October 1980, when Iran's 'artillery sank three foreign freighters and damaged two others in the port of Khorramshahr' (Danziger, 1985, p. 160). But one can assume that this was rather a war accident, as the ships were caught in crossfire, when Iranian troops charged against the advancing Iraqi forces. The Tanker War was different in strategic rationale from previous attacks on shipping, in that it aimed to hit foreign tankers, as well as Iranian vessels, to draw external actors to participate in the war, 'the Western powers in particular . . . in the hope that they would support Iraq or help to bring about a peaceful settlement' (*Strategic Survey 1985–86*, p. 126).

5.6   SADDAM'S PANACEA

Iran's 'stubborn prosecution of the war' had not enabled it to
dictate its terms for peace, and for obvious reasons Saddam
Hussein was obstinately determined to refuse these conditions.
The dilemma made it impossible for him to achieve the peace
he so eagerly sought. This impasse led to 'what many considered to be [Iraq's] trump card'. The campaign to weaken
Iran's economy was planned on the premise that Iraq would
invest in its only serious advantage over Iran, namely, the superiority of its air force (*Strategic Survey 1985–86*, pp. 127–8).
   Chubin made an interesting suggestion as to President
Hussein's motive for using the now-famous *Super-Etendard* low-
level attack fighters armed with *Exocet* missiles, which he
relates to Iraq's 'excessive faith in some technical panacea or
short cut to end the war . . . [and] a touching or desperate
belief that international pressures could be effective in bringing war to an end' (1986, p. 312). In writing these words, he
may have had in mind Saddam Hussein's comment, on 20 June
1982, when he said: 'It is strange that the superpowers . . .
made no tangible effort to stop the war . . . raging in one of
the most dangerous and vital regions of the world' (in Hiro,
1989, pp. 84–5). There is also little doubt that the Iraqi military were impressed by the performance of the French fighter
aircraft during the Falkland/Malvinas war, when the
Argentinians sank the British destroyer *Sheffield* and the container ship *Atlantic Conveyor*, in May 1982.
   France remained Iraq's major Western arms procurer
throughout the war, and sold Baghdad arms worth $5.6
billion, up to 1983. As production of the *Super-Etendard* had
ceased, Paris leased five of its own to Iraq. According to
reports, Deputy Prime Minister Taha Yasseen Ramadan had
been able to persuade the French Government to permit
Iraq to use these against Iran (*Navy International*, May 1984,
p. 310). During the first half of 1983, the French Minister of
Defence, Charles Hernu, was in Baghdad twice, and Iraq's
Foreign Minister, Tariq 'Aziz, visited Paris three times, ostensibly working on the arrangement. The deal, agreed upon in
Baghdad by the French Foreign Minister, Claude Cheysson, on
12 February 1983, was followed by an oil-for-arms barter
arrangement on 23 May. This was confirmed by 'Aziz on 20

July, in a news conference published in the independent French paper *Le Monde*, in which he warned that Iraq was 'determined to threaten Iranian economic and petroleum interests in the Gulf' (24 June 1983). Six days later, the Iranian government vouched 'to destroy the security of the Gulf' if Iraq carried out its threat, and dispatched troops and guns to Sirri Island in September, estimated to be around 600 men by US Satellite Intelligence (Sat-Int). On 5 October, the SDC, chaired by Khomeini for the first time in three years, issued a communiqué in which it signalled its determination to retaliate if Iraq tried to cripple Iran's oil industry. The plan included the closure of the Gulf to international shipping, the destruction of Western oil interests in the region and attacks on the Kirkuk oilfields in northern Iraq. On 9 October, in reaction to these threats, the French government embarked on an airlift of military supplies to Iraq. It dispatched a new consignment of 30 *Exocets*, and an undisclosed number of anti-tank missiles and high-explosive bombs, in addition to 100 AMX-30 tanks. It also brought forward the transfer of the remaining 29 *Mirage* F-1s to spring 1984 (29 *Keesing's 1983*, pp. 32954–5; *Navy International*, January 1984, p. 44; and O'Ballance, 1988, pp. 127–8).

As mentioned earlier, Iraqi officials had travelled to Washington in August 1983 to deliver a brief on the course of the war. They explained that the closure of the Gulf in the face of Iraqi exports of oil had seriously weakened the economy, and that unless Baghdad had the capability of increasing the cost for Tehran, fighting would continue. At the time, arms sales to both countries were embargoed, and the US government's officially declared position on the issue seemed to be firm. Unofficially, America sanctioned the sale of arms to Iraq but discouraged its allies from doing the same for Iran. The French government then approached the Reagan Administration to elicit its support for the *Super-Etendard* deal, arguing that reinforcing Iraqi military capabilities would forestall a defeat that could jeopardize the security of other Arab Gulf countries in the future. In addition, using the 'French-supplied planes and missiles against the oil tankers whose cargo financed the Iranian war effort' may force Iran to desist from prosecuting the war (Rubin, 1987/88, p. 122; and Saunders in Naff [ed.], 1985, p. 72).

International reaction, fuelled by Tehran, led to a delay in the delivery of the aircraft, but they reached their destination on 29 October. Observers assumed that French reticence was overcome by the massacre of their servicemen in Beirut (see Section 3.6). Their transfer was not made public until six days later, and President Hussein confirmed their arrival in an interview published in *Le Matin* (3 November 1983). Iraq had also bought an undisclosed number of radar-homing AM-39 *Exocet* anti-ship missiles. It took the Iraqi pilots about six-months' training in France on the use of these fighters against naval targets. In November, anticipating the start of operations, Iraq warned that it considered the northern tip of the Gulf a war zone. Baghdad had already declared the same area a *Maritime Exclusion Zone* from 12 August 1982. Twice, on 15 August 1983 and 29 January 1984, Iraq renewed its warning and declared the area around Kharg dangerous for all naval vessels (Danziger, 1985, p. 163; Karsh, 1987, pp. 29, 45; King, 1987, pp. 55–6; Brown-Humes, 1988, p. 17; and O'Ballance, 1988, pp. 123–4, 128).

Saddam's centrepiece for the Tanker War was the *Super-Etendard* Mach-1 fighter aircraft, manufactured by Dassault, with a range of 530 miles. 'Given the 300-mile distance from Nassiriyah air base to Kharg Island, this range is more than adequate for the fighter to carry out its assigned missions . . . Despite its incompleteness, the available information reflects the actual missile hits fairly accurately' (Danziger, 1985, pp. 163, 166). The aircraft has two external tanks, although it usually carries one *Exocet*. Manufactured by the French company Aerospatiale, the smart and agile missile has the capacity to 'fire and forget', and dashes towards its target at a low altitude (O'Ballance, 1988, p. 124). As the missile is launched from a distance of 30 to 50 miles, the jet is at times safely out of range of the enemy's anti-air defence systems. (Incidentally, the *Exocet* was most suitably named after a warm sea fish which propels itself out of the sea and skims across the water surface to evade its predators).

Arms transfers to LDCs at war are usually embargoed at the time when they need them most. France made no secret of its strong ties with Iraq and, unlike other global and major powers, made no pretence of neutrality. The embargo on arms shipments, imposed at the start of the war, was lifted by

President Giscard d'Estaing at the end of January 1981. Under pressure from arms manufacturers, he sanctioned the delivery of 60 *Mirage*-F1 fighter-aircraft, fitted with missiles, which Iraq had ordered in 1977. These were part of a $1.6 billion weapons package which also included tanks, anti-tank weapons, radar systems and PBs (O'Ballance, 1988, p. 52).

France's policy was dictated by political, military, strategic and economic considerations. Viewing an Iranian victory as a threat to Western interests and to political stability in the region, it backed the Iraqi war effort at the cost of incurring Tehran's wrath. Paris ensured the financial survival of the regime by providing additional credits to Baghdad, whose outstanding debts to France had reached between $6 to $8 billion by the end of 1983, of which $2 billion were owed to French companies. The government also prevailed on French creditors to renegotiate the terms of their loans, accede to a deferral and allow partial repayment in the form of oil shipments from Saudi Arabia. The reasoning was that by making more loans available to Iraq, Paris would save its initial investment. Helping to maintain Saddam Hussein against the Iranians' aim to remove him would ensure payments, whereas a pro-Tehran successor regime may wish to default – a blow which could devastate the French arms industry (Hiro, 1989, pp. 123–4; Johnstone, 1987, p. 8; and O'Ballance, 1988, p. 52).

Claude Cheysson, France's former Minister of Foreign Affairs, disclosed that 'all Arab countries begged France to sell arms to Iraq, and at the time, the UN and the world community were scared of Iran and Muslim fundamentalism'. Since most Arab countries supported Iraq against Iran, France's stance was certain to better its relations with the Arab world, by demonstrating that a special relationship existed between them and Paris (Cheysson, televised interview, 30 August 1990). France had actively pursued this policy since the 1960s, when President de Gaulle broke off the alliance with Israel and sought a *rapprochement* with Arab countries. His two-fold strategy ensured the flow of oil and access to the lucrative Middle Eastern markets.

Arms sales accounted for 25 per cent of total French exports, of which Iraq's share amounted to 40 per cent. These sales provided France with hard currency earnings, a regular supply of oil, an opportunity to test its hardware in combat and a return on its research and development (R&D) programme which reduced, in actual terms, the costs of domestic procurement of newer generations of weaponry for its own forces. In addition, military cooperation with, and the provision of defence for its ally improved the prospects of French firms for investing in Iraq, or obtaining contracts of a military nature, such as the construction of an anti-aircraft defence system around Baghdad. 'By early 1983 about 1000 French companies were active in the Baathist republic, and between 6000 and 7000 French specialists were based there' (Hiro, 1989, p. 124; also O'Ballance, 1988, p. 128).

Within the framework of its multi-faceted policy, the decision of the French government to lease its own combat aircraft opened up the lucrative prospect of selling more of the expensive *Exocet* missiles to Baghdad. The first batch of these had reached Iraq in 1978, and they were fired from French *Super-Frelon* helicopter-gunships during the early phases of the war. The Iraqi Air Force also owned French *Mirage* F-1 interceptors armed with R-30 or super R-550 *Magic* missiles. Why the Iraqis did not arm their *Mirages* with the *Exocets* which they already had, instead of requesting the *Super-Etendard*, is still unclear. Besides being more sensible, the combination would have been more menacing, being up to date, faster and with a bigger radius. One reason may have been the *Exocet*'s effective performance in the Falklands. The excellent electronic guidance system which operates the missile homes in on the target which is hit with precision. But the Iraqis did eventually equip their fighters and gunships with *Exocets*, and the five *Super-Etendards* were returned to the French Air Force, after the two-year lease expired (King, 1987, p. 56; *Military Balance 1985–86*, p. 175; and O'Ballance, 1988, p. 124).

When they arrived, observers predicted that the combined use of the *Exocet*-fitted *Super-Etendard* would enable Iraq to bring about a slight shift in the military balance. After the ground war had stagnated for the preceding four years, they were of the view that Baghdad would coerce Tehran to accept a ceasefire after affecting its capacity to export oil (29 *Keesing's 1983*, p. 32594).

In fact, Saddam's panacea was viewed as central to the success of the Tanker War strategy.

6 The Ledger – A Chronological Survey of the Conflict

As the foundation of this work is empirical (though within a framework of strategic theory), a set of charts of Iraqi and Iranian hits was compiled, based on Table 1.11, covering the 56 months under study. To appraise the soundness of the Iraqi Tanker War strategy, numerous factors were taken into account to refute or confirm the proposed hypothesis. Cards were prepared in chronological order, bearing events of relevance to the topic, in order to answer the set of questions asked in Chapter 1 and others. Intersections were drawn on the ten charts, coinciding with each month, and incidents were entered on their respective dates. Allowing for a time-lag between cause and response, an investigation was conducted of the causal relationship between Iraqi and Iranian attacks on shipping in the Gulf and developments elsewhere. The analysis of diplomatic, political and military events related to the Tanker War, within the domestic, regional, and international settings, determined the degree to which the Iraqi escalatory strategy succeeded (see Charts A6.1–A6.10).

6.1   1984 – THE CURTAIN RISES ON THE TANKER WAR

6.1.1   January 1984

On the second day of the year, an Iraqi military communiqué announced that an aircraft destroyed five enemy naval vessels south of Bandar Khomeini. Lloyd's only logged the general dry cargo *Iran Emamat* (LT, FX), whose accommodation aft, bridge and crane were damaged by fire after the vessel was struck by a missile off Khor Musa. After discharging her cargo at Booshehr, she was towed to Bandar Abbas, then to Gadani

Beach where she was sold and broken up. Iraq confirmed Iran's claim that it lost two aircraft during the engagement.

Coinciding with the start of the campaign on tankers, Reagan provided Iraq's leadership with open backing, declaring an Iranian victory 'contrary to US interests' (King, 1987, p. 53). At the same time, Israel threatened a preemptive strike against Saudi Arabia, if it proceeded with a planned West German arms package deal. The kingdom's extended Red Sea coast and its dependence on sea trade made it especially vulnerable to potential Israeli air and naval attacks (Taha, 1984, pp. 26–7 and [2], p. 38). Therefore, the expansion and renovation of GCC navies and land-based defensive systems became a high priority, bearing in mind Israel's preemptive attacks on Egypt's, Lebanon's and Iraq's nuclear reactors (see Section 3.6).

6.1.2   February 1984

In Iraq and Iran, ground war activities meshed with other tactics, with varying degrees of success. Iraq attacked Kharg and declared an exclusion zone around it for the fourth time, used *Exocets* against naval targets and CW to repel Iranian troops between Basra and 'Amarah (Daly, 1985, pp. 150, 154–6), and the reciprocal missile and bombing war on cities ignited again, after Baghdad admitted receiving a consignment of Soviet *Scud-B* SSMs. A UN-mediated halt to the targeting of urban areas took effect in June (O'Ballance, 1988, pp. 153–5).

Three Cypriot freighters may have been the first targets attacked by Iraqi *Super-Etendards* firing *Exocets*, on the first day of the month, despite the announcement of their first combined operation later. The bulk carrier *City of Rio* (LT, CTL) and the two dry cargo ships *Neptune* (LT, SER) and *Skaros* (LT, FX, CTL), were hit near Bandar Khomeini. One was towed, sold and broken up; the second sailed for Bulgaria; and the third was tugged to Bandar Khomeini after the fire was extinguished in the engine room, where the missile lodged. Lloyd's, however, were unsure whether the *City of Rio* was damaged by a missile or a mine, while Danziger and *Navy International* concluded that she struck a mine and grounded, and the latter confirmed that the *Skaros* and the *Neptune* were damaged by *Exocets*. After a fortnight, the Liberian bulk carrier

Al Tariq (LT, FX, HM, SER) was struck by a missile while transiting the Khor Musa channel, though Danziger placed the attack at the port of Booshehr (1985, p. 165; see also *Navy International*, 1984, April, p. 232 and July, table p. 433). The explosion was followed by fire in the steering flat. When it was extinguished, she was towed to Booshehr. Two years later, on 23 February 1986, she was damaged by a missile, five miles south of Kharg (Lloyd's).

In Iran, all air and naval forces were ordered on maximum alert to obstruct passage through Hormuz of 'hostile' (Western) naval forces. In response, USN units patrolling the area sailed to the Strait to ensure that it remained open. Iranian threats to close the Gulf if the Iraqis continued their attacks on shipping were countered by thinly-veiled warnings by Washington (Daly, 1985, pp. 150–1). On the 21st, the White House Spokesman, Larry Speakes, emphasized US resolve to keep the Gulf open to trade, and confirmed press reports that a naval task force, headed by the aircraft carrier USS *Midway*, was deployed in the northern Arabian Sea. Five days later, the Defense Department announced that a destroyer used machine-guns and flares to ward off an approaching Iranian aircraft over-flying the area around the Strait, following an announcement that no aircraft would be allowed within a circle of five miles surrounding any USN vessel (see Section 3.6). The Pentagon drew up contingency plans to deal with the emergency, including the use of *Super Stallion* CH 53E minesweeping helicopters. And Britain agreed to allow *Armilla Patrol* vessels to escort convoys of merchantmen to neutral Gulf ports, and prevent attempts to obstruct the free passage of ships if Iran carried out its threat. Following the GCC ministers' concerns over the closure of the Strait, Reagan pledged US commitment to keep it open. In the meantime, Athens' Mercantile Marine Ministry warned Greek-owned ships to avoid the Gulf (30 *Keesing's 1984*, p. 33057; and *Navy International*, April 1984, p. 232).

In retaliation against Iraqi attacks on tankers and cities, Iran deployed large formations of troops along the front, launching three *human wave* offensives: *Wal Fajr-5* (Dawn) in the Mehran area, *Wal Fajr-6* near Dehloran, and *Operation Khaybar* in the Hawizeh Marshes. After initial successes, they were driven back by Iraqi artillery and tanks, supported by helicopter-gunships and combat aircraft. Back in Tehran, the Ministry of *Jihad* was formed to separate regular troops and volunteers, and restore discipline among the squabbling forces. Also, as a necessary requirement for the ongoing war, some of the professional cadres who had been dismissed or jailed were won back, but their role was still downplayed for political reasons (O'Ballance, 1988, pp. 142–6, 150–1).

The Tanker War was 'taking a serious turn for the worse', and its potential impact could be enormous on oil-producing and consuming countries; however, the departure of the multinational forces from Lebanon 'overshadowed' this news (*Navy International*, April 1984, p. 232; and see Section 3.6).

6.1.3 March 1984

The capture of the strategic island of Majnoon blocked Iraq's access to yet another area of abundant oil reserves. Its seizure was a testimony to the continued success and dynamism of the Iranians in ground battles, and to the failure of Iraq's three-pronged tactic. The outcome prompted Iraq to introduce forced recruitment to expand manpower and increase the number of divisions. It also became an incentive to further stimulate the Tanker War, especially so, after a UN report condemned the use of chemical weapons but failed to name the culpable (O'Ballance, 1988, pp. 149–50; King, 1987, Appendix I, p. 71; and see Chart A6.1 and Table 1.11).

Iraq's desperate bid to internationalize the war led it to attack a vessel of a neutral country for the first time, and two belonging to allies. Three of the four loaded freighters, struck whilst sailing in a fifteen-ship convoy under naval protection from Booshehr to Bandar Khomeini, were total losses. The Indian general dry cargo *APJ Ambika* (LT, FX, FD, SER), owned by Apeejaf Lines and under charter to Iran, carried a cargo of lead and machinery. Her engine room caught fire after the missile struck a hatch, then penetrated into the engine room bulkhead. Unable to fight the fire, her 35 hands abandoned her, but were rescued by an escort warship. She and the *Charming* sank (for the political and military impact in London, see Section 7.2). The Turkish freighter *Sema-G* (LT, FX, CTL), with a shipment of iron ingots, caught fire after an explosion in the accommodation and the cargo bay. She was towed by a tug, unloaded, then sold and broken up. Two of her seamen died and the 16 remaining hands abandoned ship, but were rescued. Eight Iranian soldiers were also reported killed during the attack. Iraq claimed seven of the ships were 'enemy naval targets', but in fact, only the *Iran Eslam* bulk carrier flew the Iranian flag (Lloyd's; *Navy International*, 1984, April, p. 233, May, p. 310 and July, table p. 433; and Hiro 1989, p. 129).

Warnings against shipping multiplied in Baghdad and Tehran, in what appeared as a contest of wills in the atmosphere of mounting hostilities. By the middle of the month, the Iraqis announced their intention to hit any ships bound for Bandar Khomeini and Booshehr, and on the 27th, for the first time, a war communiqué explicitly named the type of aircraft and weapon wielded against a target in the Tanker War. Iraq revealed the use of *Super-Etendards* firing *Exocet* missiles in attacks on Kharg and tankers in its proximity, hitting the *Filikon L* (see Chapter 5). The airraids convinced some shipping companies not to call at Iranian ports; however, despite repeated hits, very little damage was reported on Kharg, according to US Sat-Int (Daly, 1985, p. 156; Hiro, 1989, p. 129; and O'Ballance, 1988, pp. 154–5).

Two days later, two bulk carriers were damaged off Bandar Khomeini. The Greek *Iapetos* (LT, FX, SER) was first hit from the air; then a land-based missile ploughed through her engine room, causing fires to sweep through there and the accommodation, and her 16-man crew abandoned her. She was towed to Dubai, sold and broken up. Of the three vessels attacked between 27 and 29 March, only the freighter *Iran Dahr* (LT, SER), struck by missiles in Khor Musa, was an 'enemy naval target' (Lloyd's; Daly, 1985, pp. 157–8; Danziger, 1985, pp. 161, 163; Hiro, 1989, p. 129; 30 *Keesing's 1984*, p. 33058; Karsh, 1987, p. 29; and *Navy International*, July 1984, p. 432 and table p. 433).

The scare caused by the Tanker War started, with Indian and Japanese governments advising ships flying their flags not to enter the Gulf, even in protected convoys. The shipping companies, determined to avoid losses to their fleets, joined the Greeks, who had banned their tankers from the Gulf less than a month earlier. As Japan was Iran's major buyer, the Iraqi objective to attract international reaction and lessen

Iran's revenues proved successful (*Navy International*, May 1984, p. 310; Daly, 1985, p. 156).

Iraq's call for Egypt's return at the ICO summit in January, was followed by a proposed formula for its re-entry into the Arab League, during talks conducted in Baghdad by its Deputy Prime Minister. It came after Tariq 'Aziz broke ranks with Arab consensus and visited Cairo in July 1983 (*Strategic Survey 1988–89*, p. 180). One should recall that at the Baghdad Arab summit President Hussein had viewed the Egyptian–Israeli peace agreement as a sell-out. Until the invasion of Kuwait, Cairo and other capitals considered Iraq the Eastern flank of the Arab World and the defender of Arab interests in the Gulf. By contrast, on the whole, Iranian–Egyptian relations were strained, except for short intervals: once, when their monarchies allied by marriage; then in the 1970s, relations flourished, and both states co-sponsored a proposal for a nuclear-free Middle East to be permanently recorded on the UN General Assembly agenda, on 15 July 1974; and two years later, the Shah agreed to furnish Egypt's navy with hovercraft. The breaking-point with the IRI came with Egypt's invitation to the ailing Shah, who died on 27 July 1980 and was given a state funeral with full military honours by President Sadat – though few of the monarch's allies attended his burial alongside Egypt's monarchs. *Vis-à-vis* each other, Cairo's and Tehran's prevailing perceptions remain that of regional rivalry.

The eagerness shown to readmit Egypt into the Muslim and Arab folds was based on the potential benefits that Iraq hoped to gain by renewed bilateral relations. Baghdad could depend on Cairo's diplomatic backing, once it had regained its previous leading political rank; draw on Egypt's large reservoir of skilled and unskilled labour to compensate for gaps caused by conscription, and draft some into its own army; and use the expertise of strategists and pilots to design new tactics and train its own pilots. The resumption of relations also opened the prospects for formal and clandestine trade. As we now know, Saddam Hussein established a secret international procurement organization, geared to provide Iraq with a bomb-making potential; fuses, shells and rocket parts were seized in the late 1980s and early 1990s in custom raids in Western air and sea ports. In addition to the transactions that Iraq arranged officially, the network assembled arms-manufacturing tools and purchased military hardware. It was likely that Egypt could either provide arms, or act as a conduit or end-user for Iraqi purchases of military materiel.

Previous months witnessed active American involvement in the area, whereby Washington conducted a *realpolitik* strategy. It repeatedly proclaimed its neutrality, stated its interests and clear objectives in the Gulf, hand in hand with a concealed agenda, the blueprint of which combined the leaning towards Iraq, with the yet undisclosed licensing of arms sales. During the first quarter of the year, the Kremlin reinvigorated its own engagement in the Gulf, in a policy that equally demonstrated a pragmatic approach. In order to maintain friendly relations with the two countries at war with each other, the USSR performed a balancing act, whereby, on the one hand, it confirmed its acceptance to fund an Iranian nuclear reactor (Daly, 1985, p. 150), and on the other, it discussed nuclear co-operation with Baghdad (O'Ballance, 1988, p. 159). It also dispatched a delegation, including arms export officials, granted $2 billion 'in long-term loans for economic projects', and resumed deliveries of war supplies. To signal its support for Tehran, Baghdad's closest non-Arab ally remained neutral and curtailed arms shipments to Iraq from 1980 to 1982, in keeping with its official policy of resolving conflicts peacefully and opposing regional wars. When Iranian troops crossed into Iraqi territory, the ban was partial up to 1984; then it was totally lifted, and weapons flowed to Baghdad through the Red Sea port of 'Aqaba. For the duration of the war, Jordan's only harbour served as entrepot for goods bound for Iraq, and Soviet ships delivered their cargoes of hardware at a daily rate of nearly 200 lorry-loads. At the end of March 1984, over 20 ships were seen unloading (King, 1987, p. 49; *Navy International,* July 1984, p. 432; and see Section 4.4).

6.1.4 April–May 1984

While two rounds of parliamentary elections to Iran's second *majlis* were conducted in April and May, resulting in a relative advantage for the 'fundamentalists' over the 'conservatives' and independents, the US and UK governments agreed to suspend shipments of chemical ingredients to Iraq, after the publication of the UN report on its use the previous month; it took West Germany until 7 August to follow suit. But the two allies differed on war-related links with Iran. On 2 April, the UK government confirmed that it was training Iranians in Britain 'on anti-aircraft control systems', and in the face of US government objections to the export of spareparts for Iran's *Chieftain* tanks, *Rapier* and *Tiger Cat* missiles, and Rolls-Royce aircraft engines for its *Phantoms*, Britain replied that it considered them as 'non-lethal', and therefore not covered by the embargo (O'Ballance, 1988, pp. 150, 151, 153).

In the unfolding Tanker War, Saudi ships found themselves under attack from both Iran and Iraq. Tehran started retaliating against its enemy's Gulf Arab allies, particularly Saudi Arabia and Kuwait, and Iraqi pilots increasingly shifted their sphere of operations southward to Kharg and flew as far as Booshehr, hitting two Saudi tankers, the *Safina Al Arab*, loaded with oil from Kharg to France, and the *Al Ahood* (see Chapter 5). Throughout its war against Iran, Iraq was given political, diplomatic, logistical and – most importantly – financial support by the UAE, Kuwait and Saudi Arabia. However, in early May, Saddam Hussein threatened that tankers near Kharg would be attacked even if they belonged to 'Arab brothers', and warned them not to trade with Iran. Accordingly, at an OAPEC meeting in Kuwait, Sheikh Ahmad Zaki Yamani, who served as Saudi Oil Minister from 1962 to December 1986, struck a note of caution about tankers sailing to Kharg (*Navy International*, July 1984, p. 434; and *Wall Street Journal*, 10 May 1984). Also, with Iran's restraint to escalate activities in the Gulf, the only way left for Iraq was to hit Saudi targets, and draw the US into the conflict, assuming that its fleet would rush to assist its ally.

Iraqi aircraft mainly kept to a confined zone during the first two months. Now they exhibited more daring. Out of eight targets hit, three were at Kharg and one further south at Booshehr. This could either be ascribed to the pilots' increased confidence in handling their newly acquired fighters, or to the fact that they were still flying *Super-Frelon* helicopters armed with *Exocets* during the earlier phase, something they had been doing since the onset of the Iran–Iraq War. This meant that they started attacks with the French jet fighters on the day the military command announced the news. The 500-mile combat radius of the helicopter-gunships would allow them to fly from Nassiriyah air-base to beyond Kharg. But on a long-range mission, they could have become an easy prey for Iranian interceptor-planes and would hardly survive an aerial dogfight. Therefore, they possibly preferred to deploy them at locations closer to their home base, against targets in Bandar Khomeini and Khor Musa.

13 May marked the day when Iran launched its retaliation in the Tanker War, 18 weeks after Iraq started it. Ceasing to be passive while Iraqi hits nibbled at its economy, it struck back at its enemy's allies. In what seemed at first an impressive debut, Iran initiated its counterattack by hitting three tankers in three days, owned by Kuwait and Saudi Arabia. None sustained CTL. The Kuwaiti tanker *Umm Casbah* (LT, RPD), loaded with 76 560 tonnes of crude, was the first target of an F-4 *Phantom*, 85 miles north of Bahrain. The slightly damaged central tank was repaired in Bahrain, and she sailed to her destination, two days later. The following day, another Kuwaiti tanker caught fire after two of her wing tanks were struck by a missile, leaving a hole, gaping more than five square meters. After the blaze was extinguished, the *Bahrah* (LT, FX, SER), which was in ballast, was temporarily patched in Kuwait, then sailed to Dubai to enter a dry dock for further repairs on the accommodation section, the pump room and the navigation structure. Two days later, the Saudi tanker *Yanbu Pride* (LT, FX, SER), partly loaded with 128 000 tonnes of crude, was hit five miles north of al-Jubail. The missile punched a one-metre cavity in a starboard tank, and the fire spread on deck. Repairs started in Rio de Janeiro six weeks later. The Kuwaiti tanker *Kazimah* (LT, FX, RPD), sailing in ballast, was the next Arab-owned missile casualty. The fire in two of her tanks was extinguished by the crew and she limped to Bahrain on the same day, and back to Kuwait on 11 June. A few weeks earlier, two ships were accidentally damaged during hostilities with Iraq. The South Korean tug/supply ship *Heyang Ilho* (LT, FX, FD, SER) sank in Marjan Field in 45–50 metres, and was later raised by a crane vessel. She was taken first to Ras al-Ghar, then to Bahrain, thence to Gadani beach, where she was sold and broken up. On 3 April, the Indian general dry cargo *Varuna Yan* (LT, FX, SER) caught fire after being struck by a missile in the Shatt al-'Arab estuary (Lloyd's; *Navy International,* July 1984, p. 434 and table p. 433; and Danziger, 1985, p. 164). Whether a connection exists

between the degree of damage sustained by a tanker in a missile attack and the fact that she is loaded, partly loaded or in ballast would be interesting to know. In the first three cases above, the loaded tanker continued her voyage two days later, after minor repairs, and the two tankers in ballast or partly loaded were more seriously damaged. It may appear logical that a missile's thrust into a full tank of crude is blunted, and therefore causes less destruction, while a missile piercing into an empty tank, but for vapours, causes far more devastation. But the case of the *Kazimah* defied this judgment.

Once Iran started retaliating after the IRGCN became operational, the Tanker War became a serious threat to the area (see Section 7.1). To defend the kingdom from Iranian and Israeli attacks (see Section 6.1.1), King Fahd, who had urgently requested 1200 US *Stingers,* was only granted 400 missiles and 200 launchers (*Strategic Survey 1984–85,* p. 69), and warned that he would search for other sources. However, the American president made two alternative proposals to the Saudi monarch, both of which were rejected. He indicated his willingness to grant air cover and dispatch US forces if they were invited, reasoning that the arrival in the Gulf of a few naval units would have a great impact, especially if provided with air protection (King, 1987, p. 53; and *Navy International,* July 1984, p. 434). The impression was gaining ground in the area that he was hopeful to have US access to naval and air bases in the Gulf, or that his patience was running out because the Saudi deal was reduced. Unable to intervene directly, Reagan decided to support Iraq officially, with a public display of understanding for its tactics, coupled with a condemnation of Iran. Seen from Tehran, the apparent arbitrariness provoked its suspicion about US motives. Was the policy designed as a reprimand to Iran? Was it meant to persuade it to agree to a ceasefire and start negotiations? Or was it a convenient way to fan the flames of hatred against its style of Islamic government?

Emboldened by Washington's open expression of support, and to increase pressure on Iran, Saddam Hussein disclosed that Baghdad received information on Iranian ground-troop movements from US Sat-Int (King, 1987, p. 53). However, others believed that US covert negotiations with Tehran, followed by substantial arms sales in 1985–6, were in fact important psychological factors in the ongoing war; they boosted the

Iranian troops' morale and offset the US–Iraq intelligence association and Washington's 'military, diplomatic, or economic support' for Iraq (Axelgard, 1987, pp. 124–6).

6.1.5 June–July 1984

International, regional and local developments became hectic. Spotlights were first on New York, with the adoption of SCR 552. It requested – as had SCR 540 on 31 October 1983 – a halt to raids on civilian centres, condemned attacks on Saudi and Kuwaiti ships, and called for free navigation in the Gulf (*Navy International,* January 1984, p. 44; Daly, 1985, p. 160; and Karsh, 1987, p. 37). In Washington, Assistant Secretary of State Richard Murphy, the first American official to explicitly express US policy towards the Gulf conflict, said that a victory by Iran or Iraq was not militarily feasible nor strategically desirable (King, 1987, p. 53). Asked about the statement six years later, he confirmed it during a personal communication (Murphy, Interview, 8 March 1990).

In the Gulf area, Saudi pilots shot down two IRI *Phantoms,* and Riyadh received the first consignment of US *Stinger* launchers and missiles. A similar request by Kuwait was blocked, and it turned to Moscow instead, signing a $325 million arms deal (*Strategic Survey 1984–85*, p. 69; 'Abdel-Halim, 1986, pp. 11, 44 and 1985, p. 67; Daly, 1985, p. 150; O'Ballance, 1988, p. 155; and King, 1987, pp. 52–3). Across the Gulf, Tehran prepared for an offensive, planned for the month of Ramadan, and news was released that Khomeini suffered a heart attack, followed by an eight-hour coma. Intertwining diplomacy with military activities, an Iranian commission visited Moscow, and Tehran hosted a return visit by the highest-ranking Soviet delegation since 1979. Though these were signs that relations warmed up, Iran failed to persuade its neighbour to the north to halt arms exports to Iraq. This did not rule out the possibility that they broached topics, beneficial to both countries, such as the export of Iranian gas, reduced by Moscow over differences on the Afghan issue. Tehran may have also sought Moscow's good offices to exert leverage on its ally – a role that presented the USSR with the opportunity to become a major player in the Gulf, alongside the US (*Time,* 17 August 1987, pp. 4–10; 'Abdel-Halim, 1985, pp. 29, 79; and King, 1987, p. 50).

In a clear challenge to the Council's resolution, Baghdad staged more attacks in the Gulf, and figures for the year showed its highest score during the month of July (see Chart A6.2 and Table 1.11). As more and more of its aircraft took to the air, one-third of the jetties at Kharg were damaged. The island accounted for over 80 per cent of oil exports, and the hits were effective in reducing them dramatically to 0.7mbd (Aryan, 1989, p. 183; and Danziger, 1985, p. 160). Thus Iraq managed to partly meet one of its intermediate aims of cutting back Iran's revenues. With increased attacks, insurance premiums peaked on merchant ships sailing to the war risk zone, estimated at between 7.5 and 12 per cent for hulls and five for cargo (O'Ballance, 1988, p. 157; 'Abdel-Halim, 1985, p. 9; and *Navy International*, July 1984, p. 435).

Hans-Dietrich Genscher arrived in Tehran – the first visit by a senior Western dignitary to post-revolutionary Iran. West Germany was the only major Western country to maintain full diplomatic relations with Iran, and in September 1980, its Foreign Minister had hosted talks between US Deputy Secretary of State Warren Christopher and Sadeq Tabatabai, Khomeini's aide, for the release of American embassy hostages. In the years to come, Bonn developed its relations with Tehran, and supplanted the US as its biggest trading partner (*Time*, 11 January 1988). The visit came as a result of a policy shift, whereby Tehran concluded that it had to cultivate its links with the West, as the policy of isolation worked against it. This was a signal that it was firmly set on the path of joining the outside world, after it realized that Iraqi hits against neutral shipping and its use of chemical weapons did not attract world condemnation. Its launch of the diplomatic counteroffensive clearly suggested Iraq's tactic was proving effective.

6.1.6   August–October 1984

Iran and Iraq were waging an economic war against each other, in which oil became the main tool. But both were determined to continue supplying their coffers with foreign earnings by resolving their difficulties by whatever means available – Iran by organizing convoys of shuttle tankers that hugged the coast, and Iraq by increasing overland oil exports. To counter the refusal of ships to enter the Gulf, Tehran announced plans to tranport oil away from the preferred 'hunting area' of Iraqi pilots to the lower Gulf, beyond the reach of their aircraft. By having its warships escort the chartered tankers 630 miles southward and guarding them with shore-based missiles, Iran presented itself to the international community as a credible protector of neutral shipping. Tankers that ceased to lift oil from Kharg could thus be persuaded to make the shorter and relatively safer journey from Hormuz to Sirri – a clear set-back for Iraq. Succeeding the Iraqi–Turkish deal to build a second pipeline a month earlier, an Iraqi–Saudi commission unveiled plans in September to link up an Iraqi pipeline with the trans-Saudi Petroline (King, 1987, p. 45; O'Ballance, 1988, pp. 151, 158, 171; and Karsh, 1987, p. 30).

Following the failure of the *Khaybar* thrust in August, the IRI Defence Minister was sacked, and while Iraq held parliamentary elections in late October, Iran launched *Operation Wal Fajr-7*, around Mehran in the Iranian Kurdish area. In the central sector, its troops routed the Iraqis' and re-took parts of the disputed border territory. Gaining ground, after seizing Fao and Majnoon in previous operations, Tehran's foreign policy was able to release itself from the siege mentality, and Khomeini issued a statement allowing relations with all governments except 'a few'. Setting in motion the pattern established in May 1983, Turkish troops crossed again into northern Iraq to pursue the Kurds (King, 1987, pp. 25, 45; O'Ballance, 1988, pp. 151, 153; and see Section 3.6).

In what was becoming standard Iraqi behaviour after any military or diplomatic reverses, its hits against tankers intensified, matching the figures in March, the second-highest after July. These actions could also be regarded as a last-ditch pounding to discourage foreign tanker owners from leasing their vessels to Iran for the planned shuttle.

6.1.7   November–December 1984

November 1984 was the first lull in the Tanker War. The subdued behaviour of both adversaries seemed related to their foreign policies. US–Iraqi diplomatic relations, severed by Baghdad over US backing for Israel in June 1967, were resumed towards the end of the month, and Iraq was careful not to jeopardize the back-channel negotiations that were under way with Washington. Iran, whose spiritual leader had announced that the country was on its way to improve relations with the outside world, did not wish to be cited as the guilty party in the maritime conflict. By ceasing attacks, Tehran had a better chance to frustrate Iraq's objectives to gain more diplomatic and military support and prod the US to enhance their naval presence in the Gulf.

The GCC announced its decision to establish a rapid deployment force, in case the war between their two powerful neighbours spilled over the borders. The declaration was followed in early December by Iranian assurances that no attempt would be made to close Hormuz or attack states that supported Iraq – motivated by Tehran's firm intention to thaw relations with the world community.

Iraqi attacks resumed in December, albeit moderately, while Iran's increased radically, reaching the year's highest, in reaction to Iraq's diplomatic triumph. Except in May, its response to Iraqi attacks were few, and missiles were the prevalent medium. The assaults on vessels trading with Arab harbours usually ranged between one and two a month, but increased to six in December. Missiles struck the Greek cargo *Aegis Cosmic* (LT, SER), loaded with agricultural products, and four tankers: the Kuwaiti *Tariq* (LT, FX, SER) and the Bahamian *B T Investor* (LT, RPD), both in ballast; the Greek *Ninemia* (LT, FX, SER, HM and LT, FX, CTL), also in ballast but hit twice in two days; and the Indian *Kanchenjunga* (LT, FX, SER), loaded with 258 000 tonnes of crude. The *Ninemia* was sold and broken up, while the other four vessels suffered more or less serious damage, but were repaired and returned to service – the *Aegis Cosmic* sailing under the new name of *Alpha Cosmic* (Lloyd's).

Iran's oil exports dropped briefly during the year, but Iraqi hits failed to halt them altogether. These were sufficient, so far, for its war effort. However, the IRI budget for 1984–5 disclosed falling revenues and imports, and reduced Tehran's ability to launch major offensives, or to purchase arms to compensate for the depletion caused to its stockpile. This proved that Iraq's strategy had some success. Given that Saudi Arabia was partly funding Iraq's war costs, it is also worth noting that Riyadh was forced to draw heavily on its financial reserves, after oil revenues dropped from $114 billion in 1982, to $74 billion the year after, then to $53 billion in 1984 ('Abdel-Halim, 1985, p. 9; and King, 1987, p. 26).

During the first year of the Tanker War, both superpowers seemed inclined towards Iraq. Whilst Baghdad and Moscow celebrated the 12th anniversary of their treaty, the USSR resumed arms transfers to its ally and increased Iraqi and Saudi oil imports. It discontinued those from Iran, in spite of the exchange of diplomatic visits in June. The US launched *Operation Staunch*, a campaign to dissuade its Western allies from selling arms to Iran, and granted Iraq $840 million commodity credits for food. The loans were allowed to increase beyond $5 billion, used for the purchase of arms and the development of arm-making capabilities, as subsequently revealed by the inquest into the dealings of the Atlanta branch of the Italian Banca Nazionale del Lavoro (BNL). France also continued weapon sales to Iraq, including 30 new *Mirage* F-1s. But despite Iraq's improved position by the end of the year, Iran still retained an edge in the large reservoir of highly indoctrinated manpower, ready to offer themselves for the defence of their new ideology (Daly, 1985, pp. 150, 155; Cockburn, 1992; Darwish, 1993; *Independent*, 10 December 1992 and 14 July 1993; and Axelgard, 1987, p. 124).

6.2   1985 – ON STAGE AND BACKSTAGE TUG-OF-WAR

6.2.1   January–February 1985

Unlike the previous one, the beginning of this year was not auspicious for the Iraqi regime. In the first such undertaking since 1980, Iraqi troops embarked on two small-scale offensives against Majnoon and near Qasr-e-Shirin, in the central sector, towards the end of January. They failed to recapture the southern island and merely regained a toehold which they lost later, and on the whole, both ground operations were unsuccessful. On 22 February, a political initiative launched by the Iraqi government nine days earlier was also in vain, when the PUK and *al-Da'wah* spurned an offer to grant an amnesty to all 'illegal' opposition parties, even those in exile.

In the Gulf, Iran scored its highest hits for the year in February (see Chart A6.3 and Table 1.11). Four missiles struck the Kuwaiti container *Al Manakh* (LT, SER), with a cargo of aluminium ingots, causing a four-metre opening in the port side, and another missile hit the Sri Lankan *Royal Colombo* (LT, RPD), loaded with 125 000 tonnes of crude. The Saudi tanker *Mohammed Al Bakri X* (LT, RPD), in ballast, was attacked in the southern Gulf by a light aircraft, dropping an explosive device which detonated 600 yards off the starboard bow. And the *Captain John G P Livanos* was attacked by mistake (see Chapter 5). The case of the Saudi tanker was the first mention by Lloyd's of the platform used in an Iranian attack.

Also during February, Iran embarked on the Kharg–Sirri shuttle. Using its own as well as chartered tankers, it attempted to foil any victory that Baghdad may claim from stepping up airraids on Kharg, especially after its oil output dropped because of intensive attacks. By bringing the crude down the Gulf and closer to Hormuz, the newly launched service countered the neutral ships' plans to avoid entering the Gulf altogether, and emphasized Tehran's determination to present the country as one which limits any damage that may befall international shipping. As a result, its oil output rebounded, and Iraqi successes proved short-lived.

6.2.2 March 1985

In defiance of the shuttle service, Iraq claimed hitting 30 Iranian tankers since the beginning of the year, but Lloyd's registered only 15, with the highest score this month. While it resorted to muscle-flexing in the Gulf, it declared a *Military Exclusion Zone* over Iranian airspace, and sparked anew the war of the cities. Its pilots rocketed Bakhtaran (formerly Kermanshah), a major city in western Iran, Bandar Khomeini, on the northern tip of the Gulf, Borujerd in Lorestan province, and the provincial capital of Qarvin. The operations involved 415 aircraft and 320 helicopter-gunship sorties – the most massive mission since the start of the war. Iranian jet fighters retaliated by raiding residential areas around and in Baghdad, and Saddam City, a poor residential neighbourhood on Basra's western edge. It escalated eight days later by firing the first *Scud-B* missile at Baghdad, after forces of *Operation Badr* across the Hawizeh Marshes were driven back by Iraqi counterattacks. Hundreds of their civilians were killed or wounded, according to both official news agencies. In a show of solidarity, King Hussein and President Husni Mubarak flew to Baghdad, the first such visit by an Egyptian leader since 1979 (King, 1987, p. 43; *International Herald Tribune*, 12 and 16–17 March 1985; *Strategic Survey 1984–85*, p. 69; Karsh, 1987, p. 31; and O'Ballance, 1988, pp. 160–4, 169).

Although embassies had not recommended evacuation, Alitalia and Lufthansa airlines organized flights for their nationals fleeing the outbreak of rocket attacks (*International Herald Tribune*, 16–17 March 1985), and airlifted most of the evacuees out of Tehran by April. At UN headquarters, the SC's President voiced his alarm over the targeting of civilian areas on 5 March, followed by another statement ten days later. Using the *Scud* strike on his capital to attract worldwide sympathy and appeal for mediation, Iraqi Foreign Minister Tariq 'Aziz called for direct peace negotiations under the aegis of the UN Secretary-General. He also suggested the creation of a UN Force to oversee the truce, since similar ceasefires had collapsed before, and rejected an appeal by Tokyo to halt the war on cities (*International Herald Tribune*, 12 March 1985; see other calls for a UN patrol in Ramazani, 1988, p. 87; and McNaugher and Richardson in Taylor and Francis, 1988, pp. 303, 312–13; and in Sections 6.4.1, 6.4.7 and 7.1).

Despite a plea by the Indian prime minister's emissary, the onslaught on urban areas continued. Six *Scud* strikes and aerial raids on Basra were countered by Iraqi helicopter-gunship attacks in the Eastern Dejla River region, destroying 22 boats ferrying soldiers. Iran struck back by shelling seven Iraqi cities, and carried out three airraids. By the third week, Iran's press speculated that deterrent measures against the ports of Iraq's Arab allies were inevitable. While government circles favoured a partial ceasefire to protect cities and shipping, they rejected new peace proposals. Khomeini opposed halting the war altogether, unless his conditions were met, and had no intention of changing his previously stated objectives. He announced that combat would continue until the world 'accepts Iran's right to punish the aggressor'. It became a war of the 'good' against the 'evil', of God against the devil (*International Herald Tribune*, 16–17 March, 27 March and 2 April 1985).

6.2.3   April–June 1985

Inactivity in the Tanker War appeared linked to the planned visit by the UN Secretary-General. Eventually also, missile hits on cities ceased in April, as Perez de Cuellar held emergency talks in Baghdad and Tehran, explaining that sanctions would be catastrophic for both countries. The *démarche* was followed by a statement voicing the Council's dismay at the use of CW against Iranian troops in March, without specifically indicting Iraq (King, 1987, appendices I and II, pp. 71, 76).

In May, in order to extricate Iraq from its economic and military crises, the Saudis approved earlier plans for the Red Sea pipeline, with a projected capacity of 1.6mbd, and dispatched their foreign minister to Tehran, to arrange for a truce during the holy month of Ramadan. But his plea for peace fell on hostile ears. Because of Tehran's rigidity and the stagnation on all fronts, Iraq initiated a new bout of reciprocal hits on cities. In Kuwait, an assassination attempt on the ruler failed (O'Ballance, 1988, p. 169; King, 1987, pp. 18, 30, 34; and see Section 7.2).

In June, Tehran allowed Turkish troops on its soil for the first time in years to pursue the KDPI, an Iranian Kurdish faction; and Saddam Hussein announced a unilateral two-week moratorium of the war on cities. During a pro-government rally in Tehran, Khomeini ordered the adoption of *defensive jihad*, away from *human wave* tactics. The method of throwing wave after wave of teenaged *baseej* into the inferno of ground battles had not achieved victory, rather, it had cost the lives of thousands on the battlefield, and resulted in public displays of discontent. Along the disputed border, Iranian troops carried out several minor attacks near the Hawizeh Marshes and on Majnoon in the south, and near Qasr-e-Shirin, Mandali and Marivan in the northern and central zones. These were not met by any Iraqi responses, either on the ground, where its forces were in disarray in most areas, or over the waters of the Gulf (O'Ballance, 1988, p. 166, 168, 170; King, 1987, pp. 25, 30 and Appendix II, p. 76; and Karsh, 1987, pp. 50–1).

6.2.4   July–August 1985

Iran's ground and naval offensives became increasingly daring. Putting pressure on Iraq again, its troops attacked near Fakkeh, attempting to penetrate Basra's defences, and entered Iraqi Kurdistan, where they seized a few border villages, with help from KDP *Peshmerga* (O'Ballance, 1988, p. 167). With more Iraqi territory occupied by Iran, Iraqi opposition figures started gambling on Saddam Hussein's fall.

'Stop-and-search' operations in the Gulf were stepped up, following the appointment of Captain Mohammed Hussein Malek-Zadegan as C-in-C, IRIN, on 27 June. During the first two weeks of his command, the navy inspected 42 ships for contraband (see Sections 7.1 and 7.2), and on 2 August, carried out its first helicopter attack against a naval target, 60 miles off Qatar. The second reference by Lloyd's of the platform used in an Iranian attack mentioned that the damage sustained by the Panamanian *Stelios* (LT, RPD), loaded with crude, was slight, as the missile exploded at sea (*Middle East Journal 1986*, p. 120).

In mid-August, Iraq's fiercest air-strikes against Kharg destroyed the two main eastern and western jetties, but left the third intact. The timing of the effective airraids, lasting intensively for 12 days during the last stages of Iran's presidential election campaign, was intended to undermine Tehran's regime. In effect, it turned out to be the opposite. It rallied the people around their leadership and tipped the balance in favour of President Ali Khamenei, who was re-elected for a second term.

6.2.5   September 1985

Iranian troops failed again to seize Basra and Sumar, but made modest gains in Kurdistan. Iraqi pilots continued their large-scale attacks on Kharg, and on the 19th, their missiles struck the North Korean *Son Bong* (LT, FX, CTL, FD) whilst loading at the oil terminal. It caught fire and became the only VLCC to sink as a result of an Iraqi aerial attack during the length of the Tanker War (Lloyd's). For the second month running, Iraqi raids on Kharg succeeded in sharply reducing Iran's oil exports by two-thirds (King, 1987, p. 26; and O'Ballance, 1988, pp. 168, 171).

In a secret deal, known as the Iran–Contra or Irangate affair, Iran received a consignment of 508 US tube-launched optically tracked wire-guided (TOW) missiles, despite *Operation Staunch*, launched by Washington, which was meant to activate an arms embargo during the Iran–Iraq War. In fact, it instead created a thriving black market in arms (see Sections 2.1 and 3.6). 'Ironically, the US supplied Hawks and spare parts to Iran in two shipments in 1985 and 1986, organized by Oliver North as part of the Reagan administration's abortive effort to ransom hostages in Beirut' (*Independent,* 2 March 1995; *Middle East Journal 1986,* p. 121; Hersh, 1992; and see Sections 6.3.4, 6.4.2, 6.4.3 and 7.2). The evidence casted doubts on Washington's neutrality in the war, and highlighted its double-barrelled policy of providing both warring nations with arms, having granted Iraq agriculture loans, spent on weaponry (see Section 6.3.2).

Alarmed by Iran's gains in the war and Iraq's failure to deliver a victory after five years, two Gulf sheikhdoms established diplomatic relations with Moscow, Oman this month, and the UAE the following November, which presented the USSR with a window of opportunity to enhance its diplomatic and political role in the area, and gain new markets for arms sales.

6.2.6 October–December 1985

At the end of October, Colonel Mohammed Hussein Jalali was appointed IRI Defence Minister in Musavi's new cabinet, and about three weeks later, the Assembly of Experts selected Ayatollah Hussein Ali Montazeri as Khomeini's successor. On the southern shores of the Gulf, at a summit in late November, the GCC heads of state expressed their desire for improved relations with Iran. The following month, keen to expand his circle of influential allies, Oman's Sultan Qabus echoed Sun Tsu's counsel, saying that 'in the end Iran is a neighbouring country and we want good relations with it' (in King, 1987, p. 39; *Strategic Survey 1985–86,* p. 128; and O'Ballance, 1988, p. 169).

In September, in retaliation to Iraq's intensive airraids on Kharg since mid-August, numbering 44, the IRIN had inspected 300 ships in the Gulf, under the policy announced in July. But on 24 November, it ushered a portentous mode of action which gave foreign navies a justification to escort their merchant ships. The Kuwaiti cargo *Ibn Al Beitar,* loaded with iron and steaming in the Gulf of Oman, was seized by Iranian units and taken first to Bandar Abbas and then to Bandar Khomeini, where she was detained. Thirteen months later, she sank during a missile attack, presumably carried out by an Iraqi aircraft (Lloyd's; *Strategic Survey 1985–86*, p. 128; Karsh, 1987, pp. 31–2; O'Ballance, 1988, p. 171; and see Sections 7.1 and 7.2).

Policy directions *vis-à-vis* the Iran–Iraq War had started to take shape by early summer, and activity for mediation intensified, especially in private. Generally speaking, there was a will to end the war, though that was conditional: the international community wanted no victor, and Iran, whose troops were gaining ground, was not keen for a ceasefire, although Rafsanjani expressed his wish that a diplomatic solution should be sought. Baghdad awaited international mediation efforts to come to fruition, displaying its first serious attempt to sue for an armistice, as shown by the fairly subdued level of attacks on tankers for most of the year, except in March. Disillusioned with international diplomacy, Iraq was to veer again towards air strikes (see Chart A6.4 and Table 1.11).

The year closed with the political landscape in the area unaffected by hostilities on the front, although both Tehran and Baghdad stepped up operations during each other's elections in August and October, respectively, in an attempt to sway voters away from their governments. Both increasingly relied on Turkish troops to quell their Kurdish minorities. And both collaborated with each other's Kurdish factions – Tehran with the KDP's Barzani and the PUK's Talabani, and Baghdad with the KDPI's Ghassemlou. The strategic situation was also largely unchanged. Iraq tried to mesh several tactics, but while its airpower was six- or sevenfold Iran's, it failed to exploit its superiority. In so far as Iraq's hits against its enemy's oil installations and shipping did not drive Iran to close the Strait of Hormuz and draw foreign powers into the conflict, its strategy miscarried. Iran remained successful on the ground, and the moderate level of the Tanker War allowed it to gain $16 billion in oil revenues. By the year's end, Iraq's debts had risen to $40 billion, although it was able to double its exports to 1.5mbd of oil. Anti-war demonstrations were staged in Tehran's streets, the most notable in April and mid-May; and bombs, for which Islamic *Jihad* claimed responsibility, blew up in Kuwait and Saudi Arabia. Both foes had almost consumed their stocks of missiles in their war of cities, forcing them to seek new sources for their depleted arsenals – Iraq having hurled 135 *Scuds* against Iranian cities from the start of hostilities until 1985, 82 during that year alone, and Iran having fired 14 *Scuds* and exhausted most of the Libyan and Syrian consignments. Oil prices fell by about 60 per cent, reaching a low of $27 a barrel, which increased the pressures on Iran's and Iraq's economies. Prices had rocketed from $2 a barrel in 1970 to $11 in 1974, and surged spectacularly again in 1981 to approach $40 a barrel. They were to have a further free fall to below $10 a barrel the following April (*Strategic Survey 1985–86*, p. 129; Zaloga, 1988, p. 1424 and table p. 1427; King, 1987, p. 29 and note p. 66; *Independent*, 5 April 1993; Karsh, 1987, p. 50; and O'Ballance, 1988, p. 167–8).

6.3   1986 – WARFARE OVER STARDOM IN THE GULF

6.3.1   January 1986

The year unfolded favourably for Iran, militarily, economically and strategically. On the battleground, the attempt by Iraqi troops to regain Majnoon was foiled, but its pilots succeeded in wrecking an oil-storage tanker moored near Larak. To counteract the throttling of its economy, Tehran unveiled plans to establish three new oil installations out of range of enemy bombers, one at Jask, on the Arabian Sea, the other two within the Gulf, close to Hormuz, on Qishm Island and at Bandar Lengeh. Given its policy of national sovereignty and non-intervention in Gulf affairs, its navy reinforced its posture in the area, warned naval craft to sail clear of its *Naval Advice Zone* and continued its inspection of ships (O'Ballance, 1988, pp. 182–4, 194; and see Sections 6.2.4, 7.1 and 7.2).

Promoting the policy of no victor and no loser, both superpowers wooed Tehran with practical measures, one covertly, the other overtly. President Reagan authorized the CIA to purchase 4000 TOW missiles from the Defence Department, of which 1000 were delivered through Israel at the end of the following month. Additional hardware, also sanctioned by the US, reached Tehran by July, where the leadership could have hardly concealed their delight that American envoys were secretly negotiating arms transfers with them. Moscow agreed to resume Iranian gas imports and dispatched a Soviet delegation to Tehran in February. Beside weakening the Soviet–Iraqi alliance, improved relations with the other superpower enhanced Iran's chances for diplomatic backing in international debates on the war, and counterbalanced US support for Iraq.

6.3.2   February 1986

On the battlefield, Iranian troops carried out several successful offensives, one of which dealt the Iraqi troops a decisive defeat. In the north, during *Operation Wal Fajr-9* in the Sulaymaniyah area, they were able to control a thin strip in Kurdistan until early March, again aided by Kurdish *Peshmerga*. More importantly, they launched a two-pronged diversionary attack north of the Hawizeh Marshes beforehand, to coincide with *Wal Fajr-8*. The amphibious operation to seize Fao, the strategically located peninsula, resulted in the threatening of Basra from the south (O'Ballance, 1988, pp. 173–6, 179–80; and Karsh, 1987, p. 32). Its loss was a grave one for Iraq, further limiting its oil wealth and restricting its coast. It was also a serious blow to the West and to adjoining countries, as the southern region was of great significance in so far as it might secede and join Iran – a 'nightmare' scenario from their viewpoints.

The success of the Iranian infantry, in that particular battle, energized a secret international network of government agencies and private banks that upgraded Iraq's military capabilities. The surprise capture of Fao motivated Baghdad to expand its Republican Guards from three brigades to 25 in the following two years, and to accelerate a programme to develop and extend the range of an SSM that could reach the Iranian capital and other locations. Whilst oil prices had plunged, the Iraqis found a window of opportunity in credits extended by the BNL, under a US Department of Agriculture programme. They 'ultimately totalled $5bn', including $100 million which funded Project 395, 'the *Condor II* ballistic missile with a range of 600 miles' (Cockburn, 1992; and see Section 6.1.3).

Desperate because the Tanker War had not borne the fruits they expected during the last ten months, and keen to offset their losses in ground battles, Iraqi pilots shot down an Iranian C-130, killing all 40 VIP passengers, bombed other strategic targets, such as a bridge and a refinery, the following month, a train carrying military personnel north of Dezful and an arms factory near Tehran in May (O'Ballance, 1988, pp. 181–2; and *Middle East Journal 1987*, p. 488).

The escalation of Iraqi hostilities against international shipping set the UN in motion. SCR 582 was unanimously adopted, and a UN team of experts visited Iran, after Iraq's allegations that its troops had used CW. World reaction was also prompted by the failure of the Indian prime minister's envoy, who had the unenviable task of negotiating a ceasefire.

The glut in the world oil market required output cuts to drain stockpiles and maintain or propel prices. The prospect of a collapse in prices once again caused alarm in Iran. As it needed to raise its earnings to fund the war effort, it diminished oil exports to 0.75mbd from 1.6mbd the previous month, hoping that by decreasing the burgeoning oversupply on the market they would bolster prices and stave off another free fall (King, 1987, p. 27; and see Sections 6.3.6 and 6.4.5).

6.3.3 March 1986

Following the publication of the UN experts' report, the SC condemned Baghdad for its repeated use of CW against Iranian troops and called for mediation to end the fighting. Subsequently, the Council's President was strongly critical of Baghdad. Undaunted by the UN's grave charge, and having failed to recapture Fao, Iraq responded by keeping up pressure on Iran's communications and productive power. Although Iran's air capability was no match for its own, Iraq's attacks against naval vessels decreased, but its aircraft concentrated on raiding strategic targets, such as the Isphahan refinery in central Iran, and the Qotar Bridge on the Turkish border. Successful hits on a few tankers and on the plant forced Iran to import refined oil products up to early May, and the bombing of the bridge disrupted the usual heavy traffic (O'Ballance, 1988, p. 182).

In retaliation for Iraqi assaults on the Sirri shuttle, Tehran escalated its own attacks over the Gulf waters, producing its best results so far. Its operations in the Gulf remained low-key until March, when they reached eight hits. Most of the vessels struck flew non-Arab flags, except for the Qatari tanker *Zor*, and were attacked off the coast of Qatar. Whilst seven were missile attacks – three of which were fired from helicopter-gunships – one was an assault with machine-gun fire, presumably from an FAC. The incidents resulted in five seamen killed and eight injured. None of the ships sustained CTL, and all continued in service after repairs. In two cases, the missiles failed to explode, giving substance to allegations that Israel had sold Iran obsolete missile parts, in November 1985, in a secret arms deal (*Washington Post*, 12 January 1986). The *Zor* sailed to Jebel 'Ali under her own steam, with the unexploded missile lodged in a cabin; and the Norwegian tanker *Berge King* proceeded with her voyage to Ras Tanura anchorage, where the missile was removed from the air-conditioning room with the assistance of the Saudi Navy (Lloyd's; and see Chart A6.5 and Table 1.11).

6.3.4 April–May 1986

Iraqi aircraft struck an Iranian troop train at Haft Tappeh in May, and ground troops punched their way into the border town of Mehran. An offer to exchange it for Fao was rejected by Iran, since the latter had obviously more strategic value, being an outlet to the Gulf, in addition to its proximity to Basra, Majnoon and Kuwait. Both enemies charged into Iraqi Kurdistan with limited success, the Iranians aided by Kurdish guerrillas, and the Iraqis supported by Kurdish pro-government fighters, the *Jash* – a word meaning 'mercenary' in Kurdish, and 'baby donkey' in Arabic, and used derisorily in the latter connotation by Baghdad's Iraqi opponents (O'Ballance, 1988, pp. 179–80, 189; see also Karsh, 1987, p. 32).

In April, Vice-President George Bush announced that the US would not wait for an invitation from any of the Gulf states in case of an emergency, and at the end of May, Reagan warned that he would not allow Hormuz to be closed. The American administration thus escalated the confrontation with Iran, and appeared to side further with Iraq. The policy was prompted by a growing perception of threat, as both countries' operations in the Gulf were amplified, Iran's success on the ground increased, Kurdish activities in northern Iraq were stepped up, and Iraq failed to recapture the vital areas of Majnoon and Fao.

Oil prices went into a downward spiral, falling below $10 a barrel from $27 in December. Logic would have suggested that prices would rise with increased Iraqi and Iranian attacks on tankers, but Iran suspected that it was being punished in response to its military exploits and hard-line policy towards the 'Great Satan'. US resolve to penalize Iran was further demonstrated with a new policy option in May, which underscored the statements made by Reagan and Bush: a USN warship intercepted an IRIN frigate to prevent it from seizing a US cargo, ostensibly destined for the UAE (see Section 7.2). Almost a decade later, reports suggested that the UAE was cited in end-user certificates for Iraqi purchases of weapons (see Section 7.1).

Reagan's special envoys, Lieutenant-Colonel Oliver North, a White House aide, and Colonel Robert McFarlane, a National Security Advisor, secretly visited Tehran on Irish passports on 28 May. A power struggle between Rafsanjani and Montazeri turned the political component of the mission into a fiasco. However, the military aspect resulted in the transfer of at least 2008 TOW anti-tank and 235 *Hawk* anti-aircraft missiles, and other military items, which US Congressman Jim Wright said Israel shipped with US approval (*New York Times*, 21 November 1986; also O'Ballance, 1988, p. 193; *Time*, 17 August 1987, pp. 4–10; and see Sections 6.2.5, 6.3.1, 6.4.2, 6.4.3 and 7.2). It was the same McFarlane who instructed USN marines and ships to open fire in defence of US allies in Lebanon, and thus led to the loss of credibility of the multinational force. American, Israeli and West European nationals were arrested the month before, for their involvement in two arms deals for Iran worth $2.38 billion, including combat and transport aircraft, TOW and *Hawk* missiles, tanks, and guided bombs, although a US-sanctioned consignment of TOW missiles had reached Tehran in November 1985 and February 1986, and seven tons of arms were scheduled to be dispatched via Yugoslavia and Spain the following July. And a year earlier, on 15 July 1985, five men were charged in San Diego for selling spare parts for Iran's F-14s (*New York Times*, 16 July 1985; and see Sections 6.3.3 and 6.3.8).

6.3.5 June–July 1986

In Iran and Iraq, six years of war had taken their toll. Heavy casualties on the battlefield, economic hardship, and power and water shortages affected internal cohesion in Iran, leading to anti-war demonstrations. Internal discontent forced Rafsanjani to admit that 'two powerful factions' polarized Iranian politics concerning Iran's strategy in the war, the economy and foreign policy (*Strategic Survey 1986–87*, pp. 128–9; *Time*, 17 August 1987; King, 1987, pp. 23–4; and 'Abdel-Halim, 1985, p. 79).

For the second consecutive July, Iran did not venture any attacks in the Gulf, but as a countermeasure to successful Iraqi hits against its installations, it stationed a new floating oil terminal at Larak, after some VLCCs refused to sail to Kharg. On the war front, it launched *Operation Karbala-1*, driving Iraqi forces from Mehran, less than two months after seizing it. In response to the routing of its ground troops, Iraq sought a different means to hurt Iran's capabilities. Its aircraft bombed the Ground Satellite Communication Centre at Assad Abad, which disrupted communication links (Lloyd's; King, 1987, p. 27; and O'Ballance, 1988, pp. 180, 182–3).

In the Iraqi capital, morale deteriorated after the capture of Fao and the loss of Mehran. Saddam Hussein reshuffled the RCC, the RC and the cabinet, during a meeting of the extra-ordinary Congress of the Ba'th Party. The top-level meeting was designed to tighten his control and show that he was far from cowed by the drawn-out war, and to evaluate reversals on the ground, following the loss of Mehran. He was asked to step down or resign temporarily, to enable his entourage to set up a provisional government, in accordance with Iran's conditions for a ceasefire. Because he lacked military expertise, he was also criticized by a number of ministers and accused of by-passing military commanders in the conduct of war, and in his appointments to command positions, bought political loyalty rather than efficiency. The meeting was the climax of several years of a power struggle, waged by the military to retain control of war-related decision-making. Saddam Hussein then decided to loosen his control, to escape bearing any responsibility for failures due to his interference (*Strategic Survey 1986–87*, pp. 126, 130; and O'Ballance, 1988, p. 185).

Co-opted by Baghdad, Massoud Rajavi, who thus far was in control of the MKO, a small private army of fighters, left Paris for Baghdad, which he had secretly visited on former occasions (King, 1987, p. 56; and O'Ballance, 1988, pp. 130, 189). He roped hundreds of Iranians into his feud with the regime, and was to form the National Liberation Army (NLA), a year later (*Middle East Journal 1987*, pp. 602, 699; and see Sections 6.3.9 and 6.4.4). The MKO, who have members in London, Paris, Stockholm and other European cities, increasingly came under suspicion of being responsible for bomb explosions, including the one at Tehran University, in mid-March 1985, during a Friday sermon by President Khamenei, broadcast live on Tehran Radio (IRNA and Reuter in *International Herald Tribune*, 16–17 March 1985; and Velayati interview in *Independent on Sunday*, 10 March 1996).

6.3.6   August 1986

Iran's government officials admitted their inability to fund the growing costs of war, which forced them to adopt austerity measures. The depletion of the state's coffers resulted from the combination of a collapse in world prices of oil, reaching $14 a barrel, a drop in production, and the lowering of its price to $4.80 a barrel, to compensate buyers who paid higher insurance premiums (see Section 6.1.5). At an OPEC meeting, Iran and Saudi Arabia closed ranks to harmonize policies on restricting production, to reestablish prices at $16 a barrel. They also agreed on Saudi exports of refined petroleum products to the IRI (O'Ballance, 1988, p. 183; Axelgard, 1987, p. 90; King, 1987, p. 30; and see Sections 6.3.2 and 6.4.5). Although Riyadh remained cautious of Tehran's intent, overlapping economic interests overwhelmed the Iraqi–Saudi alliance, despite Saddam Hussein's posture as the Gulf states' defender against Iran.

So far, the Iraqi ruler was in charge of the failed Iran–Iraq War strategy and could not be expected to turn into the advocate of a change of direction. But for him, ending the war was foremost among his political priorities, and he still had faith in diplomacy and international pressure. However, he was incapable of dictating the stream of events, which seemed to flow against his interests. Iran and his two main allies, the USSR and

Saudi Arabia, collaborated with each other – Moscow resumed Iranian gas imports, and the Saudis prevailed upon Hussein to reach a settlement, as the drop in oil revenues made the war funding too costly for them. Also, Iran's own campaign against international shipping was becoming as fierce as Iraq's, with eight hits this month. There was also another factor adding to the pressure: the Iraqi troops' reversals, especially their ejection from Fao and Mehran, led to divisions within the RCC and the RC, and forced the Iraqi president to reconsider his stance. To take the moral high ground and appeal to public opinion, he proposed a four-point peace plan, which basically restated his initial demands. But his call found no favour in Tehran, where previous conditions were reiterated, and war reparations raised to $309 billion (O'Ballance, 1988, p. 185). It is doubtful that Khomeini could see in the Iraqi president the negotiator he would face, unless Saddam Hussein held a better hand and the spiritual leader had a stake in initiating a dialogue.

Tehran's refusal of the peace offer resulted in the intensification of the Tanker War on both sides, with Iran matching the number of vessels hit by its enemy and by itself the previous March (see Chart A6.6 and Table 1.11). The Iranians demonstrated that they were not giving in, and the Iraqis vented their frustration. They raided Farsi on two consecutive days, and carried out their first attack on Sirri, with four *Mirage* F-1s, 450 miles away from base. The assaults signalled to Iran that its strategic targets were within easy reach, and that the surveillance on Farsi and the hit-and-run attacks carried out by the IRGCN from there, as well as oil exports from Sirri, could be disrupted at will. In the aftermath, Iran was driven to relocate oil exports to the Larak terminal, 120 miles east of Sirri (King, 1987, p. 27; O'Ballance, 1988, pp. 183–4; and Karsh, 1987, p. 33).

At the end of this eventful month, Iran initiated *Operation Karbala-2* near Haj 'Omran. Aided by Kurdish fighters, its troops were successful in this limited offensive. About six weeks later, they collaborated again in a commando raid on the Iraqi pipeline near Kirkuk. This incident, among others, demonstrated that overland oil exports were vulnerable to sabotage, airraids and missile attacks. Moreover, whilst regarded safer than the chaotic Gulf waters, oil traffic across borders could be plugged by personal enmity between rulers or embargoes, as for instance, the Iraqi in Syria in 1982 and after 1990, and civil war, such as the Saudi in Lebanon in 1983.

This period marked the start of a schism within the Iraqi opposition movement, which had remained hitherto more or less cohesive. For the first time since the onset of war, divisions appeared between the main parties over the 'Defence of the Fatherland'. Arab Nationalists, democrats and communists asserted that the protection of Iraq did not in itself signify sustaining the government, but entailed the preservation of the country's territorial integrity against the aggression of an invading power. They called for an immediate ceasefire, and maintained that all Iraqis, whatever their ethnic, religious or political loyalties, should avoid aiding foreign troops in overrunning their country in the hope of ousting the regime. On the other side of the divide, the KDP and the PUK, the two main Kurdish parties, allied with the *Shi'ah* in the south. Anticipating that an Iranian victory would rid them of Saddam Hussein, they hoped the war would continue until that goal was reached (see Section 2.2).

6.3.7   September 1986

Iran mounted separate offensives, *Karbala-2* and *Karbala-3*, in which it relied on commando frogmen to attack al-'Amaya offshore radar, al-Bakr oil platform, Mehran and Majnoon. Troops built another pontoon over al-Shatt in the zone of Fao to assert control over the area and fortify their positions, by easing the movement of troops and the deployment of additional weapons (O'Ballance, 1988, p. 189; and Karsh, 1987, p. 33).

The Gulf waters were turbulent and the skies above were rumbling. Iraq extended the *Naval Exclusion Zone* to incorporate all Iranian ports and oil terminals, claimed its aircraft had carried out 120 sorties against Kharg since 1 September 1985, and raided the faraway Lavan oil terminal. The IRIN protected its shuttle tankers, one of its frigates attacked a Kuwaiti target for the first time, and a helicopter-gunship fired missiles at a British merchant vessel. Western warships escorted their own merchant fleets, allowing ships flying other flags to tag behind, and a Soviet man-of-war forced the IRIN to release two of its merchant ships (Gamlen, 1989, p. 47; and O'Ballance, 1988,

p. 184). The war was on its way to being internationalized, with Kuwait's request for re-flagging (see Section 7.2).

6.3.8 October–November 1986

In New York, SCR 588 was passed unanimously, summoning Tehran and Baghdad to implement SCR 582, and requesting the Secretary-General to reactivate mediation efforts. In Iran, fuel and power shortages forced the authorities to declare conservation, and declining revenues to $6 billion, compelled them to cancel the planned Ganaveh and Asaluyeh pipelines. Despite shortages, they resumed export of 2.5m tons of oil at concessionary rates to Syria, halted when payments were delayed (King, 1987, pp. 27, 42).

The following month, the Lebanese weekly magazine *Al-Shira'* revealed the American arms-for-hostages deal with Iran, news of which was leaked by Montazeri's office. One day later, the White House spokesman warned that as long as the Islamic republic advocated terrorism, the US would continue the 1979 arms embargo. Embarrassed by the disclosures, the American president toned down the belligerent stance taken by his spokesman, and made conciliatory remarks about Iran. These drew a predictable gust of rhetorical scorn from Khomeini and Rafsanjani, whose revelations added fuel to fire and forced the US administration to reveal the 18-months secret barter, which included the provision of arms and intelligence to Iran (*Time*, 17 August 1987, pp. 4–10; *Middle East Journal 1987*, pp. 259, 260–3; *Strategic Survey 1986–87*, p. 129; and King, 1987, p. 54). In the meantime, US courts were dealing with 40 cases of weapons' smuggling (see Section 6.3.4).

The first Lloyd's account confirming the IRIN's involvement in retaliatory attacks came on 18 November, when a warship launched missiles at the Liberian tanker *Crown Hope* (LT, SER), whilst it was unloaded and anchored off Sharjah. Because the crew abandoned ship, the fires were extinguished with the aid of a tug, and she was towed to Dubai for repairs. A few other minor incidents, related to Iranian assaults in 1986, deserved highlighting in the evolution of the Tanker War. These were on 13 March, against the Liberian tanker *Gogo Regent* (LT, RPD), which received a salvo of machine-gun fire;

on 1 August, the Greek tanker *Ethnic* (LT, SER) was blasted by cannon fire; on 16 September, the Kuwaiti tanker *Al Funtas* (LT, SER) was hit with a burst of six shells fired from a gunboat (or a frigate); and on 15 November, the UAE bulk carrier *Shaam* (LT, FX, SER) was attacked by two gunboats (Lloyd's). In all four cases damage seemed negligible, however, these episodes heralded a change in Iran's tactics, with the extensive use of FACs manned by sailors, presumed to be members of the IRGCN. It became the norm at a later stage in the war, when the *Pasdars'* activities expanded, and they established themselves as the key actors in naval skirmishes (see Section 7.1).

This month witnessed the second-highest number of Iraqi hits since the start of the Tanker War, after July 1984, and the farthest airraid. The round trip of 1560 miles to Larak was either due to the introduction of air-refuelling capability, or to its aircraft being allowed to re-fill in other Arab airfields, as Tehran suspected (King, 1987, p. 27; O'Ballance, 1988, pp. 184–5; and see Section 7.2). The extent and range of the attacks were provoked by Iraqi aggravation at the news of the triangular relationship involving the US, Israel and Iran. In Baghdad's view, the arms shipments increased Iran's offensive capabilities and risked to prolong the war, therefore the need to exert added pressure (see statements by Iraq's foreign minister, Tariq 'Aziz on 22 November 1986 in *Middle East Journal 1987*, p. 259; by its UN Ambassador, Nizar Hamdoun, in *Washington Post*, 24 November 1986; by Egypt's President Husni Mubarak in *Al-Ittihad*, in *Middle East Journal 1987*, p. 420; see also McNaugher in Taylor and Francis, 1988, p. 300; *Strategic Survey 1986–87*, pp. 127–8; and Gamlen, 1989, pp. 87–9).

6.3.9   December 1986

Following Iraq's dynamic campaign against merchant ships, attention converged again on the UNSC, where its President voiced concern over the widening conflict, continued ground fighting, and attacks on civilian shipping and oil installations, all of which endangered the interests of the world community.

In response to the miscarriage of *Operation Karbala-4* against Basra, SAIRI held a conference in Tehran to form a government-in-exile and call for armed struggle against Saddam Hussein. But since spring, Khomeini already had grave doubts about a *Da'wah*-led *Shi'ah* revolt. Irritated by the autonomous stance taken by the organization and the continuous squabbling within it, he privately supported the easing-out of its leader, Hojatolislam Mohammad al-Hakeem. Consequently, as a substitute irritant to the *Ba'th* regime, Tehran increasingly cooperated with Kurdish *Peshmerga* in its operations in Iraqi Kurdistan, and provided them with full backing. It is worth noting that Saddam Hussein subsequently followed suit. Having failed to unseat the Iranian government himself, he started relying on Rajavi's guerillas by summer, lavishing on them MBTs, artillery and every possible financial and logistical support (O'Ballance, 1988, pp. 130, 189, 204; and *Middle East Journal 1987*, p. 259).

Despite Iran's failure to seize Basra, Iraq's set-backs on the battle-front alarmed international observers. Iran was perceived as a potent threat in a region where the West had major interests, and in their view, its victory and the downfall of the *Ba'th* regime jeopardized Iraq's territorial integrity. They feared the strengthening of *Shi'ah*-inspired secessionist movements and the creation of a pro-Tehran entity in parts or all of Iraq. Perceived to be in a precarious position because of the military and political onslaught of Iranians, Kurds and *Shi'ah*, the US administration decided on new policy steps. Increasingly passionate arguments within the US administration, about which procedures to activate, resulted in open support for Iraq, coupled with a vigorous confrontation with Iran. It was also disclosed that the CIA was providing Iraq with Sat-Int information on the location of Iranian oil and power plants (*Washington Post*, 15 December 1986). The following two years witnessed increased US threats in response to Iran's escalation in attacks on naval targets, the enlargement of the US fleet in the Gulf region and virulent air and naval engagements between Iran and the US (see Section 7.4).

Starting in 1986, and continuing into the following years, problems developed over manpower and the economy in Iraq and Iran. Despite earlier pronouncements by Saddam Hussein, pledging that youngsters under the age of 18 would not be sent to the front, universities were closed from August 1986 to February 1987, while teachers and students were drafted.

In Iran, with young men increasingly dodging conscription altogether or using family connections to avoid service on the front, the *majlis* ruled in January that all would spend a year in forward areas. Lecturers were drafted when universities were closed in September, and in November, 14-year-old boys and girls underwent military training. The politicization of the ranks, especially among the *Pasdar*, and the encroachment of political figures upon war-related decision-making in both states, led to resentment within the ranks (O'Ballance, 1988, pp. 185–8, 190, 199; and *Time*, 17 August 1987, pp. 4–10).

From 1981 to 1986, Iraq became the first LDC in arms imports, in spite of the decline in oil exports, averaging 1.7mbd to 1.8mbd. Oil revenues, which were approximately one-quarter to one-third of pre-war levels, earned Baghdad from $5 to $8 billion, and its debts rose to between $60 and $80 billion, forcing it to adopt austerity measures and defer debt repayments. By the end of the year, Iraqi effective air strikes reduced Iranian oil exports to 0.7mbd, and statements by the Iranian leadership indicated their recognition that the Tanker War was harming the country's economy. However, Iran's successful ground offensives – especially the capture of Fao – balanced the Iraqi momentum (Sluglett-Farouk and Sluglett, 1990, pp. 273–4; King, 1987, pp. 18, 27; Cockburn, 1992; *Strategic Survey 1986–87*, p. 130; and see Section 6.3.6).

6.4   1987 – THE INFLAMED GULF WATERS

6.4.1   January 1987

Despite an improvement in their 'antitank warfare and air-defense capability', ascribed to the effect of earlier arms transfers, the Iranians' attempt to capture Basra during *Operation Karbala-5*, was yet another in a string of foiled assaults on the city. While official Washington claimed that the equipment sent was valued at a mere $12 million, Gary Sick, a former National Security Council official, 'estimated that Iran received between $500 million and $1 billion in arms from Israel and the United States in 1985–86' (in Axelgard, 1987, p. 124). Arms transfers from various sources, including MBTs, fighter aircraft, SAMs and RPGs, became valuable assets. In addition, shipments of spare parts made many platforms battleworthy again, and explained how Iran was able to continue its campaign for so long.

The persistence of the Iranians to occupy Basra, and the tenacity of the Iraqis to defend it, derived from its geostrategic significance, and the consequences of its surrender were incalculable. Apart from being an important link between the interior of Iraq and the outside world through the Gulf, the outcome of their swordplay could have seriously impacted on the regional balance of power, and affected the morale of troops and populations on both banks of al-Shatt. Basra, the capital of the south, is Iraq's second largest town, its main port and naval base, and has a large concentration of *Shi'ah*. Its fall could have eventually led to the seizure of the whole southern area, and Iranian troops could then have easily crossed the Kuwaiti border, marched across the flat desert and beyond, in the same way Iraq's Republican Guards did with impunity on 2 August 1990. After the onslaught on Basra, Iran launched another offensive in the central sector, near Qasr-e-Shirin, and strikes on cities resumed.

Iraqi pilots again escalated attacks on vessels sailing in the Gulf. For its part, Iran energized its maritime campaign, which had remained moderate for the last quarter of the previous year, and an IRIN unit fired a *Sea-Killer* missile at a tanker loaded with Kuwaiti oil, when she failed to stop to be searched. Estimating that 180 attacks on ships had killed 100 sailors and destroyed 6m DWTs, the Chairman of the International Chamber of Shipping in London declared that conditions in the Gulf warranted the creation of a UN naval unit. His plea was countered the following day by assurances from Washington to implement the Carter Doctrine to keep Hormuz open (O'Ballance, 1988, p. 194; and see other calls for a UN patrol in Sections 6.2.2, 6.4.7 and 7.2). With both enemies' intense actions endangering shipping, a Soviet frigate escorted four of its merchant ships, loaded with arms for Iraq, and Shultz disclosed that the USN deployed five of its units in the northern Gulf and an aircraft carrier task force in the Arabian Sea (*Middle East Journal 1987*, p. 418; and see Chart A6.7 and Table 1.11).

In Tehran, Rafsanjani urged the Gulf states to withdraw their support for Iraq, explaining that Iran had no interest in expanding the war to them (*Middle East Journal 1987*, p. 418).

The Tanker war seemed to be straining Iran (see Sections 6.3.6 and 6.3.9), and by comparing its actions against Arab oil interests in the Gulf, hitting their tankers and facilities, and the GCC leaders' statements, one could assume that while Tehran attempted to intimidate these states and thus mobilize them to put political pressure on Iraq, it also tried to provoke a rift between them and their ally. The following day, at the ICO summit in Kuwait, the UN Secretary-General called for the setting up of a panel to decide on responsibility for starting the war, in keeping with Khomeini's conditions (*Middle East Journal 1987*, p. 418). Iraq was perceived as having weakened on the war front, and the campaign on shipping by both foes continued unabated, threatening the interests of the worldwide Muslim community, most of whom are oil-importers. With uncertainties mounting about the outcome of the conflict, the delegates curried favour with post-revolutionary Iran – the first such public support since the war began.

6.4.2   February–March 1987

On both sides of the border, leaders realized their countries' inability to gain an overall victory over each other, and a war of words began along these lines. Khomeini explained in February that war was a 'divine cause' rather than a 'single final offensive', and Saddam Hussein vouched a month later that Iran would meet 'slow defeat through attrition'. On *neyrouz*, the Iranian New Year, passions ran high on the streets of Baghdad, when crowds were brought into the game. Rallies were organized by the Iraqi government to celebrate Khomeini's failure to use his mass call for arms to turn 1986 into his proclaimed 'Year of Victory', ending on 21 March (O'Ballance, 1988, pp. 187, 200).

Operation Fatah–4, in the Haj 'Omran area in Kurdistan, was followed by two offensives seven miles from Basra. The sounds of explosions were heard by its residents, who panicked and abandoned the city, after the surrounding area had been economically devastated. During that time, the IRI declared the end of *Karbala-5*, and Baghdad suspended missile attacks on cities at the Kremlin's behest. As Iraq's airforce had sustained considerable losses, the Tanker War was at a low level, but the IRGCN used FACs to carry out their first attack.

The Tower Commission, which investigated the Irangate affair in the US, judged that what began 'as a search for a strategic opening . . . became "a series of arms-for-hostages deals"' (King, 1987, p. 54). While the West usually associates the term 'convoluted politics' with the Middle East, the congressional inquiry concluded in November 1987 that the full details of the episode may never be known (see Sections 6.2.5, 6.3.1, 6.3.4, 6.4.3 and 7.2).

In March, Moscow agreed to lease three tankers to Kuwait, hoping to maximize its involvement in the operation, after which Reagan acceded to the Kuwaiti request to re-register and escort its tankers (see Sections 7.2 and 7.3). Both agreements were not finalized until the following month, as the West and the USSR were hesitant to get too involved in ongoing hostilities. While negotiations were under way, attacks on tankers were subdued, which enabled Iran to export 2mbd of oil for the following few months – a level sufficient for its war effort. Neither Iran nor Iraq were prepared to take the onus for ships' casualties, one because it rejected the concept of draping Kuwaiti tankers in US flags, and did not wish to give outsiders a reason to enlarge their naval presence, and the other was uncommonly careful not to jeopardize the talks.

A fortnight later, the US administration voiced concern at the installation on Qishm and near Kuhestak of Iranian antiship missiles. The Chinese-made *Silkworm* was a replica 'of the Soviet SS-2-N (*Styx*), which had gone down in naval history as being the first ship-to-ship missile to sink an enemy ship in action; the Israeli destroyer, *Eilat*, in October 1967'. The testing of the missiles near Hormuz was shortly followed by the first vessel to be hit by a mine in the Gulf. During a visit to Beijing the same month, US Secretary of State George Shultz was given assurances by his hosts that no weapons were exported to Iran (O'Ballance, 1988, pp. 204–5; and for a detailed description of missiles in Iraq's and Iran's arsenals, see Zaloga, 1988, pp. 1424–7).

Kurdistan was the focus of *Operation Karbala-7*, where Iranian troops participated with Kurdish fighters and scored limited gains. On the same day, in accordance with the 1983 Iraqi–Turkish border security agreement, Turkish aircraft carpet-bombed Iraqi Kurdish villages – their 20th airraid since 1984, in addition to two ground assaults, during which its troops combed the area for suspected PKK camps. Beside routing the PKK and warning Iran and its collaborators, the incursions were meant to relieve pressure on Iraqi troops in the north, who could then be deployed elsewhere (see Sections 2.3 and 3.6). In its aftermath, news was floated that Talabani and Barzani agreed to collaborate in toppling the regime in Baghdad but not to allow Tehran to manipulate them, since Kurds alone suffered Turkish reprisals (O'Ballance, 1988, pp. 201–2). But events in the ongoing war, showing that Kurdish elements continued to take part in later Iranian operations, belied the report.

6.4.3 April–May 1987

Following the Iranian test-firing of an HY-2 *Silkworm* missile, warnings from Washington not to disrupt the flow of oil were countered by Rafsanjani's threats against American targets around the world if the US intervened in the Gulf and by the Iranian UN envoy's pledge to hinder supplies from reaching Iraq (*Middle East Journal 1987*, pp. 419–20). Nonetheless, USN and RN operations escalated in level, intensity and scope. Weinberger ordered USN warships to extend their stay in the Gulf and to patrol the waters further north, and battle groups were instructed to join the aircraft carrier USS *Kitty Hawk* in the Arabian Sea (Ciarocchi, 1987, pp. 5–6; and see Maps 6.1 and 6.2). Also, after a senior RN officer confirmed that the test had been carried out 'around the turn of the year', units of the *Armilla Patrol* shifted to a 'high-alert status' whenever they were within range of the missile (*Jane's Defence Weekly*, 2 July 1987, p. 1417; also see *Strategic Survey 1987–88*, Table p. 130; and Section 7.2 and Appendix A10). In the meantime, the GCC conducted their first joint naval manoeuvres, code-named *Al-Tadhamun* ('Solidarity') (*Middle East Journal 1987*, p. 418).

While lengthy negotiations on re-flagging Kuwaiti tankers were under way (see Section 7.2 and Appendix A7), Iran made headway on the ground and in the Gulf. In April, troops taking part in *Operation Karbala-8* pounded Basra and drained the city's protective water barriers, *Operation Karbala-9* targeted the Qasr-e-Shirin area, and an Iranian outfit, aided by *Peshmerga*, seized strategic heights near Sulaymaniyah and

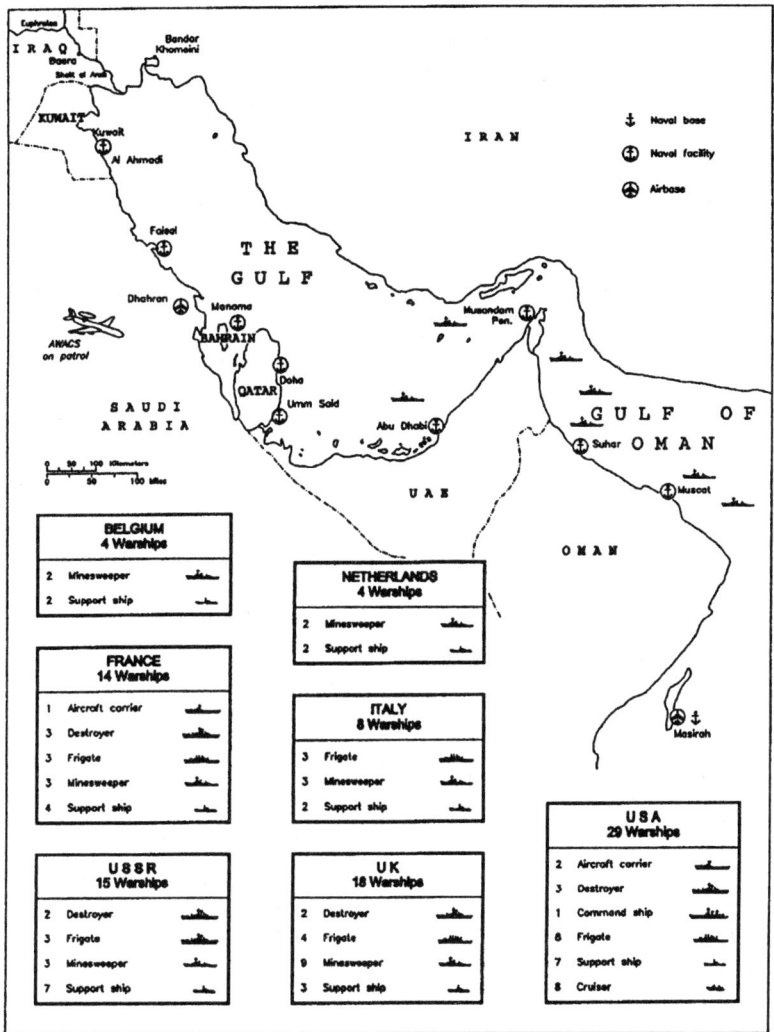

Map 6.1   Foreign Naval Presence and Facilities in the Gulf (Winter 1987)

areas near Mawet and Qala Diza in Kurdistan (O'Ballance, 1988, pp. 203–4). One month later, Iraqi soldiers were about to destroy the hydro-electric dam on Darbandi Khan Lake to flood the Sulaymaniyah region, but the Iranians and the

Peshmerga defended the dam and seized the surrounding grounds, according to an Iraqi source.

Good fortune favoured Saddam Hussein during these two months. He escaped an assassination attempt on his life near the northern city of Mosul, specific details of which were given in a personal communication, and his long-awaited dream of drawing foreign powers into his dispute with Iran became virtually guaranteed, paradoxically, after one of his pilots disabled the USS *Stark* (see Sections 7.2 and 7.3).

On Capitol Hill, both houses refused to investigate Israel's role in covert arms sales to Iran – the first funds of which ($300 000) were provided by Texas billionaire and 1992 presidential contender H. Ross Perot – despite McFarlane's Congressional testimony 'that Israeli Defence Minister Yitzhak Rabin visited [him] at the White House to discuss US replenishment of Hawk missiles to Israel should Israel ship the ones it possessed to Iran' (see Sections 6.2.5, 6.3.1, 6.3.4 and 6.4.2). And whereas Shultz pacified Arab League delegates by assuring them that the US would continue to deny Tehran any arms until it agreed to negotiate, Washington turned down Riyadh's request for *Maverick* ASMs, essential for the defence of the kingdom against potential Iranian and Israeli attacks (Angrand and Rabier, 1989, note p. 101; *Middle East Journal 1987*, p. 592; and see Sections 4.6 and 6.1.1).

The creation of the main IRGCN base on Farsi Island in May, and the reinforcement of the one on Abu Musa Island, heightened the level of attacks by the *Pasdar* and the IRIN, with hits totalling eight. US officials pointed out that they 'posed a "whole galaxy of threats" to shipping and US forces in the Gulf' (*Jane's Defence Weekly*, 4 July 1987, p. 1417). Iran's indignation at Moscow's immediate response to Kuwait's request to charter tankers, and its willingness to order its warships to escort them, triggered a series of attacks on Soviet vessels. Amongst the casualties were a freighter attacked by an Iranian gunboat, another fired on by IRIN units, using machine-guns and RPGs, and a tanker damaged by a mine (Lloyd's; and see Chart A6.7, Table 1.11 and Sections 7.2, 7.3, 7.4).

In mid-May, Oman's Yussef Bin-'Alawi Bin-'Abdallah, one of the longest-serving Gulf Ministers of Foreign Affairs, Iran's Ali Akbar Velayati (the other being), met with Premier Musavi in Tehran. At the end of the four-day visit, during which regional developments were discussed – with the re-flagging project foremost among the issues – he was told that security in the Gulf could only be achieved 'by not supporting Iraq' (*Middle East Journal 1987*, p. 592). Beside the UAE and Qatar, Oman was less involved in the war than other Gulf states, in part because of its geographic remoteness and the near-absence of a *Shi'ah* community that could be manipulated by others. Thus, it was the most likely to play a mediating role in regional disputes, and although it was not a member in OPEC, its envoys repeatedly played the roles of emissary and broker in disagreements between members of the oil cartel. Relations were generally poor between both countries since the downfall of the Shah and the bitter political attacks of Iran's new rulers on Oman's government. But Oman, the UAE and Qatar increasingly disapproved of Kuwaiti actions and sought an overture with the Islamic republic (Chubin and Tripp, 1989, p. 159; Khalaf, 1987, p. 33; King, 1987, p. 36; and McNaugher in Karsh [ed.], 1989, p. 179).

6.4.4 June–July 1987

In Tehran, Khomeini dissolved the ruling IRP, and while conscription for the IRGC was announced, one of its outfits landed on Abu Musa Island. Nearby, around Hormuz and further away, in the Gulf of Oman, the IRIN conducted large-scale manoeuvres. On the war front, Iraqi Kurdish guerrillas took the opportunity of Iraqi troops being absorbed elsewhere to mount a series of commando raids around Sulaymaniyah, with logistical Iranian support. Iraq responded by attacking the IRGCN base on Farsi Island twice in two days, and by supporting the formation of Rajavi's NLA (*Middle East Journal 1987*, pp. 595, 602–3).

But attention focused far away, with critical decisions being taken by outside powers. Slowly, but quite relentlessly, the causal relationship between the Tanker War and military, political, economic and diplomatic aspects became obvious, and the solid connection between the campaign on tankers and other factors showed that the internationalization of the conflict was being fostered.

Determined to increase diplomatic pressure, especially on Tehran, the UNSC demanded that Iran and Iraq 'observe an immediate ceasefire, discontinue all military actions on land, at sea and in the air, and withdraw all forces to the internationally recognized boundaries without delay'. Adopted unanimously on 20 July, and instantly accepted by Iraq, SCR 598 was drafted with active West German involvement, and became the basis of a truce one year later (*Time*, 11 January 1988). As Iran had achieved territorial gains in Kurdistan and around Basra, it saw no advantage to acquiesce to a ceasefire, while Iraq was the party that would gain the most. Sanctions against Iran, proposed by the three permanent members of the UN Security Council (US, UK and France, also referred to as the perm3) were renounced because of Soviet and Chinese refusal (Axelgard, 1987, p. 126). Beside being partners in the crusade against US 'hegemony', Beijing had become Iran's biggest arms supplier, particularly after signing an oil-for-arms deal on 23 May, consisting of aircraft, MBTs, artillery pieces, missiles and spare parts for ex-Soviet arms, and the building of four factories in Kerman to manufacture 'ammunition, rockets and tank spare parts' (*Middle East Journal 1987*, p. 593). They also collaborated in a nuclear programme, and China's coffers benefited from sales of *Silkworms* to Tehran and Riyadh (*Time*, 11 January 1988). Their cooperation was certain to expand after the PRC called for the clause on war reparations to Iran to be implemented (Zaloga, 1988, p. 1427; and *Independent*, 1 November 1991). Moscow declined to offend its two allies for a variety of reasons, involving its own national interests too. Baghdad was its partner in an agreement and its main client for weapons exports; and it was involved with Tehran in a gas deal and in plans to build a second rail link from Iran to Soviet Central Asia. The refusal was also influenced by Tehran's pledge to discontinue its support for Afghani *mujahedeen*, and cease rousing Muslims in neighbouring Soviet republics (*Guardian*, 13 December 1987).

France severed diplomatic relations with Iran, following the strafing of the freighter *Ville d'Anvers* by two gunboats in the Gulf. The move came also after the gendarmes, surrounding the Iranian mission in Paris, failed to convince Tehran's envoys to hand over their translator, Wahid Gordji, wanted for questioning in connection with a wave of bombings that shook the French capital last September. Believed to be a senior intelligence officer in Western Europe, Gordji was suspected to have masterminded and financed the explosions. In retaliation, Tehran summoned the French consul before an Islamic revolutionary court, charging him with espionage, drug trafficking and subversion, each of which carried the death penalty. The breakdown marked the collapse of Prime Minister Jacques Chirac's policy of *rapprochement* with Tehran, illustrated by part payments worth $330 million of the $1 billion loaned by the Shah, arms exports, and the deportation of Massoud Rajavi. In the preceding quarter, Tunisia broke off its relations, Egypt closed the Iranian Interest Section, and London and Tehran were represented by one diplomat each, thus increasing Iran's isolation. Commenting during a sermon, Rafsanjani said that 'the issue of the war of the embassies is inseparable from the Gulf War'. He was proved right. One week later, the French 32 000-ton aircraft carrier *Clemenceau*, surrounded by her battle group, steamed to the Gulf of Oman with 40 aircraft aboard, including 12 *Super-Etendards* (*Time*, 17 August 1987, pp. 4–10; *Newsweek*, 27 July and 24 August 1987, p. 10; *Washington Post*, 20 November 1988; *Middle East Journal 1987*, p. 595; *Strategic Survey 1986–87*, p. 131; Ramazani, 1988, p. 224; O'Ballance, 1988, p. 189; and King, 1987, p. 56).

For its part, the US 'tilt' towards Iraq proved ephemeral, and was beneficial to Iran in the short term. The expansion in the USN's presence moderated Iraqi actions during the month of July and assisted Iran to export 2mbd of its oil, the largest purchaser of which was America itself. This month alone, it provided Tehran's treasury with a sum in excess of $350 million. After the *Washington Post* disclosed that Iran was the US' second largest supplier of oil, the Senate banned imports from Iran, including crude, on 28 September. Furthermore, in early 1987, US officials denied press reports that 'misleading intelligence' on troops' strengths was 'passed to both Iraq and Iran', but it became clear that they had drawn the Iraqis' attention to concentrations of Iranian troops away from Fao, prior to its capture (Axelgard, 1987, pp. 125–6; also O'Ballance, 1988, p. 198; and see Chart A6.8 and Table 1.11).

6.4.5 August 1987

In the wake of the Mecca riots, mobs ransacked the Saudi and Kuwaiti embassies in Tehran, and an explosion that rocked the Saudi Aramco gas plant raised fears that Iran was stepping up its military and political campaign against Iraq's allies. Particularly so, after Rafsanjani called for the elimination of the Saudi royal family, whom Khomeini described as 'inept and spineless' in a talk on Tehran Radio (*Time*, 17 August 1987, pp. 4–10). A few months later, news surfaced that Riyadh, which severed relations with Tehran after the Mecca incident, had pressured Syria, one of Iran's few Arab allies, to follow suit, but that President Asad found that the war was being 'complicated by the presence of the fleets in the Gulf . . . it is possible to reach results with Iran through friendly dialogue, and . . . not . . . through the use of force or pressures'. He disclosed that he met the Iraqi president in April, but that it did not cause any policy changes (interview in *Newsweek*, 28 September 1987, pp. 20–1).

In the Gulf, the IRIN conducted navy manoeuvres labelled *Operation Martyrdom* in remembrance of at least 275 of Iranian pilgrims killed in Mecca on 31 July, and in protest against the re-flagging operation. During the war-games, which lasted four days, Khomeini promised to settle the score. In the waters off Fujairah, hitherto safe, a vessel was hit by a mine as far down as the Gulf of Oman, for the first time. The incident prompted a change of policy by the British and French governments, who now agreed to an earlier request by US Secretary of Defense Frank Carlucci, to send warships to the Gulf. Seven British and three French minesweepers sailed to the troubled waters. Undaunted, the IRGCN continued attacks with FACs and mines, not only in retaliation against the foreign navies' presence, but also as a subterfuge to cover up Tehran's acute embarrassment at having secretly negotiated with the 'Great Satan', and accepted arms from the 'Zionist enemy'. Tehran aimed at restoring its credibility among Iranians, who were closely watching the Irangate Congressional Hearings in the world media (Dainville, 1988, p. 63; *Newsweek*, 24 August 1987, p. 10; *Time*, 17 and 28 August 1987; and see Appendix A.10).

These events coincided with a less-publicized development. Iraqi oil flowed to the port of Iskenderun, thus raising its export volume to the Turkish coast from 1mbd to 1.5mbd. Four months earlier, the Iraqi–Saudi Petroline had increased Iraqi sales from 1.8mb to 3.2mb, and another Iraqi pipeline was being built to the port of Yanbu', with a capacity of 1.6mb. Thus the government avoided bankruptcy and partly funded its war effort with these much-needed foreign earnings. To circumvent attacks on Kharg, Iran was assembling a line to the port of Jask, beyond the Strait of Hormuz, and negotiating with the Soviet Union to export oil to the Black Sea through a converted gas pipeline, left idle since 1980. Worried by the level of attacks, and to avoid the troubled Gulf waters, most oil producers in the area hastened to expand the network of pipelines – although these were expensive in comparison to shipping, even when costly insurance premiums on tankers were added. Their plans contemplated shipping half the Gulf oil to Mediterranean and Red sea ports overland, in spite of an estimated cost of \$2 billion each for the Iraqi and Iranian lines, and \$5 billion for the Petroline (*Time*, 24 August 1987).

Oil production as well as prices surged, induced by fears of a widening war. At \$20 a barrel, Kuwait earned \$8 million a day more than four months earlier, Iran \$20 million more than a year ago, and total Gulf production grew to 7.4mbd from 5mbd in May, in response to 'panic buying' in the West. Most Gulf countries overproduced and pumped 2.8mbd more than the 16.6mbd ceiling agreed by OPEC in June, with Iran doubling its exports. Far from relieving the persisting 'oil glut', over-production was bound to drive prices lower in the long term (*Newsweek*, 24 August, p. 10 and 14 September 1987, pp. 16–17; and see Sections 6.3.2 and 6.3.6).

In the border area, Iranian troops benefited from the ceasefire to prepare for a new ground offensive, but shortages in manpower and supply started to affect their ability to carry out major operations. Iraqi pilots also took advantage of the lull following the adoption of SCR 598 to improve their efficiency. In order to encourage Iran to respond favourably to the resolution, they concentrated their attacks on economic installations, re-started action with 36 bombers striking Bandar Khomeini, and sank an Iranian tanker. The Tanker War continued unabated with Iran's show of force and its direct challenge to the US, hitting a Kuwaiti container ship off Dubai, followed by a missile attack on Kuwait, in early September. The Japanese, who had stopped entering the Gulf for several days, were provided with Iranian PB escorts, after which they resumed trips in convoys.

In Tehran, despite the temporary surge in oil-generated income, and support by young fanatics who still trusted Khomeini's pledge to march to Jerusalem through Iraq, there were signs of growing discontent, in particular among the affluent and the intellectuals. In their view, the ills that plagued their country under the Shah were practised by officials of the new regime, such as brutality and corruption. War-weariness produced long queues of visa seekers outside foreign embassies, especially businessmen, whose factories closed for scarcity of raw materials, and young men, who hoped to dodge the draft. Figures of deserters rose to 30 per cent, despite their inability to get jobs or travel abroad. After tens of thousands fled to Turkey, Pakistan and Gulf Arab states, the government drafted its own officials, thus causing a shortage of qualified civilian manpower. The large number of young widows, who could turn to prostitution, threatened to cause social problems. Hoarding of basic foodstuffs became widespread, however, Khomeini blocked proposals by the cabinet for harsher sentences against *bazaaris* (see section 2.3). While inflation soared, wages hardly increased, forcing most to take on extra work. Growing public discontent forced the government to fine shops selling at inflated prices, and subsidize staples and issue ration books, which permitted the needy to pay one-tenth of the market price. Thus the cost of war became burdensome, in social and economic terms (*Time*, 17 August 1987, pp. 4–10).

6.4.6   September–October 1987

Reagan pledged to the UN General Assembly to reduce the number of warships in the Gulf once the tension had lessened, and the Secretary-General, back at the UN headquarters in New York, reported that his visit to the area was a set-back in the prospects for peace. Every time an envoy held high-level talks in Baghdad and Tehran, without making any headway with Iran's leadership, Iraq gained points, because it had accepted all the proposals for a ceasefire (*Newsweek*, 5 October 1987; and Gamlen, 1989, p. 67). World public opinion, which turned increasingly in favour of Iraq and against Iran, hoped that war-like noises from Washington and a lull in Iraqi strikes would provide Iran's leaders with a chance to reconsider negotiations. If, on the other hand, they did not grab the opportunity, then the world community could avoid hard choices no longer. But as with other mediators who flocked to the Gulf, Iran spurned the options and recommendations offered by Perez de Cuellar. It had kept a consistent policy of rejecting any proposed peace plan, unless the conditions set at the very beginning of the Iran–Iraq War were met. Khomeini's ruthless policy of unconditional surrender was premised on the belief that it would cause the overthrow of Saddam Hussein and establish an administration with which peace could be settled.

Seven years into the war, Baghdad and Tehran closed their diplomatic missions to each other in October. Over the Gulf waters, conditions deteriorated to a considerable degree. Iraq, frustrated by the deadlock and Iran's refusal to comply with SCR 598, started the autumn aerial offensive. It struck five vessels on the same day, totalling eight within a week, and 12 by the end of September, including the world's largest VLCC, the Liberian *Seawise Giant*, loading at Larak, close to the Hormuz passageway. Iran matched the number of Iraqi hits, and both totals were their highest since the start of the Tanker War (Dainville, 1988, pp. 60–1; [Harare] *Herald*, 24 December 1987; Nasser, 1988, p. 1; and see Chart A6.8 and Table 1.11).

From 1985 to 1989, Admiral William Crowe, Chairman of the Joint Chiefs of Staff (JCS), held the most senior uniformed post at the Pentagon at one of the most critical times in the history of USN operations in the confined and exposed waters of the Gulf. One year before assuming his new duties, he was based in Bahrain, serving as Commander, METF. Beside personally handling the crucial negotiations on the reflagging of Kuwaiti tankers with the oil minister, Sheikh 'Ali Khalifah al-Sabbah, and events in its aftermath, he was at the pinnacle of military decisions and part of the innermost circle at the White House, involved in political debates regarding USN manoeuvres in the Gulf. Being a central figure in the inner advisory team of President Reagan, during the period covering the Tanker War, the admiral gained a reputation for being a master at harmonizing military requirements with political obligations. Subsequently, he served as one of his country's top envoys abroad. In the mid-1990s, he headed the USA mission in the UK, and was committed to keeping the US–UK 'special relationship' alive (Crowe, 25 October 1996).

During those momentous events, Admiral Crowe's diplomatic skills were revealed in the National Security Planning Group (NSPG) meetings, when the views of its members conflicted, especially when the subject of US retaliation against Iranian attacks was discussed. Howard Baker, Chief of the White House Staff and Frank Carlucci, the National Security Advisor, supported diplomatic responses, while James Baker, the Treasury Secretary, called for a firm response, and Caspar Weinberger, the Defence Secretary, was the most hawkish of the group. While Admiral Crowe personally favoured a response that would send the Iranians a firm signal, such as sinking one of their warships, he submitted a list of suggested targets, which included oil platforms, used by the Iranians as speedboat bases, Farsi Island, another of the *Pasdaran* bases, and military installations at the port of Bandar Abbas. The *Silkworm* site at Fao was ruled out, as 'there was no point in just killing a lot of date palms there', since the missile launchers were mobile. He added that in the end, it was up to the president to decide whether, when or how hard the US would respond, as the NSPG only offered advice (Crowe, Interview, 28 April 1995; see Sections 6.5.1 and 7.4).

Iran and the US became fiercely embattled, partly over attacks against America's protégés. On 21 September, US helicopter-gunships crippled the *Iran Ajr*, caught laying mines, killing five of her crew; and in retaliation for firing on US patrol helicopters, USN units destroyed three IRGCN speedboats near Farsi. Iran struck back, hurling two *Silkworms* at two tankers off the Kuwaiti port of Ahmadi: the Liberian-registered American VLCC *Sungari*, which had no USN protection, and the *Sea Isle City*, the first missile attack on a re-flagged tanker. In their blow-for-blow sparring, the USN destroyed two Iranian offshore platforms at Rashadat in the Rostam oilfield, used by the IRGCN as minor bases, as a reprisal for attacks on the VLCCs. Undeterred, another Chinese-made missile, also fired from Fao, hit the oil-loading facility at Kuwait's Sea Island terminal, setting the petroleum tanks ablaze (*Time*, 5, 19 and 26 October and 2 November 1987; *Newsweek*, 24 August and 2 November 1987; *Strategic Survey 1987–88*, p. 131; Dainville, 1988, pp. 60–2; Ramazani, 1988, pp. 86–7; Gamlen, 1989, pp. 55–7; Nasser, 1988, p. 1; and see Chapter 5).

Reviving its manoeuvre to intercept and inspect maritime traffic, a second case of forced detention by Iran occurred on

9 October. Iranian PBs attacked the Greek refrigerated cargo *Mykonos* (LT, SER) and compelled her to sail to Bandar Abbas. But the *Mykonos*' fate did not end as tragically as the *Ibn Al Beitar*'s in October 1985. Released four days later, she was able to resume her voyage to Dammam with her cargo of meat and timber (Lloyd's).

6.4.7 November–December 1987

Politicians and diplomats alike worried about the upsurge of fighting in the Gulf where, by the end of October, Iraqi pilots had targeted 11 vessels and Iran ten. The urgency to end the war became as strong as the pressures which mounted on all sides to start it, seven years earlier. Meeting in Amman, the Arab heads of state provided Iraq with a political triumph, showing unprecedented solidarity in taking a harder line towards Iran, especially Saudi Arabia, Kuwait and Bahrain. The GCC summit in Riyadh, the following month, accused Tehran of 'prevaricating' over SCR 598, and coordinated defence strategies, raising the possibility of Egyptian military assistance. Although Egyptian officers were already training Kuwaiti and Iraqi pilots and anti-missile personnel, Mubarak did not agree to station troops in the Gulf (*Time*, 11 January 1988; *Strategic Survey 1987–88*, pp. 131–2 and 1988–9, p. 180; and *Guardian*, 22 November 1987).

To demonstrate that they were prepared to lend weight to their demands, the UNSC five permanent members (P5) signed a statement endorsing an embargo against Iran if it continued to defer its decision over SCR 598. Until then, Iran's only advocates among the P5 were China and the Soviet Union, but unlike before, their delegates were prepared to agree to sanctions (see Section 6.4.4). As a reminder of the interests at stake in the area, the Soviet envoy suggested a UN naval blockade of the Gulf, but US officials were distrustful of proposals that upgraded the Soviet role there, or lessened their own (*Time*, 11 January 1988; Gamlen, 1989, pp. 42–3; and see other calls for a UN patrol in Sections 6.2.2 and 6.4.1 and Thatcher's response to the proposal in Section 7.2).

In defiance of decisions reached in the Arab and international fora, official statements out of Tehran warned Iraq's allies to cease supporting their foe. At the same time, it unleashed its forces in retaliation against them. Intense attacks on shipping continued escalating in the Gulf, and although they sank their first tanker, Iran's diplomats abroad denied any knowledge of the attack. Given the stalemate on the battlefront, anyway, where Iranian forces staged probing attacks in the Fakkeh area north of Basra again, Khomeini said he had modified Iran's tactics, and turned the war into one of attrition to deprive Iraqis of respite.

Having so far failed to break Iran's resolve, and still desperate to broaden the war and ease pressure on its ground troops, Iraq took the support given by the Arab and GCC summits and the P5 as a 'green light' to escalate its attacks on Iranian oil-related targets. Thus the last quarter of the year became a record period in the Tanker War. Combined figures of Iraqi and Iranian strikes for the months of October, November and December were the highest, totalling 72. The year also witnessed the fiercest fighting, as both countries scored 164 hits, out of 421 since May 1981, and out of the total of 490 throughout the Tanker War. But because of the foreign naval presence of around 80 vessels, the IRGCN's actions were largely limited to the area of Hormuz. Missile firings on cities were also the highest during that year, totalling 104, of which Iraq fired 25 *Scuds* and Iran 18, in addition to 61 *Oghab* missiles (Zaloga, 1988, Table p. 1427; and see Chart A6.8 and Table 1.11).

A few entries in Lloyd's during the last three months caused confusion. No activity by any IRIN man-of-war was recorded for the ten months following the attack on the *Crown Hope* in November 1986, until a loaded South Korean tanker was struck by shell fire, from what was thought to be a frigate on 1 September 1987. The wrecked boilers initially immobilized the *Astro Pegasus* (LT, SER), but she was repaired and reported in service. Six weeks later, the Kuwaiti tanker *Umm Al Jathathel* (LT, RPD), loaded with gas oil, was also assailed by a craft reported to be an IRIN frigate. She continued her voyage, as she only sustained seven small punctures in the port side and five in the afterpart of the accommodation – presumed to be caused by a fusillade of machine-guns. On 11 December, the Greek tanker *Tharaleos* (LT, RPD), in ballast, was said to have been assaulted by a frigate, but damage was minor and she proceeded to Mina Saud, and then to Philadelphia. The minimal damage described above suggested that the vessels were shot at with salvos of machine-gun fire, probably from a boat and not a frigate, as had been assumed by Lloyd's. During the course of the Tanker War, this form of attack had become more and more familiar, especially after the creation of the IRGCN's base on Farsi Island, and their increased usage of swarms of lightly armed FACs.

Two other recordings in the register on 15 December were also puzzling, one of which concerned the Greek tanker *Ariadne* (LT, RPD and LT, FD, HM, WS, SER). The first attack was carried out at dawn, off the Omani coast near the Strait, when she was strafed by machine-gun fire from a gunboat. Later in the day, eight miles north of Jebel 'Ali, she was assaulted by a frigate. A massive explosion in the pump room ripped open the ship's deck, and fires raged in the accommodation area. She listed to starboard, then was stranded the following day (Lloyd's). These two offensives conveyed the impression that the IRIN and the IRGCN carried out combined operations, despite Tehran's repeated denials.

From the beginning of the Tanker War, the superpowers had been ambivalent in their policies towards Iran and Iraq. Officially neutral, they called for restraint and a ceasefire, and at the same time, each provided them both with hardware. But tension was rising between them, motivated principally by Washington's equal concerns about the expansion of Soviet influence in the Gulf and the 'hegemonic' designs of Iran, especially after Gorbachev deferred setting a date for a summit with Reagan. While the White House appeared to attach itself more closely to Iraq, the Kremlin had a dynamic and flexible Gulf policy. The US implicitly sanctioned Iraq's attacks on strategic Iranian targets, denounced Iran over the continuation of the conflict, and constantly called for UN-mandated sanctions against it. These proposals were invariably opposed by the USSR and the PRC, and whereas Gorbachev called for the departure of the foreign armada and a diplomatic solution, and in effect kept the Soviet Navy at its former level, Washington applied the sheer military might of its seapower against Iran's (see Section 4.5). On the other hand, the Kremlin shrewdly manoeuvred to make inroads into the area. Diplomatic pressures on Baghdad to suspend missile attacks on cities were successful in February; in March, it rapidly approved leasing three tankers to Kuwait with an understanding that its warships would engage in escort operations (see Section 7.2);

and in August, it successfully negotiated plans with Tehran to reactivate pipelines and construct another rail line from Iran to Central Asia (see Section 6.4.5). As fears arose in GCC capitals that the USSR took advantage of the war to lay foundations for solid economic relations with Iran, Kuwait's oil minister, Sheikh 'Ali Khalifah al-Sabbah, visited Moscow in November. One month later, the Saudi foreign minister followed in his trail, and also held talks in Washington (Dainville, 1988, p. 64; *Time*, 19 October 1987; and *Guardian*, 1 November 1987).

6.5   1988 – IRAN SAILS INTO A SEA OF TROUBLES

6.5.1   January–March 1988

As the conflict continued, Syria's foreign policy became difficult to evaluate. Although it still supported Iran publicly, their relations appeared to decline. In March 1987, Tehran halted oil sales to Damascus at reduced prices, and both capitals' policies in Lebanon no longer coincided. By the fall of 1987, Asad's link with Moscow had loosened, and he offered to mediate the release of Western hostages held in Lebanon. Taking advantage of the emerging trend, Jordan's King Hussein proposed to use his good offices again to reconcile the two *Ba'thi* rulers, which threatened to increase Iran's isolation (*Newsweek*, 28 September 1987, pp. 20–1; *Middle East Journal 1987*, p. 591; Dainville, 1988, p. 64; and see Section 6.4.4).

Another major regional development had more implications for the Tanker War. It lent itself to a myriad of explanations but was less publicized. The USS *Iowa* sailed from the region and was not replaced, thus reducing the US naval presence (Dainville, 1988, p. 63). Optimists implied that the USN restructured the size of its fleet because peace was within reach, and cynics remarked she left the area because she was too large and attractive a target for Iranian attacks. Her withdrawal was seen by some as being motivated largely by the need to lower the estimated annual cost to the American taxpayer of $200 million for the armada (or $240 million, according to Richardson in Taylor and Francis, 1988, p. 311), 'described in Washington as supporting the diplomatic campaign to pressure Iran to begin peace talks with Iraq or suffer sanctions'

(*Guardian*, 13 December 1987). Although Reagan had pledged at the UN that once 'the tension diminishes, so will our presence' (*Newsweek*, 5 October 1987), some thought he reduced the American fleet on patrol duty in the Gulf to appease Gorbachev and secure the Kremlin's consent to join the US, the UK and France in their call for an embargo against Iran (see Sections 4.5 and 6.4.7). Hints by the GCC Secretary-General to 'lower the profile' of the USN, and predictions by Kuwait's defence minister that 'foreign navies will now withdraw', entered the equation (Gamlen, 1989, pp. 39–40). Another view was that Europe's battle fleet compensated for the departure of the American cruiser (see Maps 6.1 and 6.2).

During a 70-minute interview with Admiral Crowe, one of the questions asked was the motive for withdrawing the USS *Iowa* and its support flotilla, thus reducing the size of the USN in the region. He explained that there was no need for her in the area any longer, since the USN had achieved its double objective of neutralizing the capabilities of Iran's ports and airfields and establishing free unchallenged navigation, and that the situation in the Gulf had become relatively calm (Crowe, Interview, 28 April 1995; see Section 6.4.6 and 7.4).

Over the Gulf waters, Iran scored 27 hits, the second highest figure in one quarter, after the total of 37 in the last three months of the previous year (see Chart A6.9 and Table 1.11). Iraq struck 17 ships, compared to 35 the previous quarter, including two shuttle tankers at Kharg, causing the highest loss of life in one raid.

In mid-January, a frigate accompanied by a FAC hit the Liberian tanker *Petrobulk Pioneer* (LT, SER), sailing in ballast. Her bunker tanks were perforated and her superstructure was damaged by shell fire. She proceeded to Dubai, then to Jebel 'Ali, and was seen at the Hormuz terminal six weeks later. Again, on 18 March, the Panamanian liquid gas carrier *Maria 2* (LT, FX, FX, SER) caught fire in the engine room and the accommodation, after an attack by a frigate, eight miles off Dubai. Two of her tanks were holed and leaked. After being extinguished, the fires reignited, gutting her bridge, and she was towed to Singapore. The last mention of an Iranian frigate assailing a vessel was registered on the last day of the same month, when the Cypriot tanker *Haven* (LT, FX, WS, SER), loaded with light oil, caught fire and stranded one mile off

Mina Saqr. Her accommodation and a tank were severely damaged by fire. A fortnight later, she was re-floated and towed to Fujairah and then to Singapore (Lloyd's). Apart from those referred to before, the incidents reported here, involving Iranian maritime attacks, seemed questionable. Were the attacking ships indisputably identified as frigates, or were they large boats, mistaken for frigates, as was suggested earlier (see Section 6.4.7)? If they indeed were frigates, then it would follow that the IRIN and the IRGCN cooperated in combined operations. In which case, Iran was violating international law by attacking ships of non-belligerent countries sailing in international waters. That would place into doubt official Iranian statements claiming the *Pasdaran* and the navy did not collaborate. It would also call into question the navy headquarters' assertion that the IRIN neither commanded nor was able to control the activities of naval volunteer forces. However, if the craft reported in these attacks were not frigates, but large PBs, one could guardedly conclude that these were operated independently by the volunteers. And the IRIN restricted its operations to coastal and escort patrols of convoys shuttling between Kharg and the lower end of the Gulf. By dissociating itself from the volunteers' actions, the IRIN was able to pretend that the IRGCN could not be curbed, in which case Tehran discovered an ingenious method to attain its aim – with gain and no pain.

Iraq renewed the war of the cities, amid news from Iran that it could produce CW and long-range missiles (*Time*, 11 January 1988), combined with frustration over the battlefield deadlock and Tehran's refusal to endorse SCR 598. The firing of 90 long-range SSMs in ten days against Tehran, Qom and other towns marked their first use by Iraq. The barrage of modified *Scud-B* missiles, countered by Iranian attacks, also aimed to further delay any major Iranian ground offensive, and by delivering a psychological blow to the Iranian people's morale, restrict the enlisting of volunteers and provoke a wave of popular support for a peace settlement. World attention focused on the area again, after shifting to crisis areas in Afghanistan and Israel. While Washington still pressed for UN sanctions against Tehran, Gulf rulers counselled against the missile volley, as it depicted Iraq as the belligerent (*International Herald Tribune*, 14 March 1988; and *Strategic Survey 1988–89*, p. 174).

Iran launched minor ground offensives in two areas in Kurdistan and occupied 540 square miles, while the Kurds reportedly controlled 4000 square miles of rural Kurdistan. Aided by *Peshmerga*, Iranian troops were about to enter Halabja, the harmless and previously obscure town, when Iraqi aircraft dropped CW, killing 4000 people in a few minutes, to implicate Iran in the use of chemicals (Korn, 1992, pp. 157–60; and *Strategic Survey 1988–89*, p. 174). Unfortunately for the Kurds and the Iranian troops, the vicious incident was under-reported, at the time, and left no mark on public opinion, contrary to the media exposure and images of despair offered to television viewers during the second Kurdish exodus in 1991. Consequently, there were no public debates, or commissions of inquiry, nor sanctions. The international inertia reflected the lack of political will, and the war was made bloodier and more vicious, inflicting unbelievable suffering, particularly on Kurdish women and children, and teenage *baseej*.

6.5.2 April–August 1988

Conditions in the final four months were pivotal in ending the Iran–Iraq War. Momentous political and military factors fused and brought about Iran's acceptance of SCR 598, passed the year before. One of the reasons was the change in attitude among Iranians, whose will to fight was exhausted. The second was the combination of diverse military tactics implemented by Iraq. Finally, the USN's escalation in anti-Iranian operations played a decisive role, with Tehran's accurate perception that the US was intervening on Iraq's side.

Following the convening of the third *majlis*, Khomeini appointed Rafsanjani acting chief of the armed forces. The pragmatic parliamentary speaker, who had been discharged from the Imperial army, had a fair knowledge of military tactics. He gauged public opinion to assess whether it was worthwhile to proceed with warfare, especially so when divisions soon emerged within the newly elected house. A large group of members opposed the continuation of war and called for a ceasefire, aware that most of the population had been driven to the limit of endurance. Daily hardship, caused by economic strains, had led to public unrest. According to Graham Fuller,

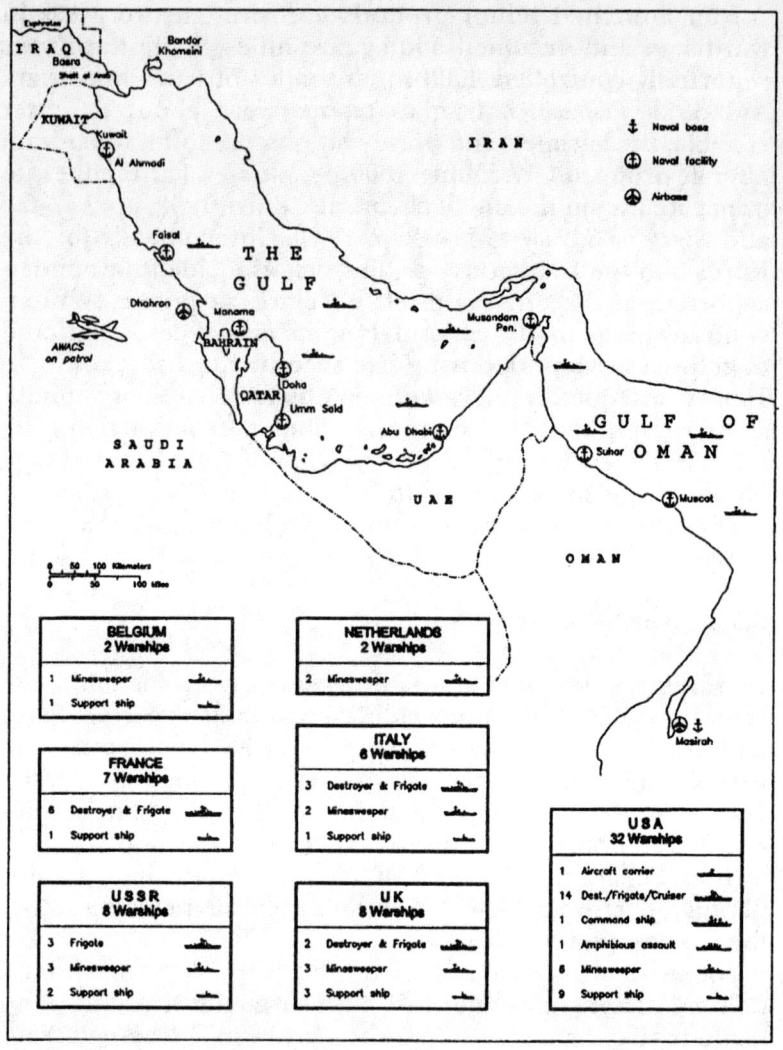

Map 6.2 Foreign Naval Presence and Facilities in the Gulf (Summer 1988)

former Vice-President of the US National Intelligence Council and senior analyst at the Rand Corporation, the Iranians 'were close to the breaking point politically' (in *Washington Post,* 26 October 1988; also *Strategic Survey 1988–89,* p. 175; and see Section 6.4.5).

The shower of rockets finally ceased, after Iraq hurled 200 long-range SSMs against its foe's cities and Iran responded with 77 (according to Zaloga, 1988, table p. 1427, from January to the end of May, Iraq fired 193 *Scuds* and Iran 231, in addition to 104 *Oghab* missiles). On the main battlefront, Iranian troops made limited attacks on Penjwin and penetrated Shalamja, but retreated, as the tides of war turned in favour of Iraq. Iran, which throughout the war dominated ground battles, found itself losing, within a short time, territories that took several years to capture and hold on to. Iraq increased its pressure in all three sectors, and its troops mounted several offensives along the border. Using CW extensively, they seized some Iranian territories in the Penjwin district and the Musian border area, and regained Fao, Majnoon, Mawet and Shalamjah. Mehran, which they also overwhelmed, was handed over to Rajavi's NLA (O'Ballance, 1988, p. 189; and *Washington Report on Middle East Affairs*, August 1988, p. 31).

Despite Tehran's acceptance of SCR 598 on 18 July, both countries played for higher stakes, and fighting persisted up to the eleventh hour in small enclaves along the border. Iraqi and Iranian operations were staged to acquire the ability to negotiate from a position of strength, and to have better cards during the forthcoming talks. The Iraqi army achieved breakthroughs in the central and southern fronts, but its attempts to make headway in the north failed. Shortly before the war drew to a close, when the ceasefire was implemented on 20 August, the Iranian army recaptured Mehran and territories it had lost in the south near Ahvaz.

Iran's reversals on the ground were compounded by losses at sea, weakening its conventional and volunteer navies. Their freedom of action was curtailed by Reagan's instructions to USN commanders and pilots to protect all neutral vessels and strictly observe the rules of engagement (ROE) (see Appendix A9 and Sections 7.3 and 7.4). US–Iranian naval and aerial clashes escalated (see Map 7.3), with a mine attack on the USS *Samuel B Roberts*, avenged at a later date with attacks on Sirri and Sassam, countered 15 minutes later with an assault on an American oil platform and two merchant ships. Conditions became uncontrollable with heavy casualties on both sides. They culminated with the downing of Iran Air Flight 655 on 3 July, with 290 civilians aboard, by the *Aegis*-class missile cruiser, the USS *Vincennes*, following skirmishes with Iranian FACs. During the fray, Iraqi pilots hit three tankers (CTL), including the world's largest, recorded as the most costly single raid for insurers (see Chart A6.10 and Table 1.11), and Saddam Hussein repeated his five-point peace plan on the 20th anniversary of the *Ba'thi* coup (Dainville, 1988, pp. 64–5; Gamlen, 1989, pp. 58–60; and *Washington Report on Middle East Affairs*, August 1988, p. 31).

The following day, Tehran endorsed SCR 598, and two days later, Khomeini gave his famed 'poison chalice' speech to justify the government's acceptance of the UN-mandated ceasefire. He explained to his followers that they had to renounce the *jihad*, launched years ago, as he was conscious of the enormous economic pressures on his people. Most notably, he also declared that he was anxious not to provoke deeper Western involvement in the Gulf, or lay the country open to US air attacks.

Iraq and Iran pursued an excessively lengthy and static war, with high casualties, and troops in close proximity to each other in areas around their common border at all times. Both relied on trench warfare, especially Iraq, with Iran using infantry attacks and *human wave* tactics, backed by a large reservoir of manpower. Each attempted to break the deadlock, with sporadic ground fighting erupting on the battlefront, but with little success. Both had large arsenals of land and sea mines which they used immoderately, and both were able to circumvent the weapons embargo and procure missiles, artillery, spare parts, light arms and ammunition. Occasionally, bomb and missile volleys targeted each other's urban areas, to induce war-fatigue among the people, with the aim of creating enough pressure on their governments to agree to a negotiated settlement. From 1984, Iraq, followed by Iran, took the war to the waters of the Gulf and conducted a campaign against shipping. Iraq used its airpower and Iran relied on a mix of regular and volunteer forces, using a combination of fixed-wing and rotary aircraft with a fleet of FACs and conventional naval craft. But neither had adequate airpower or seapower to alter the military balance and bring about a decisive victory. On the domestic scene, consumer goods were scarce and retail prices spiralled in both states. A new breed of *nouveaux riches* traders, mostly related to members of the regimes, carved a niche for themselves, profiting from the war. Thus both governments were forced to introduce controls and subsidize basic food staples, after growing alienation among the poor. Both regimes reexamined their ideology and modified their posture, on the one hand to monopolize the slogan of nationalism and undercut the rising tide of opposition, and on the other, to hijack world backing from their foe. Shortly after the ceasefire, and before the year's end, Baghdad and Tehran clamped down on their opposition at home. Iraq gassed Kurdish villages, and across the Shatt, a wave of large-scale summary arrests and executions of political prisoners, targeting the MKO, led to the massacre of mainly leftist Iranian dissenters; the detainees, running into thousands, were accused of advocating armed rebellion (*New York Times*, 30 November 1988; Gamlen, 1989, p. 64; and *Strategic Survey 1988–89*, p. 176).

On 25 August 1988, peace negotiations were launched in Geneva, chaired by the UN Secretary-General, after Iraq withdrew its demand for direct discussions with Iran. But talks stalled until 15 August 1990, when Baghdad renounced its claim over the eastern bank of al-Shatt and accepted the status quo *ante bellum*, less than a fortnight after its invasion of Kuwait. Although several exchanges of prisoners of war (POWs) took place between them, each side alleged that large numbers of those who remained had applied for political asylum. Baghdad's repeated requests to clear al-Shatt and open Basra to shipping were always countered by Tehran's insistence on the signing of a treaty that legalized its claim over half the waterway, tracing the boundary along the *thalweg*, as stated in the 1975 Algiers agreement. But uncertainty still hovers over the issue of the border dispute, as no workable peace plan has materialized yet between Iraq and Iran. Whether the conflict will be allowed to rest is open to question, but past history does not give cause for optimism.

7 Iran's Silent Force and the US Navy Take Centre Stage

7.1 *KITMAN VA MAKR*

In the Tanker War, Iraqi pilots focused on Iranian strategic targets. These included its fleet and oil-export facilities, foreign chartered tankers which operated in the shuttle service, and those lifting Iranian oil. Iranian retaliatory assaults had been unable to restrain Iraq's onslaught. Quite the contrary, it escalated relentlessly as the war continued, and curiously, did not attract world condemnation, whereas Iran's attacks were increasingly denounced as endangering international shipping, especially by Washington. Circumstances suggested that it became evident to Iran that it needed to orchestrate a different response.

In an article in the French journal *Defense Nationale*, Chardin had a fascinating theory on the reasons for Iran's success in profiting from circumstances, by manipulating countries it perceived as hostile to its interests. He explained that the nation which is reputed to have invented the game of chess a long time ago, had revealed itself as an extremely efficacious, though dangerous, adversary. It combined military action with terrorism and economic blackmail, profited from US–USSR antagonism, divulged sensational news that harmed certain countries' governments, and played off President Jimmy Carter and President-elect Ronald Reagan against each other during the hostage crisis and the election campaign. In short, he wrote, Iran used a blend of duplicity (*takiga*), concealment (*kitman*) and deviousness (*makr*) in pursuing its policies (Chardin, 1987, p. 59). Needless to say, Iran's method of reprisal in the Tanker War will be added to Chardin's list along with the examples cited.

Geopolitical and geostrategic realities dictated Tehran's oblique course. It had to use a 'silent force' to counter the obstacles it faced. Iraq's attacks were against Iranian targets or tankers lifting oil from its ports. On most occasions, these were in the war zones, in Iranian territorial waters or within the Iraqi-declared maritime exclusion zone. But Iran faced a dilemma. Its enemy had been landlocked since the first weeks of operations in 1980. All its crude was exported overland, through neighbouring countries, via pipelines and in tanker trucks. Its imports, including arms shipments, also came across Kuwait, Saudi Arabia, Turkey and Jordan. As Iraq's neighbouring countries were not at war with Iran, its military command had to devise ways and means to retaliate. This it accomplished by attacking Iraq's Gulf allies first, especially Saudi Arabia and Kuwait, then at a later stage, any tanker flying the flag of a country perceived to be siding with Baghdad.

Another course of action was to close the Strait of Hormuz in the face of all ships bound to the harbours of Iraq's allies. Were this tactic workable, the overland routes across countries adjoining Iraq would still remain available to Baghdad, with ships unloading at Mediterranean and Red Sea ports. As discussed in Section 4.2, there were practical difficulties for the IRIN in securing total obstruction. In earlier operations, at least two destroyers, two frigates, two PBs and a corvette were seriously damaged, and two PBs and two minesweepers were lost; and, according to an Iranian naval officer who emigrated in the mid-1980s, its only surviving minesweeper was stationed in the Caspian Sea. Also, some of the sophisticated weaponry was inoperable because of the lack of maintenance, and its stock of SSMs and SAMs was depleted. Notwithstanding the fact that it had suffered significant losses since the start of the war, Iran's navy still remained the largest Gulf seapower. But using it to blockade a vital SLOC would have alienated the world community and created massive problems for Iran. Hence the decision to avert international denunciation. Tehran created a non-regular volunteer force, which designed an unorthodox and flexible strategy, operated rocket-armed FACs, used sea-mines, and resorted to suicide attacks in some operations.

Under international law, the rules of naval warfare permit a country at war to 'stop and search' ships, in other words, to intercept and inspect neutral vessels to ascertain whether they were loaded with cargoes destined to its enemy. Accordingly, the IRIN stepped up its operations from random inspection of 'shipping, to a full-scale programme of intercepting, boarding and searching vessels suspected of carrying arms and other supplies for Iraq'. In July 1985, it announced that it planned to exercise its legal right regularly, in order to impede the flow of goods to its enemy. Thus, from the following September, approximately 300 ships were inspected, up to mid-November (Aryan, 1989, p. 189). Why the Iranian Navy did not practice its prerogative earlier is unclear.

The arms embargo was another problem Iran had to resolve. The war had run into several years, and stockpiles of spare parts and ammunition had either been depleted or become obsolete. Iran was able to partially circumvent the arms embargo, as is now known from books and newspaper reports on cases of clandestine arms shipments. Although it acquired at highly inflated prices some of the weapons it needed for the conduct of the war, the quantity and type it was able to purchase hinged very much on whether they were obtainable on the black market. This depended, among other factors, on the willingness of manufacturers to provide Tehran with the items it requested, and on the availability of a third party that would consent to be cited as the end-user on the contract. (The end-user certificate is the guarantee by an importing country that arms received will not be re-exported, but requests for an international register of these licences, which would verify their authenticity, have never been seriously considered by any government.) Also, big platforms can hardly be the stuff for contraband, although it was reported that a British arms merchant was arrested in the US in 1983, trying to ship 100 American tanks to Iran, citing the UAE as end-user (*Wall Street Journal*, 10 May 1984; and see Section 6.4.3).

Besides facing these difficulties, Iran had to defend its economic lifeline too. Intense bouts of Iraqi strikes on Kharg and tanker convoys started to affect its earnings from oil sales. Usually, these attacks were followed by instructions to foreign vessels from their companies or national labour unions not to sail near Iranian oil facilities. In some instances, the ships' masters were instructed not to enter the Gulf at all. Oil revenues dropped, at a time when these were crucial to sustain the war economy, and to fund the import of consumer goods for a population that had become increasingly restive as the war endured.

Also, as the Tanker War intensified, insurance premiums on cargoes and hulls escalated because of the risks involved in lifting crude from Iranian oil terminals. For instance, war risk insurance rates on ships entering the Gulf rose to 7.5 per cent of a tanker's value in June 1984, and Lloyd's of London increased them again by 50 per cent in the fall of 1987 (Daly, 1985, p. 157; and *Newsweek*, 14 September 1987, pp. 16–17). Keeping the crude priced at the level indicated by OPEC's index, while buyers were bearing the new premiums, made Iranian oil prices uncompetitive. It was likely, as a consequence, that it risked losing its market-share.

To counter increased Iraqi assaults, Iran formed the IRGCN in 1986, and relied on volunteers for its manpower. There was no shortage of recruits, though they knew they would either perish or, at the very least, suffer under harsh conditions in their day-to-day life. Resources were scarce at first, but motivation among the *Pasdar* was high. Tehran started recruiting this new type of legion, with the double purpose of de-emphasizing the role of officers commissioned under the *ancien régime*, and tightening control over the fighters. As the war unfolded, the *Pasdar* became the enduring image of Iranian victory. The stories about these war heroes are now part of the folklore saga. The battlefield accounts of heroic exploits went straight from the soldiers' mouths into national legend.

The IRGCN started operating from its base on Farsi Island, by 6 May 1987, and the same month witnessed a sudden burst of tit-for-tat attacks. Its units began assaulting civilian shipping in international waters or in territorial waters of non-belligerent countries, and the last quarter of 1987 saw the highest number of strikes by Iran, culminating in 17 hits in December alone (see Table 1.11). According to a former IRIN officer, in a personal communication, their squadrons mainly used FACs and claimed to have operated independently of the regular navy, although they received their training and part of their hardware from it. Irrespective of their flags, the ships they struck were either tankers in ballast, or cargoes loaded with goods, all steaming to Arab harbours. The targets also included tankers that had lifted oil from Arab terminals, but Saudi and Kuwaiti facilities and tankers took the brunt of the attacks. Both countries were known to have substantially aided Iraq's war effort, and the government in Tehran made its point: each attack was yet another warning that they should halt support for its enemy. The core of Iran's policy of retaliation seemed to have been its confidence that if their economies were hurt to a degree that became untenable for them, they would ultimately exert pressure on Iraq to stop hitting tankers, or even sue for peace.

It took Iran about two years to establish an operational naval force that eventually grew larger than its navy, totalling 20 000 *Pasdar*, whose spirit of daring was often demonstrated in their engagements. Commanded by Mohsen Rezai, the IRGCN was fitted out with a fleet of around 800 speedboats, in addition to about 80 Swedish-made interceptor *Boghammer* craft, which could be effective in suicide attacks. Nicknamed 'Boston Whalers', they are highly manoeuverable and fast, with speeds of up to 60 mph, and armed with inexpensive weapons (*Time*, 19 October 1987). These agile boats were appropriate for operations in archipelagos and crowded waters, studded with a large number of small islands. They proved effective in implementing their strategy, at a cost that was low in political and financial terms. To a considerable degree, their use of *Zodiac* boats denoted their creativity and good sense in overcoming their shortage in resources and the international political constraints.

First of all, the arms embargo had to be bypassed. As *Zodiacs* could be used for non-military purposes, ordering them in large numbers would not arouse the manufacturers' suspicions. Secondly, their cost was far lower than traditional craft, which allowed Iran to purchase a larger number within the limitations set for budgeting. Thirdly, small rubber boats are lightweight and can easily be delivered by airfreight and consequently reach their destination quickly. Fourthly, instruction on their use is simple to absorb, therefore trainees can operate them in a short time. Fifthly, they combine the advantages of speed, a high degree of manoeuvrability and the difficulty of detection on radar screens, with the various possibilities of arming them with recoilless rifles, machine-guns and RPG launchers. In the constricted waters of the Gulf, interspersed with reefs, they were suitable for low-intensity missions. Lastly, and not least importantly, they had been tested in an earlier operation, when the Iranian infantry occupied al-Fao.

The fleet of speedboats, often unmarked, made hit-and-run attacks against vessels. They were each manned by four to eight *Pasdar* and became Iran's chief retaliatory weapon in the Tanker War. Their tactics relied on harassing US warships without directly confronting them, and they carefully targeted tag-along tankers, which trailed behind the escorted convoys but technically fell beyond their protection (*Time*, 14 September 1987, pp. 12–13; and *Newsweek*, 24 August 1987, pp. 8–9).

According to an Iranian naval officer, who asked for anonymity, and whose information was in part corroborated by a former Iranian merchant marine officer (Pourzanjani, Interview, 17 May 1991), the IRGCN established its headquarters on Farsi Island, a barren atoll which also had surveillance and tracking installations. They also set up smaller reinforced bases on the islands of Hormuz, Sirri, Larak, Abu Musa, the two Tunbs and Halu, about 1000-strong each. They deployed some minor forces on oil platforms too, mainly those damaged by Iraqi attacks. While some of these were used for radar surveillance to report on convoy movements, others were launching pads for attacks against naval targets. He also said that the Revolutionary Guards were trained in suicide attacks at Nowshahr Naval Academy on the Caspian Sea, and instructed in simple techniques of naval warfare, such as ramming a ship, at Bandar Abbas naval base. Using a boat loaded with high explosives, which blasts upon contact with the target, was devised between 800 and 850 BC; the tactic was refined during the wars between Persian and Hellenic forces, and relied on extensively in the wars involving Sparta and Athens between 431 and 400 BC (for a historical account of ramming, see Abou-Zikry, 1986, pp. 16–18, 20–1).

Besides their large fleet of small boats, the IRGCN were provided with an air defence/offense capability, in the form of around 40 Swiss *Pilatus* PC-7 light training/attack aircraft, helicopters and Chinese F-6 and F-7 fighter aircraft. Their arsenal was bolstered with 35 to 50 of the famous Chinese *Silkworm* missiles, some mounted on hardened sites on the mainland

and on Qishm Island, at the mouth of the Gulf, and others mobile on Fao (Cordesman, 1988, p. 27; and see Map 7.1). The *Pasdar* also had a number of potent US *Stingers*, empty packing cases of which were found on one of three speedboats disabled by US machine-gun fire in the fall of 1987. The shoulder-fired missiles were used with devastating effect by the *mujahedeen* in Afghanistan against Soviet helicopters and fixed-wing aircraft. According to a Pentagon investigation, they were either purchased from American-aided guerrillas in Afghanistan, or the IRGC had managed to seize them. The discovery faced strategists in Washington with the alarming likelihood of USAF aircraft in the Gulf being shot down by US-made missiles (*Time*, 19 and 26 October 1987; and *Newsweek*, 26 August 1987).

Mine warfare was another tactic used by Iran to resolve its dilemma in reciprocating, having the dual advantage of being exemplary for the Gulf theatre of operations, and leaving no 'fingerprints' (see Map 7.2). The use of its regular navy would have invited world opprobrium for violating international law by attacking ships of non-belligerent countries sailing in international waters. And, according to a retired Iranian naval officer, the IRIN command was also faced with the unwillingness of regular officers to attack merchant ships, which they felt to be unethical. The problem was resolved by laying mines, using simple craft, such as cargoes or even wooden dhows. They were camouflaged on the boats' decks, or attached beneath the hulls, and laid under the cover of darkness. When a target was hit, Tehran rarely exulted in its victory, nor acknowledged its success. During the course of hostilities, mines were detected along open-water channels, and off the shores of Saudi Arabia, Kuwait, Bahrain and Oman. Whether they were planted there deliberately or had floated towards these waters, was unclear. At the height of the Tanker War, they became 'the greatest single threat to shipping' in the Gulf, but being indiscriminate, they also endangered tankers lifting Iranian oil, a fact that was emphasized by the fate of the *Texaco Caribbean* (see Chapter 1). At a later stage in the war, while suggesting that the US or Iraq had also deployed mines, the Iranian leadership admitted planting them for purely defensive reasons. At Tehran's War Information Centre, Kamal Kharazi explained to members of the foreign press that 'it is quite natural to use such means to block

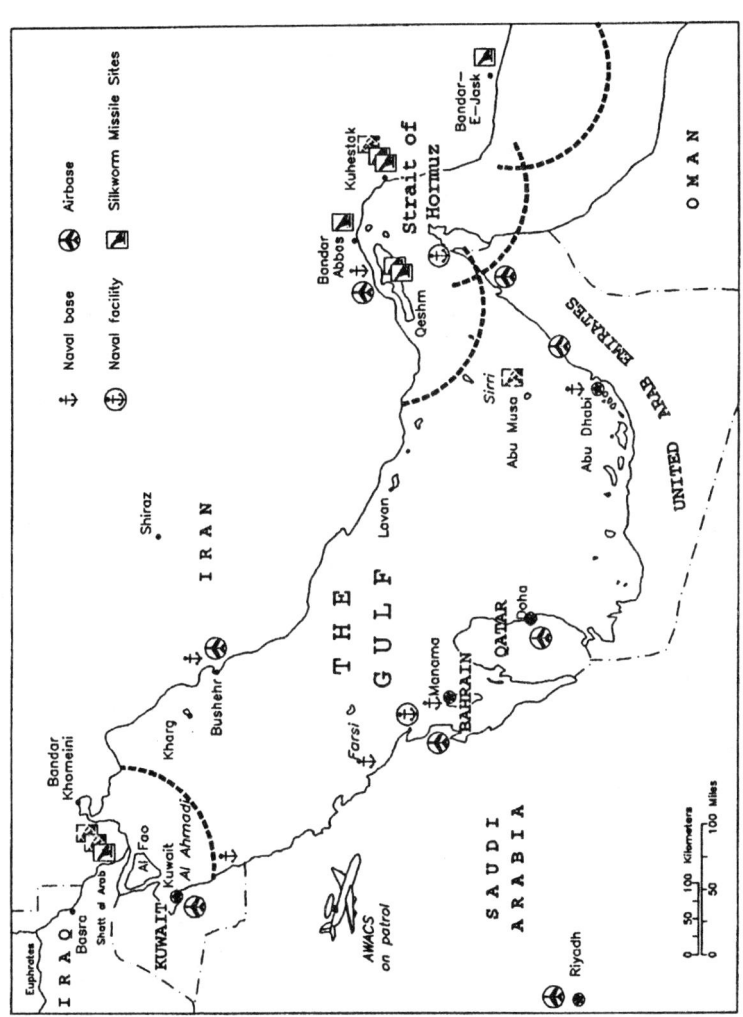

Map 7.1 Iranian Naval and Air Facilities and Silkworm Sites

approaches' (*Newsweek*, 24 August 1987, pp. 8–9; see also Ayad, 1988, pp. 7–8; and Cordesman, 1988, p. 26).

At the time, the Iranian naval mine arsenal was estimated at around 1000. Most were old Soviet M-08s of early-1900s vintage, with contact and chemical horns. The floating contact mines held 240 pounds of explosives and were bottom-moored at a depth of up to 350 feet. Reconditioned, they were bought from North Korea which, from 1982 to 1987, provided Iran with weapons worth $5 billion, using Pakistan as a bridge with China. The link that united Tehran and Pyongyang was their anti-Western policy, in addition to strategic and financial interests. The first contested any foreign military presence, especially US political and military dominance in the Gulf, and the second was exasperated by the West's blockade, while both were highly conditioned against any foreign association – and in Iran's case, even Western economic assistance was often regarded as dubious. The earliest entry in Lloyd's of a ship striking a mine, presumably laid by Iran, was on 5 January 1987, when the Liberian tanker *Solena* (LT, RPD) sustained a dent in the bow, while sailing off Ras Tanura (also *Middle East Journal 1987*, p. 88; *Proceedings/Naval Review 1988*, p. 52; and Cordesman, 1988, pp. 33–4).

Because of their simplicity, it was suspected that some mines were manufactured locally, especially after Hojjatul-Islam Hashemi Rafsanjani, the Speaker of Parliament, stated that Iran can 'produce mines like seeds', and sow them throughout the Gulf. As foreign navies expanded their fleets in the Gulf, Iranian mines became their greatest single threat. According to *Newsweek*,

> chastened American convoys now move at a crawl up and down the Gulf, paced by Sea-King helicopters scanning and patrolling the waters . . . The scourge of America's high-tech Navy is a 'weapons system' stunning in its simplicity: high explosive mines so rudimentary they could be made in a garage, planted from teak-hulled boats of a design so ancient that Marco Polo marvelled they could sail at all. Meanwhile, the Americans . . . are geared for Star Wars (31 August 1987).

The Iranians also displayed ingenuity when they adopted defensive tactics to counter the difficulties they faced. Foreign tankers that ran the risk of the Gulf run were organized into convoys escorted by units of the IRIN, sometimes given air support by helicopters. Iran also operated shuttle services from Kharg to the mouth of the Gulf, then from other oil terminals in the north, when some foreign tankers refused to lift oil within the exclusion zone, or from facilities that had increasingly been fired at by Iraqi pilots. Moreover, when world demand on its crude declined, Iran offered a discount of $3 per barrel on the sale price of its oil to offset the rise of $2.33 per barrel in the insurance premium on cargoes to the war zone, and was thus able to remain within the competitive market (Aryan, 1989, pp. 187–8). But it faced the danger that the longer the war continued and the fiercer it became, the higher the chances that the long-term competitiveness of its oil could be damaged. On the other hand, the longer the authorities lowered the price, the weaker the economy became; its tight cash position then limited its ability to catch up with Iraq's imports of arms.

In 1983, Iran's oil exports were 1.77mbd, dropping slightly to 1.57mbd in 1984, and climbing somewhat to 1.6mbd the year after, despite fierce Iraqi aerial raids on Kharg, numbering 77 between mid-August and late December, and totalling 120 during the year. Kharg Island provided 1.6mbd, during the first half year of the Tanker War, but plunged to around 600 000bd, which deprived its treasury of about $25 million daily. These revenues were partly counterbalanced by earnings from the sale of 200 000bd from its offshore wells at Sirri and Lavan (Aryan, 1989, p. 187).

The retired Iranian naval officer explained that the physical countermeasures which Iran resorted to included a large array. Reflectors on buoys were reinforced, in order to deflect incoming missiles from attacking tankers; 'fire-fish', which were remote control boats for gunnery practice, were also stationed within Iraqi 'hunting zones' to attract incoming missiles; and PBs that guarded tanker convoys towed rafts, carrying large radar reflectors, to lure incoming enemy missiles away from their intended targets. Furthermore, submersible buoys (SMB), linked to flexible underwater pipelines at terminals, were connected to oil-loading tankers about one to one-and-a-half miles from the platforms. These decreased the danger of attack and ensured that at least one tanker a day was loaded. The electronic countermeasures hinged on the air force, which kept two aircraft in the air, 24 hours a day over Kharg, deployed from Isphahan air base up to 1983. After that, because of the inability to replace losses and spare parts, the overflights were decreased. Asked why the Iraqi airraids were unsuccessful in totally crippling Kharg despite their intensity, the Iranian officer replied that it was due to a combination of incompetence on the part of Iraqi pilots, and the efficiency of Iranian air defence at the vital facility, and that proper training would have sharpened the Iraqis' performance. Even when several of the jetties were damaged, the sale of one tanker's oil cargo a day covered the war costs and the country's needs, he said.

When Tehran decided to counter Iraqi strikes in an unconventional manner, it devised a strategy that basically drew from *Shi'ah* teachings for its overall approach. Its military command pursued a deliberate policy of *kitman* (silence or concealment) and *makr* (cunning), which are dominant themes in *Shi'ah* Islam. Iran's officials in Tehran and diplomats abroad were careful not to admit culpability for any damage caused to merchant shipping, especially when it came to acts for which the Revolutionary Guards were responsible. As a rule, the Iranian media abstained from reporting attacks on foreign ships, and on the rare occasions when they did, few details were disclosed, and none of the armed services claimed credit for them. Even when proof emerged of their involvement in a specific attack, the IRIN command alleged that they had no knowledge of the episode, and neither commanded nor controlled any of the *Pasdar* naval squadrons.

While Iran's leadership issued statements denying they were behind attacks on international shipping, the government resolved its rack of problems in imaginative ways, and operations had the hallmark of a well-designed and cost-beneficial strategy. Circumstances dictated the development of novel maritime tactics to counter Iraq's increasing success in the Tanker War, and forms of reprisal and protection were devised that proved both adequate and tolerable, taking into consideration the medley of political and financial restraints that Iran was subjected to.

7.2   THE ISSUE OF PROTECTING KUWAITI TANKERS

Kuwait's merchant fleet sustained hits against four of its tankers among a total of 72 vessels hit in the Gulf by both belligerents in 1984, one tanker and two cargo ships among 49 the year after, and two tankers and one freighter out of a total of 100 the following year. In 1987, two each of its tankers and cargo ships were attacked among 165, and no losses were recorded in the final year of the Tanker War (see Tables 1.1–1.4 and 1.6–1.9).

Casualties during the first three years of the Tanker War were the reason given for Kuwait's request to re-flag its tanker fleet in September 1986. The tiny state lacked the seapower appropriate for the defence of its approaches, whilst Soviet and most Western merchant ships were afforded the protection of their warships. By hiring American, Soviet and British tankers, Kuwait harboured the hope that these would be entitled to escorts, or that the mere presence of foreign men-of-war would foreclose an Iranian attack. If they were assaulted, then the war would expand.

Kuwait informally approached both superpowers through the government-owned Kuwaiti Oil Tanker Company (KOTC) to seek a mode of protection, and justified the *démarche* on the grounds of increased Iranian attacks on its tankers. It contemplated to have this task almost equally shared, whereby six tankers would hoist the *Stars and Stripes,* and the other five the red *Star, Hammer and Sickle* (US Senate Foreign Relations Committee on 18 October 1987, in Ramazani, 1988, p. 61; see also Cordesman, 1988, p. 28).

It was reported later that all P5 were invited to share in the exercise. It is hard to resist the view that Kuwait, presumably at the behest of Iraq, thus attempted to internationalize the war – the reasoning being that an increase in the foreign naval presence in the Gulf would either precipitate a showdown between Iran and the major seapowers, or motivate both superpowers to compel Iran to end the conflict (Ciarocchi, 1987, p. 7; Dainville, 1988, p. 56; Gamlen, 1989, pp. 12–13; 33 *Keesing's 1987*, p. 35597; and *Middle East Journal 1987*, p. 595).

Kuwait's motive to seek protection for economic reasons was doubtful, and US Senator Sam Nunn, the Chairman of the

Armed Services Committee, observed later that Kuwait's request was 'to draw superpowers into the Iran/Iraq war . . . to force a negotiated end; . . . there is no economic motive' (26 *ILM 1987*, pp. 1464–78). Before the ceasefire, Rubin had already foreseen the scheme, writing that the 'real objective of Kuwait and Iraq is to draw in Washington and Moscow so deeply that they will be forced to move decisively to end the war' (Rubin, 1987/88, p. 130).

This assumption was supported by the fact that whereas Kuwait originally opposed any foreign involvement in the Gulf, it shifted its position subsequently. Earlier pronouncements by its foreign and defence ministers, during GCC meetings in April 1981, then on 20 February 1984, indicated that Kuwait 'shall resist any foreign intervention at all levels' (*Navy International*, April 1984, p. 232; see also King, 1987, p. 36). The strategic guidelines, laid down at the founding of the GCC, affirmed that security arrangements in the Gulf were the 'responsibility of its peoples', rejected foreign military bases and any foreign military encroachment in the area, especially by the superpowers, and opposed membership in any international coalition. These views were restated during the 1982 summit, with the establishment of a joint rapid deployment force under a unified command, and agreement to coordinate policies on weapons acquisition (Khalaf, 1987, pp. 20–2). It could conceivably be argued that Kuwait's volte-face in 1986, on the question of self-reliance, was attributable to Iraqi pressure.

Asked to explain the motive for approaching all five permanent members of the UN Security Council, and whether Saddam Hussein had any role in convincing his government to do so, a former senior Kuwaiti official, at the centre of reflagging negotiations, indicated that public opinion was the main concern. Speaking on condition not to be identified, he said that his government was careful not to project an image that would link it too closely to the US alone. Therefore, Kuwait approached all five permanent members of the UN Security Council, in order to deflect political criticism domestically and regionally for having sought the protection of a country that firmly stood behind Israel. This discussion took place in the aftermath of the 1991 Gulf War. It was not surprising, of course, that a member of the ruling family would be uneasy to admit that he and his kinsmen were ever associated, in any manner, with earlier Iraqi plans.

Originally, Kuwait planned to charter tankers from both superpowers to lift its oil crude, but requested similar assistance from other major powers later. Whereas France and China declined to take part, Britain offered protection to two re-flagged tankers and re-registered three more, after a formal request by Kuwait on 15 July 1987; for the previous six years, the RN had quietly escorted British tankers through the Gulf. From 1985, each of the three RN units on patrol in the Gulf had been fitted with two laser weapons. Viewed 'as an additional defence, particularly against suicidal Iranians in fighters or on fast PBs', it was furnished by the USN a year earlier, after successful tests (*Sunday Times*, 7 January 1990; see also Gamlen, 1989, p. 13; and *Time*, 17 August 1987; for names, details, dates and areas of deployment of ships of the *Armilla Patrol* from 1980 to early 1989, see Cox in *Warships* 94, pp. 32–7, 3–6; for changes in its role from 1980 to date, see Appendix A10; see also Section 6.4.3).

Examples of how seriously the major powers regarded the twin matters of the security of SLOCs and the safety of their merchant fleets were first given on 18 October 1985, when a French warship intercepted an Iranian PB to prevent her crew from inspecting a French freighter (O'Ballance, 1988, p. 172); and in early May 1986, units of the USN intercepted an Iranian frigate in the Gulf of Oman to thwart her attempt to seize an American cargo ship sailing to the UAE. Frustrated at being prevented from exercising their right to check whether contraband goods were bound for Iraq, Muhammed Hussein Malek-Zadegan, the Navy C-in-C, declared that Iran would 'resolutely enter action' if US and French warships interfered in the navy's operations. Nonetheless, units of the METF escorted ships loaded with military materiel for Bahrain in February and May 1987 (*Middle East Journal 1986*, pp. 693, 697; Ciarocchi, 1987, p. 6; and see Section 6.2.4).

The Soviet Navy also demonstrated its resolve in early September 1986, when two merchant ships were boarded, searched and detained, and one forced to unload at Bandar Abbas, for a thorough inspection. Their release was secured by the dispatch of a Soviet man-of-war to the Gulf. They showed their determination again in mid-January 1987, when a *Krivak*-class missile frigate (FFG) escorted four cargo ships, loaded with arms for Iraq (Cordesman, 1988, p. 27; and *Middle East Journal 1988*, p. 80). Both operations were widely seen by Iranians as defiant acts.

Iraq's strike on the British bulk carrier *Charming* (LT, FX, WS, CTL) on 1 March 1984, caused an uproar in London. Loaded with alumina, it was owned by the Prince Shipping Company of Sark, but flying under a flag of convenience. The engine room and the accommodation were completely gutted when she caught fire, and she ran aground in Khor Musa channel, with her funnel showing above water level. Her crew were rescued with minor injuries, and an IRIN tug towing her was also hit and abandoned her. She was subsequently refloated, sold and broken up (see Section 6.1.3). After the Iraqi ambassador was summoned to the Foreign Office and handed a memorandum of protest, the incident was reviewed at the HoC. During the debate, David Owen, the Leader of the Social Democratic Party, called for the establishment of a UN maritime peacekeeping force to protect merchant shipping. Probably fearing the inclusion of Soviet ships in the operation, Prime Minister Margaret Thatcher countered that this would be 'extremely difficult if not impossible'. An Iranian rocket attack on the British tanker *Pawnee* (LT, FX, RPD), followed by an official protest on 24 September 1986, brought on an increase in RN patrols in the Gulf, from 30 November (*Middle East Journal 1987*, pp. 80, 259; and *Navy International*, May 1984, p. 310).

At the time of the Kuwaiti request, attacks on tankers were not considered as threatening the economic well-being of the world community. There was no sign of urgency, since Gulf oil shipments were not interrupted, and an 'oil glut' even caused a decline in prices. By the end of 1986, 221 vessels had been hit since the start of the Tanker War, of which only ten were Kuwaiti. In comparison to the number of tankers that sailed through the Gulf every month, totalling a low of 169 to a high of 196, the percentage of Kuwaiti tankers hit was minimal, and amounted to less than one per cent. Therefore, the level of hostilities during that period was not of major concern, and did not warrant an increase in foreign naval activity (Lloyd's; also Cordesman, 1988, pp. 27–8; and Ramazani, 1988, p. 62).

Nevertheless, the KOTC floated the idea again in December, asking to place their ships under the US flag. This was followed up with an official request by the Kuwaiti Oil Minister, Sheikh Ali Khalifah al-Sabbah, in January 1987, at which time Washington gave its qualified approval. Although in principle not opposed to the idea, the US government stated that the matter was not an intergovernmental issue. Kuwait was told that its tankers had to submit to the stringent regulations of the US Coast Guards' (USCG) code, but were neither offered nor promised naval protection.

In a personal communication, a highly-placed Kuwaiti source, closely linked to the negotiations, disclosed that although the idea of re-flagging was not off-handedly rejected, the hesitation and the ensuing slow process were due to fears that the powerful American labour unions would insist on re-flagged tankers to be wholly or partly manned by US crews, which the KOTC hoped to avoid doing. Normally, all officers, including the captain, and 75 per cent of the crew have to be US citizens. Moreover, Congress members were concerned that American shipping companies, who operated tankers registered elsewhere, such as Panama or Liberia, and flying 'flags of convenience', would lobby them and demand that protection be extended to their vessels as well. Furthermore, it was feared that the Pentagon would oppose such a move on grounds that this task would overtax the METF in financial terms, and overstretch its capabilities, in terms of materiel and manpower.

Coincident to these developments, USSR–Kuwaiti negotiations progressed. As early as January 1987, specific details were discussed in Moscow with a representative of the KOTC, and the Soviets made it clear that they were ready to participate immediately. Originally, the Kuwaitis had planned to charter three long-haul Soviet tankers, but none was large enough among those available for hiring. Thus, an agreement was reached to re-flag three Kuwaiti tankers and provide them with escorts; drawn up by 2 March, it was scheduled to be signed ten days later.

Upon hearing about these plans, President Reagan gave his approval for the protection of all 11 Kuwaiti tankers on 7 March, and instructed various departments to finesse details. In return, Kuwait was asked to pledge that its port facilities and those of other Gulf Arab states would not be made available to the Soviet fleet (Ciarocchi, 1987, p. 7). The Soviet presence in the area would thus be undercut, and an increase in their naval activity in the Gulf forestalled, which would have been necessary for the protection of Kuwait's re-flagged tankers. The suddenness of the shift signalled Reagan's determination to exclude the Soviets from sharing in the re-flagging operation, and was a clear indication of his obsessive preoccupation with the threat of their enhanced influence in the Gulf.

Reports were also circulated that Washington tried to use its leverage on Kuwait to withdraw its request for Soviet protection. The *démarche* was explained on the grounds that, firstly, the administration thus continued to implement the policy of containment by restricting the role of the Soviet Navy in the Gulf, to the degree possible. Secondly, it was hoped that the militarily weak Gulf states would come to regard America as their sole protector. Needless to add that after the overthrow of the Shah of Iran, and the dramatic blow to the *twin-pillar* policy, the security and stability of the Gulf Arab states was viewed by Washington as being of overriding interest. Lastly, it was unequivocally to America's interests to guarantee the unimpeded flow of Gulf oil at an internationally-acceptable price, by seeking and ensuring the cooperation of Arab oil-producing states. Especially so, after the embarrassment caused in the aftermath of the scandal, which uncovered a triangular clandestine arms network, linking Washington and Tehran to Tel Aviv (for coverage of the Irangate affair, see, *inter alia*, *New York Times* and *Washington Post*, from early November 1986 to Summer 1987; and *Middle East Journal 1986–87*, pp. 260–3, 420–2, 596–7; see also Section 6.3.8).

Kuwait proceeded, however, with the signing of its contract with Moscow. It also reached a secret agreement, on 1 April, to lease an additional number of tankers, in the event that US–Kuwaiti talks failed. Whether the KOTC went ahead with its plan because doubts surrounded the prospects of an arrangement with the Americans, or whether this was a deliberate tactical move because negotiations with Washington were slow, is a matter for conjecture. The move could also be seen as an attempt to secure the backing of both superpowers against Tehran, as part of a scheme to check the perceived dangers of its exhortations to Kuwaitis to emulate the Iranian revolution. Invited to comment on the reasons behind the two-track policy, and whether it was a manoeuvre to force the USG to act more promptly, the authoritative Kuwaiti source merely smiled enigmatically, and neither confirmed nor disclaimed the assumption.

Three weeks later, on 21 April, the US State Department announced that negotiations were under way to re-register a number of Kuwaiti tankers, while other sources indicated that Kuwait rejected America's counteroffer to hire their ships, at the end of April. This was followed by an announcement, a fortnight later, that 11 Kuwaiti tankers would be re-flagged, as soon as the USCG had inspected them in Kuwait. On 15 May, the Santa Fe International Corporation, wholly owned by the KOTC, which itself was owned by the government's Kuwaiti Oil Corporation, established the Delaware Corporation, Chesapeake Shipping Incorporated, with a subsidiary in the US. Once the requirement of American ownership was fulfilled, the ships were subject to US law, and consequently entitled to protection. While most executives at the Delaware branch and all the tankers' captains were American citizens, regulations were waived for officers and crews. In return, the Kuwaitis agreed to an American request to fire all Eastern Bloc sailors, and replaced them with European and Arab officers and Filipino crews. Next, the tankers, basically Kuwaiti owned, were chartered by the KOTC. As Margaret Wachenfeld accurately remarked, 'there is very little about the tankers that is American. Neither their true owners, their management, nor their crew are by majority United States citizens . . . the transparent manipulation of statutes designed to address the peculiarities of maritime commerce [was] to serve immediate political goals' (1988, pp. 183–7; see also *Middle East Journal 1987*, pp. 591–2; and O'Ballance, 1988, p. 205; and for a chronology of the US–Kuwaiti shipping protection issue, published by the US Defense Department, see Appendix A7).

The re-flagging of Kuwaiti tankers was generally seen as a purely military response to military threats, and viewed by Washington as 'an unusual measure to meet an extraordinary situation'. Some of the American public, however, opposed the administration's decision to offer protection to Kuwaiti tankers, and criticized the plan which used 'cellophane flags for extension of the use of force' ('International Shipping and the Iran–Iraq War', US Department of State, 1987, and letters to the editor, in *New York Times*, 26 July 1987 in Wachenfeld, 1988, pp. 177, 183). But the reasons that prompted the Kuwaitis to request protection and the underlying motives of the USG to grant it were more complex. It is arguable that the re-flagging operation was the result of the congruence in American, Kuwaiti and Iraqi strategic, military and political interests.

Kuwait's *démarche* may have been dictated by internal and external security considerations, prompting it to press seriously for superpower protection. Firstly, its close alliance with Iraq in the war exacerbated existing tensions between the majority ruling *Sunnah* and the minority *Shi'ah* communities. It was hoped that a swift end to the conflict would defuse domestic political strains and halt acts of sabotage and internal terrorism. Islamic *Jihad* claimed responsibility for the bombings in 1983 and the attempt on the ruler's life in March 1985. Among those arrested were *Shi'ah* members of the outlawed Iraqi *Da'wah* party. Kuwait's fears and unease were further heightened by three explosions on 19 January 1987, followed by the arrest of *Shi'ah* Kuwaitis and the discovery of a large cache of arms and explosives (King, 1987, note p. 66; and Ramazani, 1988, p. 62).

Secondly, Kuwait's financial and logistical assistance for the Iraqi war effort brought forth a stream of Iranian political attacks. Kuwait had allowed Baghdad's imports of war materiel through the port of Shu'aibah (not to be mistaken with the Iraqi southern airfield of She'eibah), and its airspace was open to Iraqi fighters on their way to hit Iranian vessels and oil facilities. Student demonstrations in Tehran on 11 March 1986, protesting against Kuwaiti and Saudi support for Iraq, were followed two days later by official warnings that Arab Gulf states may 'become the target of a military option'. On 27 July, in an article in *Pasdar-i Islam*, Rafsanjani threatened that 'Iran would attack any Persian Gulf country giving money to Iraq to hit Iranian oil installations'. Then on 29 November, President Ali Khamenei said that attacks on Larak Island were made possible because Iraq had access to air bases in 'reactionary countries' (*Middle East Journal 1986*, pp. 79, 489 and *1987*, p. 259; also Cordesman, 1988, p. 34 and note p. 6; King, 1987, p. 31; and see Section 6.3.8).

Lastly, Kuwait perceived Iranian troops, deployed around Basra and at al-Fao since February 1986, as posing a very real threat to its security – even before – but increasingly after the deployment of *Silkworms* on the peninsula. Its limited air-defence capability justified its fears; and its reliance on power and desalinisation plants for normal life and industrial operations made it particularly vulnerable to air and missile attacks. Also, its 12 000-strong army, largely made up of uneducated *bedoun*, who enlisted to acquire Kuwaiti citizenship, was not sufficiently trained in the use of their 'high-tech' hardware to deal with such a threat.

Kuwait voiced its concerns over the safety of shipping in the Gulf at a GCC meeting on 1 November 1986. Although it is unlikely that the re-flagging plan was not discussed, especially with the authorities in Riyadh, no evidence of any such discussion can be found. No official statement was made public, which was by no means astonishing, bearing in mind the Saudis' traditional caution and their preference for discreet diplomacy.

In regard to Iraq's position on the issue, the Minister of Information, Latif Jasim, evasively claimed that it was a matter that concerned Kuwait alone (press conference on 7 September 1987, reported in Mylroie, 1988, p. 343). But Tariq 'Aziz, the Minister of Foreign Affairs, openly admitted that 'reflagging would be of mutual benefit', during a meeting with American officials (in Gamlen, 1989, p. 37).

Iran's reaction to Kuwait's plans came as early as mid-April 1987. The chartered Soviet tankers were seen as creating 'a very dangerous situation', and on the 20th of the same month, Rafsanjani denounced the US. Four days later, Khamenei addressed the crowds assembled for Friday prayers, and censured Kuwait for seeking superpower protection for its tanker fleet (*Washington Post*, 16 and 21 April 1987; and *Middle East Journal 1987*, p. 420). On 1 June, Ali Akbar Velayati, Iran's Foreign Minister, warned the two superpowers against intervention in the Gulf, and dispatched the Deputy Minister of Foreign Affairs, Muhammad Javad Larijani, to West European capitals, a few days before the summit, grouping the seven most industrialized countries (G7). His task was to discourage America's allies from taking part in policing the Gulf, and underline the dangers of an escalation in the USN presence. The selection of Larijani for the mission almost insured a successful outcome. In addition to being a US-educated mathematician and philosopher, he had an excellent command of the English language, and more importantly, understood the Western mentality (*Middle East Journal 1987*, pp. 592–3).

Reagan and Weinberger had written to European allies in May to elicit active tactical participation or financial burden-sharing in a Gulf task force. Their cautious response at the Venice Summit revealed their lack of enthusiasm for the plan. After refusing to commit themselves, Reagan announced that the US would foot the bill alone and not seek joint action (*Middle East Journal 1987*, p. 593).

On 9 June 1987, the leaders of the seven richest democracies (US, Canada, Japan, Britain, France, Germany and Italy) ended the Venice Economic Summit and issued a communiqué, in which they requested the international community to renew its efforts to end the war, which threatened to spread to neighbouring countries; called upon Iran and Iraq to seek a negotiated settlement; supported mediation efforts by the UN Secretary-General and urged the UNSC to adopt effective measures to bring about a just peace; reaffirmed the vital importance of the unimpeded flow of oil and trade; and endorsed the principle of freedom of navigation in the Gulf (reproduced from the *Weekly Compilation of Presidential Documents*, Vol. 23, No. 24, 22 June 1987, pp. 647–8 in 33 *ILM 1987*, p. 1431; and *Middle East Journal 1987*, p. 594). Larijani's mission seemed successful, given that Washington's request to issue a strong warning to Iran was not included in their statement.

US interests in the Gulf area were specified by Weinberger, in an extensive report to Congress on security arrangements in the Gulf, on 15 June 1987, as being the unimpeded flow of oil, the security and stability of moderate states in the region, and freedom of navigation in the Gulf. Policy aims were to contain the influence of the Soviet Union and limit Iran's attempts at hegemony in the area (reproduced from text provided by US Department of Defense in 26 *ILM 1987*, pp. 1433–63). The following day, his ideas were defined in a testimony before the Senate Foreign Relations Committee by the Under Secretary of State for Political Affairs, Michael H. Armacost, who also detailed the plan to protect Kuwaiti tankers in the Gulf (reproduced from US Department of State, 'US Policy in the Persian Gulf', Special Report No. 166, July 1987, pp. 10–12 in 26 *ILM 1987*, pp. 1429–31).

Over the years, the Pentagon was faced with the Gulf Arab states' reluctance to establish foreign bases. Although Kuwait was the most notable example in that respect, the conduct of the Iran–Iraq War seemed to have altered its position and prompted its request for foreign naval protection for its tankers. Re-flagging offered a potential source of mutual benefit, and US strategic requirements could at last be met and result in the establishment of permanent bases, vital for a constant and long-term military presence in the region. Washington was not about to lose such an opportunity, and Weinberger made that point clear by demanding the provision of naval bases and aircraft landing rights in the GCC states to protect shipping (*New York Times*, 24 May 1987).

But on 5 June, in an attempt to discourage them from acquiescing to such a demand, Rafsanjani threatened that Iran would 'occupy that base and port and drive the Americans from there' (*Middle East Journal 1987*, p. 594). Clearly, Iranian military power was in no way comparable to that of the US, and the challenge was designed as a shot fired across the bows of Iran's Gulf neighbours. Anyway, regardless of all the political cross-currents in the capitals surrounding the Gulf then, the Pentagon's cherished ambition was fulfilled when these states signed bilateral military memoranda, yielding basing rights to US forces, in the aftermath of the second Gulf War.

The process of negotiations and formalities for the re-flagging operation had taken eight months and were not yet concluded, and the War Powers Act seemed to be the stumbling-block. Approved in November 1973, it required the president to inform Congress within 48 hours whenever he ordered combat troops to be deployed in foreign countries or substantially enlarged the size of their contingent, and to provide Congress with half-yearly reports on all developments. Troops stationed in areas where military confrontation was a likely possibility must be withdrawn within two months, unless Congress authorized them to remain, but the president can obtain a one-month extension by claiming 'unavoidable military necessity' (for instances when the act was implemented, see Cordesman, 1988, notes p. 34).

Furthermore, Congress members had proposed several bills to obstruct the government's decision to allow the re-flagging to proceed, unless approval was extracted from Kuwait to allow the basing of US minesweepers in its ports. However, the US government was able to preempt opposition from Congress after the *Stark* incident. As Weinberger pointed out, the 'debate in the wake of the . . . attack on the USS *Stark* . . . heightened perceptions' among Americans that conditions in the Gulf had deteriorated, 'focused attention on United States policies in this key region of the world', and raised questions as to the nature of the future line of conduct (reproduced from text provided by US Department of Defense in 26 *ILM 1987*, pp. 1433–63; and Wachenfeld, 1988, note p. 188).

In the summer of 1987, the expansion in the size of naval forces deployed in the Gulf theatre, and the escalation in their activity, mirrored increased US concern for the security of the area. Reagan altered US Gulf policy from its original intention of containing Soviet influence; it was now aimed at creating a significantly potent force, devised to curb Iranian attacks. To this end, Reagan approved raising the number of the METF ships from six to nine, 12 days after the attack on the USS *Stark* revealed the vulnerability of US warships. It is interesting to note that a request made in the previous spring by Admiral Crowe, the Chairman of the JCS, to increase the ships from six to eight was opposed by the president's advisors (Ciarocchi, 1987, pp. 8–9).

7.3   WHAT WAS THE *STARK* REALITY?

On the evening of Sunday 17 May 1987, a layer of dusty haze hung in the humid air over the Gulf, and the atmosphere was thick and heavy. The summer monsoon had started, and the weather was still sweltering and damp, although the sun had collapsed behind the seemingly endless rows of dunes. Enveloped in the darkness of the night, an aircraft flew south. No enemy fighters chased its tail, and no ground troops fired at it – only a hot wind blustered across the vast sweep of desert to its right. Out of the aircraft window, as far as the pilot's eyes could see, the landscape was of parched wilderness and naked dunes – an unforgiving expanse beset by sand storms and scalding summers. On the meandering beach, the tides had left their patterned mark on the sand, and in some parts, the fine particles of shells shimmered.

Further south, a ship was steaming on a north north-western course, about 70 to 85 miles north-east of Bahrain. The humidity was condensing stickily on her body, as she plied the waters in the central Gulf. Other than the intermittent creak and the rippling of waves against her prow and at her stern, she was surrounded by stillness. A huge pall of dust hung in the air draping her, and gave an eerie air of premonition.

The aircraft flew from the northern tip of the Gulf, and rather than penetrating the skies over the water surface, it skirted the Kuwaiti and Saudi eastern coasts. Facing an-Nuayriyah, it veered east, then tacked in a south-easterly course to Ad-Dammam, whence it swung east again. Its flight path suggested a pre-determined plan and indicated caution. Instead of its usual load of one missile, it was fitted with two. The aircraft was bound on a clandestine assignment that was to spark controversy and raise a myriad of interpretations. Although there was no shortage of wild speculation later, the mystery of its mission remains unsolved to this day, and it may be long before the truth is known.

The bow of the American frigate cleaved the waves in a course tangential to the maritime advisory (not exclusion) zone in the southern Gulf, imposed by Iran at the start of the conflict, and 60 miles south of the Iraqi-declared exclusion zone around Kharg. On board the FFG-31 USS *Stark*, the approach of the aircraft went unnoticed at first. When warned by the USS *Coontz*, patrolling the area further north, the ship's company were not apprehensive, regarding Iraqis as 'virtual allies'.

At 2112 hours, two *Exocets* slammed into the ship, and the attack took the entire crew by surprise. After the Iraqi *Mirage* F-1EQ delivered its missiles, it swerved, dashed northwards and disappeared over the horizon. Back at the former British airbase of al-She'eibah, near Basra, it remained grounded for over a month, along with all Iraqi aircraft.

The following detailed description is worthwhile in order to compare the effect of attacks with *Exocet* missiles on different types of vessels in the conclusion. The narrative offered here will help to clarify the picture, by showing how these missiles were rather ineffective in their use by the Iraqi Air Force in their attacks on tankers, whilst highly effective when operated against warships.

The first missile punched a hole in the forward port side of the hull, six feet above the water line, went through the crew's forward berthing area, the Radar and Combat Information Centre (CIC) Equipment Room (RICER), then exited on the starboard side without exploding. Parts of its warhead were found later on the second deck. The second one hit a little higher, and exploded immediately after impact. Within seconds, the ship became a graveyard, strewn with twisted fragments of melted metal, while the survivors emerged from their ripped accommodation. As the fire started to rage, the overexcited men were sent into a frenzy, as they tried to explain the effects of an assault, the ferocity of which they had singularly failed to predict.

The blaze swept through the forward area and gutted it, then spread to the hull and bulkheads. The licking flames destroyed everything in their path, and melted portions of the superstructure and decking, with temperatures reaching 1800 degrees. Fire-fighting efforts were at first hampered because the water main on the port side was ruptured, but the crew managed later to rig hoses to the aft water mains.

The ship's difficulties were further compounded by the accumulation of water in the port area, which caused a list of 17 degrees – dangerously close to the angle at which the ship could capsize. Pitted in an unequal struggle against the seemingly endless raging fire, the damage control group nevertheless managed to stabilize her. While fighting to contain the blaze, the ship's company took the crippled frigate back to base, but had to reduce her speed to 15 knots. Finally, she limped back to Bahrain with a speed of just five knots.

The human casualty toll was the highest on any one ship since the start of the Tanker War. Of the 58 casualties, 36 were killed and one listed as missing, presumed dead. The injured, some badly burnt, numbered 21, two of whom were critical ('Report on the Staff Investigation into the Iraqi Attack on the USS *Stark* of the Committee on Armed Services House of Representatives' [HASC], June 1987, pp. 1–28; see also Brown-Humes, 1988, p. 28; Cordesman, 1988, p. 28; 26 *ILM 1987*, p. 1423; 33 *Keesing's 1987*, p. 35597; Adam, 1987, pp. 26–9; and Ramazani, 1988, p. 86).

A discrepancy existed among reports by several investigative committees as to which of the two missiles caused the most damage. One report claimed that the conflagration was the result of the second missile's explosion, which ignited the propellant it still carried, having been fired from close range. This conclusion was based on accounts by sailors, stationed on the bridge and lookout decks, who testified that they did not hear an explosion nor see flames after the first impact (HASC report 1987, pp. 1–28).

The findings of a classified report, shown confidentially, appeared to be more accurate, given the specialized nature of the investigators' background. It concluded that whilst the first missile's impact was inwards, the second was outwards; and although the first one did not explode, it ignited the intense blaze. The report argued that most of the 300 pounds of propellant fuel that the missile carried was unspent. This was projected inside the area traversed, and lit the fires which raged intermittently for about 20 hours.

Whilst the annual review of naval developments, published in *Proceedings*, summed up the incident as 'an IFF [identification friend or foe] error by a very tired Iraqi pilot' (in Friedman, 1988, p. 220), rumours surrounding the affair abounded. There were many theories, but no evidence. To this day, many questions remain unanswered: What was the Iraqi fighter-aircraft doing in an area away from its usual 'hunting zones', and why was it carrying two missiles instead of its usual load of one? The frigate had intercept equipment that should have detected that an attack was in process, so why did the ship's close-in-weapon system (CIWS) not lock unto the approaching missiles? Assuming that the captain was aware of Iranian vessels patrolling the area, did he give orders to switch off his ship's electronic countermeasures (ECM) systems to forestall the shooting down of the Iraqi *Mirage* and thus enable its pilot to hit an IRIN target?

Did the pilot mistake the USS *Stark* for one of the American-built Iranian frigates, as the Iraqi Foreign Minister, Tariq 'Aziz, implied three days later? Or did Tehran intend to 'muddy' the waters between Baghdad and Washington by paying the Iraqi pilot and ordering him to hit the *Stark*, as a *Pasdaran* official hinted in the *New York Times* on 8 June? But the information available discounts the two possibilities. The ship was beyond visual range and, normally, Iraqi pilots did not carry out target identification before attacking, neither by maritime nor by air reconnaissance. The USS *Stark* was hit by night and must have appeared on the pilot's radar screen as a tiny 'blip' which does not reveal the type – let alone the flag – of a ship. The only possibility of knowing that it was indeed one of the USN vessels was simple. If they had a constant route along which they patrolled this particular area, and if the frigate was following that exact course at precisely the same time as usual, she would be an easy target. With the knowledge of the route coordinates, the patrol time schedule and the ship's speed, it was purely a mathematical operation to determine her location. Using data computed from a map, the chances are high that a pilot or a ship's crew can hit a target without seeing it directly.

Was the Iraqi military command impatient with the lengthy procedures and preparations for the re-flagging operation? And hence, did Saddam Hussein issue orders to his airforce chief to hit a USN ship so as to precipitate events and force the Americans to augment their naval presence in the Gulf? Was this a deliberate Iraqi ploy to draw the superpowers into the conflict, as an Iranian spokesman suggested on the day after the attack (in 33 *Keesing's 1987*, p. 35597)? Was the US trapped by Iraq, as the Israeli Defence Minister, Yitzhak Rabin, alleged (in *Washington Post*, 29 October 1987)? More importantly, did Washington take the 'bait' and leap into the trap because this served its strategic interests and held the potential of establishing permanent bases in the Gulf?

On 22 May, Iraq agreed to a request by the US to dispatch a group of investigators to interview the pilot who attacked the American frigate, and an inquiry opened in Baghdad on 25 May. However, they were not allowed to interview him; instead, they were informed by Iraqi officials that as he had not received any signal from the ship, he therefore believed her to be an enemy target. The group left three days later, after an agreement on measures to prevent similar accidents. Conflicting rumours floated at the time, claiming that the pilot was sent into early and comfortable retirement, or alleging that he was executed, in fear that he may acknowledge the inadmissible. In the morbidly secretive *Ba'thi* Iraq, yet another veil was drawn.

Revelations surfaced later about a dispute over signals, with the Americans claiming that the frigate radioed two warnings to the approaching aircraft, after being alerted by the USS *Coontz*. Another bone of contention was the location of the stricken vessel. The Iraqis insisted that she was sailing ten miles within the declared war zone in the southern Gulf, while the Americans asserted that she was ten to 15 miles outside that area. All the ship's written and magnetic records had been destroyed by fire, heat or water. Hence, the investigating committee had to rely on the memory of the surviving crew members for an eyewitness account of harrowing events. Their assessment was linked to the degree of accuracy of the crew's chronological description and to their relevance, their ability to use precise language, and the significance of each statement. Their findings were also based on the filing of facts for the record, taking into consideration the stressful conditions. The conclusions on the highly contentious issue of the timing between the ship's radioed warnings and the release of the attacking missiles by the Iraqi pilot were therefore speculative.

When in Bahrain on 23 May to inquire into the attack, the investigators were allowed to interview almost all the survivors. But, as in Baghdad, they were not allowed to meet those directly responsible, namely, the USS *Stark*'s Commanding Officer, the Executive Officer, the Tactical Action Officer (TAO) and the Weapons Control Officer. They had been named as parties by the Navy Board of Inquiry, and their counsel advised them not to submit to questioning by others, nor to give interviews. But a statement by the master of the ship, Captain G. R. Brindel, appeared as an appendix at the end of the report (HASC report, 1987, pp. 1–28 and appendix pp. 29–30; and *Middle East Journal 1987*, pp. 593–4).

It transpired later that Captain Brindel and the First Officer of the USS *Stark* were retired from active service at the end of July, as their negligence had increased the vulnerability of the vessel entrusted to them and endangered the lives of all those aboard. An aircraft can fly within a ship's missile range in a matter of minutes or less after its 'blip' appears on the radar screen; a few seconds' hesitation in identifying it as one with hostile intent could lose a ship and its crew. The Navy Board of Inquiry found that the captain and the first officer had not complied with basic defensive procedures governing similar ships on patrol duty, which possess the capability of locking unto and destroying incoming missiles before they hit their target (33 *Keesing's 1987*, p. 35597; for Rules of Engagement [ROE] governing ships of the METF, see Appendix A9).

When confidential military documents will be declassified in Iraq, the secret behind the attack on the USS *Stark* may be revealed to the world at last – assuming, naturally, that records are kept by a government as autocratic as the *Ba'thi* one. Such an assertion also presupposes that Saddam Hussein would have such a lack of foresight as to record an action as incriminating as giving the order to hit a warship from the most powerful navy in the world. The question will remain whether there is a possibility, albeit remote, that the pilot's *tasking sheet*, in which he logged his instructions, will be found.

The matter was dealt with swiftly by the highest authorities in Washington and Baghdad, and the episode was discarded in a matter of hours. The Iraqi government offered an apology, and promised to compensate for human and material losses. The closing of this dossier corresponded almost exactly to the incident involving the USS *Liberty*, sunk in the eastern Mediterranean, after being struck by an Israeli combat-aircraft, during the June 1967 Arab–Israeli war. In both instances, the accidents were alleged to be unintentional, and still remain subjects of speculation, in spite of the official versions.

Nonetheless, it deserved thorough exploration, within the framework of a study related to military operations in the Gulf, at this particular moment in the evolution of the Iran–Iraq War. The incident instigated a flurry of meetings, briefings and hearings, followed by statements and reports by US administration officials, in which anti-Iranian rhetoric coincided with arguments in favour of protecting Kuwaiti tankers. In a most curious way, it helped to accelerate a train of events that was to assist the Iraqi leadership to attain its objective of ending the war. Because of its timing and the combination of concomitant circumstances, its military/political impact far outreached the few days it took to shut this file.

On 17 May, the Secretary of State announced the attack on the USS *Stark* in the opening words of an address delivered before AIPAC, the pro-Israel umbrella organization. He told members of the Jewish lobbying groups that the president had been informed, and consultations were taking place with the

Secretary of Defense Caspar Weinberger, the White House Chief of Staff, Howard Baker, and the National Security Advisor, Frank Carlucci (*Department of State Bulletin*, 1987, No. 2124, July 1987, pp. 58–63 in 26 *ILM 1987*, p. 1423).

A day after, President Reagan issued a statement in which he expressed anger over the tragedy, sympathies to the families of the men killed and injured, and gratitude to Saudi Arabia and Bahrain for their prompt assistance in the rescue and evacuation operation which ensued. He underscored his administration's commitment to ensure 'the free flow of oil through the Strait of Hormuz' and support the 'self-defense of our friends in the Gulf', and said the navy's mission to safeguard US interests was crucial. Most importantly for the Iraqis, he called on the international community to increase their diplomatic efforts and hasten a peaceful settlement of the Iran–Iraq War (text from *Weekly Compilation of Presidential Documents*, 25 May 1987 in *ILM 1987*, p. 1423).

On the same day, he held a 75-minute meeting in the Situation Room with the NSPG, and ordered a higher state of alert for USN vessels in the area (see Appendix A8). Iran and Iraq were notified of this change of status and warned that should their approaching aircraft be in a formation indicating hostile intent, these were to be shot down, unless they provided 'adequate notification of their intentions'. Vigorous protests were issued to the government of Iraq, demanding reparations for the loss of life and the ship's damage (White House Statement, 18 May 1987 text from *Weekly Compilation of Presidential Documents*, 25 May 1987 in 26 *ILM 1987*, p. 1423; and *Middle East Journal 1987*, p. 592).

The Assistant Secretary of State, Richard Murphy, appeared before the Subcommittee on Europe and the Middle East of the House Foreign Affairs Committee (HFAC) on the following day. He reiterated the policy of successive US administrations, all of which estimated the Gulf to be an area of major interest strategically, economically and politically. He also affirmed that US relations with Iraq and the GCC states were friendly, pledged the administration's support for the self-defence of these states, and urged the international community to intensify efforts to bring the conflict to an end (26 *ILM 1987*, pp. 1423–5).

On 20 May, Charles Redman, the State Department Spokesman, read a prepared statement which gave credit to the

Saudi air and naval forces for dispatching helicopters and a naval vessel to lend support in the search-and-rescue operation and assist the USS *Stark*, and for placing the military hospital at Dhahran on disaster alert status to receive casualties, noting that these measures were taken despite the fact that there was no pre-arranged plan for Saudi forces to aid US vessels in the Gulf. He also explained that just prior to the attack on the frigate, two Royal Saudi F-15s, based at Dhahran, were scrambled to fly in a formation with an AWACS on a routine combat air patrol (CAP) mission over the Saudi coastline. These missions, he said, were part of a Saudi–American arrangement to defend the Saudi coastline, as well as the American surveillance aircraft. When the Saudi controller on board the E-3A spotted the disabled frigate, he requested his command to commit the two F-15s to intercept the Iraqi F-1 and force it down on Saudi territory. By the time his chief sought approval from higher authorities, the *Mirage* was well on its way back to its base. The statement commended the Saudi Air Force's command and control system for its discipline (26 *ILM 1987*, p. 1425).

In reality, at the outbreak of the Iran–Iraq war in 1980, Washington had asked Riyadh to request the dispatch of four AWACS E-3As, to monitor the operations round the clock. With a range of about 250 miles, the four AWACS, designed to track high-performance military aircraft in combat, landed at Dhahran air base on 30 September, along with 2 KC-135 refuelling and a few C-141 transport planes, and 300 support personnel (Stork, 1987, p. 4; O'Ballance, 1988, p. 56; and Angrand and Rabier, 1989, p. 107).

A different version of events disclosed that 'US Defense Department sources revealed that two Saudi F-15 fighters refused a US request to intercept the Iraqi jet that attacked the USS *Stark*' (*Middle East Journal 1987*, p. 593). This report was confirmed by others, whose chronological accounts were at variance with the State Department, by showing that the two F-15s were scrambled to pursue the Iraqi jet after the surveillance aircraft had spotted the stricken naval vessel, and that the two Saudi pilots had indeed refused a US request to intercept the Iraqi *Mirage* in the absence of such orders from their base commander. On 21 May, presumably as a protest against the Saudis for failing to intercept the Iraqi fighter, the US administration delayed the proposed sale of further F-15s to the Royal Saudi Air Force (33 *Keesing's 1987*, p. 35597).

On the same day, George Shultz sent identical letters to the President of the Senate, George Bush, and to the Speaker of the House of Representatives, Jim Wright. The Secretary of State informed the Congressional leadership of the attack on the USS *Stark* and gave assurances that the navy's presence in the Gulf was within Washington's right under international law. He reassured them that the fleet remained neutral in the Iran–Iraq War and had taken no action that could be perceived as hostile by either state. He also briefed Congress on the diplomatic and military developments so far, as well as procedural matters, such as contacts between Washington and Baghdad, Saddam Hussein's letter of apology, the higher state of alert in the Gulf, and instructions to ships' commanders there, enabling them to take their own initiative to protect their vessels from attack. He added that an agreement had been reached between the US and Iraq to jointly investigate the circumstances leading to the attack, although the administration had no reason to believe that it was intentional nor that it will recur. Shultz then singled out Iran as the party responsible for threatening 'the free flow of oil' and 'freedom of navigation', and for spreading the conflict 'geographically to the lower Gulf', thus heightening the 'risk to all littoral states'. In concluding, he informed Congress of the administration's decision to proceed with plans to protect a number of Kuwaiti tankers, and to press for international action to end the war (26 *ILM 1987*, pp. 1425–6).

US support for Iraq against Iran was made explicit when the Assistant Secretary of Defense, Richard Armitage, stated on 29 May: 'We can't stand to see Iraq defeated' (Hiro, 1989, p. 186; and Stork, 1987, p. 4). Thus he sealed the death certificate of US neutrality in the Iran–Iraq War, and this myth was officially laid to rest. There was no record of the impact of all this news on President Hussein of Iraq; but one can imagine how absolutely delighted he was. However, the fact that retaliation against the Iraqis for the attack on the USS *Stark* was never under any consideration, and that, instead, Washington's wrath was directed against Tehran, brought forth a disparaging remark by Rafsanjani, who declared that the 'US Navy was a paper tiger and posed no threat to Iran' (*Middle East Journal 1987*, p. 592).

American statements, communiqués and reports revealed the unfolding of a distinct anti-Iran and pro-Iraq course. The assault on the USS *Stark* could have pitted US forces against Iraq. Instead, it almost immediately accelerated the mechanism for the escort operation code-named *Earnest Will* to start.

7.4   *OPERATION EARNEST WILL*

On 21 July 1987, the *Stars and Stripes* were hoisted up the flagpoles of two Kuwaiti vessels. After several rehearsals, *Operation Earnest Will* was finally launched. The reregistered 401 382 deadweight-ton (DWT) VLCC *Al Rekkah*, renamed *Bridgeton*, prepared herself for the heavily-guarded and well-orchestrated voyage. She was joined by the 48 233-ton gas tanker *Gas Prince*, which was to become the first US re-flagged Kuwaiti tanker to complete a round-trip through the Gulf.

The convoy started on schedule, one day after the flags were unfurled. It transited the Strait of Hormuz, sailed safely past the *Silkworm* missiles guarding the mouth of the Gulf, and un-harmed, reached the halfway point one day later. Convinced that the plan was effective, Rear Admiral Harold Bernsen, Commander, METF, declared in an interview that 'so far it has gone exactly as I thought it would – smoothly, without any confrontation on the part of Iran'. He explained that the plan was successful because 'the Iranian Air Force and Navy are not strong. It would not be in their best interest to utilize their forces in a direct confrontation' (in *New York Times*, 25 July 1987).

At the end of a meeting with President Reagan, a group of politicians posed in front of a set of microphones, and an-nounced to the world that the convoy was on its way (*Proceedings/Naval Review 1988*, p. 52). The Iranians, thousands of miles away, were thus duly alerted. In Washington, officials expressed relief that the passage they had most dreaded was behind them – an indication that the Chinese-made land-based SSMs were their main concern. A few hours later, however, the great publicity and fanfare that accompanied the start of the operation steered the *Bridgeton* – literally and not allegorically – into a sea of troubled waters.

At 0630 hours local time, on 24 July, a mine struck the VLCC 19 miles west of Farsi Island, the main IRGCN base, and about 50 miles north of the Juaymah departure channel. That the *Pasdaran* could speed from their nearby headquarters, under the cover of darkness, and lay a minefield at one of the many choke points between the multitude of coral reefs and tiny islands, did not seem to have been taken into account by the organizers of the convoy.

The *Bridgeton's* master, Captain Seitz, assumed that, as they were drawing about 23 feet, the mines must have been floating higher than that. The explosion ripped open a hole in her hull at the No. 1 tank, causing cracks in adjacent tanks and in a structural beam, and four of her 31 tanks were flooded. She was to be the third largest tanker to be hit during the Tanker War. In the captain's words, the impact

felt like a 500-ton hammer hit us up forward. First, you heard a metal-to-metal clank. And then you felt the same motion on the ship as you get in big ships in a heavy seaway. They undulate, as the shock wave moves back and up the ship into the bridge and superstructure. In fact, we parted all the stays on our radar mast. We all had to hold on so that this shock undulation didn't knock us off our feet. A lot of stuff went flying. So there wasn't much question that we had hit a mine . . . The plating is 27 millimeters thick, which is an inch and one-eighth or so. The hole was about ten meters long by five meters wide. Shrapnel went through several deck levels and through the main deck, about 90 feet away, which is also 27-millimeter plate (interview in *Proceedings/Naval Review 1988*, pp. 52–3).

Despite her damage, she continued her voyage to Kuwait at the slower speed of six knots instead of 15. Being the only ship in the convoy large and sturdy enough to sustain another hit by a mine, she was placed at the lead. The three escort warships trailed behind. Only then, it seems, the USS *Kidd* (DDG-993), the USS *Crommelin* (FFG-37) and the USS *Fox* (CG-33) started to activate their acoustic surveillance system (SOSUS). Their masters took another preventive measure, placing crew members on the bow, armed with rifles in order to shoot at any floating mines they could spot. The supertanker was temporarily patched-up in Kuwait, then sailed on to Dubai where permanent repairs were effected. Between 25 and 27 July, a number of other North Korean versions of Soviet mines were discovered in the same area (Lloyd's; and Cordesman, 1988, pp. 33–4).

After the accident, Admiral Bernsen admitted that despite warnings by intelligence sources, the convoy's route was not checked for mines. Only a few days earlier, an international minesweeping operation (MSO) had taken place. One of the two harbour approaches to the Kuwaiti anchorage, Mina al-Ahmadi, was cleared. The other channel was not considered, being closer to and within easier reach of potential Iranian artillery fire or air attacks. Saudi minesweepers (MCMV) and Soviet, Dutch and American experts cooperated in the exercise. Why an MSO on the convoy's route was not undertaken as well remained an enigma.

Four months of preparations, followed by three drill exercises, starting in early July, ended in chaos and embarrassment. The 600-ship navy – the world's most formidable naval power, which amassed a staggering array of potent fire-power, and with the most sophisticated equipment in the region – was humiliated by an ancient pre-World War One (1908) mine. This was an example, *par excellence*, of cost-effectiveness on the part of the Iranians.

The disabling of the *Bridgeton*, the pride of the Kuwaiti tanker fleet, was a major propaganda victory for Iran. Again, as in the 1979–81 American Embassy hostage crisis in Tehran, and the *Hizb-Ullah* bombings in Beirut, the might of the US had been challenged. And the relatively decrepit Revolutionary Guards Navy, manned by young zealots, was able to bully the strongest of the world's seapowers.

Although careful to dissociate themselves from the incident, the highest figures in the Iranian government issued a stream of statements. Prime Minister Mir Hussein Musavi gleefully estimated that it was 'an irreparable blow on America's political and military prestige'. And Rafsanjani warned that 'from now on, if our wells, installations and centres are hit, we will make the installations and centres of Iraq's partners the targets of our attacks'. The unmistakable reference to Saudi Arabia and Kuwait indicated that Iran's new policy of counterstrikes was on its way. On 27 July, Khamenei reiterated the threat. He singled out Kuwait as 'the only country in the region that openly supports Iraq in the war', and pointedly remarked that Iran's missiles could target any location in Kuwait. The following day, Khomeini announced that the war would continue as long as Saddam Hussein ruled Iraq. Unfortunately, the emotional crescendo reached a tragic climax with the deaths of hundreds of Muslims on pilgrimage to Mecca, in the 31 July riots (Cordesman, 1988, [II] p. 34; also Ramazani, 1988, p. 64; and Rubin, 1987/88, p. 127).

The operational plan for *Earnest Will* covered 80 pages. It specified the frequency of convoys; the number of tankers to be escorted each time; determined the force component of every operation, and which USN vessels were to be selected for convoying; and detailed the number and type of warships to be deployed in other areas, as well, with specific missions in defense of the escort operations. The convoys were to be fortnightly, and three to four warships were to protect two tankers in each operation. The small number of tankers selected each time may have been based on the fear of putting 'all one's eggs in the same basket'. Also, the larger the convoy, the longer its turn-around time, whilst small formations move faster and reduce sailing time. The two-week interval relieved pressure on USN crews.

Official American pronouncements had revealed that the main threat the navy's commanders perceived was that of land-based SSMs mounted on al-Fao peninsula and the shores and islands of the Strait of Hormuz. They also took into account the possibility of attacks by Iranian warships. Therefore, cruisers were to be on alert for defence against air attacks, and the destroyer USS *Fox* and the cruiser *Kidd* were selected, being equipped with 76 mm guns, with the capability of firing at naval as well as shore targets, and fitted with ECMs and CIWS.

The carrier USS *Constellation*, part of the US Indian Ocean Task Force, was deployed in the Arabian Sea to provide A-6 and F/A-18 attack aircraft, EA-6B jamming aircraft, and F-14 fighters. These were joined by USAF E-3A AWACSs to give the task force advanced warning of hostile activity. The METF was to be considerably reinforced by the addition of the battleship USS *Missouri*, two cruisers and a helicopter carrier, ordered to sail to the area.

The capability of Iran's Air Force was drastically weakened by high attrition during the course of the war, combined with a reduced ability to compensate for losses. In contrast, the force component of *Operation Earnest Will* was indeed impressive, considering that only two tankers were to be escorted at a time, with a two-week interval. The resulting US task force 'had four frigates, three cruisers and a destroyer . . . All of the US combat ships were equipped with long radar radars, data nets and Phalanx point defence guns' (Cordesman, 1988, p. 33). Nicknamed '*see-wis*', the *Phalanx* is a 'last-ditch' defence against anti-ship cruise missiles, and its CIWS functions independently of others, as it has a self-contained radar and gun system which can fire 2000 rounds a minute.

But the force lacked one essential component, namely, naval minesweeping vessels (MCMV), despite Reagan's $1.8 trillion military build-up, of which the USN's share was $592 billion (*Time*, 18 July 1988). It was indeed astonishing that such a formidable navy did not dispatch MCMVs to the Gulf – a lack made evident again in *Operation Desert Storm*. And it was precisely this 'Achilles heel' that Iran chose to exploit. Supposing that because of their slow speed of approximately 12 knots MCMVs would have taken a long time to travel from one of their bases to take up positions in the Gulf, there was ample time during the months of preparations to order them to sail there.

It is all the more remarkable that in a naval theatre of operations, where mines had been laid and detected many times, the USN did not include, in their combined operation, the other mine countermeasure (MCM) capability they had available – namely, MH-53 *Sea Dragon* and RH-53D *Sea Stallion* helicopters. Some of these were not airlifted until one week after the *Bridgeton* accident – a rather tardy correction to the initial operational error. On 1 August, five mine-hunter helicopters and 200 crew and support personnel reached the Gulf (Cordesman, 1988, pp. 33–4; *Washington Post*, 4 August 1987, revealed that they were only four; and *Time*, 17 August 1987, wrote that 8 *Sea Stallions* were sent).

Admiral Crowe, who was a key figure in the USN's Gulf operations, set himself the task to rectify the procedural shortcomings that had led to earlier disasters, such as the assaults on the *Stark* and the *Bridgeton*. He subsequently reorganized the top-heavy military command structure, overcame inter-service rivalries that complicated it, devised a shorter and more

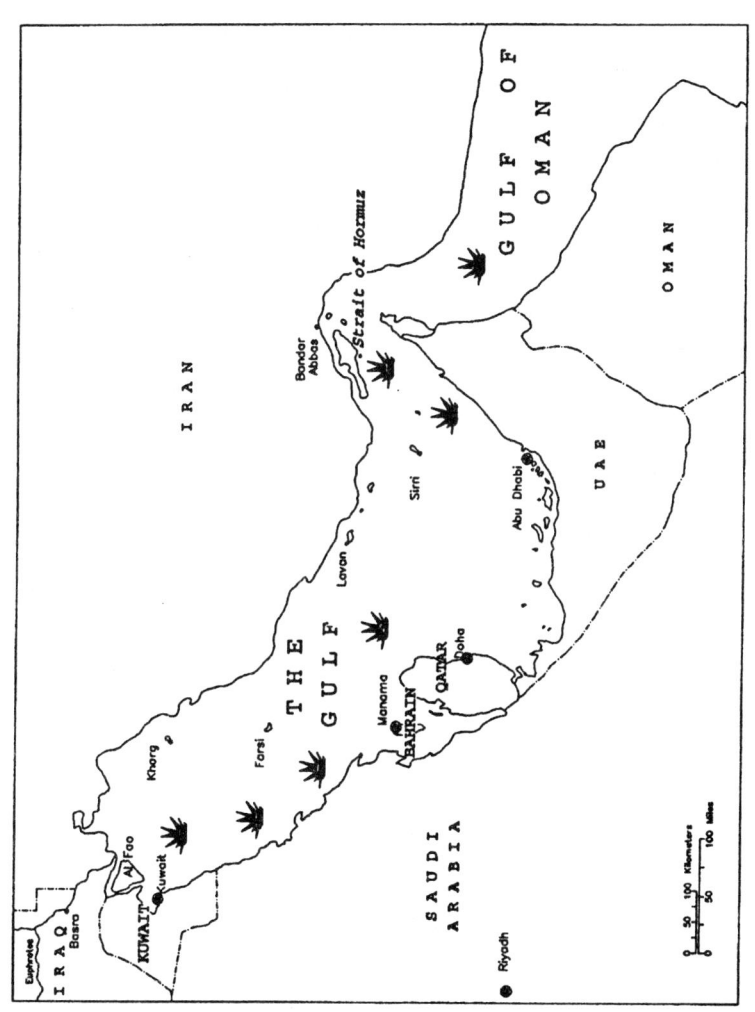

Map 7.2   Naval Mine Attacks

flexible chain of command, entrusted the resources of all the services to the commander in charge, provided the navy's Gulf theatre commanders with clear ROEs and increased their authority and freedom of action. Furthermore, he personally kept in touch with the situation in the Gulf, and from 13 to 15 September 1987, visited Admiral Bernsen on the command ship USS *La Salle*, to devise plans to trace and pursue any Iranian ships that were laying mines. He thus made it possible for the USN to accomplish their successful operations.

Some of the questions Admiral Crowe was asked, during an interview, were the following: How did the USN fail to foresee Iranian sea mine attacks on American-flagged targets? And why did the USN omit to organize and participate in a minesweeping mission before the start of the re-flagged convoys? He explained that the navy's arsenal of ocean-going minesweepers consisted of 21 Korean-War-vintage wood-hulled vessels, only three of which were operational, and that these ancient ships would have taken a very long time to sail to the Gulf. Besides, he added, almost in a whisper, the US counted on European allies to do the job. However, the navy corrected that, and dispatched the helicopters, after the offense on the *Bridgeton* (Crowe, Interview, 28 April 1995; and see Sections 6.4.6 and 6.5.1).

Albeit belatedly, the lacuna in the initial operational plan was subsequently filled with a paraphernalia of craft. The USS *Guadalcanal*, an amphibious assault ship, deployed in the Indian Ocean, sailed to Diego Garcia and took on board eight RH-53Ds. She reached the Gulf by mid-August. Additionally, a number of small craft and coastal minesweepers were dispatched there, loaded on the USS *Raleigh* and the USS *St Louis*. And on 19 August, eight ocean-going MCMVs were given orders to proceed to the Gulf. Following the increase in the naval force component, the Pentagon announced on 21 August the formation of a new joint task force to take charge in the area. Its command, on an aircraft carrier deployed in the Arabian Sea, was directly accountable to CENTCOM Headquarters in Tampa, Florida (*New York Times*, 20 August 1987; and Ciarocchi, 1987, pp. 9–10).

Every efficient convoy-and-escort operational plan depends on the scenario. Its effectiveness is conditional on many variables, a clear understanding of which determines the com-

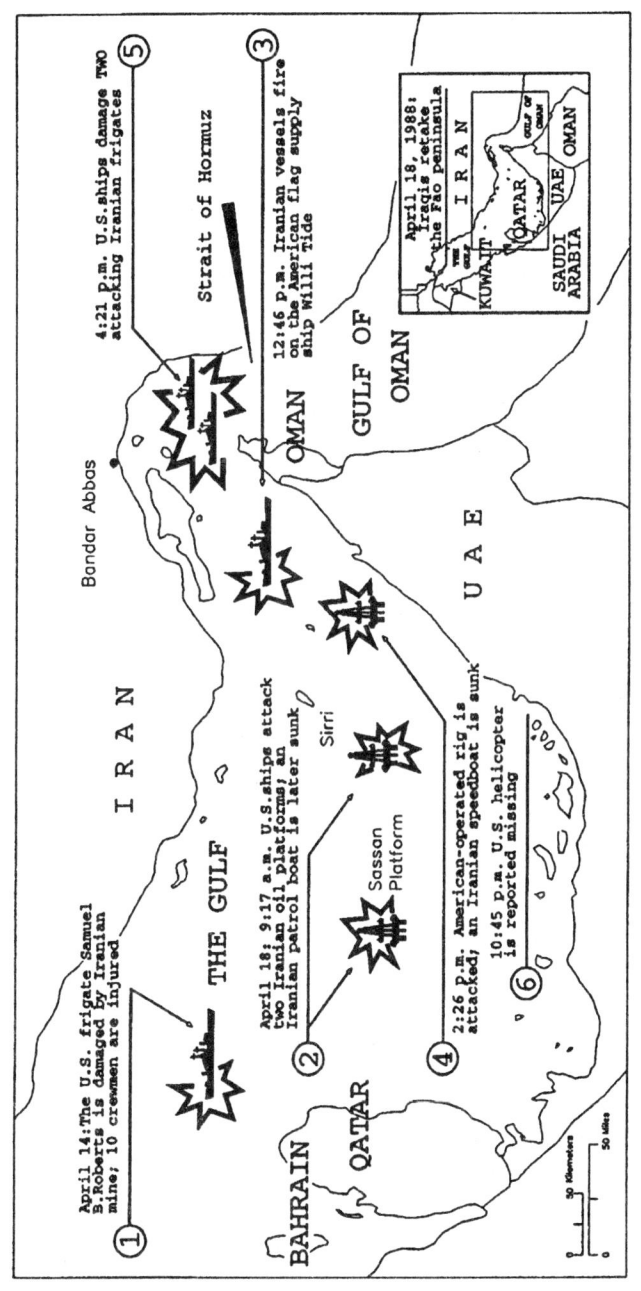

Map 7.3 US–IRI Naval Engagements

bination of forces used. The plan must take into consideration
the size of the convoy, the distance between the points of departure and arrival (in this case the Gulf of Oman to the
Kuwaiti anchorage), the geographical features of the naval
theatre of operations, such as the straits the convoy has to
transit *en route* and the approaches to the port of destination,
as well as local weather and water conditions, and most importantly, the offensive capabilities of the opponent, with the aim
of rendering them irrelevant. It is true that it is impossible to
predict with absolute certainty that the protection of shipping
will at all times be successful, especially because convoys have a
higher degree of visibility and present more targeting opportunities. But the equation must take into account one's own
means of defence/offense as well as the opponent's, to form a
cohesive force, built up by a mix of reinforcing capabilities. A
balanced force, with a wide range of operational possibilities,
can respond to almost any circumstance. The strategy then
will ensure the optimum result and neutralize the opponent's
ability to endanger the safety of the convoy. The first escort
operation exposed the USN's 'Achilles heel', which Iran immediately struck at.

The *Bridgeton* incident was not the first mine attack on
tankers. The USSR was the first of the parties, originally approached, to comply with Kuwait's request for protection. On
16 May 1987, one of the three Soviet tankers chartered by
Kuwait, was sailing 35 miles off the Kuwaiti coast, escorted by a
warship. The *Marshal Chuykov* (LT, SER), on course to Mina
al-Ahmadi, struck a mine and the explosion ripped a large
hole in her bottom. She was first towed to Kuwait for inspection, then to Dubai for repairs. Subsequently, three Soviet
minesweepers were deployed to the Gulf, and Moscow issued a
stern warning that 'force and violence' might be used in response to any future Iranian attack (*New York Times*, 18 May
1987; and *Manchester Guardian Weekly*, 7 June 1987).

Ten days later, the Liberian tanker *Primrose* (LT, SER), carrying 260 000 tons of Kuwaiti oil, also had her bottom holed,
causing an oil spill. The mine exploded off the Kuwaiti shore,
ten miles west of the location where the *Marshal Chuykov* was
hit. Two more tankers struck mines before the *Bridgeton* did.
On 9 June, the Greek tanker *Ethnic* (LT, SER) sustained underwater damage causing an oil leak; and on 20 June, another

Liberian tanker, the *Stena Explorer* (LT, RPD), was also damaged below the water-line, but was able to have her cargo of oil transshipped (Lloyd's).

Overshadowed by the disabling of the USS *Stark* the following day, the attack on the *Marshal Chuykov* did not provoke any major debate. But Moscow intensified its diplomatic contacts with Tehran to foreclose any future attacks on its vessels (*New York Times*, 30 June 1987). Nor did the other three incidents attract much attention, whereas the *Bridgeton* aroused public discussions, especially in the US. Attention had already focused on the Gulf since the *Stark* incident, and the White House faced growing opposition on Capitol Hill, where the whole subject of the convoy-and-escort operation was condemned.

Firstly, criticism concentrated on the fact that normal procedures to examine the matter by various agencies was not followed. Even when the State and Defense departments' under-secretaries appeared before Congress after the *Stark* incident, and again when Weinberger sent his report, its wording indicated a *fait accompli*. It was clear that the decision had already been taken and a commitment made without inter-agency consultations. Also, the JCS were only consulted a very short time before the operation was launched, and as the *Bridgeton* incident revealed in a glaring manner, no contingency plan addressing the threat of mine-warfare was prepared. Some observers implied that the Americans were spoiling for a fight at this stage, but the public debates, triggered by the loss of life on the USS *Stark*, followed by the *Bridgeton* incident, do not support this claim.

Secondly, the resolve to re-flag was negatively premised. It came only as a reaction to the Soviet Union's acceptance to protect Kuwaiti tankers, and was meant to contain Soviet and Iranian influence in the Gulf. On 16 June, Reagan warned that 'in a word, if we don't do the job, the Soviets will'. To which Kuwait's Under-Secretary of Foreign Affairs, Suleyman Majid al-Shaheen, responded by commenting that the 'mentality of Hollywood' affected decisions in Washington, noting that Soviet ships sailed quietly in the Gulf 'for some time', and asking 'so what has changed?' (in Rubin, 1987/88, pp. 124–5). The escort operation was an anti-Soviet reaction, clearly aimed at curtailing their attempt to have inroads into the area. Weinberger's report was cluttered with warnings about Soviet and Iranian hegemonic designs on the Gulf, and overstated current threats to US interests in the region to mobilize Congress against both countries. One could argue that American interests were not endangered in so far that access to oil, freedom of navigation and the security of the GCC states were not seriously challenged; and that although the Soviets may have wished to play a spoiler's role in an area of major significance to the Western alliance, they were likely to be constrained by the Gulf states themselves.

Thirdly, the consequences were not seriously weighed, and none of the officials seemed to have thought about whether America was wading into a quagmire. Militarily, this could Vietnamize the war – in other words, drive the US to escalate the numbers and broaden the level of activity of its forces because clear objectives and long-term plans were not defined. It could also damage the US politically: Iran – geostrategically the most important Gulf state – could ally with its neighbour, the Soviet Union, by giving them a common cause. The plan almost disregarded Iran's capabilities and willingness to retaliate, and failed to take into account the possibility that the US was engaging itself in an expanded and prolonged military operation, one from which it would be unable to extricate itself. In so far that the strategy's success was predicated on the dubious assumption of Iranian inaction, it was simplistic. The high-flying spectacle of the USN was bound to inspire revolutionary zeal and strengthen the Iranians' will to retaliate against the 'Great Satan'. *Kayhan Tehran International* confirmed this when it wrote on 28 June: 'The very possibility, though faint, that they will get an opportunity to encounter American troops in the Persian Gulf is drawing huge crowds to the recruitment centres' (in Rubin, 1987/88, p. 131).

Fourthly, the escort operation was thought to redress America's low esteem among Arab countries. US officials told Congress that Washington's political influence was damaged after the disclosures on covert arms sales to Iran. It is true that US prestige in the Middle East had been worn away by a succession of events, such as the Iranian revolution, the miscarriage of the hostage rescue operation in April, the intervention in Lebanon, the stalled Arab–Israeli peace process, and Colonel North's packaged offer to Iran, which included arms, the removal of Saddam Hussein, and the release of Palestinians imprisoned in Kuwait. However, Weinberger's plan to protect Kuwaiti tankers involved an increase in the USN presence and an attendant rise in its level of activity in the area, and also called for access to air and naval stations in the Gulf for shore-support facilities. Allowing USN and USAF to operate from bases in GCC states endangered the very existence of their brittle regimes and could have eroded their domestic support. As a matter of fact, Nunn revealed that they had 'serious reservations' about the plan (in 26 *ILM 1987*, p. 1478; and Rubin, 1987/88, p. 123).

Lastly, by aligning itself firmly with Iraq's closest ally while being hostile to Iran, Washington's claims to neutrality in the Iran–Iraq War were substantially weakened, whereas a balanced foreign policy with regard to both countries would have served US interests in the best possible manner, especially if it were founded on a strategy aimed at ending the war by mobilizing world support for an international diplomatic effort. It would have had a treble effect: enhancing America's prestige world-wide, restoring its credibility in the Middle East, and protecting its national security interests in the Gulf region – the bedrock of which were the unconstrained access to oil, the freedom of navigation, the security of moderate Gulf states and the preservation of Iran as a buffer against Soviet expansionism.

Far from appeasing Arab states in general and Gulf states in particular, the real motives behind the American tactic were questioned by America's Arab allies. Most would have favoured a multinational UN-led naval escort and an MSO, which, if brought together, could have removed doubts about American intentions.

Operation Earnest Will increased Western naval involvement in the Gulf. This in turn galvanized the will of the major powers, leading two months later (20 July 1987), to the adoption of SCR 598, calling for a ceasefire.

If the attack on the USS *Stark* were found to be intentional, the Iraqis risked, at worst, a military confrontation with the US, as the most logical outcome. At best, they endangered US–Kuwaiti negotiations on plans to provide protection for re-flagged tankers. But, in the absence of evidence proving that the attack was but an accident, the incident strengthened the USN's resolve to police the waters of the Gulf, and hastened the steps in that direction. Ironically, as events unfolded,

Washington's 'tilt' towards Baghdad increased; and its animosity against Tehran continues in the closing years of the twentieth century. In retrospect, Iraq's aim was achieved, albeit in a circuitous way. The protection of Kuwaiti tankers led to escalating tit-for-tat clashes between US and Iranian forces, and their confrontation became particularly virulent. It culminated in the tragic loss of innocent civilian lives, when the USS *Vincennes* downed an Iranian Airbus in early July 1988. Two weeks later, Iran sued for peace and accepted SCR 598.

Did the Iraqi pilot's error pave the way for an increase in the number of foreign naval vessels in the Gulf and an escalation of Iranian retaliatory activity? Could the attack on the American warship be interpreted as a move to force the US to engage themselves a great deal more? Was Saddam Hussein's objective to internationalize the war to bring it to an end finally made possible by a blunder?

Conclusion: The War Iraq could not Win and Iran could not Lose

The deliberate escalatory strategy adopted by Iraq, in what came to be known as the Tanker War, was a shift from a static war to a dynamic campaign, based on the use of ASMs to strike at countervalue targets. In general, this strategy is thought to entail fewer operational constraints, is easier to mount, and poses fewer dangers to the attackers than counterforce targeting – except in the case of highly sensitive facilities, such as Iran's Kharg oil terminal, which had a well-developed air defence system in place. Also, attacks on troop formations and military installations do not impact on public morale and do not impede the continuation of the war effort as much as strikes on strategically important economic targets; these contribute directly and effectively to a country's war-making capabilities, and their destruction often makes war too costly to prolong. Lastly, dynamic battles lift morale among attackers more than static campaigns. Why Iraq confined the scale and extent of its operations and hence failed to carry this strategy to the extreme will be discussed later.

As explained before, Iraq's desperation to see an end to the protracted war led to its adoption of a strategy based on the exploitation of its superiority in airpower. Its three intermediate objectives were to internationalize the war, weaken Iran's economy, and to a lesser degree, relieve pressure on its ground troops. The Iranian Air Force had suffered more than any of the other services from the revolution and the arms embargo, following the American hostage crisis. Its pilots had been purged or imprisoned, foreign experts responsible for upkeep and training had left, and a shortage of spare-parts had made itself felt. Based on a comparison of airpower, Iraq's war-making potential was greater than Iran's (see Section 2.3).

Another consideration at the core of Baghdad's strategy to strangle its enemy's economic lifeline was its confidence that the remainder of its own oil-export facilities were comparatively safe, barring sabotage attacks by Kurdish *Peshmerga*. It is ironic that during the early days of hostilities, when Iranian ground troops were too weak and unorganized to repel the Iraqi advance, the IRIN's success in knocking out Iraqi oil terminals and blocking access to its main ports undercut Iran's option to retaliate four years later. Iraqi pilots could thus pluck easy targets in the Gulf, virtually secure in their knowledge that their overland pipelines and tanker-trucks ran safely through Saudi Arabia, Turkey and Jordan. As these states were not at war, they were not at risk of being attacked, unless Iran allowed the war to spill into other countries and become internationalized – something it went to great lengths to avoid, much to President Hussein's chagrin.

Throughout the Iran–Iraq War, major and regional powers favoured a military stalemate, basing their judgment on the rather dubious argument that this was likely to lead to serious peace negotiations. Starting from 1982, a change in world attitude towards Iran appeared on the horizon. Muslim militancy was on the rise, and many capitals were preoccupied with Tehran's ability to act as a spoiler in other Muslim countries, as far away as Egypt. With the objective of manipulating their governments, Iran projected itself as a model to the *mustazafeen* (oppressed masses), by exerting political and social pressures on disaffected societies. Taking Kuwait as an example, tensions already existed between Kuwait's *Sunni* governing elite and the *Shi'i* community, some of whom venerated Iran's spiritual leader. Internal discord and worldwide disquiet sharpened when members of *al-Da'wah* were implicated in bombing attacks. Consensus grew that Khomeini was challenging the status quo, and the international community apprehended the consequences of instability in countries with Muslim populations, if Iran were to triumph in the war. Both superpowers came to a tacit agreement that Iraq could not be allowed to be defeated, and despite their differing agendas, displayed increasing tolerance towards it. Fearing the effect on its own Muslim population in the southern provinces, and resenting Tehran's support for the Afghani *mujahedeen*, the USSR lifted the arms ban altogether, and substantially increased the shipments of military materiel to its ally. Concerned about stability in Gulf Arab states, especially those with *Shi'i* minorities, Washington feared their collapse like a house of cards under the impact of the new ideology. Consequently, it provided Baghdad with full support, including information on Iran's power installations and ground troop movements, and following back-channel contacts, struck Iraq off the list of states supporting terrorism (see Sections 3.6, 6.1.4 and 6.3.9). Thus, the time was particularly opportune for Iraq to justify the tactic its military command advocated and secure backing for its promotion.

The argument over the effectiveness of the Tanker War strategy must engage a series of events and consequences that, on the surface at least, point to contradictory conclusions. A definitive assessment was difficult to reach because of conflicting evidence:

- Iraq's air-launched missile campaign against Kharg Island in the beginning, and Lavan, Larak and Sirri later, did not prevent oil from reaching its destination. Iran's oil-export facilities were never totally destroyed, despite persistent attacks that were occasionally intense.
- The total number of ships disabled during the Tanker War reached 463, of which the majority were tankers (see Tables 1.1–1.5, 1.6–1.10 and 1.11). Nevertheless, oil tanker traffic did not diminish, and their movement bound to and from Iranian ports was not halted. A tanker surplus induced shipping companies to compete for contracts to lift oil from overproducing states, regardless of the risks involved in sailing to the war zone, particularly after Iran offered its oil at reduced prices to compensate for increased insurance premiums.
- The Iranian people, animated by revolutionary fervour, did not overthrow their government, and in the beginning, seemed to be indifferent to the costs of the ongoing war.
- The international community was hardly affected economically by the Tanker War, and outside powers were not forced to resort to an act short of a declaration of war on the IRI.
- At the start of the Iran–Iraq War, 4mbd were removed overnight from the world market, and oil prices rose to an

astronomical $42 a barrel. But the protracted war did not lead to the feared third 'oil shock', nor to an oil shortage. On the contrary, an oil 'glut' on the international market caused the price of the commodity to plunge. All Gulf states over-produced in response to world demand, and by reducing inflation, lower oil prices benefitted the economies of oil-consuming countries.

- The re-flagging of Kuwaiti tankers, in the summer of 1987, and the increase in the number of foreign warships in the Gulf, neither safeguarded Kuwaiti shipping and its territory, nor reduced the intensity of the conflict in the short term. On the contrary, it accomplished the opposite of what was ostensibly intended, and while around 80 foreign vessels patrolled the Gulf, Iraq and Iran fought more vigorously over its waters than at any other time. Their presence did not result in an immediate armistice, and Iran refused to accept SCR 598, until one year later.

- The Tanker War did not relieve pressure on Iraqi troops on the main battlefront. In the near term, Iran made strategic breakthroughs when its troops seized part of Majnoon Island and al-Fao peninsula in 1984 and 1986, respectively, thus threatening Basra, and it took the Iraqis the first part of 1988 to regain them.

Despite these contradictions, which cannot be ignored, this study nevertheless argues that in the longer term, and in a rather roundabout manner, Baghdad did accomplish its main goal of bringing the Iran–Iraq War to a standstill. It increased the costs for Iran by achieving the transitional objectives it had set out to fulfil by implementing the strategy. Operations in the Gulf, which Iraq sparked to affect international concerns and involve outside powers in the conflict, brought on Iran's reprisals. The Kuwaitis obligingly lent themselves to Iraq's scheme and requested superpower protection. Washington was manoeuvred into re-flagging Kuwaiti tankers after the attack on the USS *Stark*, and began mobilizing Western European capitals to assist in protecting merchant shipping and mine-clearing. Although Iranian officials repeatedly warned not to intervene in the Gulf (see, *inter alia*, statement by Foreign Minister Ali Akbar Velayati in *Washington Post*, 1 June 1987), the major powers either reinforced their posture or moved ships to the area. The Soviets were the first to start escorts, soon followed by the British and the Americans; and the French, Italians, Dutch and Belgians deployed warships, minehunters and minesweepers (see Chapter 7; Section 6.4.3; and Maps 6.1 and 6.2).

The presence of off-stage navies in the Gulf region increased in number, as well as in their level of operations, approaching full-scale confrontation between the USN on the one hand, and on the other, the IRIN and the IRGCN. Rather than extinguishing the Tanker War, the Western navies' presence coincided with an increase in the level of Iraqi and Iranian attacks, with devastating effect, and both inflicted massive damage to the ships they targeted, in terms of DWTs. For the first time since the Tanker War started, the Iranians managed to sink a tanker (the Singapore-flagged *Norman Atlantic*) by using RPGs; and Iraq's ASMs caused the highest number of human casualties in merchant shipping, so far, when they struck the Iranian tanker *Susangerd* in December 1987, killing 22 of its sailors, including her Norwegian captain (see Charts A6.8 and A6.9). However, the blunt application of power by the USN, and the dramatic clashes involving its units with the IRGCN, especially from August to October 1987, climaxing with the shooting down of the Iranian airbus by the USS *Vincennes* in July 1988, appear to have played a decisive role in Tehran's decision to concede to a ceasefire, two weeks after the tragic incident.

Thus, in a most peculiar way, the strands came together. Iraq's attack on the USS *Stark*, followed by the re-flagging operation, served its plan by quickening the pace of events that was to assist its government to attain its objective of ending the war. In the meantime, Iran's economy was indeed drained as a consequence of the drop in its oil production, the fear of shipping companies to lift oil from its terminals, a plunge in the world price of oil, and the surge in insurance premiums on hulls and cargoes; and Iraq managed to recapture some of its territories in the spring of 1988. In the end, Tehran accepted SCR 598, approved a year earlier, which Iraq 'officially welcomed ... just two days after its adoption' ('Aziz, 1988, p. 145).

The Clausewitzian interpretation of warfare as 'an instrument of policy' and 'diplomacy somewhat intensified', was at the heart of Iraq's Tanker War strategy – in other words, to conduct vigorous negotiations, in which battles replace diplomatic memoranda. The logic behind Iraq's strategy had as its aim to exhaust Iran and erode its people's will to fight until its government is deposed, or alternatively, seeks peace. Few credit Saddam Hussein with rational behaviour, while many question his military competence. Nonetheless, the war waged on Iran's economy by targeting its oil-export potential was a rational instrument of national policy, through which Iraq sought opportunities to gain strategic advantages, accomplish its intermediary objectives and reach its final aim.

As discussed in the introduction, the reason for the selection of 'classics' as the theoretical framework for this book was that their content was relevant to regional wars, fought between two LDCs using conventional weapons, neither of whom were acting as proxies of either superpower. By the very fact that Iran and Iraq both lacked strong military/industrial bases, and largely relied on troops drafted from among an uneducated populace, many of whom were civilians with little or no previous military training, thus often ill-prepared for military service, their strategies and tactics were constrained by the following factors: the degree to which they could acquire arms, ammunition and spare parts from arms-manufacturing countries; their ability to train their crews on any of the platforms and weapon systems they could obtain; and the capacity to recondition their hardware in the arms-exporting states, and/or had the technological expertise and adequate experience in maintenance. Most importantly, the general management of war depended on whether they had the trained manpower essential to identify war aims and weapons best suited for their needs, select strategies, adapt tactics, structure command and control, and effectively manage the conduct of operations in a way that enabled senior and junior officers to take timely decisions.

Mahan's views on the quality of a country's 'manpower' were largely appropriate to the Tanker War, as illustrated by the discussion above and by the lack of training which affected the performance of Iraqi pilots, who flew at high altitudes and thus lacked precision in targeting, or kept close to their home bases, in the initial stages of the Tanker War. Iran's air and navy crews frequently missed the intended vessel, and their hits were often random (for two examples, see Sections 6.2.1 and 6.2.4). Moreover, in the first quarter of 1984, all Iraqi assaults were in the north-eastern tip of the Gulf, and ten out of eleven in the area leading to and around Bandar Khomeini. Given that the *Super-Etendard*'s combat radius is 530 miles, that Nassiriyah, the closest secure air base is 150 miles north-west of the Gulf and 300 miles from Kharg, it was baffling that they restricted their operations at sea to this zone. Only one attack was carried out near Kharg, although the oil terminal and the vessels anchored at its piers were the obvious choice and their initially declared prime target. Furthermore, in spite of Iraq's overwhelming aerial superiority and its unremitting onslaught on Iran's oil-export capability, it never attempted to hit any of the *Silkworm* missile sites, including the one within an earshot on al-Fao peninsula, which endangered the escort operation, its own territory and Kuwait's.

Both Mahan and Gorshkov drew attention to the influence of the nature of government on seapower, and effectively, Imperial Iran became the policeman of the Gulf, with the disproportionate strengths of the Iranian and all other Gulf Arab navies, whereas the revolutionary regime waged an ideological 'crusade'. *Ba'thi* Iraq perceived a dominant regional role shortly after Saddam Hussein assumed power, and consequently strove to be on a par with Iran and expand the navy, by placing the largest export agreement ever secured by Italian shipyards (see Section 5.2). In the IRI, the nature of government led to the full-scale indoctrination of soldiers. Disregard for death and the seeking of martyrdom – a prevalent theme in *Shi'i* belief and typical of its legacy – inflamed their spirit of daring. It was best shown by the religious zealotry that animated members of *Pasdaran* outfits and the newly commissioned officer corps and their men, whose resourcefulness was often displayed in their tactics. In Iraq, oppressive state-imposed controls, beside a rigid hierarchical military structure, compelled ground troops, air crews and commanding officers alike to adhere to a strict regimen, and forced them to operate as subordinates to a long bureaucratic chain of command (see Sections 2.1, 2.2 and 3.5).

Conditions and factors affecting seapower that impact on present-day warfare, whether military, economic or moral, the geographical features of a country, the importance of sea denial capabilities, measures to be taken in offense and defence, the defence of seaports, blockade, siege and convoying – all of which were pertinent to the Tanker War – were discussed by the American and Soviet admirals. Iran's extended coastline (see Section 4.2), with a string of relatively secure harbours, enabled it to relocate oil-export facilities, whenever the ones within reach of Iraqi aircraft were raided. It also allowed it to establish a series of naval bases, airfields and missile launchers all along its shores. Its fleets of warships, fixed-wing combat planes and helicopter gunships, which operated out of these bases, provided protection to chartered and foreign tankers from enemy attacks with relative ease, all along their route (see Sections 6.1.6, 6.2.1, 6.3.1, 6.3.5 and 6.3.6). Iran's maritime control of the northern Gulf, reinforced by Iraq's restricted coast, handicapped its navy, which was denied the means to enter action in any meaningful manner, and effectively impeded Iraq's sea-borne trade. However, goods offloaded at neighbouring ports, and transported overland, moderated the effect of Iran's blockade (see Sections 4.1, 4.3.2 and 5.3).

Additional themes raised by both strategists were the relationship between seapower and a sound economy, and the correlation between a country's interests and the size of its seapower. The military-economic link was addressed earlier, in relation to Iran's and Iraq's race to enlarge their navies, at a time when higher oil prices and regional conditions enabled them to expand their role in the Gulf in accordance with their interests and ambitions (see Sections 5.1 and 5.2). The strategic value of controlling straits and the methodology of naval battles and combined operations were also discussed beforehand (see Section 4.2). Another concept discussed by Gorshkov, and relevant to operations in the Tanker War, was his recognition that aircraft were critical in naval battles, but he stressed the necessity of attaching them to the naval command. They must be part of an integrated and cohesive whole, not as auxiliary forces, occasionally included in an ad hoc manner in combined operations, as Iraq and Iran repeatedly did in the few encounters when their naval units had air protection and carried out successful raids (see Sections 3.5, 4.2 and 5.3). As Sections 4.4, 4.5 and 7.3 revealed, securing sea routes, control of seas and access to foreign bases dictated US policy towards the Gulf. Also, Iranian operations in November 1980 slimmed down shipping traffic in these areas. Finally, Gorshkov's stress on the importance of communication networks was made clear by the failure of the crew on the USS *Stark* to activate their sophisticated equipment.

Clausewitz insisted on specialization and hierarchy: the military being a tool of the state, priority had to be given to the civilian authority over the military, and the roles of the statesman and the professional commander must not be combined – a warning which the leaders in both capitals failed to heed until a later stage in their conflict. In each of the two states cleaved by the Shatt, the political authorities constantly interfered with decisions taken by their military commands – in Baghdad's case the Iraqi president, and in Tehran's, the spiritual leader and his coterie of *mullahs*. Consequently, their subordinates felt impelled to prove their loyalty and their adherence to *Ba'thi* or Islamic ideology by being more rigorous than their leaders, in disregard to conditions arising in battles (see Sections 2.3 and 3.5).

Another practical contribution was the emphasis Clausewitz placed on deterrence, used by all actors during the Tanker War, either politically or militarily, some boldly and on a large scale, and others in a more restrained manner. The whole reflagging episode, its political and military escalation and its aftermath was the most conspicuous example (see Sections 7.2, 7.3 and 7.4), while Iraq's targeting of Saudi tankers to discourage them from lifting Iranian oil was rather unassertive (see Section 6.1.4). Saddam Hussein's reshuffling of the RCC twice, in 1982 when the Iraqi army was driven back across the frontier by Iranian troops, and again in 1986, after the loss of Mehran, could be viewed as political deterrence. During the latter meeting, he yielded his tight grip on war-related decisions as a ruse to lay the blame for future failures on the General Staff and the field commanders. More importantly, he caved in to their demand for change to forestall conspiracy discussions and eliminate their opposition to the reorganization of the cabinet and other councils. Suspicious of his ministers' assessment of the situation and their call for his temporary replacement, and suspecting them of fuelling a palace coup to topple him, he turned the short-lived rebellion into a presidential coup. He thus avoided being supplanted by someone acceptable to Tehran, as well as the Gulf sheikhs; these had become sceptical about Iraq's ability to vanquish Iran, and entertained thoughts of removing him, as their coffers were being drained by Iraq's demands on them (see Sections 3.6 and 6.3.5).

Iran's use of the concept proved brilliant. Again, the descendants of the countrymen who invented the game of chess reflected on every manoeuvre. First of all, Iran's attack on Kuwaiti border posts, a few weeks after the start of war, discouraged Gulf Arab states from offering military support to Iraq for as long as the conflict endured. It occasionally attacked the territories of Iraq's Gulf allies, but stopped short of all-out confrontation, and refrained from hitting their strategic targets, such as desalinization plants. Time and again, Tehran's officials reiterated stern warnings to their enemy's partners to withhold their assistance, and counselled them to adopt neutral policies towards the conflict (see Sections 6.1.7, 6.4.1, 6.4.3 and 6.4.5–6.4.7). They repeatedly reassured the GCC states that Iran would not expand the war, though it was a strategic possibility and therefore tempting. As a result, the Gulf states pursued indecisive policies towards their two powerful neighbours, depending on the situation and the potential effects it had on their interests. Their support for Baghdad was at times equivocal, and their relations with Tehran alternated between public reproach for its refusal to accept SCR 598 by the autumn of 1987, after their warming towards it by late 1985 (see Sections 6.2.6 and 6.4.3).

To discourage the US from further siding with its foe by putting to sea its strategic forces, in defence of its interests, Rafsanjani threatened to target American assets around the world (see Section 6.4.3). Also, the IRIN carried out inspection of ships to hinder supplies from reaching Iraq, an acceptable and conventional mode of practice in times of war, given that it is a 'basic right of the belligerent to capture or even destroy on the high seas enemy goods or the ship which are contrabands of war and are destined to its adversary' (Brittin in Taylor and Francis, 1988, p. 220, also see explanation of legal aspect under law of naval warfare by Grunawalt, *ibid*, pp. 306–7; and Roach, 1991, pp. 598–600; and see Sections 6.2.4, 6.4.1, 6.4.6, 7.1 and 7.2). Iran's ability to judge the threshold between the militarily possible and the politically acceptable was demonstrated by the mining of the *Bridgeton*, and missile assaults on Kuwaiti and Saudi oil-loading terminals, power plants and ships within their territorial waters, some of which did not enjoy USN protection (see Sections 6.4.6 and 7.4). It rarely admitted responsibility for its acts, and in *lieu* of confrontation with the USN, had recourse to hit-and-run attacks against its units, and night-mining of the coasts of Iraq's main allies (see Sections 6.4.5 and 7.1). However, the laying of minefields off Fujairah proved to be a tactical error, since Western capitals, especially London, reversed their policies and agreed to earlier US requests to deploy their warships in the Gulf. While it assaulted ships loaded with oil of Arab provenance, it usually avoided those who enjoyed protection by their country's warships, for two reasons: to demonstrate to Iraq and its allies that it had the will to interfere with their trade and the capability to do so without attracting retaliation; and to challenge the claim of foreign navies that their presence was merely due to preserve free trade and shipping.

The Iran–Iraq War was instrumental in the creation of the GCC – one of the few attempts at Arab cooperation that survived for so long. To restrict Iran's role militarily, politically and socially, the Gulf states exercised deterrence by using the superpowers. At first, they were satisfied that both protagonists were engaged in weakening each other. Later on, they became alarmed when they feared the war would spread into their countries, or acts of sabotage threatened their internal stability. The GCC's strategic guidelines emphasized collective self-reliance and opposition to foreign interference and the establishment of foreign bases on their soil, but they swung around and invited intervention, when the policy was waived with Kuwait's request for the protection of its tankers (see Section 7.2). Although staunch US allies, the Gulf states played both cards, like most LDCs during the Cold War, such as Kuwait's request for re-flagging to both superpowers; Saudi and Kuwaiti purchases of Soviet weapons, when the US Congress denied them such sales; visits by their foreign ministers to Moscow and Washington; and Saudi back-channel talks with each of the superpowers on expanding the flight range over its skies for USAF AWACSs and F-15s, cooperation in minesweeping missions, and extending facilities for the USN, while licensing

Aeroflot liners to overfly its air space. During the Tanker War, they edged closer to Moscow, as its good offices were thought valuable to either pressure Iran to end the war, mediate in their favour if it defeated Iraq, or defend their sovereignty, territorial integrity and interests if those were in jeopardy (see Sections 4.4, 4.6, 6.1.4, 6.2.3, 6.2.5, 6.4.7 and 7.2).

Individually and collectively they also pursued policies designed to contain Iran. By conducting official and unpublicized bilateral relations with Tehran, they sought accommodation to preserve their own as well as regional security. Saudi Arabia cooperated with Iran within OPEC and sold it refined petroleum products, when its refinery was damaged by Iraqi raids (see Section 6.3.6), requested Syria to intercede when their tankers were targeted by Iran, and both capitals gave a low-key reporting of the downing of two Iranian *Phantoms* by Saudi combat aircraft (see Section 6.1.5). For his part, Sultan Qabus plainly stated his objective to strengthen bilateral relations with Iran, especially after Kuwait's re-flagging plan, and sent a cabinet minister to conduct high-level talks in Tehran (see Sections 6.2.6 and 6.4.3). Furthermore, as conditions in the Gulf deteriorated, they revealed the GCC's vulnerabilities and their inability to provide a credible shield to defend their national security. In return for Cairo's readmission into the Arab fold during the Amman summit in the fall of 1987, Iraq's Gulf allies were provided with the strategic depth that only Egypt could give.

Clausewitz stressed the importance of 'intangibles', such as morale and leadership. Although Iraq's and Iran's leaders had banked on the preconception that if their troops occupied each other's territory, their enemy's government would immediately collapse, nevertheless, both survived. True, their people became restless when their confrontation intensified over the waters of the Gulf, shortages were felt on the marketplace, and manpower was affected in both countries, with young men unwilling to volunteer, or even dodging conscription. But for the two recently established regimes, the war became the vehicle to introduce new policies, meant to strengthen them. Among the Iranians, the war bolstered the revolution and sustained its evolution, in spite of the war's length, astronomical human casualty figures, and the devastation it wrought on the economy. In addition to surviving its crisis with the US and the trade and arms embargo, Kurdish, *Tudeh* and *mujahedeen* rebellions, and several assassination and sabotage attempts, hostilities made possible the initiation of political, economic and social reforms to reinforce policies in the educational, social security and judiciary systems, and the industrial, agricultural and military sectors. However, as the war continued, the carnage of the *baseej* on the battlefield, the use of CW by Iraq in ground operations, the scarcity and high prices of consumer goods, and the decline in services appeared to affect the morale of troops, and the people's support for the government waned. Saddam Hussein managed to survive the war and even prosper. The country did not disintegrate, as the West and the Gulf states feared. Quite the contrary, the conflict enabled him to ensconce his new administration, greatly strengthen its military force, and also found a strong military/industrial base, in spite of the onslaught by Iranians, Kurds and *Shi'ah*.

By deciding to wage war, Saddam Hussein exploited what he perceived as chaos inside Iran, namely, a declining economy, a disintegrated military, and a political system wrought by schisms. But he failed to perceive the subliminal built-up force in the psyche of the Iranian masses. He underestimated the resilience of the Iranian revolution and the power of the armed forces, who had enough weapons to continue the war indefinitely, though at a reduced level. He also overestimated the intensity of popular disaffection and the strength of ethnic loyalties in Khuzistan, where nationalism and allegiance to Tehran proved to be immeasurably strong. In this respect, both Khomeini and Hussein speculated that religious or ethnic loyalty would override territorial nationalism, but both were proven mistaken as the war unfolded. Both also used the concept of *jihad* and fought under the banner of Islam. Iran's spiritual leader did so during the first Gulf War, to rally support among Muslims, and the Iraqi president, during the second, to destabilize Arab governments whose armies were part of the coalition against Iraq. In his quest to blend religion and politics, Saddam Hussein reversed his secular policy in 1990, and claimed to fight a holy war, ordering the phrase *Allahu Akbar* ('God is Almighty') to be written on Iraqi flags.

One aspect that Iraq's leader failed to appreciate was the danger of waging war on a revolution, and that of Khomeini's in particular. In his assessment of Iran's internal conditions, he did not take into account the supremacy of moral over material dimensions in young revolutionary states, namely, the 'intangibles' that Clausewitz judged so important. When people were successful, against all odds, in bringing down an established authority, they will rise to meet any threat to their revolution. Their first victory gives them confidence that they will triumph the second time. Revolutions have an impact on people at large, and on armed forces as well. Faith in their cause is robust. Operations carried out by the *Pasdaran* demonstrated their moral commitment. In *lieu* of sophisticated weapons, training and discipline, they were armed with initiative and *élan*, and improvisation and self-sacrifice were a salient feature in their battles.

War and the threat of war allow regimes to suppress opposition, and by appealing to their nationalism, neutralize ethnic and religious minorities. Combat is also used to justify poor economic performance and necessary austerity measures. Instead of toppling the *mullahs*, the Iran–Iraq War lent legitimacy to their holy war, and became the symbol of the revolution's resilience. It is clear that Saddam Hussein did not assess the 'psychological powers' of Iran nor the strength of Khomeini's 'opposing will'; nor was he able to foresee the extent of disarray and chaos a revolution can tolerate. Khomeini was a 'crusader' oblivious of costs. To him, the war was a zero-sum-game. If he failed to expand *Allah's ummah*, it would mean that God did not acknowledge his legitimacy. He mobilized people by using a mix of religious and patriotic sentiments. His 'moral influence' was such that people were in harmony with him, offering their lives readily at his command. The notion of *istishhad* (martyrdom, as an act of faith, rather than fanaticism, as defined by a number of Western writers) was constantly referred to in speeches and Friday sermons. Exhortations for the honour to die in the defence of Islam and ensure a path to heaven were used to enlist the people's support, encourage men to volunteer and console the fallen soldiers' families.

A number of Sun Tsu's views, thought to be modern, but found to be particularly relevant to this study were the relationship between inflation and a protracted war, the importance of internal stability for a country at war, in addition to concepts on organization, discipline, sound planning, logistics, surprise and deception, expediency, flexibility and moderation. Details in Sections 7.3.5, 7.4.5 and 7.5.2, amply demonstrated how the unending war reflected on internal conditions in Iran. Mounting war-weariness was illustrated by street demonstrations, draft-dodging soaring to unprecedented levels, and growing arguments in the *majlis* and even within the governing elite. Radicals disagreed with the Council of Guardians over economic policies regarding private property, and disputes also arose between the Council and the *majlis* and between the Militant Clergy Association and one of its factions, the Tehran Militant Clergy, leading to intra-clerical skirmishes in several cities. Therefore, one may reasonably deduce that Iraq's continuous application of military power against Iran's oil sector bore its fruits.

While little was known about the degree of 'organization' in both military camps, 'discipline' among Iraqi pilots seemed to be sound, probably due to the autocratic character of the regime. Its secretive nature, however, faced researchers with the difficulty of obtaining any information on the situation. In regard to 'organization' in Iran's military, it emerged later that the powerful minister of the legendary *Pasdaran*, Muhsin Rafiqdust, was subsequently dismissed, after revelations about his inefficiency in commanding the guards, squandering the IRGC's resources in procuring arms at inflated prices, while keeping his troops under-equipped on the battlefront. He was also accused of carelessness in logistics, which included stocking CWs in high-risk areas and alarmingly close to Tehran, and endangering peoples' lives while transporting munitions to the front. Beside confirming that Iran stockpiled CW, these revelations somewhat explained the IRGC's reverses on the battlefield, during the few months preceding the ceasefire. This does not alter the fact that Iraq's own use of CW also turned the ground war around, and enabled its troops to liberate its territories; in spite of repeated denials by Baghdad, a UN investigative committee reported in August 1988, that it made extensive use of CW in spring and summer operations. As for 'discipline', the literature on the Iranian military highlighted chasms within and between the regular forces and the voluntary militia, thus undercutting their potential effectiveness in ground and naval operations. Continuous competition between regular army and *Pasdaran* commanders, rivalries in the regular forces between *ancien régime* and newly commissioned officers, and the absence of inter-service collaboration weakened the performance of all branches. After the ceasefire, reports indicated that some of Iran's leaders criticized the government's military, diplomatic and economic war strategies.

'Sound planning', 'logistics' and 'economy of force' were obviously the hallmark of the IRGCN's counterstrategy in achieving its objective. Its great reliance on a large fleet of lightly-armed FACs in the shallow and crowded waters of the Gulf, among the multitude of islands, islets and coral reefs, were particularly suited for their operations. Also, the extensive use of mines in confined areas caused serious disruption at very low cost; on some occasions, mines halted traffic on the world's most crowded oil highway, and while the fleets of tankers and warships lay at anchor in the Gulf of Oman, the area looked like a floating crowded parking plot. They were appropriate, since the 1907 Law of the Sea (LOS) Convention was applicable to Iran, which 'as a belligerent had the right to lay' them, and was under no obligation to notify neutral ships. As USN warships and helicopters scuttled the *Iran Ajr* on 21 September 1987, killing a number of its crew and capturing the survivors, it 'raises the question as to whether a neutral has the right to use force against a belligerent for authorized activity on high seas' (Brittin in Taylor and Francis, 1988, p. 319; for a view on the legitimacy of USN action, see Gamlen, 1989, p. 55; and for a discussion on the legality of Iran's minelaying and the USN's counterattacks, see Wachenfeld, 1988, pp. 199–202). They also displayed resourcefulness when they cannibalized their equipment and were able to make some of them operational again. However, in so far that the Iraqis insisted on the use of the five *Super-Etendard* fighters as the basic instrument to implement their strategy in the beginning, they went against the precept that requires a powerful force at the critical time to be concentrated at the proper location for as long as operations demanded. They placed themselves in a precarious situation, if for instance, two of these aircraft had been downed in a dog-fight with Iranian *Phantoms*, or by anti-aircraft defence systems on Kharg or other sites they raided. Their position would have become quite untenable, and in fact, the whole Tanker War tactic would have floundered.

Sun Tsu's views on the choice and careful study of the geographical area in order to prevail in combat, and the use of 'surprise' and 'deception' were illustrated by later Iraqi attacks on the make-shift terminals on Sirri and Larak. This they did by either acquiring mid-air refuelling capabilities, questioned by military observers on the basis of their lack of technical abilities in this field, or re-filling in other Gulf airfields, as the Iranians suspected. Iran, which had moved its oil-loading facilities near the mouth of the Gulf, had not expected enemy aircraft to reach that far. Hence, the Iraqis were able to capitalize on their enemy's lack of preparedness. Their surprise attacks indicated to Iran that its strategic assets were within easy reach, and that its oil exports could be interfered with at will, despite its patrolled convoys of shuttle tankers, ferrying oil away from the exclusion zone and closer to the Strait. Roach made an interesting point arguing that Iraqi attacks on Iranian oil facilities were in the nature of a blockade, and could be regarded as legitimate (1991, pp. 606–8; also see Sections 6.3.6 and 6.3.8). The Iranians were successful in this respect too. Taking one of the more publicized incidents as an example, the IRGCN certainly selected the appropriate geographical area and weapon when they planted their minefields 18 miles off Farsi Island, and lay ambush to the re-flagged Kuwaiti tanker. By avoiding the use of *Silkworm* missiles against the *Bridgeton*, which the USN anticipated, Iran escaped immediate retaliation. Despite the side-effect of the damaging of the *Texaco Caribbean* by one of their own mines, the political repercussions and psychological effect of the first operation eclipsed the second by far (see Chapter 1 and Section 7.4). Awkward currents or rough waters are not typical of the Gulf, but the IRGCN mainly relied on light craft in their hit-and-run missions, and the study of meteorological conditions was essential for their retaliatory attacks.

The Chinese strategist's notions of 'expediency', 'flexibility' and 'moderation' in warfare explained that in some cases enemies were neighbours, such as Iran and Iraq in this study, and might later become allies. (At one point during the second Gulf War, especially when Iraqi military and civilian aircraft were flown to Iranian airports, this became a nightmare scenario in the minds of the coalition's strategic planners.) Moderation, advocated by Sun Tsu and ridiculed by

Clausewitz was disregarded by Iraq in its use of CW in the ground war, and by both belligerents in their bombing and missile attacks on cities, extraordinarily violent during the last quarter of 1987 and the first of 1988 (see Sections 6.1.2, 6.2.2, 6.2.3, 6.4.1, and especially 6.4.7, 6.5.1 and 6.5.2). But both opponents showed a degree of restraint in the Tanker War. Iraq did not destroy Iran's oil export facilities completely, especially the one on Kharg, and Iran did not block Hormuz, despite some rhetoric out of Tehran, sometimes rather fierce. Iranian politicians played up their tough stance to appeal to domestic opinion and enlist popular support for the continuation of armed conflict, and avoided any drastic military measures that the Iraqis, it is believed, intended them to resort to. By not being entrapped into escalating operations to the extent of closing the Strait in the face of commercial traffic, the IRI's policy coincided with US interests.

Some observers implied that Baghdad refrained from totally destroying its choice target, Kharg (see Sections 6.2.4 and 6.3.7), to avoid alienating segments or the whole of its *Shi'i* population, for concern over acts of sabotage; or that it feared to aggrieve the community of oil producers and consumers, and incur economic and military costs. Public opinion, at home and world-wide, much of which neutral or supportive, could have turned against Baghdad, if all Iranian oil production were halted. Most of it was exported to industrialized countries, whose economies relied on the uninterrupted flow of this strategic mineral. The full-scale destruction of Iran's platforms and the resulting inability to export oil could have steered it towards an escalation of military operations and the eventual closure of the Strait. This would have caused a sizeable drop in the quantity of oil on the international market, and a rise in the price of the commodity, leading to inflation on a global scale. Faced with such a crisis, the international community would have acted promptly and decisively to intervene in the war, by either mandating economic sanctions, or by bringing their military power into play. This policy was made clear by Warren Christopher, the US Deputy Secretary of State, who warned that Washington would use any means, even military action, to foil the obstruction of Hormuz. These scenarios Iran avoided at great length, the first for obvious reasons, and the latter in support of its policy of non-intervention in the Gulf by any foreign powers.

From the purely self-interest aspect, Iraq had to balance the advantage of crippling its enemy's life-line against the interests at stake and the potential political/military impact. Had it totally wrecked Iran's oil facilities, Iraq's own, as well as its allies', would be laying themselves open to destruction. Baghdad would not only forfeit their patronage, but most certainly unleash their hostility. In this respect, it is also worth noting that Iran spent millions to renovate its oil reservoirs and outlets in the lower Gulf's harbours, out of reach of Iraqi attacks, which indicated its determination to keep its exports flowing. Also, bearing in mind Soviet and Chinese refusal to participate in a possible UN-mandated arms embargo against Iran (see Sections 6.4.4 and 6.4.7), one should not discount the fact that had any of the two warring countries shunned moderation, they would have created an international consensus for their isolation, and their appeals for world support were likely to fail.

Sun Tsu and Lidell Hart, among other strategists, highlighted the value of forming new alliances and preserving old ones, whether economic, military, diplomatic or social, to achieve the political objectives of war. During the Tanker War, new coalitions were formed and old ones strengthened. These either involved bilateral associations or a coalition of countries whose rulers shared a unanimous perception of threat, or where beside the political convergence of parties, economic interests associated them. In this regard, both Iraq and Iran were able to maximize benefits out of their relations with their allies. Given that the US fully supported Iraq's campaign in the Gulf, militarily, by targeting Iran's naval and air craft only and providing Baghdad with US Sat-Int information, economically, by extending loans and participating vigorously in building pipelines to ship Iraqi oil to the Red Sea, while subjecting Iran to an embargo, and diplomatically, by repeatedly calling for UN-mandated sanctions against Iran alone, Iraq thus had an unfettered hand – not merely in the Tanker War – but in the war at large, to the extent of using CW with impunity. One is tempted to argue that in its confrontation with its enemy, it was given the opportunity to manipulate the pace of the Tanker War, and to a certain extent, govern Iranian and USN actions and counteractions. Furthermore, in spite of the devastation of its oil and export facilities, and although it became debt-ridden, Iraq was able to pursue the protracted war at relative ease, due principally to the Gulf sheikh's cheque-book diplomacy. These were in the form of 0.3 mbd to 0.4 mbd of Saudi and Kuwaiti oil, sold on Iraq's behalf, in addition to loans, which in the case of Riyadh, totalled $25 billion by the end of the war (Sheridan, 1994; and King, 1987, p. 33). Consequently, social tensions, caused by economic hardship, were mild and manageable in comparison to Iran's. And while its enemy had to pay highly inflated prices for the hardware it managed to acquire on the black market, Iraq was given loans for major arms purchases by Moscow, Paris, Washington and others, thus enabling it to vastly enlarge its army (see Section 3.5).

One of the interesting aspects of alliance formation and preservation was the relationship governing Moscow with the two countries at war, which was almost similar to the American position in the Arab–Israeli conflict. Despite its 1972 Friendship Treaty with Iraq, the USSR had nuclear collaboration arrangements with both, and in the early days of the Iran–Iraq War gave the 'green light' to Syria, Libya and North Korea to provide Iran's arsenal with hardware (it has even been claimed that a North Korean factory was set up for the sole purpose of changing the matrix on Soviet weapons to show instead they were made in the country). By contrast, during the first two years of the Iran–Iraq War, it halted weapon transfers to its ally as a gesture in support of Iran, and only resumed major transfers when the tides of war changed. As the conflict endured, it stopped Iranian gas and oil trade, and increased Iraqi and Saudi oil imports, then resumed those from Iran again (see Sections 3.6 and 6.4.4). Despite high-level pressure from Washington, in the pursuance of the 1990s 'dual containment' policy, Moscow reinforced its symmetrical relationship, and continued to play on the Middle Eastern chessboard. It offered to cooperate with Tehran to reconstruct its nuclear reactor in Booshehr, built with German technology but damaged during the Iran–Iraq War. And it reached a $10 billion deal with its long-standing ally, to develop Iraq's gas and oil fields; although under US pressure the Kremlin agreed not to go ahead while sanctions were enforced, Russia's Foreign Minister, Yevgeny Primakov – *Pravda*'s former Middle East analyst, who travelled frequently to Iraq for the past 25 years and became Saddam Hussein's personal friend – has repeatedly called for their lifting.

The 1980s policy had many advantages for USSR national interests. On the one hand, with Iran absorbed in the war, it could not give appropriate attention to the subversion of Soviet Muslims. On the other, Moscow enhanced its image in the majority of Muslim and Arab states, tarnished after its invasion of Afghanistan, by siding with Tehran at the UN on the issues of sanctions and a UN naval patrol to replace foreign navies, and also facilitating arms procurement. Moreover, as *Ba'thi* Iraq no longer towed the Soviet line and edged closer to the US, its weakening would make it more compliant *vis-à-vis* its former patron (see Sections 6.1.3, 6.3.1, 6.3.9 and 6.4.4). Beside Iran's military and economic gains, bilateral relations held the prospect of diluting the Soviet–Iraqi alliance, counterbalanced US support for Iraq, and improved chances for diplomatic backing. One of the most consequential outcomes of the Moscow–Tehran alliance and the projects contracted between them during the Tanker War, was the railway line between former Soviet Central Asia and Iran. Labelled by Rafsanjani the 'Twenty-First-Century Silk Route', the first section of which was inaugurated in May 1996 by leaders of ten nations, it will link the hearts of Europe and Asia, the Mediterranean with the Gulf, and the Black Sea with the Indian and Pacific oceans. When completed, it will stretch all the way from London to Beijing, through Paris, Stuttgart, Budapest, Sofia, Ankara, Tehran, Mashhad, Tejen, Alma Ata, Aktogay and Urumchi, and will most certainly have far-reaching strategic, economic and social effects, well beyond this century.

The Iran–Iraq War introduced the other Communist giant into the area, who so far had a rather confined role there. Beside mutual strategic interests, agreement on contesting US 'hegemony' brought China and Iran together. Beijing became Tehran's major arms procurer, especially after signing an arms-for-oil deal in 1987, which, beside 50 J-6 fighters, also included substantial quantities of hardware and spare parts for ex-Soviet weapons. The PRC also upgraded Iran's indigenous military industry, by assisting in constructing four factories for the manufacture of rockets, ammunition, and tank spare parts. While it transferred the dreaded *Silkworm* missiles to its client, it also provided Saudi Arabia with the same. During the Tanker war, it constantly sided with Tehran against proposals for embargoes by the US, the UK and France and for war compensation to be

paid by Iraq (see Sections 4.6 and 6.4.4). The nuclear cooperation arrangements reached by Iran with Beijing and Moscow at
the time, culminated a decade later in the establishment of the
Asian Fund for Nuclear Power Research, grouping the three, in
addition to India.

Turkey is a regional power equal to Egypt and Iran, with a
population of 58 million people. Its dominion over essential
water supplies to Iraq and Syria, its control of vital oil routes
from Iraq, and its strategic relations with the US as a NATO
member, enhanced its regional role, reinforced during and
after the Second Gulf War, when it became the guarantor of
the Gulf countries' security, especially Kuwait and Saudi
Arabia. Tehran's and Baghdad's collaboration with Ankara,
whose official policy towards their conflict was said to be
neutral, was beneficial to the three parties' strategic interests
in the short and long terms. A border security agreement with
Iraq and a similar understanding with Iran enabled all three
to suppress resistance by their Kurdish minorities. Baghdad
and Tehran relied on Ankara's troops and combat planes to
target KDP, PUK and KDPI camps, while Turkish troops periodically pursued the PKK across the Iraqi border, causing over
18 000 human casualties between 1984 and 1996. Commercial
interests were advantageous to all in the short and medium
terms. Iraq's overland oil exports proved mutually beneficial,
awarding it revenues essential to sustain its war economy, and
rewarding Turkey with the toll levied on its passage.
Transactions were amplified, and Turkey's surge in exports
wiped out its deficit with Iraq, while it became Iran's second
largest customer and exporter. Its thriving trade with Iraq and
Iran led to a surplus of $1.8 billion in the late 1980s.

However, while the first Gulf War was beneficial to Turkey's
economy, it suffered seriously under the embargo mandated
against Iraq in 1990. But despite its failing economy, its set-
backs in Central Asia, its tensions with Greece over the Aegean
and in Cyprus, its frequent incursions into northern Iraq, and
its ruthless campaign against its Kurds, and although in the
post-Cold War world Turkey's role seems nonessential to
NATO, it was provided with free heavy weapons, which, in a
way, eventually enabled it to boast the second largest army in
NATO by 1993. Under the programme known as *Cascade*, inaugurated in August 1992, Nato member-states, whose forces

exceed limits set by the Conventional Forces in Europe (CFE) treaty, gave away, free of charge, surplus weapon systems to allies. At that time, Turkey had almost 4000 tanks and by July 1993 it received over 1000, a nearly 27 per cent increase.

The Tanker War had a detrimental impact on Iraq's and Iran's economies (for the costs of the war on both countries, see Chubin and Tripp, 1989, pp. 111, 129–30 and table p. 125), but affected the financial status of some of its neighbours in a beneficial manner, primarily Jordan's and Turkey's; and Pakistan, whose trade with Iran multiplied ten-folds, became its biggest commercial partner. Countries adjacent to Iraq thrived on trade and the levying of transit taxes on goods imported through their ports and dispatched overland. Goods, including arms shipments, came across Kuwait, Saudi Arabia, Turkey and Jordan, with ships unloading at Mediterranean and Red Sea ports, and Iraq's crude oil was exported overland via pipelines and tanker trucks. Hemmed in by the Iranian naval blockade, it had to solve the problem of imports and exports. This it did by using the Jordanian and Turkish borders, in particular. Consequently, harbours such as 'Aqaba became vital to Baghdad's war efforts. The substantial upgrading and modernization of the seaport's infrastructure and the highway leading to Baghdad, as well as a significant fleet of trucks and petrol tankers, were made possible with Iraqi money. During the 1980s, half of Jordan's exports went to Iraq, excluding phosphate, and the 'Aqaba–Baghdad road became one of the busiest highways in the Middle East, while thousands of jobs were created in Jordan around the sharp increase in trade links and the related services sector. However, Jordan became heavily dependent on Iraq for its oil supplies, and its economy was vulnerable to Iraqi economic and political pressures – a factor limiting its freedom of manoeuvre. It vindicated King Hussein, whose muted reaction at the time of the Second Gulf War attracted fierce criticism and disparaging commentaries from the press. With his country's reliance on Iraqi oil at concessionary prices, trade, and remittances from Jordanians employed in Iraq, his course of action was the only conceivable one. The large Palestinian population in Jordan is the other factor that should not be overlooked. They regarded President Hussein as the only Arab leader who was seriously determined to champion their cause, and indeed had the military clout to challenge Israel. In their eyes, he proved his credentials and became a symbol of their fight for liberation when he hit Tel Aviv with *Scuds* – the first Arab ruler to dare to do so. Militarily ineffective, the missiles were nevertheless psychologically powerful and politically impressive, and in a way, were large-scale *intifadah* stones that stirred the Palestinians' imagination. In the occupied West Bank, they watched from their rooftops in the same manner that the French cheered from their balconies when the allies attacked Nazi forces during the Second World War. When they took to the streets of Amman to demonstrate their support in 1991, King Hussein had to apply *realpolitik* and steer his country carefully to avoid unrest. However, from 8 August 1995, relations deteriorated between Amman and Baghdad, when Lieutenant-General Hussein Kamel al-Majeed and his brother, Colonel Saddam Kamel, Saddam Hussein's two sons-in-law, defected to Jordan with their wives and a large retinue of officers. Following their assassination, after their return to Baghdad in February, the Jordanian monarch called for the removal of the Iraqi leader, in his quest to reach a *rapprochement* with the GCC states and the West, and a peace agreement with Israel.

Iraq's marriage of convenience with Egypt proved mutually advantageous, and as the military conflict and the 'wars of the embassies' broadened, Egypt closed Iran's Interest Section in Cairo, as a token of its support for Baghdad (see Section 6.4.4). The arrangement placed Egypt on the world map as a newly-emerging state in sales of conventional weapons, spareparts and ammunition. Cairo supplied Baghdad with locally-manufactured *Saqr Eye* portable SAMs, ex-Soviet MBTs, armoured personnel carriers (APCs) and fighter aircraft. It also cooperated with Iraq and Argentina in the development of the *Condor II*, renamed *Badr 2000* (Schmidt, 1991, p. 9; and *Independent on Sunday*, 26 August 1990). For the first time after many years, Egypt's balance of trade showed an improvement because of extensive arms sales, 89 per cent of which it sold Iraq (Sampson, 1988, p. xxiv).

The Egyptian arms industry was working full time producing ammunition for the Iraqis, with US blessing. A former US military official recalls: 'I looked over those plants. They were producing 130 mm and other artillery based on Soviet designs. The Egyptians sold them to the Iraqis. It was one way of getting money for the Egyptians and lowering the amount it cost us to keep their economy going' (Cockburn, 1992).

Egyptian farmers and labourers filled the gap caused by the upgrading of Iraq's troops to one million under arms, and the consequent depletion of its own work force. From Egypt's viewpoint, exporting labour reduced unemployment and socio-economic strains, and their remittances became its primary foreign-currency source. They totalled $10 billion in the 1980s, ahead of revenues from tourism and Suez Canal duties on ships, the latter of which netted $1.96 billion in 1993. It is worth noting that Egypt's expatriate community in Iraq became its largest anywhere in the world, numbering over 2 million by the late 1980s (Mubarak, Interview, 2 April 1993; and Sha'ban, 26 February 1992).

Iraqi commanders were chafing under the charge that their ground troops lost most of the territory, gained during the first few weeks, and that their pilots had failed to exploit their superiority in airpower as compared to Iran's. Most importantly for the Tanker War, the renewed association with Cairo provided the Iraqis with the opportunity to call upon Egyptian pilots, one of whom said his group took part in prolonged training of Iraqi aviators, along with other nationals (Touman, Interview, 17 August 1988). Iraq also drew on the expertise of Egyptian strategists, who became involved, at a later stage of the war, in planning for the seizure of al-Fao. Although the following may or may not have been envisaged by the Iraqi leadership at the time of renewed bilateral relations, a number of Egyptian workers were forcibly drafted into the Iraqi army, while others were attracted by offers of high salaries, and took part in the recapture of al-Fao. Some were taken as POWs, 16 of which were released by Iran shortly after the ceasefire (Velayati, 1988, p. 71).

Syria generally viewed Iraq as providing it with strategic depth, and its president warned Iran in late January 1987, that if it seized Iraqi territory or attacked its Gulf neighbours, he would withdraw his support for Tehran. Their strategic interests also coincided on the Kurdish and the Faurat and Dejla water issues, all of which increasingly involved Turkey. But relations were eroded by personal animosity between Asad and Hussein, with Syria backing Iran in the war and cooperating with it in Lebanon. The Syrian *'Alawi* minority, who dominate the socio-economic and political structure within the country, are essentially *Shi'ah*. Converging with Iran's interests to topple Saddam Hussein, Syria revealed the realism of a small state, whose ruler was on the look-out for a supporter against him. Syria's backing of Iran was also founded on their resentment of US foreign policy in the area, given its unflinching support for Israel, and its collaboration with Baghdad in backing Maronite Christians in Lebanon. The Iranians had influence among the *mustazafeen*, the *Shi'ah* in southern Lebanon, and Lebanon's *Hizb-Ullah*, and in that respect, cooperated with Syria, the dominant power in the country. At the very start of the war, Damascus provided Tehran with missiles, and two years later, plugged the Kirkuk-Baniyas pipeline, thus reducing Iraqi oil exports. Distrust between the two *Ba'thi* leaders was so potent, that Iraq had to station at least two to three divisions in the north at all times during the war (see Sections 3.5 and 3.6). Syria was amply rewarded by Iran for its support, by allowing it to import oil at reduced prices, even when Tehran had shortages and was forced to start conservation (see Section 6.3.8). Their collaboration during the Iran–Iraq War drove a wedge in the Arab coalition supporting Iraq. But Asad's foreign policy appeared to shift towards ambivalence in the later stages of the Tanker War. While he continued to support Iran publicly, their relations seemed to decline, at a time when his alliance with the Soviet Union was coming apart. In March 1987, Tehran had halted oil sales to Damascus at a discount, and both capitals were in disagreement over policies regarding the proxy war fought on Lebanese soil. Starting in the fall of 1987, Asad edged towards conciliation with the US, by offering to mediate the release of hostages held in Beirut, and at the Amman Arab summit in November 1987, went so far as to condemn Iran (see Sections 6.4.5 and 6.5.1).

Syria was a loser after Iran accepted SCR 598, and when the Soviet Empire collapsed. It could no longer aspire to play the leading role of the intermediary in the area, and lost the political backing of a superpower. Whilst a peace settlement had not materialized and Israel's military capabilities were continuously developed, the termination of Soviet military aid forced Damascus to search for other countries willing to sell arms, but without the soft terms it enjoyed with Moscow. In the meantime, America still considered Syria a sponsor of terrorism, and did not lift sanctions against it, although Damascus succeeded in mediating for the release of Western hostages held in Beirut, eased constraints on Syrian Jews and issued those who wished to leave with exit visas, and proposed to assist Israel to locate soldiers missing in action in Lebanon. Most importantly, in Prince Khalid Bin-Sultan's view, it was one of 'the Arab members of the coalition, whose very presence demonstrated Arab unity against Saddam – an important psychological and political ingredient of *Desert Storm*' (Bin-Sultan, 1993, p. 2). But while its economic squeeze led to its decline, it still remained one of the major players in the ongoing Arab–Israeli peace process, by its entrenchment in Lebanon. Its open door policy attracted some foreign investment, especially from Lebanese nationals, and its nascent oil industry cushioned the negative effects of the loosened alliance with Iran. Strengthened during the Iran–Iraq War, it may not endure, once the threat that brought them together disappeared, namely, a strengthened Iraq, ruled by Saddam Hussein.

Apart from inter-state coalitions, minor indigenous as well as cross-border alliances with an assortment of organizations and ethnic groups were worked out prior to and during the Tanker War, most of which survive until now. But as a result of fighting their governments from neighbouring countries' bases, these opposition groups lost credibility among their people. Also, by serving their patrons' interests at the expense of their own countries', they failed to achieve any of their objectives. Iran, Iraq, Syria and Turkey manipulated Kurdish parties, each according to their own agenda, nurturing and sustaining them to destabilize their neighbour's regime and/or create skirmishes with its troops. Until now, Tehran gives succour to Muhammad Baqer al-Hakeem's SAIRI and other *Shi'ah* opposition groupings, and created *al-Badr* Brigade, who intimidate other militia groups in Iraqi Kurdistan. Baghdad, despite the burden of the

1990 UN-mandated sanctions, still provides Rajavi's MKO and its military arm, the NLA, with massive financial and logistical support. They operate from Iraqi territory and carry out armed resistance against the post-revolutionary regime, continuing the struggle initiated in the early 1960s. Under the Shah, and until 1975, then again since the start of Iran–Iraq hostilities, Iran occasionally relied on Barzani's KDP and Talabani's PUK *Peshmerga* to carry out sabotage and commando missions in Iraqi Kurdistan, or to constrain cross-border movements by Ghassemlou's KDPI; and the Kurdish *Jash* collaborated with Baghdad in the northern sector (see Sections 4.3, 6.2.6, 6.3.5, 6.3.9, 6.4.4 and 6.5.2). Syria, and to a lesser degree, Iran, were accused by Turkey of sheltering the PKK and allowing them to set up training camps, and Ankara exploits the water issue as a card to play with against Syria and Iraq, especially when its campaign against its Kurds faces problems. Whether in media campaigns or bilateral and multi-lateral talks, whenever one subject is discussed, the other automatically bounces back.

The intruding powers also manipulated minorities in the Gulf region to destabilize and weaken central governments. Ethnic groups were covertly encouraged and financed when it suited their purposes, or abandoned and ignored when an arrangement was imposed. In the nineteenth century, this was true in Persia, and in the twentieth, it took place in both Iran and Iraq. The Kurds are the example, *par excellence*, when they were used in the early 1970s against the Iraqi government, perceived to be a Soviet surrogate. CIA agents shored up the illusion that the US will always be behind them, while they had no intention of seeing their movement succeed. It is interesting to note that congressional investigations surrounding Henry Kissinger's and the CIA's roles in providing US support for Kurdish guerilla activities before the Algiers agreement led to reforms within the intelligence agency and to the selection of George Bush as its director.

These policies could back-fire, and the 'Kurdish Question' has the potential to develop into a drawn-out freedom fight, not only in Iraq and Turkey, but also in Syria and Iran. Despite assurances from Kurdish leaders, denying that their ultimate aim was the unification and control of all territories inhabited by ethnic Kurds, regional and major powers are intent on preventing this process, for fear of encouraging minorities elsewhere. Were this to happen, according to their 'nightmare scenario', Baluchis, Khuzistanis, Iraqi *Shi'ah*, and others would emulate them and activate latent territorial ambitions, and the whole region, with its oil, would burn.

A sovereign Kurdistan is not a prospect welcomed by regional powers, and there is widespread consensus against its establishment. Fearing the effect on their own minorities, Iran, Turkey and Syria have repeatedly proclaimed their commitment to the territorial integrity of Iraq, and since November 1992, their foreign ministers have regular discussions. It was speculated that Ankara and Tehran sought Syrian support to keep up pressure on the PKK, the *Mujahedeen-e-Khalq* and the KDPI, which operate in Iraqi Kurdistan, despite denials by Kurdish leaders. In spite of the establishment of an Iraqi Kurdish local government in 1992, preceded by parliamentary elections, the foreign ministers' final communique noted 'chaos and a total absence of authority', and denounced terrorist actions. In this respect, Damascus conducted a complex geopolitical game: while it allowed the PKK leader to announce his war cry on Syrian-controlled soil in Lebanon's Beqa' Valley, its Foreign Minister Farouq al-Shara' endorsed increased pressure on the PKK in the statement. It was suspected that Syria was anxious to conclude a water arrangement with Turkey, and in return, showed a willingness to dismantle PKK camps in the Beqa', agreed to exchange intelligence about the Kurds with Turkey, and that it manoeuvred with this card for that end.

Most major powers also oppose the creation of a Kurdish state on geostrategic and geopolitical grounds. A country situated near Central Asia and adjacent to several states, with a large population that could grow to more than 25 million after the influx from neighbouring countries and Europe, would suddenly create a new regional power, given its strategic mineral resources, such as uranium, copper and phosphate, beside its large reserves of petroleum. It is inhabited by a resilient people, who made enormous sacrifices, and do not mind sustaining hardship in order to achieve their final aims. Its mountainous landscape makes it easily defensible, and the sizable force of *Peshmerga* was hardened in battle and resistance-fighting. But their armaments do not make them a serious threat to neighbouring countries, since their arsenal mainly consists of mortars and hand-held rocket launchers, in addition to some simple heavy weapons, such as artillery pieces, and a few MBTs, captured from Iraqi forces.

Iraq's natural wealth is unevenly distributed, and Baghdad is likely to starve if the country were carved up. Sandwiched between two oil-rich regions, it would not be able to subsist on its own. Baghdad boasts its historical and cultural heritage, but Kurdistan and Basra are the key provinces. Apart from potential resistance by the central government, some members of the Iraqi political opposition movement contest the idea of a break-up. On the one hand, the pan-Arab *Ba'th* and *Qawmiyun* – for ideological reasons – in addition to some liberal and leftist groups, oppose the creation of a sovereign Kurdish state; and the main *Shi'ah* party, *al-Da'wah*, does not sanction the dismemberment of Iraq, despite Islamists' strong belief in *al-ummah al-Islamiyah* (Muslim nation) and *la qawmiyah fil-Islam* (no nation-state in Islam, namely, the rejection of the concept of state, boundaries, etc.). On the other, some leftists side with Kurds, and assert the right of all people, who share the same territory, heritage and economy to claim self-determination; in the long-term, they hope to create an independent state, after reaching an amicable agreement with all parties concerned. But for the time being, most Iraqi Kurds would settle to play a more active role, and have the same career opportunities as the *Sunni* Arabs in business enterprises, the army and academia. After being discriminated against, they are determined to participate on an equal basis and be integrated into the socio-economic and political structures, with full rights and representation in the legislative, executive and judicial systems.

Since the founding of their first front in 1988, Iraqi Kurdish leaders retreated from seeking a sovereign Kurdistan, and espoused the concept of a federated entity, within a truly democratic state. Barzani made it unequivocally clear that he no longer envisaged statehood, and only raised demands that conformed with 'geopolitical realities, one of which is that we live in a land-locked area, and despite that our *Peshmerga* have a long history of armed struggle, violence is counterproductive to the movement and would destroy us' (Barzani, 1992).

These thoughts were enshrined in the draft constitution, where a balance was kept between the sovereignty and integrity of Iraq, and the Kurds' own culture, history and traditions. Discussed within Iraqi Kurdish circles in 1992, it provides for three autonomous regions within a democratic constitutional and federal presidential republic (Clauses 1, 2 and 25 [3]), with equal rights for men and women of all races and beliefs, as proclaimed by the UN Charter (Clauses 3 and 10–13), sharing one capital, Baghdad (Clause 19), one flag, national anthem, and currency (Clause 21) and one nationality (Clause 23). Beside provincial legislative councils, cabinets and prime ministers (Clause 24), the central government has two legislative chambers (Clause 25 [1a and b]), an executive president, two vice-presidents from the two other provinces (Clause 25 [2]), and a cabinet headed by the president (Clause 25 [3]). A close examination of the document confirmed the Kurds' unwillingness to continue to live in an under-developed province in a highly-centralized country. This thread ran distinctly throughout the fabric of the text, and the clauses repeatedly asserted the adoption of the concept of a federated Iraq, where the Kurds – in regard to some affairs – share responsibilities and power with the central government. The idea was denounced by Turkey and Iran, and became a bone of contention among the Iraqi opposition. It could fertilize the seeds of future conflicts, with national entities fighting each other. However, the Kurds' prolonged ordeal validated their misgivings.

The richer a nation in natural resources and cultural heritage, the more reluctant its people to be integrated within a centralized state, where the government absorbs their revenues and dissolves their identity. As has been the case in the 1990s, the Kurds made the most of an embargoed and weakened Baghdad to seize greater autonomy. The longer the present conditions prevail in an Iraq under sanctions, the more rapidly the chauvinist tendency will spread among Iraqi Kurds, but the more precarious their conditions become, the weaker their negotiating position will be *vis-à-vis* to the government and other opposition parties.

Authoritarian governments characterize most regimes in the Middle East. But Iraq – and Turkey also – will only hold together if they became more pluralistic countries, where diverse ethnic, social, and cultural interests exist and develop together. This settlement is definitely the only one to avert the disaster scenario, advanced in Baghdad, Ankara, Tehran and Damascus, of a descent into civil war, Yugoslavia-style, with factions fighting – not only the central government – but each other over issues of borders for their ethnic communities, and the regions rich in natural resources.

The experience gained from the Iran–Iraq War furnishes a few guidelines, some applicable to the Gulf region, while other lessons learnt could serve in the Middle East, in LDCs and elsewhere.

Stability in the Gulf region is dependent on collective security arrangements entered into by all countries bordering its waters, and whereas Iran's and Iraq's roles are indispensable, Yemen's inclusion should be seriously considered. While it is true that relations were badly frayed by two Gulf wars, and that the GCC states are apprehensive of Baghdad's and Tehran's predominance in the area, their security concerns coincide and 'constitute a firm basis for their solidarity and their gathering together within a single regional system to guarantee and safeguard their common interests' (Velayati, 1988, p. 73). The creation of a joint naval force, that includes all the complementary elements available in each country, is essential in order to cease dependence on alien flags for their defence. A credible seapower, based on cost-saving collaboration, and combining naval as well as air craft, will be capable of protecting their vital routes of approach, especially in restricted areas such as the straits of Hormuz and Bab al-Mandab (see Section 5.1).

The Iranian non-traditional model is appropriate for an LDC confronting lesser-developed as well as superior navies, and it is in the best interests of Arab naval commanders to review its successful low-intensity maritime operations, using mines and FACs; train their forces along the lines of Iran's tactics; and acquire the means best suited for carrying them out; and as an addendum, study LOS clauses on their use. They should also acquire mine warfare countermeasures, in defence of their coasts and harbours.

The establishment of a regional industrial/military base is also indispensable. One such project started in Egypt, but was not allowed to fully develop for political reasons. To lessen dependence on foreign arms manufacturers, indigenous industrial capabilities, such as Iraq's and Iran's, which developed reasonably well during their war and continued to do so afterwards, should also be incorporated.

Middle Eastern states should seriously urge for the banning of NBC weapons in the area. Fortunately for Iraq's neighbours, its large arsenal of chemical and biological weapons has been exterminated, and innocent civilians no longer live in fear of meeting the fate of the inhabitants of Halabja. However, Israel's nuclear capability threatens security in the area, and despite Iran's and Egypt's collaboration as early as 1974, proposing a nuclear-free Middle East to the UN General Assembly, the issue has yet to be addressed by the major powers, and should not be met by the world's complicity and silence.

The provision of arms to Iran and Iraq during their war followed the rationale that neither should be allowed a total victory, and the chasm it reveals between policies and politics and the message it sends verges on conspiracy. In the realm of *realpolitik*, policy decisions are rarely dictated by considerations of what is honourable, and scruples hardly ever play a role in this domain. Wisdom would have suggested not to arm belligerents so as to prevent the war from escalating, but instead, all actors backed the assumed winner. In international relations, more often than not, states uphold the right of the strongest, and make their armed presence at the victor's side. When the eight-year war finally ended, its outcome was inconclusive. The two countries fought each other to a bloody impasse until they finally realized that neither side had the ability to win outright. While neither had triumphed, as was planned by the dominant international players, Baghdad and Tehran both declared victory, but the whole region plunged into a state of uncertainty, in a world that is more unstable and unpredictable than ever. Although it was a draw, it could be argued that Iraq won by avoiding defeat.

Whereas there is no definitive evidence, so far, to ascertain that these clandestinely sold weapons were decisive in the final outcome of the war, they were nonetheless highly instrumental in delaying its termination. It is suspected, however, that they were vital in some battles, though an accurate analysis cannot be made in the context of this study, as this, in itself, would be far too lengthy, and should become the subject of another book. Revelations surfaced in the international press about clandestine arms deals involving the major arms-manufacturing countries, as well as LDCs. But the information did not always disclose the types and quantities of weapons sold and the exact dates of deliveries. This impeded the research on that particular question. Furthermore, results of the assessment would nevertheless remain indefinite, until all the details that have remained camouflaged, so far, are uncovered. The data should involve the specific types, the precise quantities, the accurate dates of deliveries, and the training of crews in order to enable any analyst to establish a relationship between the effective assimilation and use by the troops of the newly acquired weapons, and their consequent impact on each battle. Short of these prerequisites, there is no reliable, or even unreliable, method of ascertaining their value.

Generally speaking, support for Iraq started in 1982, once the Iranians repelled the Iraqi troops. Eastern, Western, Middle Eastern, and Latin American governments and middle-men took advantage of a lucrative market, and became the main beneficiaries from the war. They contributed to the build-up of weapons arsenals, provided the technology to establish new arms and ammunition factories, or updated indigenous arms manufacturing capabilities – not only in Iraq – but also in Iran. Britain was only one among many that broke the embargo, by claiming that its exports were of non-lethal nature. But because of its democratic climate, the tip of the iceberg is starting to appear. In a written answer to a question tabled by an MP, Premier John Major revealed that Britain sold Iraq between 1987 and 1989, more machine tools than the US, Italy and France put together, totalling nearly $93 million. Italy sold $42 million-worth of equipment, France $16.8 million and the US $11.7 million (*Financial Times*, 12 January 1993). The cabinet, of which Major was a senior member, endorsed a secret policy and approved the sale to Iraq of arms and arms-manufacturing machinery for making shell fuses. Confidential documents, uncovered in court, confirmed that the cabinet authorized the transfer of 'a vast quantity of defence equipment made by major British companies, in full knowledge that it was to be used by the Iraqi Ministry of Defence and air force' (*Independent*, 10 November 1992).

Western states competed against each other and against Eastern Europeans in their pursuit of *super deals*. They clung to their traditional markets, and vied for new opportunities. The areas they targeted were the Middle East generally, and the Gulf states particularly. Sir Anthony Parsons, the former British ambassador to the UN and the *éminence grise* of British diplomacy, maintained the view that the bulk of arms transfers was contracted by the P5, and a case in point was that 85 per cent of Saddam Hussein's arsenal was supplied by them. He added that in the few months following the 1991 Gulf War, arms deals worth $30 billion were contracted. Ambassadors, military attaches and visiting officials are known to have competed for arms contracts on behalf of their countries. During her premiership, Margaret Thatcher bluntly told British diplomats posted to the Gulf region, that the government expected them to step up their pressure and actively pursue this policy of salesmanship. At the end of the televised interview, Sir Anthony remarked that sadly, the secrecy that surrounds arms deals and the protection accorded by governments to the trade has only led to wars (Parsons, 14 June and 25 November 1991; and in Sampson, 1991). The same theme was the subject of an article by Van Hollen, who aptly named it 'Don't Engulf the Gulf' (1981, pp. 1064–78).

It is not unusual for states to have a declared policy and a hidden agenda. In this respect, most of the actors involved in the Gulf, whether Middle Easterner or Western, conducted ambivalent policies. All statements from their capitals repeated their insistence that Iraq and Iran were under the obligation to respect and implement the ban on arms. At the same time, it transpired that secret bargains occurred, involving the busting of the embargo, and it seems that they thought it unlikely that the violation would incur any censure. Iraqi and Iranian forces fought with weapons which were allowed to flow from Moscow, Washington, Paris, London, Bonn, other European and some Latin American and Middle Eastern capitals, and these were just as responsible as President Hussein for the Iraqi and Iranian people's predicament, and can be considered as accomplices in the massacre or maiming of at least one million people. A number of investigations in the US, the UK and other European capitals demonstrated that an effort was made to prevent the public, and even the majority of government officials and members of the houses of representatives to get to the truth. In Britain, there were even allegations that some vital documents of the arms-to-Iraq affair may have been destroyed. The covert sales of arms to Iraq and Iran revealed, unfortunately, that secrecy in Britain and America made a mockery of the democratic accountability that liberal-minded people around the world believed were exemplary in those two particular countries.

Whether under a Republican or a Democratic administration, US foreign policy was constantly designed to prevent the emergence of a regional power, anywhere in the world (see Kissinger's memoirs *Years of Upheaval* and *White House Years*, and Brzezinski's *Power and Principle*, both of whom served as National Security Advisers, one a Republican and the other a Democrat). Shah Muhammed Reza was one of the two exceptions beside Israel, and he was allowed to play a comparatively dominant role in the area. Since his overthrow and the consequent collapse of America's *twin-pillar* policy in the Gulf, Washington reverted to its standard approach.

It is worth noting that although the US and UK governments often discouraged others, such as China's, from selling weapons to Middle Eastern clients, they themselves rarely showed restraint. To control the arms trade, they set up quasi-governmental sales organizations. Their members negotiated the deals directly, or supervised negotiations between the arms makers and the potential client-state. In his outstanding filmed report entitled 'The Two-Edged Sword', Anthony Sampson held the view that government-to-government agreements were the main manifestation of the trade, and arms dealers existed as much in the Pentagon and in Whitehall as elsewhere. Air shows and arms exhibitions in various capitals confirmed the fact. As the arms industry generated $250 billion a year, the net result was that the GNP of every country that sold them was raised. Despite an arms embargo on Iran and Iraq during the eighties, 46 countries provided them with hardware, of which 38 supplied both sides. A decade later, the second 'Gulf War gave American salesmen the kind of live commercial they'd longed for. A week after it ended, American weapons were being advertised as "combat proven", and John Major, on a visit to the Gulf, declared "we're here to sell!"' (Sampson, 1991).

In order to discredit their explanation of events, Middle Easterners are constantly branded by Westerners as likely to use 'conspiracy theory'. However, cryptic political behaviour by Western capitals, coupled with compromising reports surfacing now, force the theory upon political analysts. American, Israeli and European governments, intelligence agencies and politicians at the highest level were associated with – and some exposed by – cases labelled Arms-for-Iraq and Arms-for-Iran in Britain, Iraqgate, Irangate and October Surprise in the US, and were implicated in circuitous deals connected with the Bank of Commerce and Credit International (BCCI), and the BNL. Following the collapse of the trial of three employees of the British Matrix-Churchill company, the matter of arms sales to Iraq raised so much controversy, that the Scott Inquiry was initiated in 1992.

Given the widespread flouting of the arms embargo by the P5 and other lesser arms-manufacturing countries during the war, which was highly instrumental in delaying its termination, the compliance with the UN register for arms transfers is critical. One can foresee difficulties, such as who determines which countries are considered belligerent, and on the other hand, which countries will be entitled to purchase weapons for legitimate defence needs? What are the criteria used to calculate the types and quantities of weapons a country needs for defence purposes? What are the sanctions, if any, against offending countries or manufacturers that defy the practices laid down by the UN? What are the means to monitor the transactions, and ascertain that the information is correct? Will the documentation that indicates the quantities and qualities of weapons sold made available to the general public, such as researchers or members of the press?

Iran and Iraq are still embattled in a caustic ideological struggle and each asserts the superiority of its social, political and economic systems, while confidently anticipating the disintegration of the other. But the ceasefire seems to be holding, and peace might be at hand, though there is still cause for scepticism, because of the raft of problems brewing that separate them, and Baghdad's and Tehran's rigid bargaining positions. The issues opposing them are 'unobstructed freedom of navigation in international waters in the Arab Gulf and in the Straits of Hormuz ... [and] clearing the Shatt al-'Arab and ensuring safe navigation therein, without prejudice to the legal status of the river' (Aziz, 1988, pp. 150–1), 'the formation of an impartial body for the identification of the aggressor' (Velayati, 1988, p. 71), the exchange of POWs, frontier delineation at the *thalweg*, war reparations, Tehran's offers of support and sanctuary to *Shi'i* dissidents, and Baghdad's funding of the MKO and their provision with heavy equipment, training camps and offices in Iraq. The Second Gulf War introduced a new factor in the equation that locks them in their bitter fight: the return of Iraqi civilian and military aircraft flown to the safety of Iranian airfields during the allied campaign.

On 15 August 1990, less than a fortnight after its army invaded Kuwait, Baghdad reversed its earlier position and surrendered all its claims, by announcing that it 'conceded to a United Nations ruling on Tehran's rights over the disputed border in the Shatt al-'Arab waterway, pulled out troops from occupied Iranian territory and initiated an exchange of prisoners of war' (*Independent*, 27 August 1990). Eight years of airraids, of assaults and countercharges, of battles wasted over towns, seized and lost again, had been in vain. The loss of Iranian and Iraqi lives, and the devastation of both countries became meaningless.

Whether a lasting settlement can be reached, that is amicably agreed by the two sides and has some prospect to remain in force is anyone's guess. Whether it can lead to the final denouement of the bitter four-hundred-and-fifty-years-old border dispute is another question riddled with uncertainty.

Appendices

APPENDIX A1

Table A1   Ships Hit, 1980–4

	Iraqi Attacks			Iranian Attacks		Both
	Missile	*Rocket*	*Mine*	*Rocket*	*Ground Fire*	
1980	—	—	—	—	5	5
1981	3	1	—	—	—	4
1982	7	1	3	—	—	11
1983	8	—	—	—	—	8
1984	35	—	2	16	1	54
Total	53	2	5	16	6	82

Source: Danziger, 1985.

APPENDIX A2

Table A2   Ships Hit, 1984

Jan	—	—	—	—	—	—
Feb	4	—	1	—	—	5
Mar	5	—	—	—	—	5
Apr	3	—	—	—	1	4
May	6	—	—	4	—	10
Jun	3	—	1	1	—	5
Jul	2	—	—	2	—	4
Aug	2	—	—	3	—	5
Sep	2	—	—	2	—	4
Oct	2	—	—	2	—	4
Nov	—	—	—	—	—	—
Dec	6	—	—	4	—	10

Note: Totals corrected for March, June and July, listed as 4, 4 and 2
Source: Danziger, 1985.

APPENDIX A3

Table A3   Ships Hit, 1984–8

	Gulf Shipping Attacks		
Year	Iraq	Iran	Total
1984	44	18	62
1985	36	14	50
1986	64	42	106
1987	90	92	182
1988	36	54	90
Total	270	220	490

Source: Brown-Humes, 1988, p. 17.

APPENDIX A4   CHRONOLOGY OF SHIPS HIT, 1980–3

Iranian Attacks

1980

7 October: Three foreign freighters were sunk and two others damaged by Iranian shells in the Iranian port of Khorramshahr during an exchange of fire with attacking Iraqi forces. At least 20 crewmen were killed.

Iraqi Attacks

1981

21 May: Iraqi aircraft slightly damaged the Panamanian bulk carrier *Louise I* just outside the northern Iranian port of Bandar Khomeini.
19 October: An Iraqi missile damaged the Liberian bulk carrier *Al Tajdar* near Bandar Khomeini, and the Panamanian bulk carrier *Moira* was bombed and seriously damaged. Both were later repaired.
25 October: Iraqi missiles set the Indian bulk carrier *Rashi Vish Wamitra* ablaze near Bandar Khomeini, causing heavy damage.

1982

11 January: Two Iraqi missiles set fire to the Panamanian freighter *Success*, causing her to be abandoned. The Greek bulk carrier *Annabella* was damaged by a mine near Bandar Khomeini.

14 February: The 16 000-ton Iranian tanker *Mokran* was seriously damaged by mines laid by the Iraqis near the northern Iranian port of Bandar Mashahr.

30 May: The Turkish tanker *Atlas* was seriously damaged during an Iraqi bomb attack on Kharg Island.

6 June: The Greek 26 000-ton bulk carrier *Good Luck* was damaged by Iraqi missiles off Bandar Khomeini. Three crewmen were killed.

9 August: Iraqi missiles sank the 15 000-ton Greek freighter *Lition Bride* near Bandar Khomeini and damaged the 16 000-ton South Korean bulk carrier *Sanbow Banner* beyond repair. Eight crewmen were missing and one killed aboard the *Sanbow Banner.*

4 September: The Turkish bulk carrier *Mar Transporter* was damaged beyond repair by a direct Iraqi missile hit on her engine room near Bandar Khomeini. She was sailing in a 10-ship convoy escorted by Iranian naval vessels.

11 September: The Greek freighter *Evangelia S* struck an Iraqi mine at the entrance to Bandar Khomeini harbor, was grounded and abandoned.

21 November: The Indian bulk carrier *Archana* was slightly damaged by an Iraqi missile attack at the Iranian port of Bushire.

18 December: Iraqi missiles set fire to the Greek tanker *Scapmount* which was abandoned in the channel leading to Bandar Khomeini.

1983

2 January: Iraqi aircraft set fire to the Singapore freighter *Eastern* and the *Orient Horizon* of Liberia, causing them to run aground while in a convoy from Bandar Khomeini.

15 May: The Panamanian oil tanker *Pan Oceanic Sane* was set ablaze by an Iraqi missile attack and abandoned in the Bandar Khomeini channel.

25 May: Iraqi aircraft slightly damaged the Panamanian supply ship *Seatrans-21.*

31 May: The Indian bulk carrier *Atj Priti* was seriously damaged by Iraqi missiles near Bandar Khomeini.

31 October: The Greek freighter *Avra* was set ablaze by Iraqi missiles near Bandar Khomeini as she sailed in a convoy escorted by Iranian naval vessels.

21 November: An Iraqi missile sank the 13-ton Greek bulk carrier *Antigoni* near Bandar Khomeini as she sailed in a convoy escorted by Iranian naval vessels.

8 December: The 16 000-ton Greek bulk carrier *Iapetus* was attacked by Iraqi missiles off Bandar Khomeini and abandoned, later to be repaired. *Source*: Danziger, 1985.

APPENDIX A5

Table A5   Safety Record of Merchant Fleets, 1987–91

(Flags of convenience in bold, 2m tons and above)

Nationality	*% lost of fleet*
St Vincent/Grenadines	1.00
South Korea	0.95
Cyprus	0.90
Malta	0.81
Vanuatu	0.70
Philippines	0.58
Turkey	0.50
Greece	0.48
Panama	0.44
India	0.44
Bahamas	0.38
Italy	0.33
Norway	0.31
Indonesia	0.30
Yugoslavia	0.29
World average	0.29
Hong Kong	0.28
USA	0.23
Singapore	0.23
Liberia	0.20
Sweden	0.19
Netherlands	0.17
China	0.15
Brazil	0.15
Taiwan	0.11
Denmark	0.10
Poland	0.10
Canada	0.09
Romania	0.07
Germany	0.06
France	0.04
Bermuda	0.04
Spain	0.04
UK	0.04
Russia	0.02
Japan	0.02
Australia	0.02

Source: The Institute of London Underwriters, in Bennetto, 1993.

APPENDIX A6

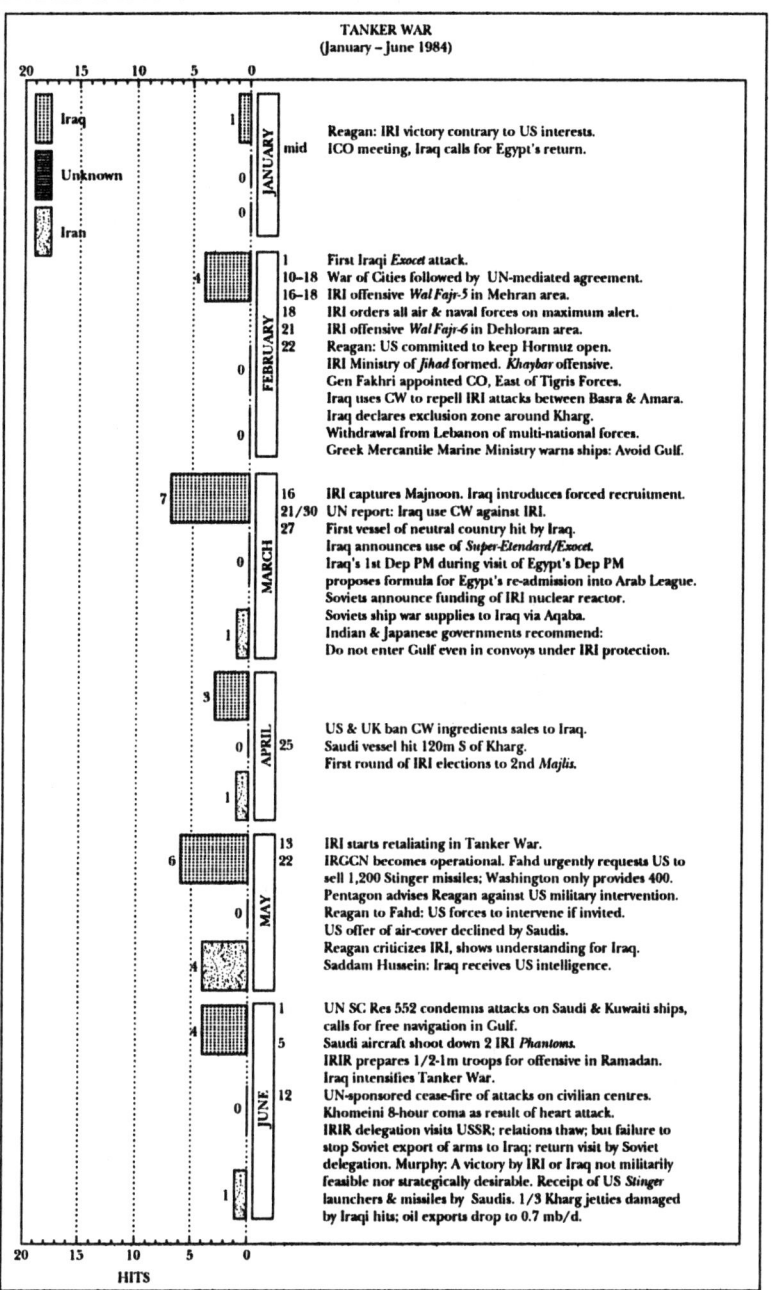

TANKER WAR
(January – June 1984)

JANUARY	1	Reagan: IRI victory contrary to US interests.
	mid	ICO meeting, Iraq calls for Egypt's return.
FEBRUARY	1	First Iraqi *Exocet* attack.
	10–18	War of Cities followed by UN-mediated agreement.
	16–18	IRI offensive *Wal Fajr-5* in Mehran area.
	18	IRI orders all air & naval forces on maximum alert.
	21	IRI offensive *Wal Fajr-6* in Dehloran area.
	22	Reagan: US committed to keep Hormuz open.
		IRI Ministry of *Jihad* formed. *Khaybar* offensive.
		Gen Fakhri appointed CO, East of Tigris Forces.
		Iraq uses CW to repel IRI attacks between Basra & Amara.
		Iraq declares exclusion zone around Kharg.
		Withdrawal from Lebanon of multi-national forces.
		Greek Mercantile Marine Ministry warns ships: Avoid Gulf.
MARCH	16	IRI captures Majnoon. Iraq introduces forced recruitment.
	21/30	UN report: Iraq use CW against IRI.
	27	First vessel of neutral country hit by Iraq.
		Iraq announces use of *Super-Etendard/Exocet.*
		Iraq's 1st Dep PM during visit of Egypt's Dep PM
		proposes formula for Egypt's re-admission into Arab League.
		Soviets announce funding of IRI nuclear reactor.
		Soviets ship war supplies to Iraq via Aqaba.
		Indian & Japanese governments recommend:
		Do not enter Gulf even in convoys under IRI protection.
APRIL	25	US & UK ban CW ingredients sales to Iraq.
		Saudi vessel hit 120m S of Kharg.
		First round of IRI elections to 2nd *Majlis.*
MAY	13	IRI starts retaliating in Tanker War.
	22	IRGCN becomes operational. Fahd urgently requests US to
		sell 1,200 Stinger missiles; Washington only provides 400.
		Pentagon advises Reagan against US military intervention.
		Reagan to Fahd: US forces to intervene if invited.
		US offer of air-cover declined by Saudis.
		Reagan criticizes IRI, shows understanding for Iraq.
		Saddam Hussein: Iraq receives US intelligence.
JUNE	1	UN SC Res 552 condemns attacks on Saudi & Kuwaiti ships,
		calls for free navigation in Gulf.
	5	Saudi aircraft shoot down 2 IRI *Phantoms.*
		IRIR prepares 1/2-1m troops for offensive in Ramadan.
		Iraq intensifies Tanker War.
	12	UN-sponsored cease-fire of attacks on civilian centres.
		Khomeini 8-hour coma as result of heart attack.
		IRIR delegation visits USSR; relations thaw; but failure to
		stop Soviet export of arms to Iraq: return visit by Soviet
		delegation. Murphy: A victory by IRI or Iraq not militarily
		feasible nor strategically desirable. Receipt of US *Stinger*
		launchers & missiles by Saudis. 1/3 Kharg jetties damaged
		by Iraqi hits; oil exports drop to 0.7 mb/d.

HITS

Iraq
Unknown
Iran

A6.1   Tanker War (January–June 1984)

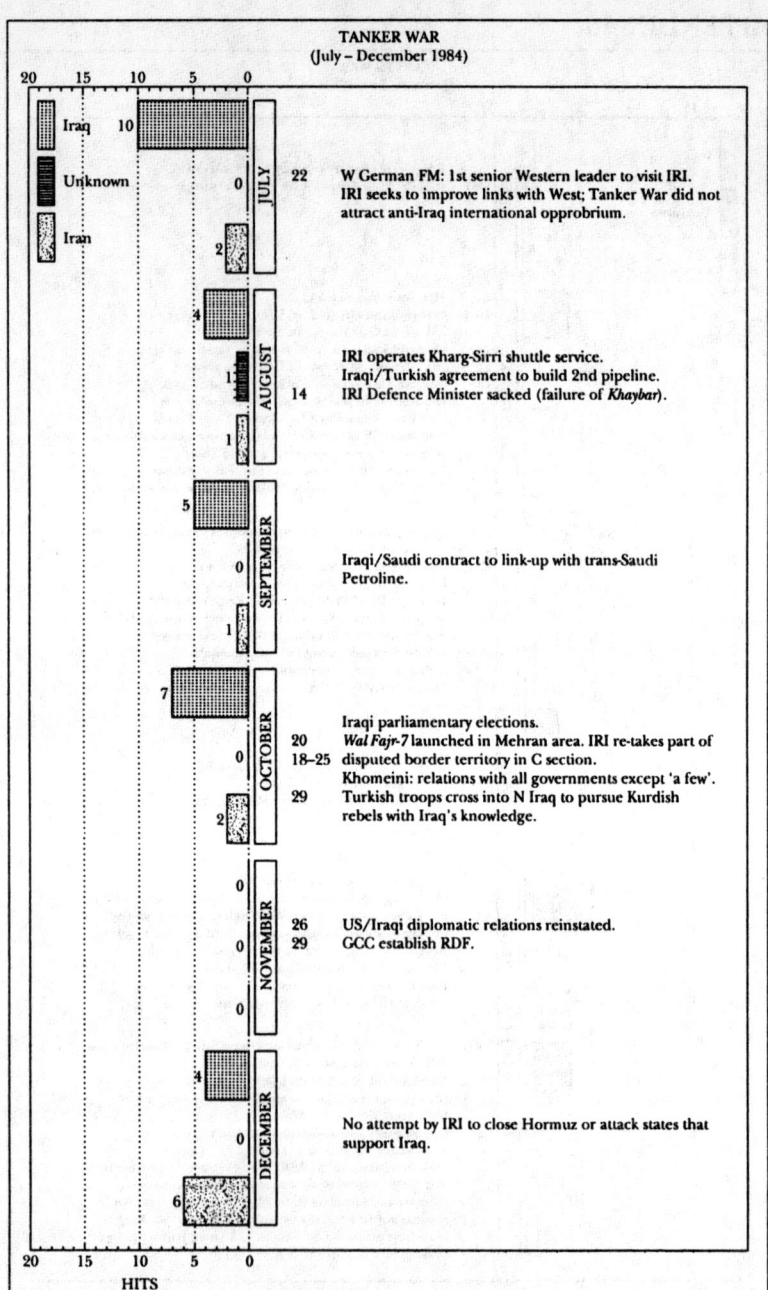

TANKER WAR
(July – December 1984)

Iraq 10
Unknown 0
Iran 2

JULY
22   W German FM: 1st senior Western leader to visit IRI. IRI seeks to improve links with West; Tanker War did not attract anti-Iraq international opprobrium.

4
11
1

AUGUST
    IRI operates Kharg-Sirri shuttle service.
    Iraqi/Turkish agreement to build 2nd pipeline.
14   IRI Defence Minister sacked (failure of *Khaybar*).

5
0
1

SEPTEMBER
    Iraqi/Saudi contract to link-up with trans-Saudi Petroline.

7
0
2

OCTOBER
    Iraqi parliamentary elections.
20   *Wal Fajr-7* launched in Mehran area. IRI re-takes part of
18–25 disputed border territory in C section.
    Khomeini: relations with all governments except 'a few'.
29   Turkish troops cross into N Iraq to pursue Kurdish rebels with Iraq's knowledge.

0
0
0

NOVEMBER
26   US/Iraqi diplomatic relations reinstated.
29   GCC establish RDF.

4
0
6

DECEMBER
    No attempt by IRI to close Hormuz or attack states that support Iraq.

HITS

A6.2   Tanker War (July–December 1984)

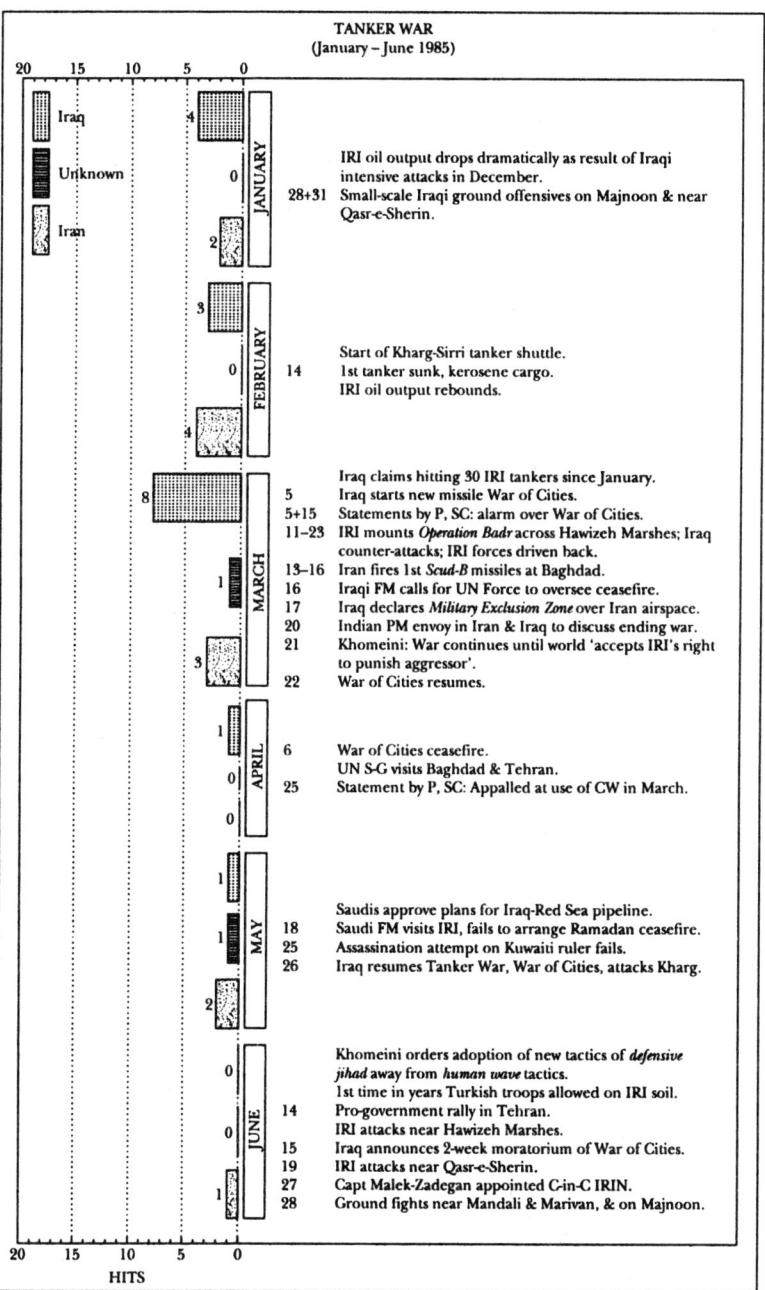

TANKER WAR
(January – June 1985)

JANUARY	IRI oil output drops dramatically as result of Iraqi intensive attacks in December.
28+31	Small-scale Iraqi ground offensives on Majnoon & near Qasr-e-Sherin.
FEBRUARY	Start of Kharg-Sirri tanker shuttle.
14	1st tanker sunk, kerosene cargo.
	IRI oil output rebounds.
MARCH	Iraq claims hitting 30 IRI tankers since January.
5	Iraq starts new missile War of Cities.
5+15	Statements by P, SC: alarm over War of Cities.
11–23	IRI mounts *Operation Badr* across Hawizeh Marshes; Iraq counter-attacks; IRI forces driven back.
13–16	Iran fires 1st *Scud-B* missiles at Baghdad.
16	Iraqi FM calls for UN Force to oversee ceasefire.
17	Iraq declares *Military Exclusion Zone* over Iran airspace.
20	Indian PM envoy in Iran & Iraq to discuss ending war.
21	Khomeini: War continues until world 'accepts IRI's right to punish aggressor'.
22	War of Cities resumes.
APRIL	War of Cities ceasefire.
6	
	UN S-G visits Baghdad & Tehran.
25	Statement by P, SC: Appalled at use of CW in March.
MAY	Saudis approve plans for Iraq-Red Sea pipeline.
18	Saudi FM visits IRI, fails to arrange Ramadan ceasefire.
25	Assassination attempt on Kuwaiti ruler fails.
26	Iraq resumes Tanker War, War of Cities, attacks Kharg.
JUNE	Khomeini orders adoption of new tactics of *defensive jihad* away from *human wave* tactics.
	1st time in years Turkish troops allowed on IRI soil.
14	Pro-government rally in Tehran.
	IRI attacks near Hawizeh Marshes.
15	Iraq announces 2-week moratorium of War of Cities.
19	IRI attacks near Qasr-e-Sherin.
27	Capt Malek-Zadegan appointed C-in-C IRIN.
28	Ground fights near Mandali & Marivan, & on Majnoon.

HITS

A6.3 Tanker War (January–June 1985)

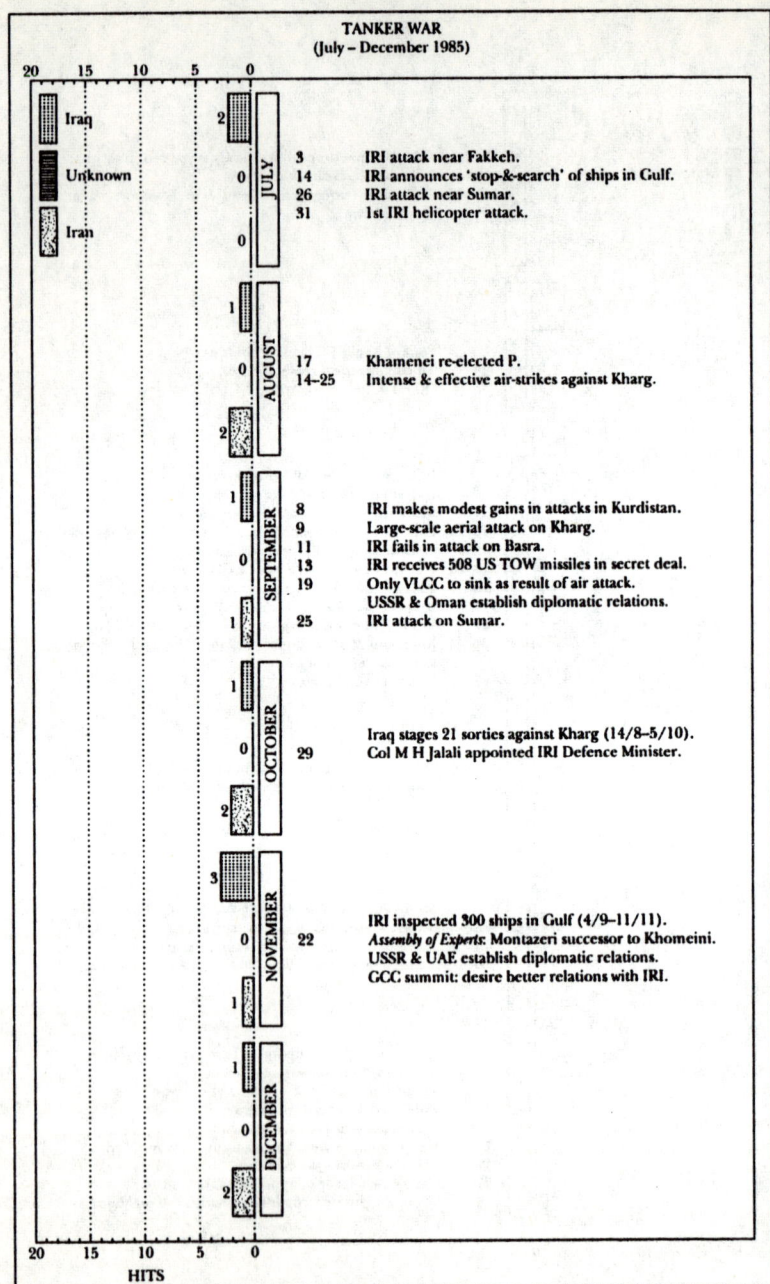

TANKER WAR
(July – December 1985)

Iraq	
Unknown	
Iran	

JULY
3   IRI attack near Fakkeh.
14   IRI announces 'stop-&-search' of ships in Gulf.
26   IRI attack near Sumar.
31   1st IRI helicopter attack.

AUGUST
17   Khamenei re-elected P.
14–25   Intense & effective air-strikes against Kharg.

SEPTEMBER
8   IRI makes modest gains in attacks in Kurdistan.
9   Large-scale aerial attack on Kharg.
11   IRI fails in attack on Basra.
13   IRI receives 508 US TOW missiles in secret deal.
19   Only VLCC to sink as result of air attack.
     USSR & Oman establish diplomatic relations.
25   IRI attack on Sumar.

OCTOBER
    Iraq stages 21 sorties against Kharg (14/8–5/10).
29   Col M H Jalali appointed IRI Defence Minister.

NOVEMBER
    IRI inspected 300 ships in Gulf (4/9–11/11).
22   *Assembly of Experts*: Montazeri successor to Khomeini.
    USSR & UAE establish diplomatic relations.
    GCC summit: desire better relations with IRI.

DECEMBER

HITS

A6.4   Tanker War (July–December 1985)

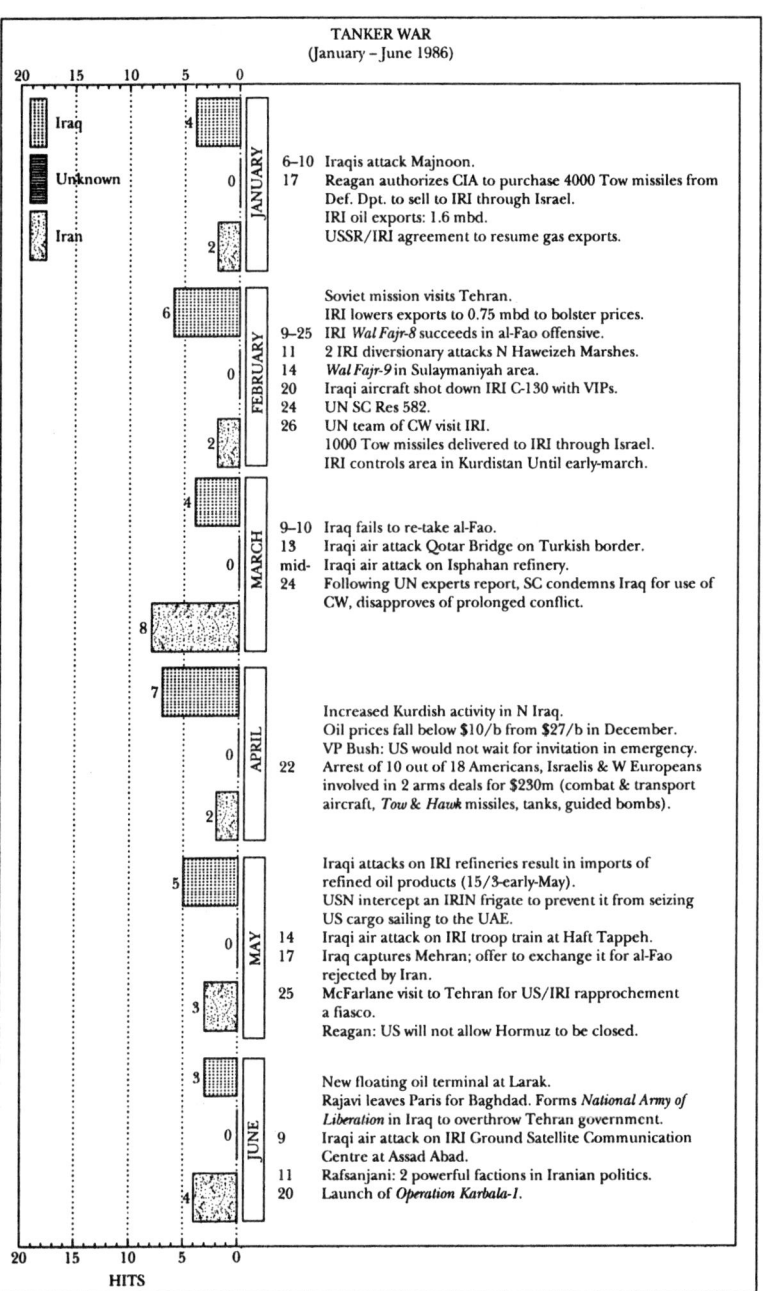

TANKER WAR
(January – June 1986)

JANUARY
6–10 Iraqis attack Majnoon.
17 Reagan authorizes CIA to purchase 4000 Tow missiles from Def. Dpt. to sell to IRI through Israel.
IRI oil exports: 1.6 mbd.
USSR/IRI agreement to resume gas exports.

FEBRUARY
Soviet mission visits Tehran.
IRI lowers exports to 0.75 mbd to bolster prices.
9–25 IRI *Wal Fajr-8* succeeds in al-Fao offensive.
11 2 IRI diversionary attacks N Haweizeh Marshes.
14 *Wal Fajr-9* in Sulaymaniyah area.
20 Iraqi aircraft shot down IRI C-130 with VIPs.
24 UN SC Res 582.
26 UN team of CW visit IRI.
1000 Tow missiles delivered to IRI through Israel.
IRI controls area in Kurdistan Until early-march.

MARCH
9–10 Iraq fails to re-take al-Fao.
13 Iraqi air attack Qotar Bridge on Turkish border.
mid- Iraqi air attack on Isphahan refinery.
24 Following UN experts report, SC condemns Iraq for use of CW, disapproves of prolonged conflict.

APRIL
Increased Kurdish activity in N Iraq.
Oil prices fall below $10/b from $27/b in December.
VP Bush: US would not wait for invitation in emergency.
22 Arrest of 10 out of 18 Americans, Israelis & W Europeans involved in 2 arms deals for $230m (combat & transport aircraft, *Tow* & *Hawk* missiles, tanks, guided bombs).

MAY
Iraqi attacks on IRI refineries result in imports of refined oil products (15/3-early-May).
USN intercept an IRIN frigate to prevent it from seizing US cargo sailing to the UAE.
14 Iraqi air attack on IRI troop train at Haft Tappeh.
17 Iraq captures Mehran; offer to exchange it for al-Fao rejected by Iran.
25 McFarlane visit to Tehran for US/IRI rapprochement a fiasco.
Reagan: US will not allow Hormuz to be closed.

JUNE
New floating oil terminal at Larak.
Rajavi leaves Paris for Baghdad. Forms *National Army of Liberation* in Iraq to overthrow Tehran government.
9 Iraqi air attack on IRI Ground Satellite Communication Centre at Assad Abad.
11 Rafsanjani: 2 powerful factions in Iranian politics.
20 Launch of *Operation Karbala-1*.

HITS

A6.5 Tanker War (January–June 1986)

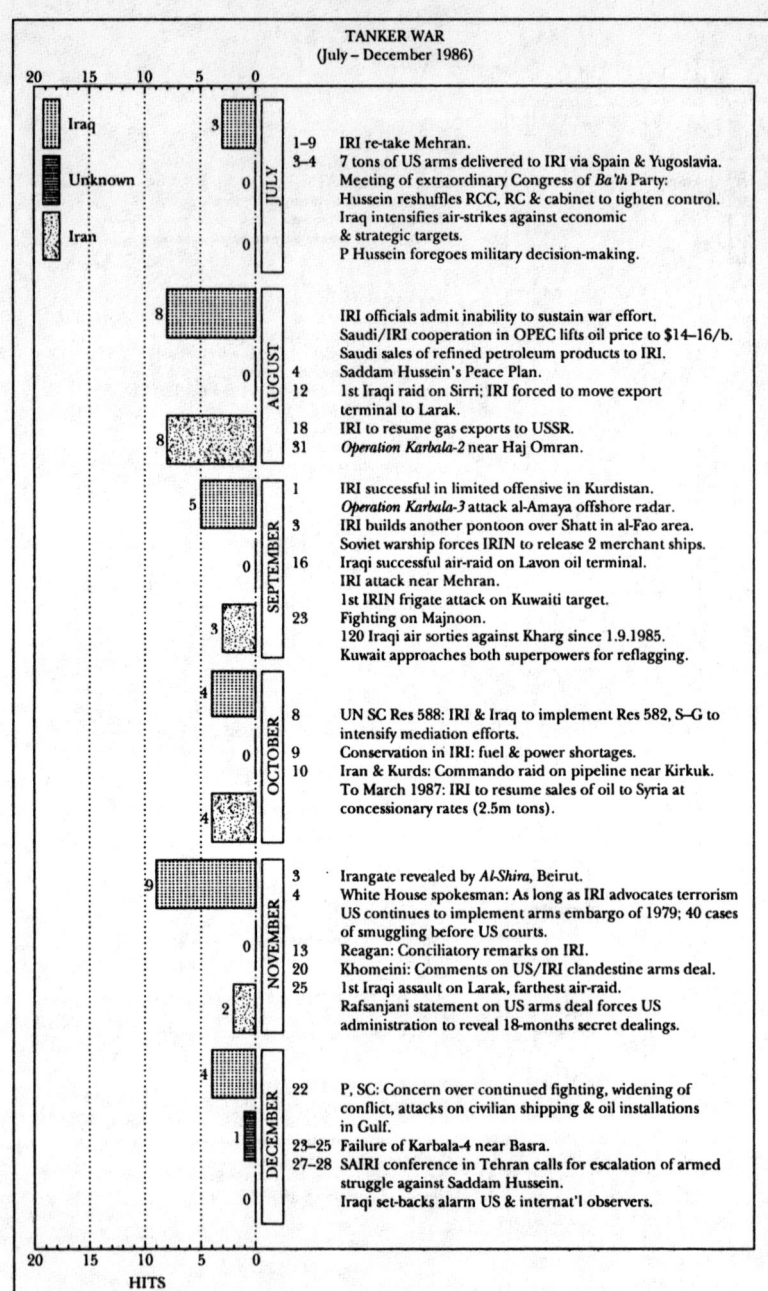

TANKER WAR
(July – December 1986)

JULY	1–9	IRI re-take Mehran.	
	3–4	7 tons of US arms delivered to IRI via Spain & Yugoslavia. Meeting of extraordinary Congress of *Ba'th* Party: Hussein reshuffles RCC, RC & cabinet to tighten control. Iraq intensifies air-strikes against economic & strategic targets. P Hussein foregoes military decision-making.	

(Bar chart data — HITS)
- Iraq: 3 (July)
- Unknown: 0 (July)
- Iran: 0 (July)

IRI officials admit inability to sustain war effort.
Saudi/IRI cooperation in OPEC lifts oil price to $14–16/b.
Saudi sales of refined petroleum products to IRI.
AUGUST
- 8 (Iraq)
- 0, 4 — Saddam Hussein's Peace Plan.
- 12 — 1st Iraqi raid on Sirri; IRI forced to move export terminal to Larak.
- 18 — IRI to resume gas exports to USSR.
- 8 — 31 — *Operation Karbala-2* near Haj Omran.

SEPTEMBER
- 5 — 1 — IRI successful in limited offensive in Kurdistan.
  Operation Karbala-3 attack al-Amaya offshore radar.
- 3 — IRI builds another pontoon over Shatt in al-Fao area.
  Soviet warship forces IRIN to release 2 merchant ships.
- 0 — 16 — Iraqi successful air-raid on Lavon oil terminal.
  IRI attack near Mehran.
  1st IRIN frigate attack on Kuwaiti target.
- 3 — 23 — Fighting on Majnoon.
  120 Iraqi air sorties against Kharg since 1.9.1985.
  Kuwait approaches both superpowers for reflagging.

OCTOBER
- 4
- 8 — UN SC Res 588: IRI & Iraq to implement Res 582, S–G to intensify mediation efforts.
- 0 — 9 — Conservation in IRI: fuel & power shortages.
- 10 — Iran & Kurds: Commando raid on pipeline near Kirkuk.
  To March 1987: IRI to resume sales of oil to Syria at concessionary rates (2.5m tons).
- 4

NOVEMBER
- 9 — 3 — Irangate revealed by *Al-Shira*, Beirut.
- 4 — White House spokesman: As long as IRI advocates terrorism US continues to implement arms embargo of 1979; 40 cases of smuggling before US courts.
- 0 — 13 — Reagan: Conciliatory remarks on IRI.
- 20 — Khomeini: Comments on US/IRI clandestine arms deal.
- 25 — 1st Iraqi assault on Larak, farthest air-raid.
- 2 — Rafsanjani statement on US arms deal forces US administration to reveal 18-months secret dealings.

DECEMBER
- 4
- 22 — P, SC: Concern over continued fighting, widening of conflict, attacks on civilian shipping & oil installations in Gulf.
- 1 — 23–25 — Failure of Karbala-4 near Basra.
- 27–28 — SAIRI conference in Tehran calls for escalation of armed struggle against Saddam Hussein.
  Iraqi set-backs alarm US & internat'l observers.
- 0

HITS

A6.6   Tanker War (July–December 1986)

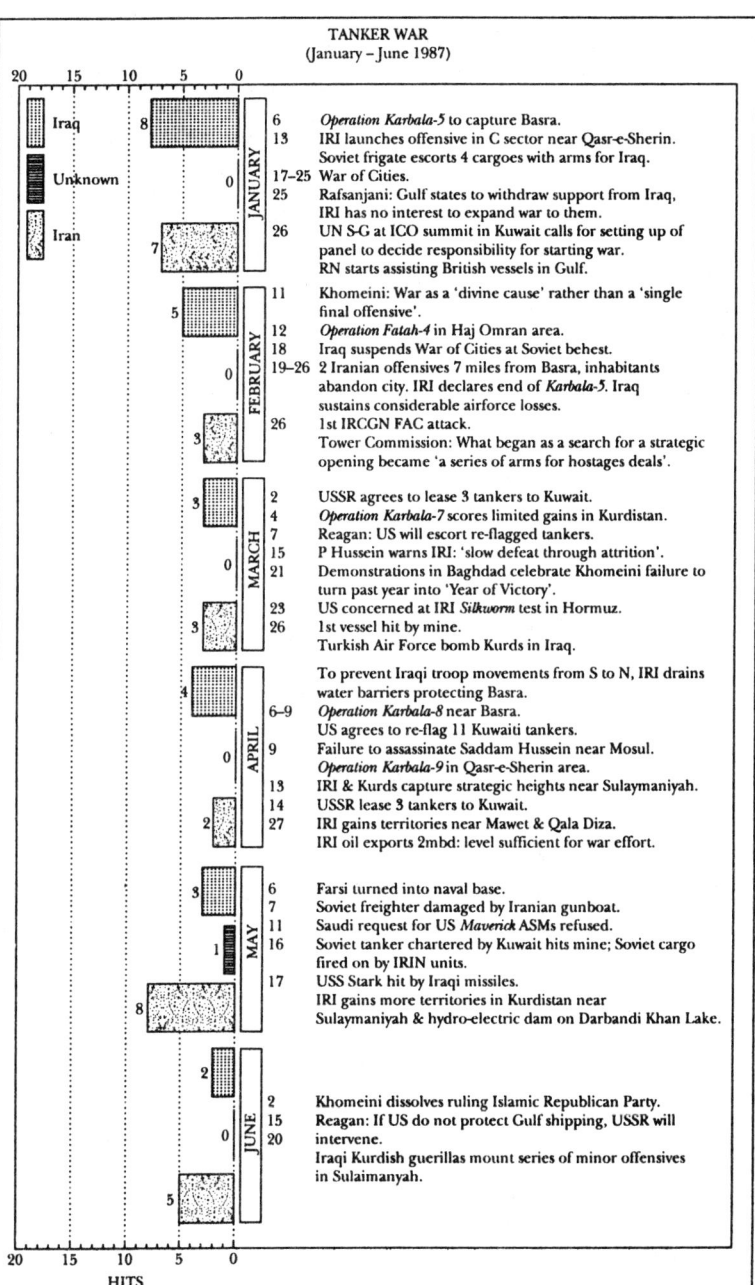

TANKER WAR
(January – June 1987)

Iraq 8

Unknown 0

Iran 7

JANUARY

6   *Operation Karbala-5* to capture Basra.
13   IRI launches offensive in C sector near Qasr-e-Sherin.
    Soviet frigate escorts 4 cargoes with arms for Iraq.
17–25   War of Cities.
25   Rafsanjani: Gulf states to withdraw support from Iraq, IRI has no interest to expand war to them.
26   UN S-G at ICO summit in Kuwait calls for setting up of panel to decide responsibility for starting war.
    RN starts assisting British vessels in Gulf.

FEBRUARY

11   Khomeini: War as a 'divine cause' rather than a 'single final offensive'.
12   *Operation Fatah-4* in Haj Omran area.
18   Iraq suspends War of Cities at Soviet behest.
19–26   2 Iranian offensives 7 miles from Basra, inhabitants abandon city. IRI declares end of *Karbala-5*. Iraq sustains considerable airforce losses.
26   1st IRCGN FAC attack.
    Tower Commission: What began as a search for a strategic opening became 'a series of arms for hostages deals'.

MARCH

2   USSR agrees to lease 3 tankers to Kuwait.
4   *Operation Karbala-7* scores limited gains in Kurdistan.
7   Reagan: US will escort re-flagged tankers.
15   P Hussein warns IRI: 'slow defeat through attrition'.
21   Demonstrations in Baghdad celebrate Khomeini failure to turn past year into 'Year of Victory'.
23   US concerned at IRI *Silkworm* test in Hormuz.
26   1st vessel hit by mine.
    Turkish Air Force bomb Kurds in Iraq.

APRIL

    To prevent Iraqi troop movements from S to N, IRI drains water barriers protecting Basra.
6–9   *Operation Karbala-8* near Basra.
    US agrees to re-flag 11 Kuwaiti tankers.
9   Failure to assassinate Saddam Hussein near Mosul.
    Operation Karbala-9 in Qasr-e-Sherin area.
13   IRI & Kurds capture strategic heights near Sulaymaniyah.
14   USSR lease 3 tankers to Kuwait.
27   IRI gains territories near Mawet & Qala Diza.
    IRI oil exports 2mbd: level sufficient for war effort.

MAY

6   Farsi turned into naval base.
7   Soviet freighter damaged by Iranian gunboat.
11   Saudi request for US *Maverick* ASMs refused.
16   Soviet tanker chartered by Kuwait hits mine; Soviet cargo fired on by IRIN units.
17   USS Stark hit by Iraqi missiles.
    IRI gains more territories in Kurdistan near Sulaymaniyah & hydro-electric dam on Darbandi Khan Lake.

JUNE

2   Khomeini dissolves ruling Islamic Republican Party.
15   Reagan: If US do not protect Gulf shipping, USSR will intervene.
20   Iraqi Kurdish guerillas mount series of minor offensives in Sulaimanyah.

HITS

A6.7   Tanker War (January–June 1987)

TANKER WAR
(July – December 1987)

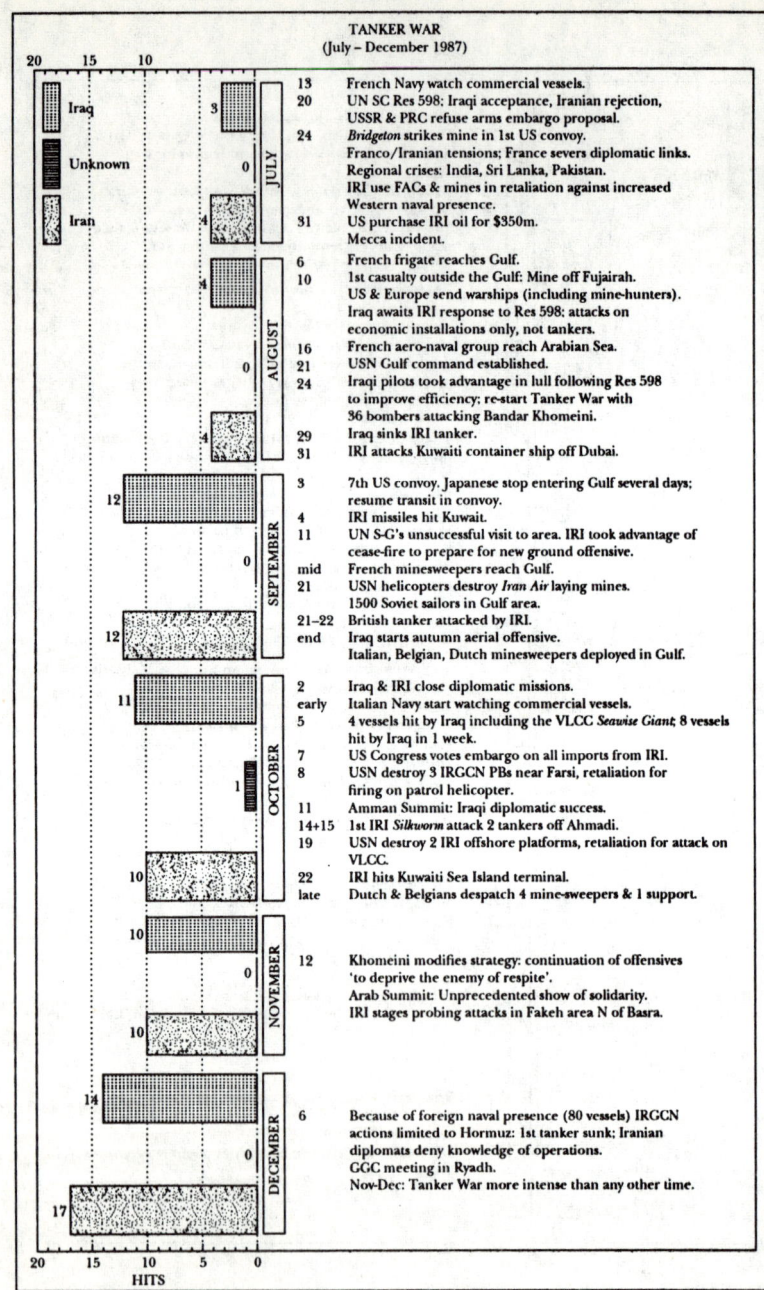

Date	Event
13	French Navy watch commercial vessels.
20	UN SC Res 598; Iraqi acceptance, Iranian rejection, USSR & PRC refuse arms embargo proposal.
24	*Bridgeton* strikes mine in 1st US convoy. Franco/Iranian tensions; France severs diplomatic links. Regional crises: India, Sri Lanka, Pakistan. IRI use FACs & mines in retaliation against increased Western naval presence.
31	US purchase IRI oil for $350m. Mecca incident.
6	French frigate reaches Gulf.
10	1st casualty outside the Gulf: Mine off Fujairah. US & Europe send warships (including mine-hunters). Iraq awaits IRI response to Res 598; attacks on economic installations only, not tankers.
16	French aero-naval group reach Arabian Sea.
21	USN Gulf command established.
24	Iraqi pilots took advantage in lull following Res 598 to improve efficiency; re-start Tanker War with 36 bombers attacking Bandar Khomeini.
29	Iraq sinks IRI tanker.
31	IRI attacks Kuwaiti container ship off Dubai.
3	7th US convoy. Japanese stop entering Gulf several days; resume transit in convoy.
4	IRI missiles hit Kuwait.
11	UN S-G's unsuccessful visit to area. IRI took advantage of cease-fire to prepare for new ground offensive.
mid	French minesweepers reach Gulf.
21	USN helicopters destroy *Iran Air* laying mines. 1500 Soviet sailors in Gulf area.
21–22	British tanker attacked by IRI.
end	Iraq starts autumn aerial offensive. Italian, Belgian, Dutch minesweepers deployed in Gulf.
2	Iraq & IRI close diplomatic missions.
early	Italian Navy start watching commercial vessels.
5	4 vessels hit by Iraq including the VLCC *Seawise Giant*; 8 vessels hit by Iraq in 1 week.
7	US Congress votes embargo on all imports from IRI.
8	USN destroy 3 IRGCN PBs near Farsi, retaliation for firing on patrol helicopter.
11	Amman Summit: Iraqi diplomatic success.
14+15	1st IRI *Silkworm* attack 2 tankers off Ahmadi.
19	USN destroy 2 IRI offshore platforms, retaliation for attack on VLCC.
22	IRI hits Kuwaiti Sea Island terminal.
late	Dutch & Belgians despatch 4 mine-sweepers & 1 support.
12	Khomeini modifies strategy: continuation of offensives 'to deprive the enemy of respite'. Arab Summit: Unprecedented show of solidarity. IRI stages probing attacks in Fakeh area N of Basra.
6	Because of foreign naval presence (80 vessels) IRGCN actions limited to Hormuz: 1st tanker sunk; Iranian diplomats deny knowledge of operations. GGC meeting in Ryadh. Nov-Dec: Tanker War more intense than any other time.

Iraq / Unknown / Iran

JULY: Iraq 3, Unknown 0, Iran 4
AUGUST: Iraq 4, Unknown 0, Iran 4
SEPTEMBER: Iraq 12, Unknown 0, Iran 12
OCTOBER: Iraq 11, Unknown 1, Iran 10
NOVEMBER: Iraq 10, Unknown 0, Iran 10
DECEMBER: Iraq 14, Unknown 0, Iran 17

HITS

A6.8   Tanker War (July–December 1987)

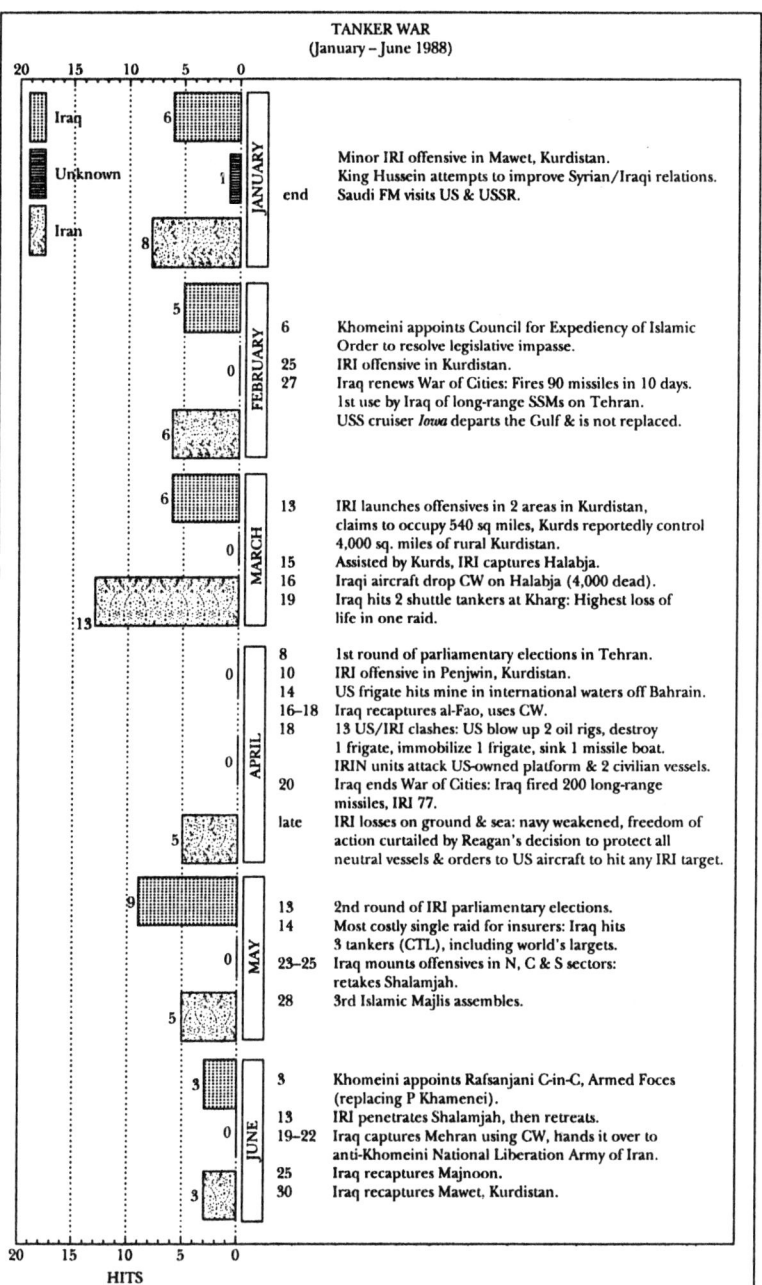

TANKER WAR
(January – June 1988)

JANUARY

end Minor IRI offensive in Mawet, Kurdistan.
King Hussein attempts to improve Syrian/Iraqi relations.
Saudi FM visits US & USSR.

FEBRUARY

6 Khomeini appoints Council for Expediency of Islamic
Order to resolve legislative impasse.
25 IRI offensive in Kurdistan.
27 Iraq renews War of Cities: Fires 90 missiles in 10 days.
1st use by Iraq of long-range SSMs on Tehran.
USS cruiser *Iowa* departs the Gulf & is not replaced.

MARCH

13 IRI launches offensives in 2 areas in Kurdistan,
claims to occupy 540 sq miles, Kurds reportedly control
4,000 sq. miles of rural Kurdistan.
15 Assisted by Kurds, IRI captures Halabja.
16 Iraqi aircraft drop CW on Halabja (4,000 dead).
19 Iraq hits 2 shuttle tankers at Kharg: Highest loss of
life in one raid.

APRIL

8 1st round of parliamentary elections in Tehran.
10 IRI offensive in Penjwin, Kurdistan.
14 US frigate hits mine in international waters off Bahrain.
16–18 Iraq recaptures al-Fao, uses CW.
18 13 US/IRI clashes: US blow up 2 oil rigs, destroy
1 frigate, immobilize 1 frigate, sink 1 missile boat.
IRIN units attack US-owned platform & 2 civilian vessels.
20 Iraq ends War of Cities: Iraq fired 200 long-range
missiles, IRI 77.
late IRI losses on ground & sea: navy weakened, freedom of
action curtailed by Reagan's decision to protect all
neutral vessels & orders to US aircraft to hit any IRI target.

MAY

13 2nd round of IRI parliamentary elections.
14 Most costly single raid for insurers: Iraq hits
3 tankers (CTL), including world's largest.
23–25 Iraq mounts offensives in N, C & S sectors:
retakes Shalamjah.
28 3rd Islamic Majlis assembles.

JUNE

3 Khomeini appoints Rafsanjani C-in-C, Armed Foces
(replacing P Khamenei).
13 IRI penetrates Shalamjah, then retreats.
19–22 Iraq captures Mehran using CW, hands it over to
anti-Khomeini National Liberation Army of Iran.
25 Iraq recaptures Majnoon.
30 Iraq recaptures Mawet, Kurdistan.

HITS

A6.9 Tanker War (January–June 1988)

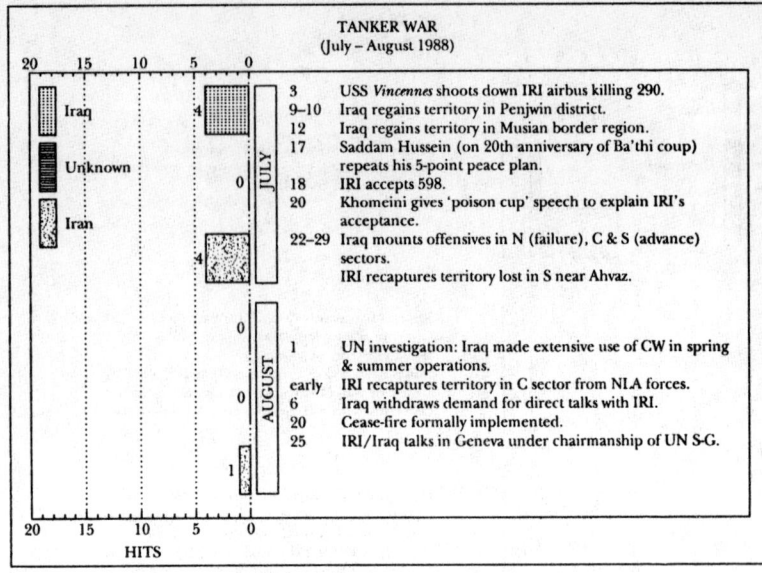

TANKER WAR
(July – August 1988)

3		USS *Vincennes* shoots down IRI airbus killing 290.
9–10		Iraq regains territory in Penjwin district.
12		Iraq regains territory in Musian border region.
17		Saddam Hussein (on 20th anniversary of Ba'thi coup) repeats his 5-point peace plan.
18		IRI accepts 598.
20		Khomeini gives 'poison cup' speech to explain IRI's acceptance.
22–29		Iraq mounts offensives in N (failure), C & S (advance) sectors. IRI recaptures territory lost in S near Ahvaz.
1		UN investigation: Iraq made extensive use of CW in spring & summer operations.
early		IRI recaptures territory in C sector from NLA forces.
6		Iraq withdraws demand for direct talks with IRI.
20		Cease-fire formally implemented.
25		IRI/Iraq talks in Geneva under chairmanship of UN S-G.

A6.10   Tanker War (July–December 1988)

APPENDIX A7   CHRONOLOGY OF KUWAITI SHIPPING ISSUE

1986

Nov 1	Kuwait raises concern about shipping at GCC Summit.
Dec 10	KOTC requests USCG to provide US flagging requirements.
Dec 23	KOTC informs US Embassy of interest in reflagging.
Dec 25	USCG informs KOTC of reflagging requirements.

1987

Jan 12	USCG sends KOTC reflagging information.
Jan 13	Kuwait asks Embassy if reflagged Kuwait-owned vessels would receive USN protection; we learn Kuwait has similar offer from Soviets.
mid-Jan	Interagency policy meetings at White House on Iran/Iraq war and Gulf.
Jan 2	Presidential statement reiterates commitment to free flow of oil through Strait, support for GCC self-defense.
Jan 29	USG reply to Jan 13 inquiry reiterates policy commitment to Gulf; Kuwait can reflag/charter if it meets US requirements.

Feb 6	We affirm to Kuwait that USN mission is to protect all US flag ships to degree possible with available assets.
mid-Feb	Interagency policy-level meetings at White House on Middle East and Gulf issues, specifically including issues of free flow of oil, SILKWORM threat and protection of Kuwaiti tankers.
Feb 25	Presidential statement reiterates USG commitment to free flow of oil, GCC states' security.
late-Feb	Successful Iranian test-firing of SILKWORM missile at Qeshm Island. We learn of USSR agreement to reflag/protect five Kuwaiti tankers.
Mar 2	KOTC asks to put six vessels under US flag.
1st week	President approves interagency recommendation March on protection of Kuwaiti tankers.
Mar 7	Kuwait informed of US offer to protect all eleven vessels in question.
Mar 10	Kuwait indicates it will accept USG offer.
Mar 12	State Department Legislative Affairs notifies Staff Directors of HFAC/SFRC Subcommittees on Europe/Middle East of USG offer to Kuwait, offers detailed briefing.
Mar 17	CJCS, Admiral Crowe, reaffirms USG offer to Kuwait.
Mar 19	Classified talking points on US/Kuwait offer delivered to HFAC/SFRC staffers.
Mar 22	KOTC/MidEast Force begin talks on protection modalities.
Mar 23	Classified talking points delivered to HASC/SASC staffers.
Mar 30	Assistant Secretary Murphy gives closed joint briefing to HFAC subcommittees on Europe/Middle East and Arms Control/International Security/Science.
Mar 31	Murphy briefs SFRC members in closed session.
Apr 2	Kuwait gives positive formal response to 3/7 offer; decides to reflag 11, limit Soviet role to charter.
early Apr	We learn Kuwait will charter three long-haul Soviet tankers.
Apr 21	Murphy in testimony to HFAC Subcommittee on Europe/Middle East refers to reflagging arrangement.
Apr 22	KOTC/USCG talks on technical details of reflagging; first step USG inspection.
early May	Soviet charters begin.
May 12	USCG inspection begins in Kuwait.
May 13	Kuwait/MidEast Force meeting on proposed system of protection.
May 14	DOD authorizes National Defense Waiver allowing vessels one year to comply with certain US-specific safety requirements and two years to comply with drydocking requirements.
May 17	Attack on USS *Stark.*

Source: *Secretary of Defense Report [Weinberger Report]* to the Congress on Security Arrangements in the Persian Gulf, 15 June 1987, in 26 *ILM 1987*, pp. 1461–3.

APPENDIX A8 READINESS CONDITIONS (USN)

CONDITION I: General Quarters, requires the manning of all weapons systems, sensors, damage control, and engineering stations. Engineering systems are configured for maximum flexibility and survivability. With all hands at General Quarters, the ship is prepared to fight at its maximum capability.

CONDITION II: Temporary relaxation of Condition I for rest and meals at battle stations.

CONDITION III: Watches require about one-third of the crew to man the weapons systems for prolonged periods. Must provide the capability to conduct or repel an urgent attack while the ship is call to General Quarters.

CONDITION IV: Watches require an adequate number of qualified personnel for the safe and efficient operation of the ship and permit the best economy of personnel assignment to watches. No weapon batteries are manned.

CONDITION V: In port during peacetime, no weapons manned. US combatants operating in the Persian Gulf remain at readiness condition III. However, when transiting the Strait of Hormuz or when confronted by an air or surface contact which closes in a threatening manner, units are required to go to condition I. All US forces in the Gulf region are at a heightened state of awareness as a result of the President's guidance, *Source: Secretary of Defense [Weinberger] Report* to Congress on Security Arrangements in the Persian Gulf, 15 June 1987 in 26 *ILM 1987*, pp. 1463, 1455.

APPENDIX A9 RULES OF ENGAGEMENT (ROE)

US Peacetime Rules of Engagement are based on the inherent right of self-defense. These rules ensure a full range of options consistent with that right and US policy. The Persian Gulf Supplement ROE have been tailored specifically for the area and provide specific guidance for threats from aircraft, surface/subsurface vessels, and land-based weapons systems such as the SILKWORM missile.

The following definitions are pertinent to understanding the ROE:

– **Hostile intent**: The threat of imminent use of force against friendly forces, for instance, any aircraft or surface ship that maneuvers into a position where it could fire a missile, drop a bomb, or use gunfire on a ship is demonstrating evidence of hostile intent. Also, a radar lock-on to a ship from any weapons system fire control radar that can guide missiles or gunfire is demonstrating hostile intent. This includes lock-on by land-based missile systems that use radar.

- **Hostile act:** Occurs whenever an aircraft, ship, or land-based weapon system actually launches a missile, shoots a gun, or drops a bomb toward a ship.

US forces in the Persian Gulf will respond as follows:

- **Self-defense:** US ships or aircraft are authorized to defend themselves against an air or surface threat whenever hostile intent or a hostile act occurs.
- **US-flagged commercial vessels:** US ships or aircraft may defend US-flagged commercial vessels against air or surface threats whenever hostile intent or a hostile act occurs.

The ROE provide authority to the on-scene commander to declare a threat hostile and engage that threat (i.e. a force demonstrating hostile intent or committing a hostile act) with all forces available to him in self-defense of his unit and US-flagged vessels. Only that force which is required to neutralize the threat or prevent a hostile act is authorized. Further, any use of force beyond that used against the immediate threat or in response to a specific hostile act must be approved by the National Command Authority. *Source: Secretary of Defense [Weinberger Report]* to Congress on Security Arrangements in the Persian Gulf, 15 June 1987 in 26 *ILM 1987*, p. 1454.

APPENDIX A10   *ARMILLA PATROL* GULF MISSIONS *THE NAVAL REVIEW*

From the Editor: Rear Admiral J. R. Hill
3 April 1994 [excerpts]

. . . instituted at the outset of the Iraq–Iran war in 1980, the patrol changed character in about 1987. Before then, it was characterised as 'for the protection of merchant shipping in the event of an escalation of the Iraq–Iran conflict' (1983), or 'to give reassurance to merchant shipping in the face of attacks inside the Gulf by both combatant-nations' (1984) . . . in 1987 . . . the role of the Armilla Patrol [was] . . . 'to reassure British merchant shipping and provide assistance if required. It was announced at the end of 1986 that the Patrol would spend more time within the Gulf west of the Strait of Hormuz . . . Typically about seven British merchant vessels have been accompanied through the Strait of Hormuz each week.' In 1988, the tempo increased: '. . . The average number of merchant ships accompanied rose . . . to peak at 79 in July 1988, with a further 27 non-entitled ships tagging on. This represents more than twice the number accompanied by all other neutral navies operating in the area' . . . the operation went as far up the Gulf as Dubai . . . some went further, but probably that was the standard run.

Reading between the lines, it is clear that the politico-military directive to the Armilla Patrol changed radically in late 1986 or early 1987. Before then, it had been distinctly a watching brief and RN ships were not allowed to escort merchantmen, of whatever flag, through the Gulf. There is confirmation of this from merchant shipping magazines such as *Seaways*, which in the years up to 1985–1986 regularly carried complaints from shipmasters that they were being attacked by missile and had no practical protection from our own naval forces. The escalation of the 'tanker war' and the introduction of a mining threat (also largely countered by RN forces) gave the necessary impetus to the British government to introduce an escorting regime – though even then they called it by another name; 'accompany' was clearly more acceptable to diplomatic sensitivities! It appears to have been confined officially to ships of British flag or under British beneficial ownership.

Incidents, once escort was introduced, there were apparently none. This may have been due to relatively tight rules of engagement . . . The Armilla Patrol continues to this day . . . .

APPENDIX A11 IRAQI ISLAMIC PARTIES

Jam'iyat Inqaz Falasteen (Save Palestine Society), the first party with a Muslim message, was created in 1947 by Mohammad Mahmoud al-Sawaf, an Azharite and member of Egypt's Muslim Brotherhood. In 1954, he was denounced for links with the Iraqi monarchy and 'colonialist powers' by 'Abdul-'Aziz al-Mudaressi and others, who formed *Hizb al-Taharur al-Islami* (Islamic Liberal Party). It affiliated with its sister party, led by Taqi-Eddin al-Banhani in Jerusalem, and became the first Islamic party to be authorized by the republican government in 1960, under the name *al-Hizb al-Islami* (Islamic Party), led by 'Abdel 'Aziz al-Badri.

Two other parties emerged in 1957: *Jama'at al-'Ulama' al-Mujahedeen al-'Iraqiyeen* (Iraqi Fighters Cleric Group), founded by Sheikh Murtadha al-Yasseen in Najaf, and *Hizb al-Da'wah al-Islamiyah* (Islamic Call or Invitation Party). The former was forced to move to Qom in 1980, headed by Mohammad Baqer al-Hakeem, and *al-Da'wah* became active only in 1968, towards the end of 'Abdul-Rahman 'Arif's regime.

They were followed by *al-Hizb al-Islami al-'Iraqi* (Iraqi Islamic Party), an extension of the Egyptian Muslim brotherhood, *Hizb al-Tahrir al-Islami* (Islamic Liberation Party) in 1960, and *Harakat Jund al-Imam* (Army of the Imam). whose founder, Sami al-Badri, had split from *al-Da'wah* in 1969. But the first was banned two years later and went underground until 1991, when it resumed its activities publicly in the UK and established a branch in Arbil in 1994, until the Iraqi troops entered Iraqi

Kurdistan, on 31 August 1996; and the second ceased to exist a decade later.

The movement gained strength with the founding by Taqi-Eddin al-Mudaressi of *Munazzamat al-'Amal al-Islami* (Islamic Action Organization) in 1968; the establishment in Damascus of *Harakat al-Mujahedeen al-'Iraqiyeen* in 1980, led by Hamzah al-Diwani, Shukry al-Bayati and 'Abdul-'Aziz al-Hakeem; and the founding of the Islamic umbrella organization, SAIRI, which has a general assembly of 77 members and a *majlis ashura* of 11.

Other Islamic parties include:

– *Al-Da'wah al-Islamiyah*, founded in 1980, after a split within the ranks of *Hizb al-Da'wah*, is led by *Haj* 'Ezz Edin Selim, and publishes a newspaper, *Al-I'tisam*, in Damascus.

– *Al-Kawader al-Islamiyah* (**Islamic Cadres**), established in 1991, also by a splinter group of *Hizb al-Da'wah*, is based in Damascus, but internal disputes affected its activities. The most prominent of its members is Muhammad 'Abdul-Jabbar (Abu Sa'di).

– *Al-Tajamu 'al-Islamic al-'Iraqi* (**Iraqi Islamic Assembly**) is a small grouping based in London, headed by the enlightened cleric Bahr al-'Ulum, who believes in a constitutional democracy.

– *Harakat Mujehedi al-Thawrah al-Islamiyah fil-'Iraq* (**Islamic Revolution Fighters' Movement in Iraq**) is a military faction, launched in southern Iraq in 1991 by *Haj* Kazem 'Abdul-Hadi (Abu Zeinab), which publishes a newspaper, *Al-Naba'*, and is supported by Iran and SAIRI.

– *Harakat al-Difa' al-Islami* (**Islamic Defence Movement**), founded in Damascus in 1980, publishes a newspaper, *Al-Wifaq al-Watani*; Sheikh Jamal al-Wakeel is its secretary general.

– *Al-Ittihad al-Islami al-Turkmani* (**Islamic Turcoman Union**), created in 1991 by *Shi'i* Turcomen loyal to *Al-Da'wah*, publishes a newspaper, *Ad-Daleel*; 'Abbas al-Bayati is its secretary general.

Lately, shifts appeared within the Iraqi secular opposition movement. On the one hand the Monarchists folded their magazine in mid-June 1997, because of 'technical problems', but according to sources, after contributions became scarce; and on 10 June, the royal pretender's political adviser and head of the political committee, Dr Khaled al-Temimi, resigned. The INC, which was funded by the CIA, also folded its paper, and a mounting number of its members are freezing their membership or resigning. On the other hand, *Al-Wifaq al-Watani*, which largely relies on former *Ba'this*, was encouraged to establish a branch in Amman, and is supported by the US, Saudi Arabia and Kuwait, among others.

On the surface, the latest changes within and among the parties may seem inconsequential to the casual eye, but if linked together are of profound significance, not only to the future of Iraq, but to the region. They indicate that Western and regional powers, with influence in the area, support the removal of Saddam Hussein, but at same time favour the preservation of the exiting political structure in Iraq, with the *Ba'th* Party in control. This can only mean that a democratic pluralistic Iraq, with a multi-party system and an accountable government, is considered undesirable.

Bibliography

INTERVIEWS

'Abdel-Halim, M. A. MoD, Cairo, 13 May and 8 June 1988.
Aboul-Gheit, A. A. Embassy of the Arab Republic of Egypt, Rome, several, 28 June to 3 July 1995.
Abou-Zikry, F. M. Abadan, Khorramshahr, Bandar Abbas, Bandar Pahlevi, Bandar Shahpour, several, January 1976.
Ayad, A. Nasser Academy for Higher Military Studies, Cairo, 14 June 1990.
Butti, F. R. London, 26 December 1994.
Day, K. Winchester, 5 January 1992.
Crowe, W. Embassy of the United States of America, London, 28 April 1995.
Murphy, R. W. Chatham House, London, 8 March 1990.
Musallam, T. A. *Ahram*, Cairo, 13, 27 April and 10 May 1988.
Parsons, A. British Council, Alexandria, 1 March 1988.
Pourzanjani, M. Exeter University, 17 May 1991.
Ramsbotham, P. Telephone Interview, 12 January 1992.
Touman, I. Alexandria, 17 August 1988.

OFFICIAL PUBLICATIONS

Armacost, M. A. 'US Policy in the Persian Gulf', Department of State, Special Report No. 166, Senate Foreign Relations Committee, July 1987, in *International Legal Materials*, XXVI (1987) 4–6.
'Aziz, T. Statement, Provisional Verbatim Record of the 17th Meeting, UN General Assembly. New York: United Nations, 4 October 1988, 145–55.
Charter of the United Nations and Statute of the International Court of Justice. New York: United Nations, December 1984.
Ciarocchi, R. J. 'US, Soviet, and West European Naval Forces in the Persian Gulf Region', *Congressional Research Service (CRS) Report to Congress*, 8 December 1987, No. 87-956.
'Overview of the Situation in the Persian Gulf', Hearings and Markup, Committee on Foreign Affairs and its Subcommittees on Arms Control, International Security and Science, and on Europe and the Middle East, House of Representatives, 100th Congress, First Session (Markup of HR 2533, H Con Res 135, H J Res 216, H Con Res 137), May 19 and June 2, 9, 10, 11 and 23, 1987, US Government Printing Office, Washington, 1987.
Report on the Staff Investigation into the Iraqi Attack on the USS *Stark*, Committee on Armed Services House of Representatives, 100th Congress, First Session, June 1987. Washington: US Government Printing Office, 1987.

'The Protection of Merchant Shipping in the Persian Gulf', House of Commons 3rd Special Report from the Defence Committee, Session 1986–87, Report and Memoranda, 13 May 1987.

Velayati, A. A. Statement, Provisional Verbatim Record of the 14th Meeting, UN General Assembly. New York: United Nations, 3 October 1988.

'War in the Gulf', Staff Report Prepared for the Committee on Foreign Relations US Senate, 98th Congress, Second Session, August 1984. Washington: US Government Printing Office, 1984.

UNPUBLISHED DATA AND PAPERS

'Abdel-Halim, A. M. 'A Conflict in the Arabian Gulf: An Overview of the Iran–Iraq War', Paper, Institute of Higher Defense Studies, National Defense University, USA, March 1985.

'*Al-Senario al-Thaleth: al-Harb fil-Masrah al-Bahari*', Paper, Symposium, 'Iran–Iraq War', War College, Nasser Academy for Higher Military Studies, Cairo, June 1988 (cited as Nasser, 1988).

Aryan, H. 'The Effects of the Islamic Revolution and the Gulf War on Iran's Economy', MA thesis, University of Durham, UK, 1989.

Ayad, A. [1], '*Al-Harb al-Bahariyah bil-Khaleej al-'Arabi: Natai'juha wa Athariha*', Paper, War College, Nasser Academy for Higher Military Studies, Cairo, 1988.

Ayad, A. [2], '*Harb al-Naqilat bil-Khaleej al-'Arabi*', Paper, War College, Nasser Academy for Higher Military Studies, Cairo, October 1988.

Bougir, G. ''*Ard Goghrafi li-Manteqat al-Harb*', no place, no date, translated, Symposium, 'Iran–Iraq War', War College, Nasser Academy for Higher Military Studies, Cairo, June 1988.

Ehteshami, A. 'Foreign Policy Making in Post-Khomeini Iran', Paper, 1993 EURAMES Conference, Inaugural Pan-European Conference for Middle Eastern Studies, 8–11 July 1993, University of Warwick, Coventry, UK.

El-Shazly, N. E. 'Huntington's Gap Hypothesis – Case Study: Muhammed Reza Pahlevi's Modernization in Iran', Paper, American University in Cairo, 22 April 1989.

Hill, J. R. letter, 3 April 1994 (excerpts, Appendix A10).

Hillier, M. '*Al-Harb al-'Iraqiyah al-Iraniyah wal-Nizam al-Iqleemi*', no place, no date, translated, Symposium, 'Iran–Iraq War', War College, Nasser Academy for Higher Military Studies, Cairo, June 1988.

Hoskins, E. 'Iraq – Children, War and Sanctions', Unpublished Draft, April 1993.

'Iraq in the 90s', Symposium, Chatham House, Royal Institute for International Affairs, March 1990.

Ismail, M. H. '*Al-Harb al-'Iraqiyah al-Iraniyah wa Ta'thiruha 'ala al-Amn al-Watani al-Masri*', Paper, Conference on Egyptian Security Issues, Cairo University, 11 March 1988.

Korn, D. *Middle East Watch Report*, 1992.

Lloyd's Register for Shipping, 1988 and 1991 (cited as Lloyd's).

Osman, A. '*Les Buts de la Guerre entre l'Iran et l'Iraq: Les Parametres du Conflit et ses Consequences Possibles*', Paper, Third International Conference on Asian Studies, Italian Asian Institute, Bari, 8–10 April 1988.

Soleyman, F. '*Al-Tashilat al-'Askariyah wa Azmet al-Khaleej*', Paper, Symposium, 'Iran–Iraq War', War College, Nasser Academy for Higher Military Studies, Cairo, June 1988.

Turner, D. J. letter, 11 December 1991.

LECTURES

Axelgard, F. W. 'The Iran–Iraq War', Faculty of Economics and Political Science, Cairo University, 15 October 1988.

Barzani, M. 'The Kurdish Issue in the Middle East', Chatham House, London, 26 February 1992.

Crowe, W. 'Transatlantic Relations: Sharing Ideals and Costs', Chatham House, London, 25 October 1996.

Ehteshami, A. 'Rafsanjani's Foreign Policy Agenda', University of Exeter, 18 November 1991.

Ehteshami, A. 'The Syrian–Iranian Alliance', School of Oriental and African Studies, London University, 5 November 1996.

Elliot, M. 'The Death of King Ghazi I – The Kuwait Crisis of 1939', School of Oriental and African Studies, London University, 18 May 1993.

Mabro, R. 'The Gulf in the 1990s', Symposium, 'The Middle East Towards the Year 2000', Oxford Town Hall, 28 May 1992.

McNaugher, T. L. 'US Policy and the Iran–Iraq War', American Cultural Center, Alexandria, 4 September 1988.

Moberly, J. 'Recent Trends in the British Policy in the Middle East', Embassy of the Islamic Republic of Iran, 27 February 1992.

Mubarak, H. Discussion meeting, Embassy of the Arab Republic of Egypt, London, 2 April 1993.

Parsons, A. 'The Iran–Iraq War: Threat to World Peace', Maritime Museum, Alexandria, 1 March 1988.

Parsons, A. 'The Middle East After the Gulf War', St Antony's College, University of Oxford, 14 June 1991.

Parsons, A. 'Future Security Regime in the Middle East', International Institute for Strategic Studies, London, 25 November 1991.

Pesaran, H. 'The Iranian Economy After the Revolution', School of Oriental and African Studies, London University, 10 December 1991.

Robins, P. 'Turkey's Relations with the Middle East', School of Oriental and African Studies, London University, 3 March 1992.

Sha'ban, M. 'Egypt and Current International Developments', House of Commons, London, 26 February 1992.

Sha'ban, M. 'The Gulf: An Egyptian Perspective', lecture, Special Meeting of Quaker Peace and Service, London Diplomats' Group, 11 March 1991.

Smolansky, O. 'Soviet Policy in the Middle East', American Cultural Centre, Alexandria, 7 April 1988.

YEARBOOKS

Al-Taqrir al-Isstratiji al-'Arabi, Al-Ahram, 1985–7.
International Legal Materials, XXVI (1987) 4–6 (cited as *ILM*).
Jane's Fighting Ships, 1984–5 (cited as *Jane's*).
Keesing's Contemporary Archives, 1978–87 (cited as *Keesing's*).
Military Balance 1985–90.
Military Technology, World Defence Almanac 1986–7.
SIPRI 1978, 1982–7, 1993.
Statesman 1986–7.
Strategic Survey 1984–9.
World Defense Almanac 1986–7.

BOOKS

Abbas, A. 'The Iraqi Armed Forces, Past and Present', 203–26 in CARDRI (ed.), *Saddam's Iraq* (London: Zed, 1986).

'Abdel-Halim, A. M. 'A Conflict in the Arabian Gulf: An Overview of the Iran–Iraq War', in *Five War Zones* (New York: Pergamon-Brassey's, 1986), 5–49.

Abou-Zikry, F. M. *Al-Bahariyah al-Misriyah* (Alexandria: Egyptian Navy Press, 1986).

Alam, A. *The Shah and I* (London: I. B. Tauris, 1991).

Al-Gheitany, G. *Man Bada'a al-Harb?* (Cairo: *Al-Lagna al-Misriyah Li-Monasarat al-'Iraq fi Masa'ih al-Silmiyah*, 1987).

Axelgard, F. W. (ed.), *Iraq in Transition* (Boulder: Praeger, 1986).

Batatu, H. *Al-'Iraq: al-Shiyu'iyun wal-Ba'thiyun wal-Dhubat al-Ahrar* (Beirut: *Mu'assassat Al-Abhath Al-'Arabiyah*, 1992).

Bulloch, J. and Morris, H. *The Gulf War* (London: Methuen, 1989).

Bullock, J. and Morris, H. *Saddam's War* (London: Faber & Faber, 1991).

Butti, F. *Al-Sahafah al-Yasariyah fil-'Iraq* (London: no publisher, 1985).

Butti, F. *Al-Mawsu'ah al-Sahafiyah al-'Iraqiyah* (Baghdad: Dar Al-Adeeb, 1976).

Butti, F. *Sahafat Tammuz wa Tatawur al-'Iraq al-Siyasi* (Baghdad: Dar Al-Adeeb, 1970).

Butti, F. *Sahafat al-Ahzab wa Tareekh al-Harakah al-Wataniyah fil-'Iraq* (Baghdad: Dar Al-Adeeb, 1969).

Carver, M. 'Conventional Warfare in the Nuclear Age', in P. Paret (ed.), *Makers of Modern Strategy* (Princeton, NJ: Princeton University Press, 1986), 779–814.

Chubin, S. and Tripp, C. *Iran and Iraq at War* (London: I. B. Tauris, 1989).

Clausewitz, C. von, *On War* (Princeton, NJ: Princeton University Press, 1968).

Corbett, J. S. *Some Principles of Maritime Strategy* (London: Longmans and Green, 1911).

Cordesman, A. H. and Wagner, A. R. *The Lessons of Modern War*, II (London: Mansell, 1990).

Dawisha, A. 'The Politics of War: Presidential Centrality, Party Power, Political Opposition', in F. W. Axelgard (ed.), *Iraq in Transition* (Boulder: Praeger, 1986), 21–32.

Devlin, J. 'Iraqi Military Policy: From Assertiveness to Defence', in T. Naff (ed.), *Gulf Security and the Iran–Iraq War* (Washington: The National Defence University Press and the Research Institute, 1985), 129–56.

Dorril, S. *The Silent Conspiracy* (London: Mandarin, 1994).

El-Shazly, N. E. 'Huntington's *Gap Hypothesis*: The Case of Iran', in *Democracy in the Middle East*. Proceedings of the BRISMES Annual Conference, (Scotland: University of St Andrews, 1992), 235–45.

Finnie, D. H. *Shifting Lines in the Sand* (London: I. B. Tauris, 1992).

Freedman, L. *Atlas of Global Strategy* (London: Macmillan, 1985).

Gamlen, E. *US Military Intervention in the Iran–Iraq War*. Peace Research Report No. 21, School of Peace Studies (Bradford: University of Bradford, 1989).

Ghareeb, E. 'Iraq in the Gulf', in F. W. Axelgard (ed.), *Iraq in Transition* (Boulder: Praeger, 1986), 59–83.

Gorshkov, S. G. *The Sea Power of the State* (Annapolis: Naval Institute Press, 1979).

Halliday, F. *Iran* (Harmondsworth: Penguin, 1979).

Hanks, R. J. and Cottrell, A. J. 'The Strait of Hormuz: Strategic Chokepoint', in A. J. Cottrell *et al.*, *Sea Power and Strategy in the Indian Ocean* (Beverly Hills: Sage, 1981), 73–116.

Heikal, M. *Iran* (New York: Pantheon, 1981).

Hersh, S. M. *The Samson Option* (London: Faber & Faber, 1991).

Hiro, D. *The Longest War* (London: Grafton, 1989).

Hunter, S. 'The Iran–Iraq War and Iran's Defence Policy', in T. Naff (ed.), *Gulf Security and the Iran–Iraq War* (Washington: The National Defence University Press & the Research Institute, 1985), 157–81.

Huntington, S. *Political Order in Changing Societies* (New Haven: Yale University Press, 1968).

Hussein, N. H. *Al-Ahammiyah al-Istratijiyah wal-Nizam al-Qanuni lil-Tareeq al-Milahi al-Bahari fil-Khaleej al-'Arabi* (Baghdad: Dar al-Rasheed lil-Nashr, 1980).

Ismael, T. Y. *Iraq and Iran* (New York: Syracuse University Press, 1982).

Keddie, N. *Roots of Revolution* (New Haven: Yale University Press, 1981).

Kupchan, C. A. *The Persian Gulf and the West* (Boston: Allen & Unwin, 1987).

Liddell-Hart, B. H. *Strategy* (London: Faber & Faber, 1967).

Limbert, J. W. *Iran at War with History* (Boulder: Westview, 1987).

Mahan, A. T. *The Influence of Seapower Upon History* (New York: Sagamore, 1957).

McNaugher, T. L. 'Walking Tightropes in the Gulf', in E. Karsh (ed.), *The Iran–Iraq War* (Basingstoke: Macmillan, 1989), 171–99.

Moorer, T. H. and Cottrell, A. J. 'A Permanent US Naval Presence in the Indian Ocean', in A. J. Cottrell *et al.*, *Sea Power and Strategy in the Indian Ocean* (Beverly Hills: Sage, 1981), 117–36.

Muhsin, J. 'The Gulf War', in Cardri (ed.), *Saddam's Iraq* (London: Zed, 1986), 227–44.

Navias, M. S. and Hooton, E. R. *Tanker War* (London: I. B. Tauris, 1996).

Nitze, P. H. *et al.*, 'Ship Vulnerability', 15, 'Soviet Expansionism', 15–17, and 'US Intervention in Third World States', 21–2 in *Securing the Seas* (Boulder: Westview, 1979).

O'Ballance, E. *The Gulf War* (London: Brassey's, 1988).

Paret, P. (ed.), *Makers of Modern Strategy* (Princeton, NJ: Princeton University Press, 1986).

Ramazani, R. K. 'The Strait of Hormuz: The Global Chokepoint', in L. W. Bowman and I. Clark, *The Indian Ocean in Global Politics* (Boulder: Westview, 1981), 7–20.

Ramazani, R. K. *The United States and Iran* (New York: Praeger, 1982).

Ramazani, R. K. *Revolutionary Iran* (Baltimore: The Johns Hopkins University Press, 1988).

Sallinger, P. and Laurent, E. *Guerre du Golfe* (Paris: Olivier Orban, 1991).

Sampson, A. *The Arms Bazaar* (London: Hodder & Stoughton, 1988).

Saunders, H. H. 'The Iran–Iraq War: Implications for US Policy', in T. Naff (ed.), *Gulf Security and the Iran–Iraq War* (Washington: The National Defence University Press and the Research Institute, 1985), 59–79.

Schofield, R. *Kuwait and Iraq* (London: Royal Institute for International Affairs, 1991).

Schmidt, R. *Global Arms Exports to Iraq* (Santa Monica: Rand, 1991).

Skeet, I. *OPEC* (Cambridge University Press, 1988).

Sluglett-Farouk, M. and Sluglett, P. *Iraq Since 1958* (London: I. B. Tauris, 1990).

Sluglett, P. 'The Kurds', in Cardri (ed.), *Saddam's Iraq* (London: Zed, 1986), 177–202.

Sterner, M. 'The Gulf Cooperation Council and Persian Gulf Security', in T. Naff (ed.), *Gulf Security and the Iran–Iraq War* (Washington: The National Defence University Press and the Research Institute, 1985), 1–23.

Sun Tsu, *The Art of War* (New York: Oxford University Press, 1976).

Till, G. *Modern Seapower* (London: Brassey's 1987).

Walters, D. *Not Always with the Pack* (London: Constable, 1989).

Yergin, D. *The Prize* (London: Simon & Schuster, 1991).

Zonis, M. *The Political Elite of Iran* (Princeton, NJ: Princeton University Press, 1971).

Zonis, M. *Majestic Failure* (Chicago: The University of Chicago Press, 1991).

ARTICLES

Abd Al-Jabbar, F. 'Why the Uprisings Failed', *MERIP*, No. 176 (May–June 1992) 2–14.

Abrahamian, E. 'Structural Causes of the Iranian Revolution', *MERIP*, No. 87 (May 1980) 21–6.

Abrahamian, E. 'Iran: The Political Crisis Intensifies', *MERIP* (March 1979) 3–6.

Abrahamian, E. 'Iran in Revolution: The Opposition Forces', *MERIP* (June 1979) 3–8.

Adam, J. A., 'USS *Stark*: What Really Happened', *IEEE Spectrum* (September 1987) 26–9.

Al-Khafaji, I. 'State Terror and the Degradation of Politics in Iraq', *MERIP*, No. 176 (May–June 1992) 15–21.

Angrand, J. and Rabier, C. 'Les Superpuissances et la Guerre du Golfe: Strategies et Enjeux', *Defense Nationale* (Janvier 1988) 95–109.

Axelgard, F. W. *World and I* (December 1987) 123–8.

Axelgard, F. W. 'Iraq and the War with Iran', *Current History*, LXXXVI, No. 517 (February 1987) 57–60, 82, 90, 91.

Bennetto, J. 'The cut-price recipe for catastrophe', *Independent on Sunday* (10 January 1993) No. 155.

Bin-Sultan, K. 'The Gulf War and its Aftermath: A Personal Perspective', *RUSI Journal*, CXXXVIII, No. 6 (December 1993) 1–5.

Bogdanor, V. 'Exorcising the Ghosts of 1914', *Independent* (1 August 1994).

Brown-Humes, C. 'Localised Conflict with Worldwide Impact', 2–3; 'Ceasefire Euphoria Gives Way to Doubts', 4–10; 'Healthier Tanker Market Emerges', 11–13; 'Tragic Human Cost of Maritime War', 14–15; 'Tactical Manoeuvres and map of Attacks', 16–22; 'Huge Loss for Underwriters', 23–5; 'Salvage Firms Fear Bleak Outlook', 26–7; 'Iran Incurs US Wrath After Iraq Mistake', 28–9; 'The Calendar of Conflict', 30–1; 'An A-Z Guide to the Gulf War' p. 32, *Lloyd's List International: After the Gulf War*, 1988.

Bruce, J. 'Iranians "Worried About US Action in Gulf"', *Jane's Defence Weekly* (4 July 1987) 1417.

Bull, H. 'Sea Power and Political Influence', *Adelphi Paper 122*, 1976.

Butti, F. '*Hal Tuhaqiq Ahzab al-Mu'aradhah al-'Iraqiyah Wehdat al-Sha'b al-Siyasiyah?*', *Hayat* (31 October 1992).

Campbell, J. C. 'Soviet Strategy in the Middle East', *American-Arab Affairs* (Spring 1984) 74–82.

Chapin, S. R. 'Countering Guerillas in the Gulf', *United States Naval Institute Proceedings* (hereafter and in text cited as *Proceedings*) (January 1988) 66–9.

Chardin, P. 'Regards sur le Conflit Irak–Iran', *Defense Nationale* (Octobre 1987) 55–62.

Chubin, S. 'Naval Competition and Security in South-West Asia', *Adelphi Paper 124*, III (Spring 1976) 22–30.

Chubin, S. 'US Security Interests in the Persian Gulf in the 1980s', *Daedalus* (Fall 1980) 31–65.

Chubin, S. 'The Soviet Union and Iran', *Foreign Affairs*, LXI, No. 4 (Spring 1983) 921–49.

Chubin, S. 'Reflections on the Gulf War', *Survival* (July–August 1986) 306–21.

Cockburn, P. 'My Enemy's Enemy ...', *Independent* (15 November 1992).

Collet, A. 'Les Missiles Tactiques', *Defense Nationale* (Novembre 1989) 151–63.

Cordesman, A. H. 'The Gulf Crisis and Strategic Interests: A Military Analaysis', *American–Arab Affairs* (Summer 1984) 8–15.

Cordesman, A. H. 'The Middle East and the Cost of the Politics of Force', *Middle East Journal*, XL, No. 1 (Winter 1986) 5–15.

Cordesman, A. H. 'Western Seapower Enters the Gulf', *Naval Forces*, IX (1988) (part 1) No. 2, 26–34; (part 2) No. 3, 34–40; (part 3) No. 4, 62–70.

Cottam, R. 'Iran – Motives Behind its Foreign Policy', *Survival* (November–December 1986) 483–95.

Dainville, A. O. de, 'Analyse de la Guerre du Golfe', *Defense Nationale* (Octobre 1988) 53–66.

Daly, T. 'The Enduring Gulf War', *Proceedings/Naval Review 1985*, 148–60.

Danziger, R. 'The Naval Race in the Persian Gulf', *Proceedings* (March 1982) 93–8.

Danziger, R. 'The Persian Gulf Tanker War', *Proceedings/Naval Review 1985*, 160–7.

Darwish, A. 'Fed eyes London link in Iraq deals', *Independent* (4 May 1993).

Defarges, P. M. 'Democratie et Diplomatie: La Doctrine Reagan Existe-t-elle?', *Defense Nationale* (Juillet 1986) 153–60.

Delcorde, R. 'Les Superpuissances dans le Golfe Arabo-Persique', *Defense Nationale* (Octobre 1986) 93–108.

Dowdy, W. L. 'Naval Warfare in the Gulf: Iraq versus Iran', *Proceedings* (June 1981) 114–17.

Doyle, L. 'Islamic Terrorist under every Arab Bed?', *Independent* (21 April 1995).

El-Shazly, N. E. 'The Quest for a Gulf Navy', *World Disarm!* No. 27 (June–July 1992) 2.

El-Shazly, N. E. 'A Restored Monarchy in Iraq: Possibility or Fantasy?', *Gulf Report*, No. 28 (April 1993) 8–9.

El-Shazly, N. E. 'Iraq: What Future?', *Sawt Al-Ittihad*, No. 105 (April 1993).

El-Shazly, N. E. 'The Boycott of Israel as a Tool of Diplomacy', *Gulf Report*, No. 28 (April 1993) 16.

El-Shazly, N. E. 'The Arab Boycott: Should it Suspend or Should it Continue?', *Sawt Al-Ittihad*, No. 106 (May 1993).

Ennes Jr, J. M. 'The Shame of the USS Liberty Cover-up', *The Washington Report on Middle East Affairs*, VII, No. 4 (August 1988) 38–9.

Fisk, R. 'A Muslim who goes to war seeks martyrdom', *Independent* (7 October 1991).

Flint, J. 'World Turns its Back as Kurds Die Quietly', *Independent on Sunday* (22 August 1993).

Frelick, B. 'The False Promise of Operation Provide Comfort', *MERIP*, No. 176, (May–June 1992) 22–7.

Friedman, N. 'World Naval Developments 1987', *Proceedings/Naval Review 1988*, 219–20.

Friedman, N. 'The *Vincennes* Incident', *Proceedings/Naval Review 1989*, 72–9.

Gabr, B. '*Samt al-Kharej wa Erhab ad-Dakhel*', *Hayat* (27 July 1993).

Garcon, J. 'La France et le Conflit Iran-Irak', *Politique Etrangere*, translated in *Al-Siyasah al-Dawliyah* (January 1988) 311–13.

Gawad, A. A. 'Moscow's Arms-for-Oil Diplomacy', *Foreign Policy*, No. 63 (Summer 1986) 147–68.

George, J. L. 'US Navy: A Pause in the Minehunting Programme', *Navy International* (January 1987) 7–8.

Ghareeb, E. 'The Forgotten War', *American-Arab Affairs* (Summer 1983) 59–75.

Golan, G. 'Gorbachev's Middle East Strategy', *Foreign Affairs*, LXVI, No. 1 (Fall 1987) 41–57.

Haeri, S. 'Iran Claims Arrest Over Shrine Blast', *Independent* (2 August 1994).

Halliday, F. 'Iran: Trade Unions and the Working Class Opposition', *MERIP* (March 1979) 7–13.

Halliday, F. 'Iran's New Grand Strategy', *MERIP*, No. 144 (January–February 1987) 7–8.

Halliday, F. 'The USSR and the Gulf War: Moscow's Growing Concern', *MERIP*, No. 148, (September–October 1987) 10–11.

Helms, C. M. 'The Iraqi Dilemma: Political Objectives Versus Military Strategy', *American–Arab Affairs* (Summer 1983) 75–85.

Hersh, S. M. 'US Covert Aid Sent to Iraq in 1982', *San Diego Union* (26 January 1992).

Hirst, D. 'Kuwait Caught in a Deadly Trap', *Guardian* (15 November 1987).

Hooglund, E. 'Iran and the Gulf War', *MERIP*, No. 148 (September–October 1987) 12–18.

Hooton, T. 'The Tanker War in the Gulf, 1984–88', *Jane's Intelligence Review* (May 1992) 218–21.

'In Gulf, US Navy "Snipes" have Extra-Hot Job', *Christian Science Monitor* (12 October 1988).

Jabber, P. 'US Interests and Regional Security in the Middle East', *Daedalus* (Fall 1980) 67–96.

Jabber, P. 'Forces of Change in the Middle East', *Middle East Journal*, XLII, No. 1 (Winter 1988) 7–15.

Jawdat, N. A. 'Reflections on the Gulf War', *American–Arab Affairs* (Summer 1983) 86–98.

Johnson, T. M. and Barrett, R. T. 'The Rapid Deployment Joint Task Force', *Proceedings* (November 1980) 95–8.

Johnstone, D. '"Little Satan" Stuck in the Arms Export Trap', *MERIP*, No. 148, (September–October 1987) 8–9.

Jordan, J. 'The Iranian Navy', *Jane's Intelligence Review* (May 1992) 213–17.

Jordan, K. B. 'Naval Diplomacy in the Persian Gulf', *Proceedings* (November 1981) 27–31.

Karadaghi, K. '*Mash'an Rakkad al-Dhamen al-Jabburi 'an Saddam Hussein al-Takriti wa Tassalotuhu*', *Hayat* (25 April 1993).

Karsh, E. 'The Iran–Iraq War: A Military Analysis', *Adelphi Paper 220* (Spring 1987).

Khalaf, A. 'The Elusive Quest for Gulf Security', *MERIP*, No. 148 (September–October 1987) 19–22.

King, R. 'The Iran–Iraq War: The Political Implications', *Adelphi Paper 219* (Spring, 1987).

Langston, B. and Bringle, D. 'Operation Praying Mantis', *Proceedings/Naval Review 1989*, 54–65.

Matthews, R. 'Saddam Pushed UN Resolve to the Limit', *Financial Times* (12 January 1993).

McCrystal, C. 'Tide of History turns on River of Steel', *Independent on Sunday* (16 May 1993).

McDonald, W. L. 'The Convoy Mission', *Proceedings/Naval Review 1988*, 36–44.

'Missile War in the Gulf', *US News and World Report* (14 March 1988) 36.

Mylroie, L. 'The Baghdad Alternative', *ORBIS* (Summer 1988) 339–54.

Neumann, R. G. and Hunter, S. T. 'Crisis in the Gulf: Reasons for Concern but not Panic', *American–Arab Affairs* (Summer 1984) 16–21.

O'Rourke, R. 'The Tanker War', *Proceedings/Naval Review 1988*, 29–34.

O'Rourke, R. 'Gulf Ops', *Proceedings/Naval Review 1989*, 42–50.

Patrizia, C. A. 'US Policy in the Arabian Gulf – A Long-Term View', *American-Arab Affairs* (Fall 1987) 45–55.

Pryce-Jones, D. 'Monde Arabe', *Politique Internationale*, No. 53 (Automne 1991) 303–20.

Quandt, W. B. 'The Gulf War: Policy Options and Regional Implications', *American–Arab Affairs* (Summer 1984) 1–7.

Rafsanjani, A. A. H. 'Yes to Revolution and to Moderation', interview in *Time*, CXLI, No. 21 (24 May 1993) 48–51.

Ramazani, R. K. 'Iran: Burying the Hatchet', *Foreign Policy*, No. 60 (Fall 1985) 52–74.

Ramazani, R. K. 'The Iran–Iraq War and the Persian Gulf Crisis', *Current History* (February 1988) 61–4, 86–8.

Richards, C. 'Border Gate Opens New Era for Israel and Jordan', *Independent* (9 August 1994).

Roach, J. A. 'Missiles on Target: Targeting and Defense Zones in the Tanker War', *Virginia Journal of International Law*, XXXI, No. 4 (1991) 593–610.

Rondot, P. 'La Logique de Saddam Hussein', *Defense Nationale* (Novembre 1990) 45–59.

Rubin, B. 'Drowning in the Gulf', *Foreign Policy*, No. 69 (Winter 1987/88) 120–34.

Sciolino, E. 'Iran's Durable Revolution', *Foreign Affairs*, LXI, No. 4 (Spring 1983) 893–920.

Sheridan, M. 'Saudi Rulers Learn to Live with Fewer Millions', *Independent* (13 December 1994).

Sick, G. 'La Revolution Iranienne et les Grandes Puissances', *Politique Etrangere* II (1987) translated in *Al-Siyasah Al-Dawliyah* (January 1988) 307–10.

'SS *Bridgeton*: The First Convoy', Interview, *Proceedings/Naval Review 1988*, 52–7.

Stork, J. 'Arms Industries in the Middle East', *MERIP*, No. 144 (January–February 1987) 12–16.

Stork, J. 'Reagan Re-Flags the Gulf', *MERIP*, No. 148 (September–October 1987) 3–5.

Stork, J. 'AWACS in the Gulf', *MERIP*, No. 148 (September–October 1987) 38.

Taha, A. 'Naval Development in the Persian Gulf', *Naval Forces*, V, No. 3 (1984) 22–9.

Taha, A. 'The Navies of the Persian Gulf', *Naval Forces*, V, No. 4 (1984) 34–43.

Taylor and Francis, 'The Persian/Arab Gulf Tanker War: International Law or International Chaos', Conference Report, Council on Law and The Law of the Sea Institute, Carnegie Endowment for International Peace, *Ocean Development and International Law*, XIX (1988) 299–321.

Theberge, R. 'Iran: Ten Years After the "White Revolution"', *MERIP* (June 1974) 3–22.

The Echo of Iran, 'The White Revolution and Iran's Independent National Policy', Foreign Policy Series No. 2 (January 1973).

'US Arms Sales to Iran 1973–78, by Quantity and Manufacture', *MERIP*, No. 71 (March 1979) 22–3.

Van Hollen, C. 'Don't Engulf the Gulf', *Foreign Affairs*, No. 5 (Summer 1981) 1064–78.
Viorst, M. 'Iraq at War', *Foreign Affairs*, LXV, No. 2 (Winter 1986/87) 349–65.
Vlahos, M. 'The *Stark* Report', *Proceedings/Naval Review 1988*, 63–7.
Wachenfeld, M. G. 'Reflagging Kuwaiti Tankers: A US Response in the Persian Gulf', *Duke Law Journal*, No. 1 (1988) 175–202.
'War between Iran and Iraq', *Survival* (January–February 1981) 42.
Wright, C. 'Implications of the Iraq–Iran War', *Foreign Affairs*, LIX, No. 2 (Winter 1980/81) 275–303.
Zaloga, S. 'Ballistic Missiles in the Third World', *International Defence Review*, XXI, (11/1988) 1423–7.

NEWSPAPERS

Al-Ahram
Al-Ahram International
Al-Akhbar
Al-'Amal Al-Islami
Al-'Arab
Al-Daleel
Al-Ghad Al-Demuqrati
Al-Hayat
Al-'Iraq
Al-'Iraq Al-Hur
Al-Jihad
Al-Jumhuriyah
Al-Majrasha
Al-Mostaqil
Al-Mautamar
Al-Muhajir
Al-Nadhrah Al-'Arabiyah
Al-Quds
Al-Shahadah
Al-Wafd
Al-Warkaa
Al-Watan
Al-Wefaq
Asharq Al-Awsat

Babil
Baghdad
The Financial Times
The Guardian
The Guardian Weekly
The Independent
The Independent on Sunday
The International Herald Tribune
Iraqi Issues
Kayhan Al-'Arabi
Lewa' Al-Sadr
Le Matin
Le Monde
Nida Al-Rafedhayn
Rikay Kurdistan
Tareeq Al-Sha'b
The San Diego Union
Sawt Al-Ittihad
Sout Al-'Iraq
Sout Al-Jamaheer
Tareeq Al-Sha'b
The Times
The Wall Street Journal

MAGAZINES AND JOURNALS

Al-Dasturiyah
Al-Demoqrati
Al-Ghad

MERIP
Middle East Journal
Naval Forces

Al-Malakiyah al-Dasturiah	
Al-Muntada	Navy International
Al-Siyasah Al-Dawliyah	Newsweek
Al-Wasat	ORBIS
American-Arab Affairs	Politique Internationale
Current History	Proceedings
Defense Nationale	Survival
Foreign Affairs	The Economist
Foreign Policy	The Middle East Journal
International Defence Review	Risalat Al-'Iraq
International Security	Time
Jane's Defence Weekly	Washington Report on Middle East Affairs

VIDEO FILMS, TELEVIZED INTERVIEWS AND BROADCASTS

Albright, M. Interview in BBC 1, 18 June 1993.

Cheysson, C. Interview in *Newsnight*, BBC 2, 30 August 1990.

'Death of a Principle', *Panorama*, BBC 1, 1 April 1996.

Gale, Interview in 'Birds of Death', *Secret History*, Channel 4, 6 July 1992 and 21 April 1996.

Hopkins, A. 'Human Rights, Human Wrongs', BBC, 6 December 1993.

Panorama, BBC Radio, Arabic Section, 19 November 1996.

Parsons, A. Interview in Sampson, 13 December 1991.

Sampson, A. 'The Two-Edged Sword', BBC 2, 13 December 1991.

'The Great Gulf Cover-up', *Dispatches*, Channel 4, 15 May 1997.

'The Last Shah', *Reputations*, BBC 2, 18 April 1996.

Wars in Peace, 'Iran and Iraq', ITN video film, March 1992.

'What has Become of Us?', Channel 4, 11 December 1994.

Index